W9-CIJ-990

DISCARD

THE AVENGERS

WRITER
BRIAN MICHAEL BENDIS

PENCILER
JOHN ROMITA JR.

INKER
KLAUS JANSON
WITH **TOM PALMER** (ISSUES #5-6)

COLORIST
DEAN WHITE

LETTERER
VC'S CORY PETIT

ASSOCIATE EDITOR
LAUREN SANKOVITCH

EDITOR
TOM BREVOORT

Collection Editor: JENNIFER GRÜNWALD • Editorial Assistants: JAMES EMMETT & JOE HOCHSTEIN
Assistant Editors: ALEX STARBUCK & NELSON RIBEIRO • Editor, Special Projects: MARK D. BEAZLEY
Senior Editor, Special Projects: JEFF YOUNGQUIST • Senior Vice President of Sales: DAVID GABRIEL
Book Design: JEFF POWELL

Editor in Chief: JOE QUESADA • Publisher: DAN BUCKLEY • Executive Producer: ALAN FINE

AVENGERS BY BRIAN MICHAEL BENDIS VOL. 1. Contains material originally published in magazine form as AVENGERS #1-6. First printing 2011. ISBN# 978-0-7851-4500-4. Published by MARVEL WORLDWIDE, INC., a subsidiary of MARVEL ENTERTAINMENT, LLC. OFFICE OF PUBLICATION: 135 West 50th Street, New York, NY 10020. $24.99 per copy in the U.S. and $27.99 in Canada (GST #R127032852); Canadian Agreement #40668537. **Printed in the U.S.A.** ALAN FINE, EVP - Office of the President, Marvel Worldwide, Inc. and EVP & CMO Marvel Characters B.V.; DAN BUCKLEY, Chief Executive Officer and Publisher - Print, Animation & Digital Media; JIM SOKOLOWSKI, Chief Operating Officer; DAVID GABRIEL, SVP of Publishing Sales & Circulation; DAVID BOGART, SVP of Business Affairs & Talent Management; MICHAEL PASCIULLO, VP Merchandising & Communications; JIM O'KEEFE, VP of Operations & Logistics; DAN CARR, Executive Director of Publishing Technology; JUSTIN F. GABRIE, Director of Publishing & Editorial Operations; SUSAN CRESPI, Editorial Operations Manager; ALEX MORALES, Publishing Operations Manager; STAN LEE, Chairman Emeritus. For information regarding advertising in Marvel Comics or on Marvel.com, please contact Ron Stern, VP of Business Development, at rstern@marvel.com. For Marvel subscription inquiries, please call 800-217-9158. **Manufactured between 12/13/10 and 1/10/11 by R.R. DONNELLEY, INC., SALEM, VA, USA.**

10 9 8 7 6 5 4 3 2 1

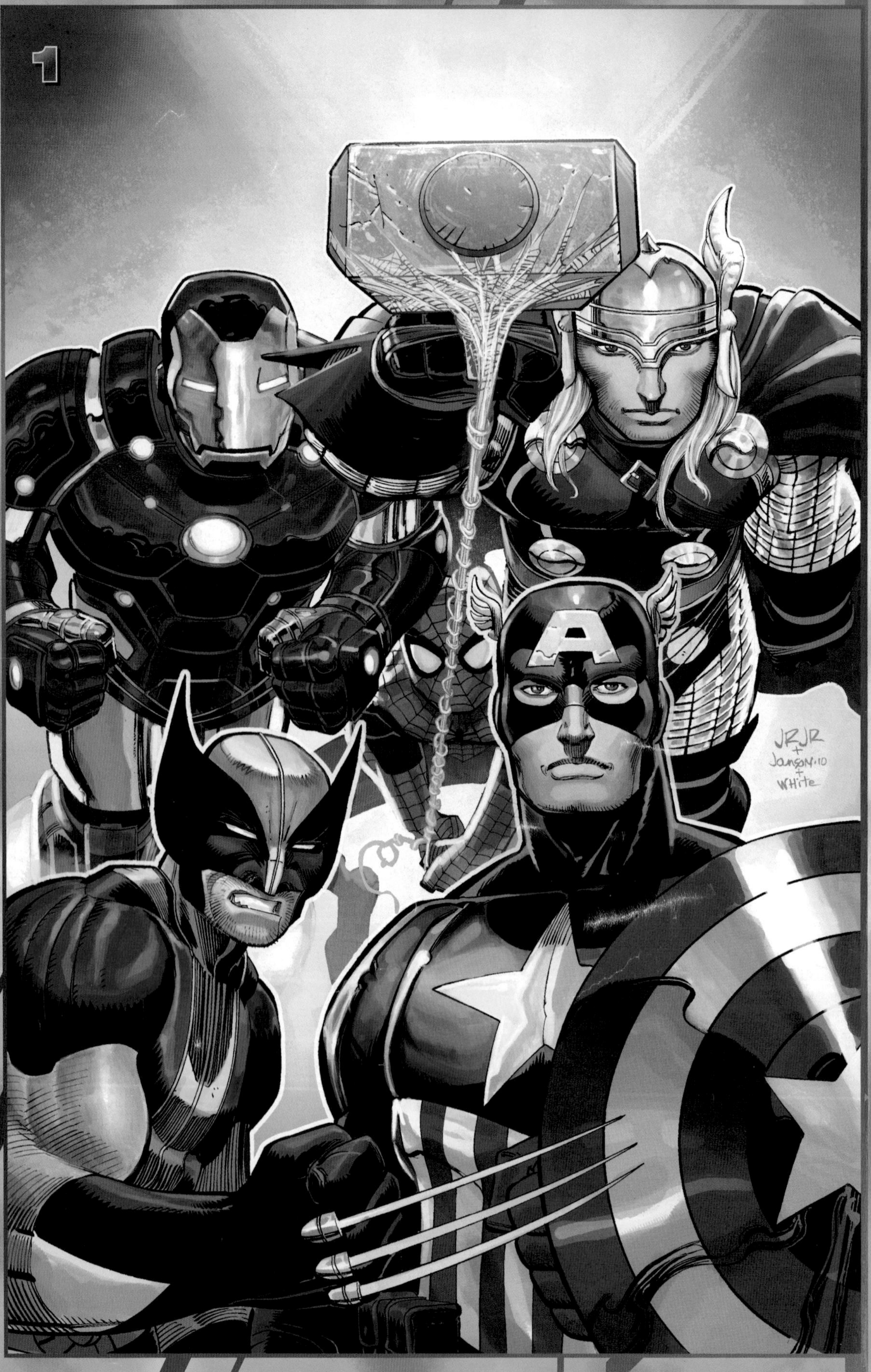
1
JRJR + Janson.10 + White

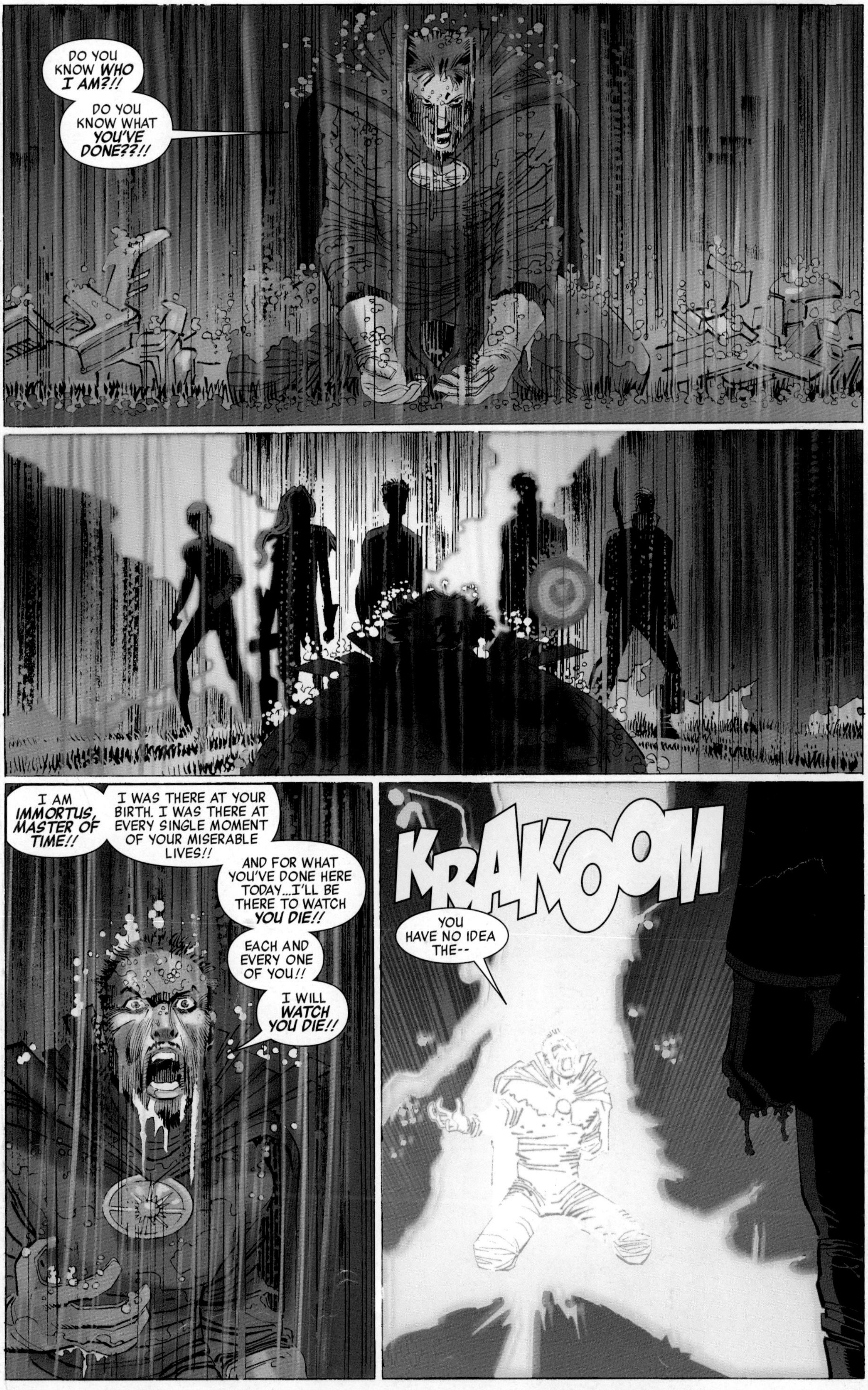
DO YOU KNOW WHO I AM?!!
DO YOU KNOW WHAT YOU'VE DONE??!!
I AM IMMORTUS, MASTER OF TIME!!
I WAS THERE AT YOUR BIRTH. I WAS THERE AT EVERY SINGLE MOMENT OF YOUR MISERABLE LIVES!!
AND FOR WHAT YOU'VE DONE HERE TODAY...I'LL BE THERE TO WATCH YOU DIE!!
EACH AND EVERY ONE OF YOU!!
I WILL WATCH YOU DIE!!
KRAKOOM
YOU HAVE NO IDEA THE--

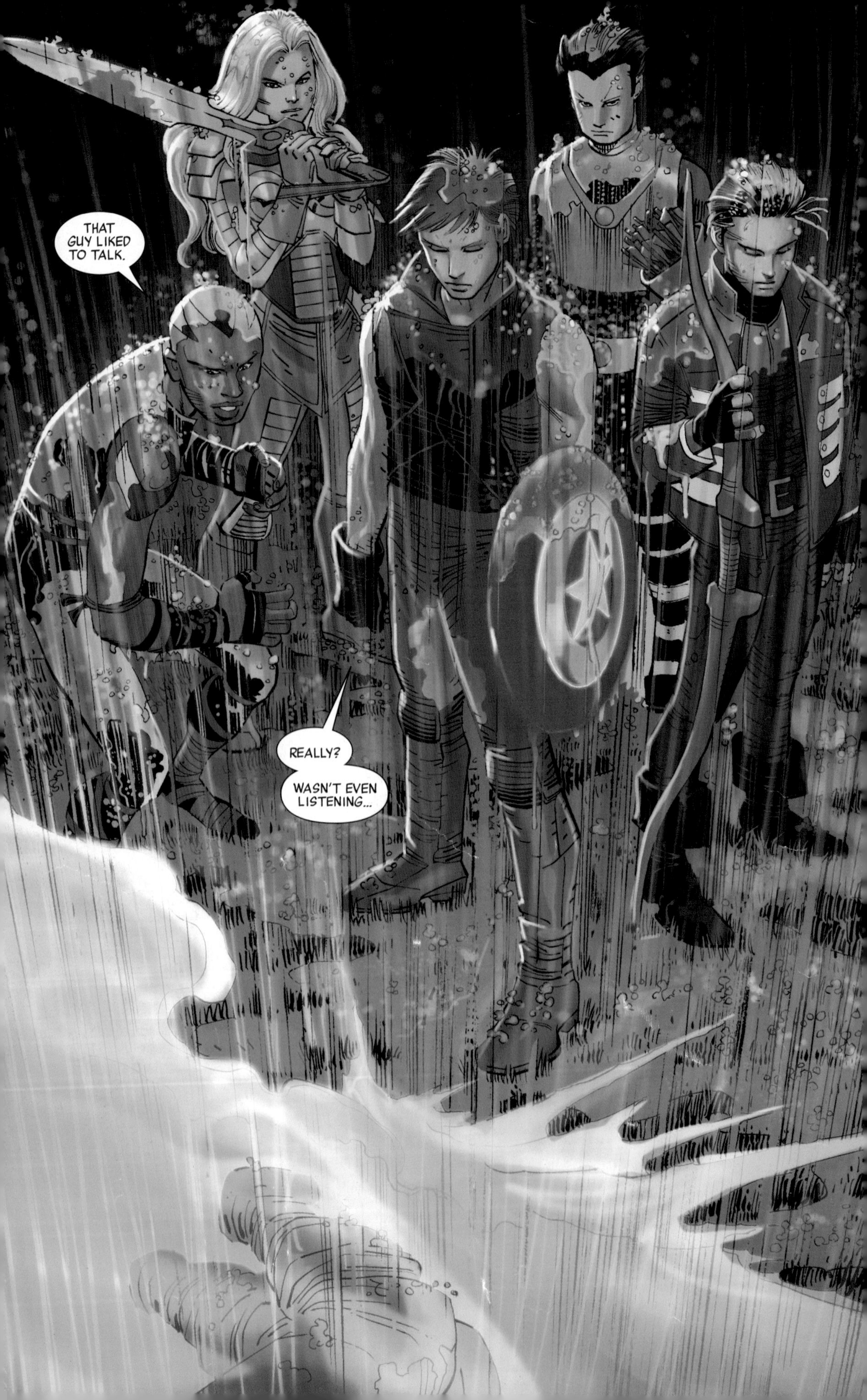
THAT GUY LIKED TO TALK.
REALLY?
WASN'T EVEN LISTENING...

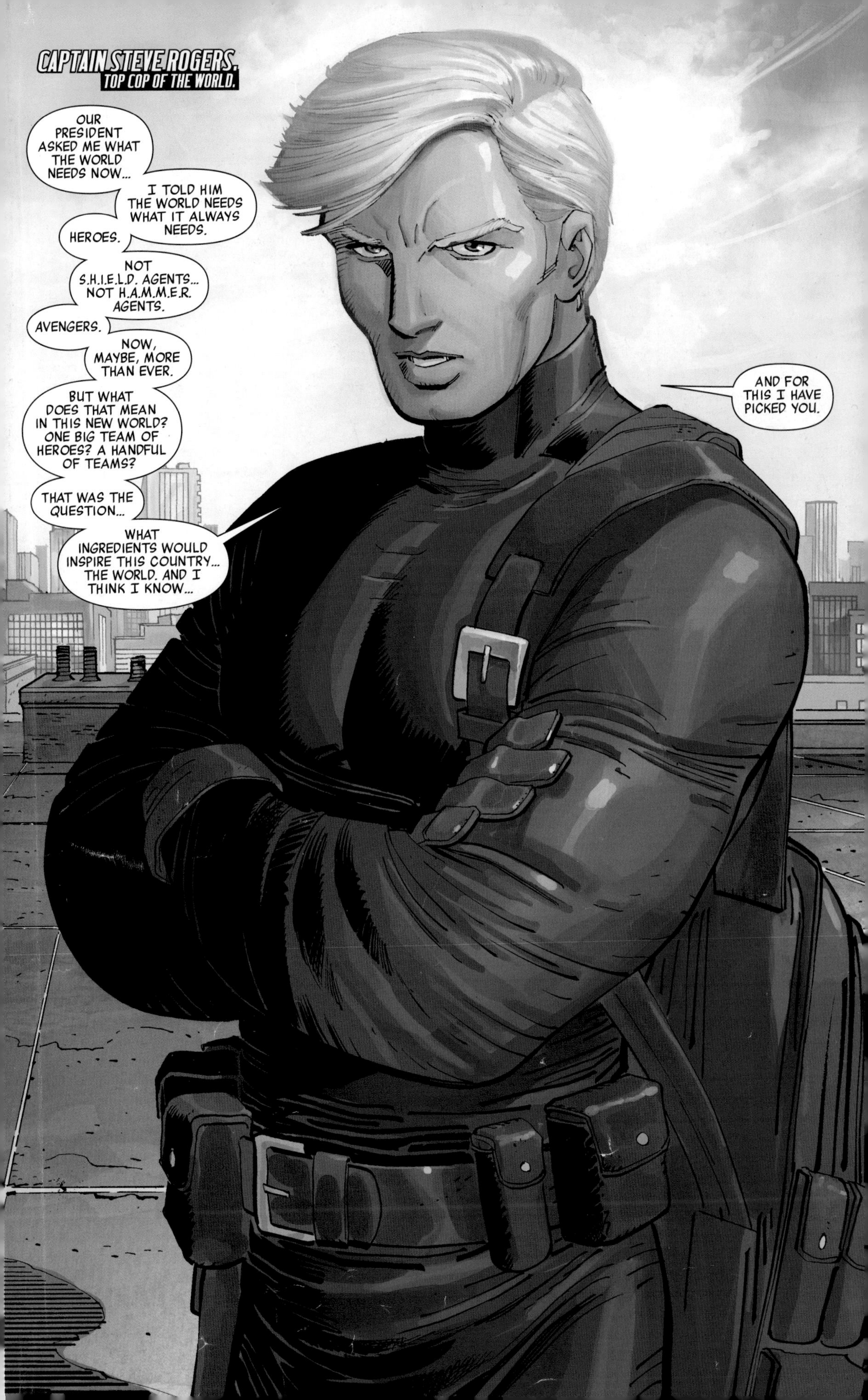
CAPTAIN STEVE ROGERS.
TOP COP OF THE WORLD.
OUR PRESIDENT ASKED ME WHAT THE WORLD NEEDS NOW...
I TOLD HIM THE WORLD NEEDS WHAT IT ALWAYS NEEDS.
HEROES.
NOT S.H.I.E.L.D. AGENTS... NOT H.A.M.M.E.R. AGENTS.
AVENGERS.
NOW, MAYBE, MORE THAN EVER.
BUT WHAT DOES THAT MEAN IN THIS NEW WORLD? ONE BIG TEAM OF HEROES? A HANDFUL OF TEAMS?
THAT WAS THE QUESTION...
WHAT INGREDIENTS WOULD INSPIRE THIS COUNTRY... THE WORLD. AND I THINK I KNOW...
AND FOR THIS I HAVE PICKED YOU.

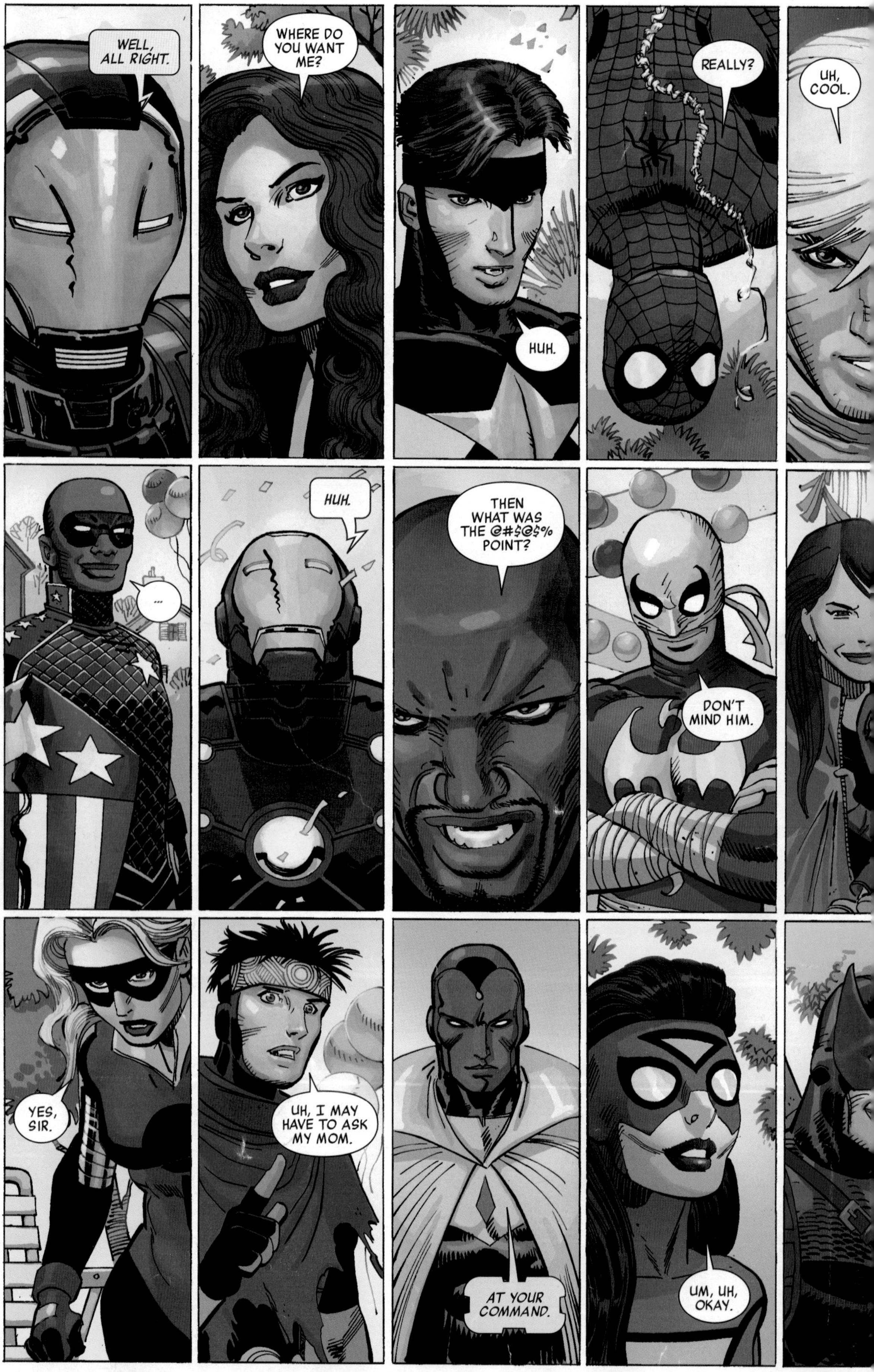
WELL, ALL RIGHT.
WHERE DO YOU WANT ME?
HUH.
REALLY?
UH, COOL.
...
HUH.
THEN WHAT WAS THE @#$@$% POINT?
DON'T MIND HIM.
YES, SIR.
UH, I MAY HAVE TO ASK MY MOM.
AT YOUR COMMAND.
UM, UH, OKAY.

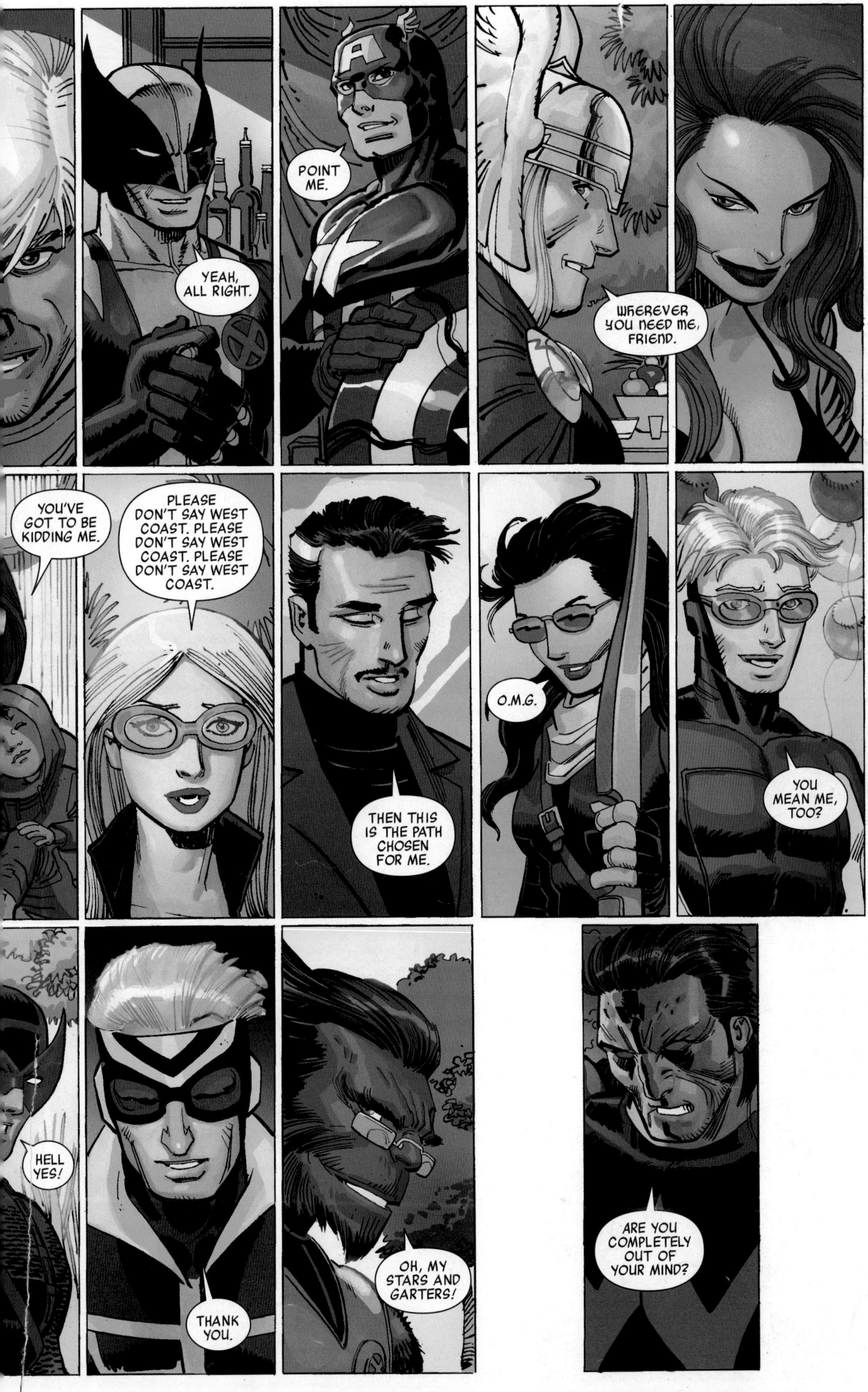
YEAH, ALL RIGHT.
POINT ME.
WHEREVER YOU NEED ME, FRIEND.
YOU'VE GOT TO BE KIDDING ME.
PLEASE DON'T SAY WEST COAST. PLEASE DON'T SAY WEST COAST. PLEASE DON'T SAY WEST COAST.
THEN THIS IS THE PATH CHOSEN FOR ME.
O.M.G.
YOU MEAN ME, TOO?
HELL YES!
THANK YOU.
OH, MY STARS AND GARTERS!
ARE YOU COMPLETELY OUT OF YOUR MIND?

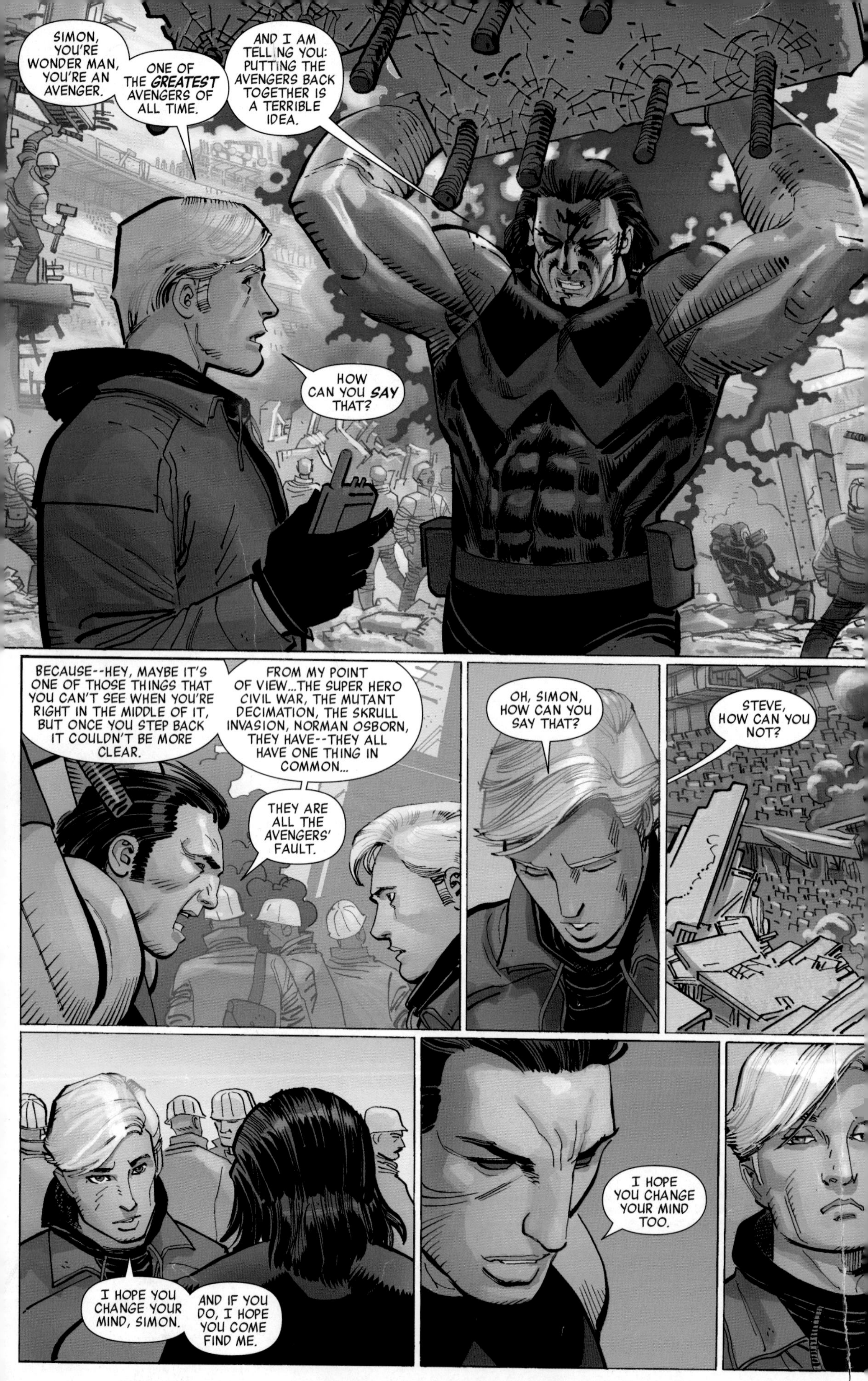
SIMON, YOU'RE WONDER MAN, YOU'RE AN AVENGER.
ONE OF THE GREATEST AVENGERS OF ALL TIME.
AND I AM TELLING YOU: PUTTING THE AVENGERS BACK TOGETHER IS A TERRIBLE IDEA.
HOW CAN YOU SAY THAT?
BECAUSE--HEY, MAYBE IT'S ONE OF THOSE THINGS THAT YOU CAN'T SEE WHEN YOU'RE RIGHT IN THE MIDDLE OF IT, BUT ONCE YOU STEP BACK IT COULDN'T BE MORE CLEAR.
FROM MY POINT OF VIEW...THE SUPER HERO CIVIL WAR, THE MUTANT DECIMATION, THE SKRULL INVASION, NORMAN OSBORN, THEY HAVE--THEY ALL HAVE ONE THING IN COMMON...
THEY ARE ALL THE AVENGERS' FAULT.
OH, SIMON, HOW CAN YOU SAY THAT?
STEVE, HOW CAN YOU NOT?
I HOPE YOU CHANGE YOUR MIND, SIMON.
AND IF YOU DO, I HOPE YOU COME FIND ME.
I HOPE YOU CHANGE YOUR MIND TOO.

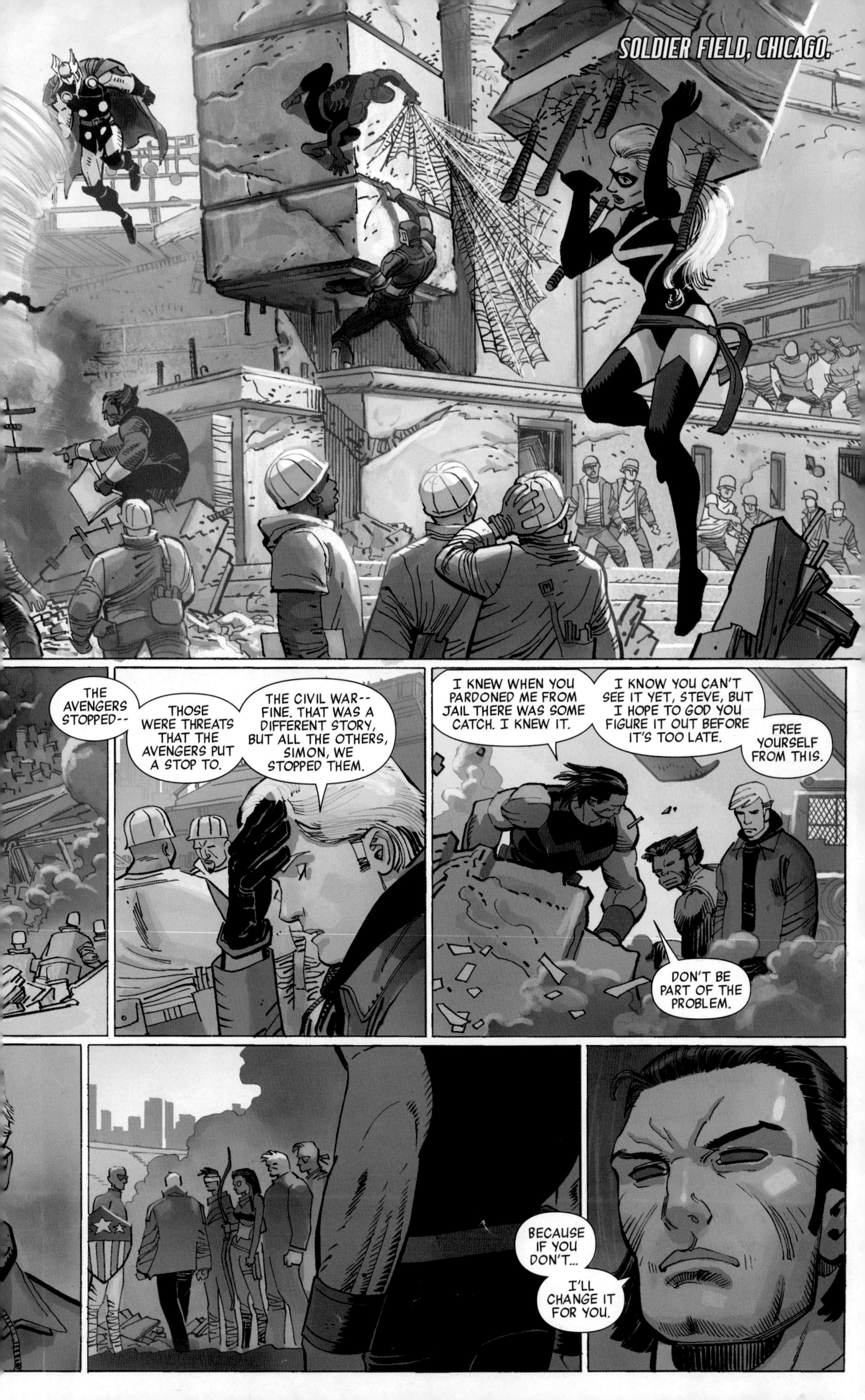
SOLDIER FIELD, CHICAGO.
THE AVENGERS STOPPED--
THOSE WERE THREATS THAT THE AVENGERS PUT A STOP TO.
THE CIVIL WAR--FINE. THAT WAS A DIFFERENT STORY, BUT ALL THE OTHERS, SIMON, WE STOPPED THEM.
I KNEW WHEN YOU PARDONED ME FROM JAIL THERE WAS SOME CATCH. I KNEW IT.
I KNOW YOU CAN'T SEE IT YET, STEVE, BUT I HOPE TO GOD YOU FIGURE IT OUT BEFORE IT'S TOO LATE.
FREE YOURSELF FROM THIS.
DON'T BE PART OF THE PROBLEM.
BECAUSE IF YOU DON'T...
I'LL CHANGE IT FOR YOU.

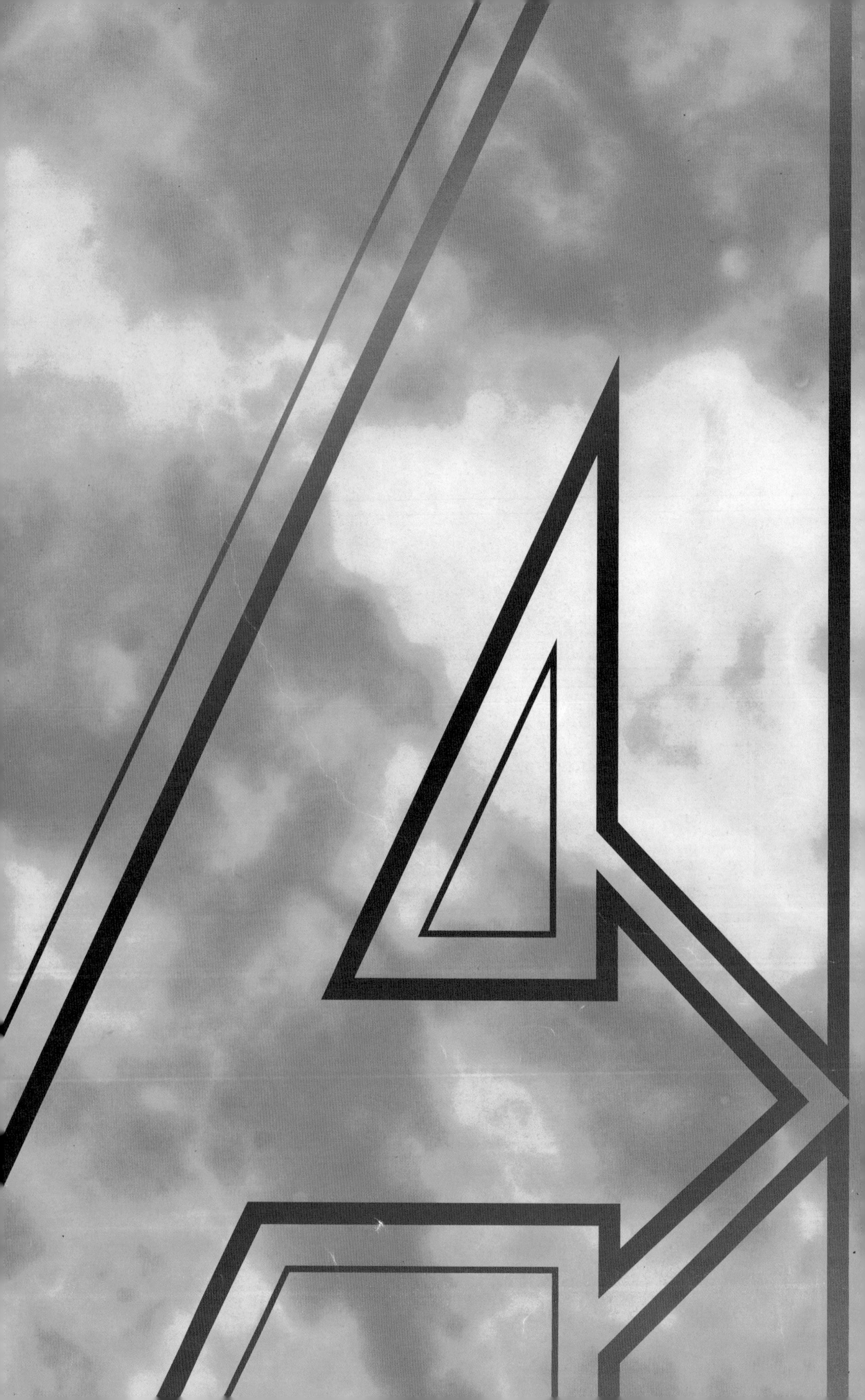

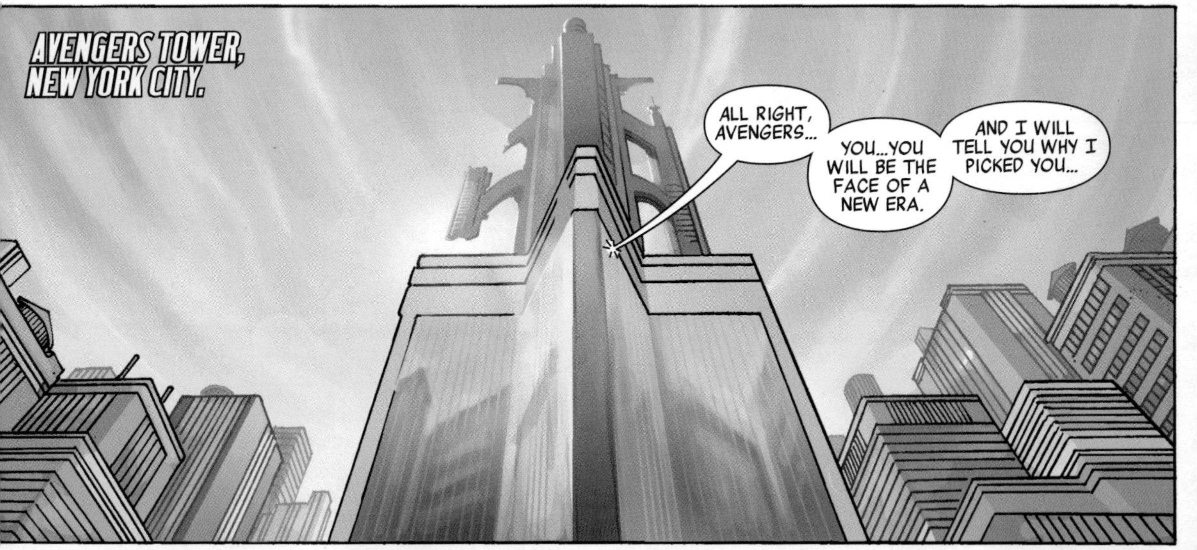
AVENGERS TOWER, NEW YORK CITY.
ALL RIGHT, AVENGERS...
YOU...YOU WILL BE THE FACE OF A NEW ERA.
AND I WILL TELL YOU WHY I PICKED YOU...

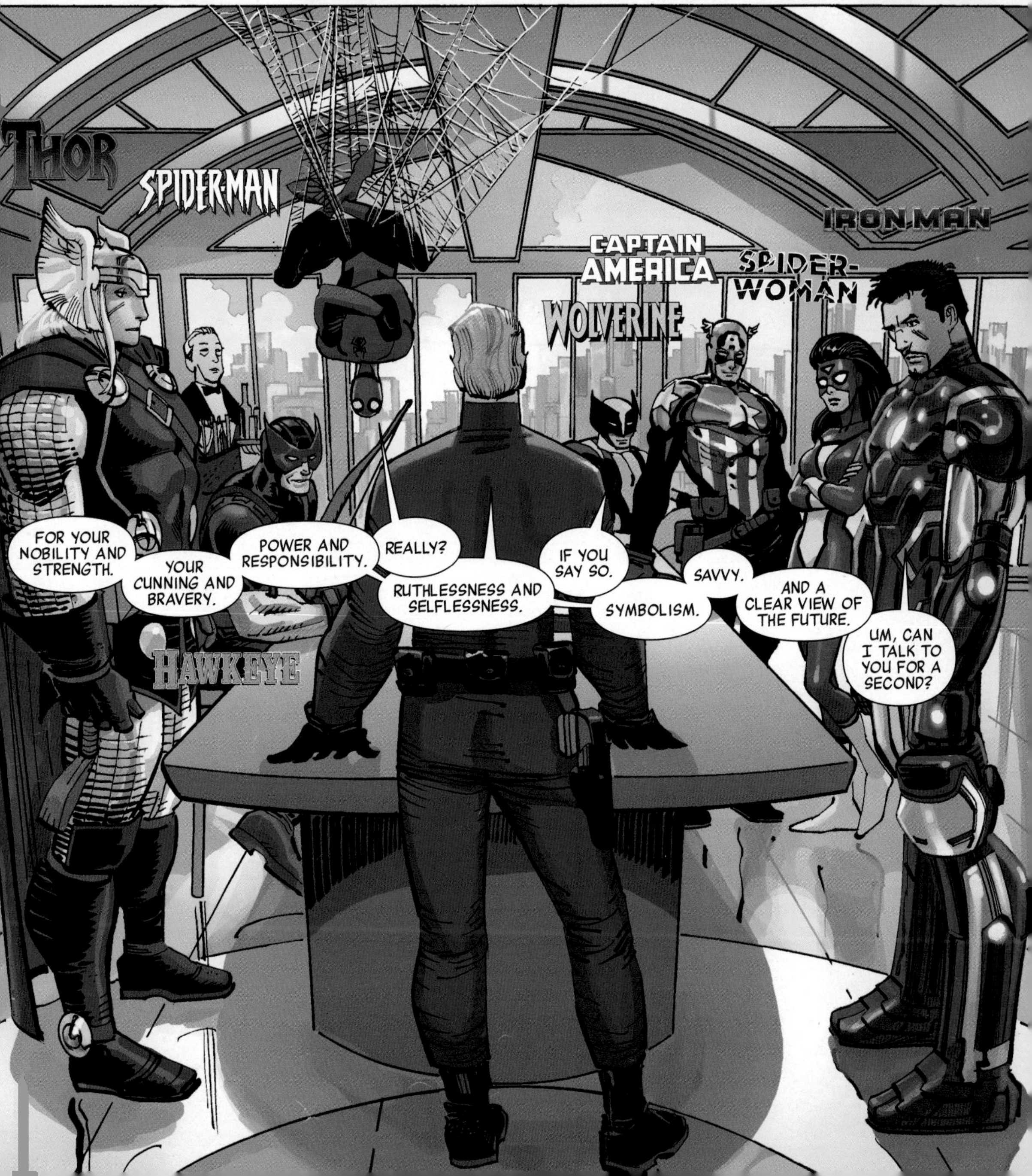
THOR
SPIDER-MAN
CAPTAIN AMERICA
WOLVERINE
SPIDER-WOMAN
IRON MAN
HAWKEYE
FOR YOUR NOBILITY AND STRENGTH.
YOUR CUNNING AND BRAVERY.
POWER AND RESPONSIBILITY.
REALLY?
RUTHLESSNESS AND SELFLESSNESS.
IF YOU SAY SO.
SYMBOLISM.
SAVVY.
AND A CLEAR VIEW OF THE FUTURE.
UM, CAN I TALK TO YOU FOR A SECOND?

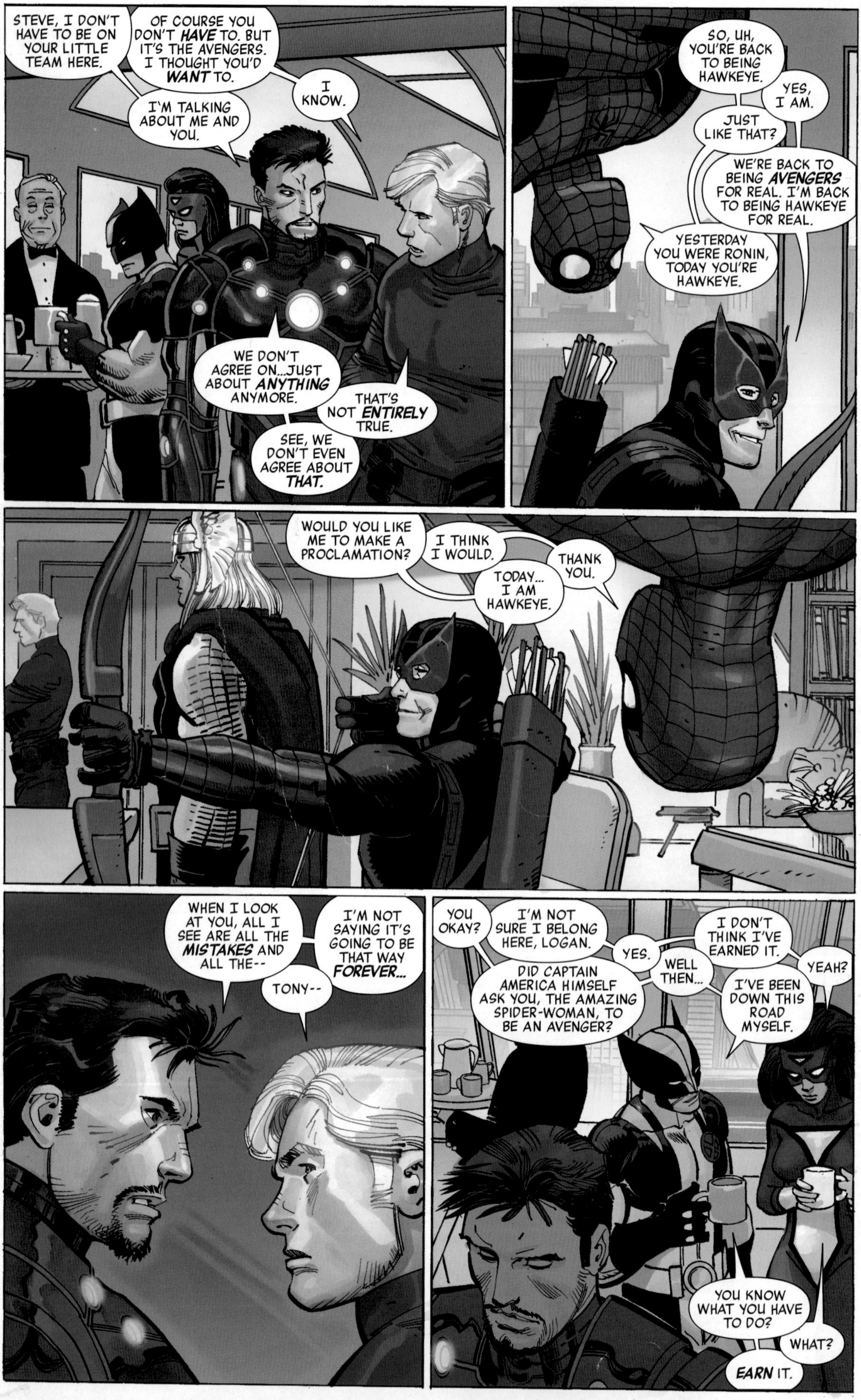
STEVE, I DON'T HAVE TO BE ON YOUR LITTLE TEAM HERE.
OF COURSE YOU DON'T HAVE TO. BUT IT'S THE AVENGERS. I THOUGHT YOU'D WANT TO.
I'M TALKING ABOUT ME AND YOU.
I KNOW.
WE DON'T AGREE ON...JUST ABOUT ANYTHING ANYMORE.
THAT'S NOT ENTIRELY TRUE.
SEE, WE DON'T EVEN AGREE ABOUT THAT.
SO, UH, YOU'RE BACK TO BEING HAWKEYE.
YES, I AM.
JUST LIKE THAT?
WE'RE BACK TO BEING AVENGERS FOR REAL. I'M BACK TO BEING HAWKEYE FOR REAL.
YESTERDAY YOU WERE RONIN, TODAY YOU'RE HAWKEYE.
WOULD YOU LIKE ME TO MAKE A PROCLAMATION?
I THINK I WOULD.
TODAY... I AM HAWKEYE.
THANK YOU.
WHEN I LOOK AT YOU, ALL I SEE ARE ALL THE MISTAKES AND ALL THE--
TONY--
I'M NOT SAYING IT'S GOING TO BE THAT WAY FOREVER...
YOU OKAY?
I'M NOT SURE I BELONG HERE, LOGAN.
YES.
DID CAPTAIN AMERICA HIMSELF ASK YOU, THE AMAZING SPIDER-WOMAN, TO BE AN AVENGER?
WELL THEN...
I DON'T THINK I'VE EARNED IT.
YEAH?
I'VE BEEN DOWN THIS ROAD MYSELF.
YOU KNOW WHAT YOU HAVE TO DO?
WHAT?
EARN IT.

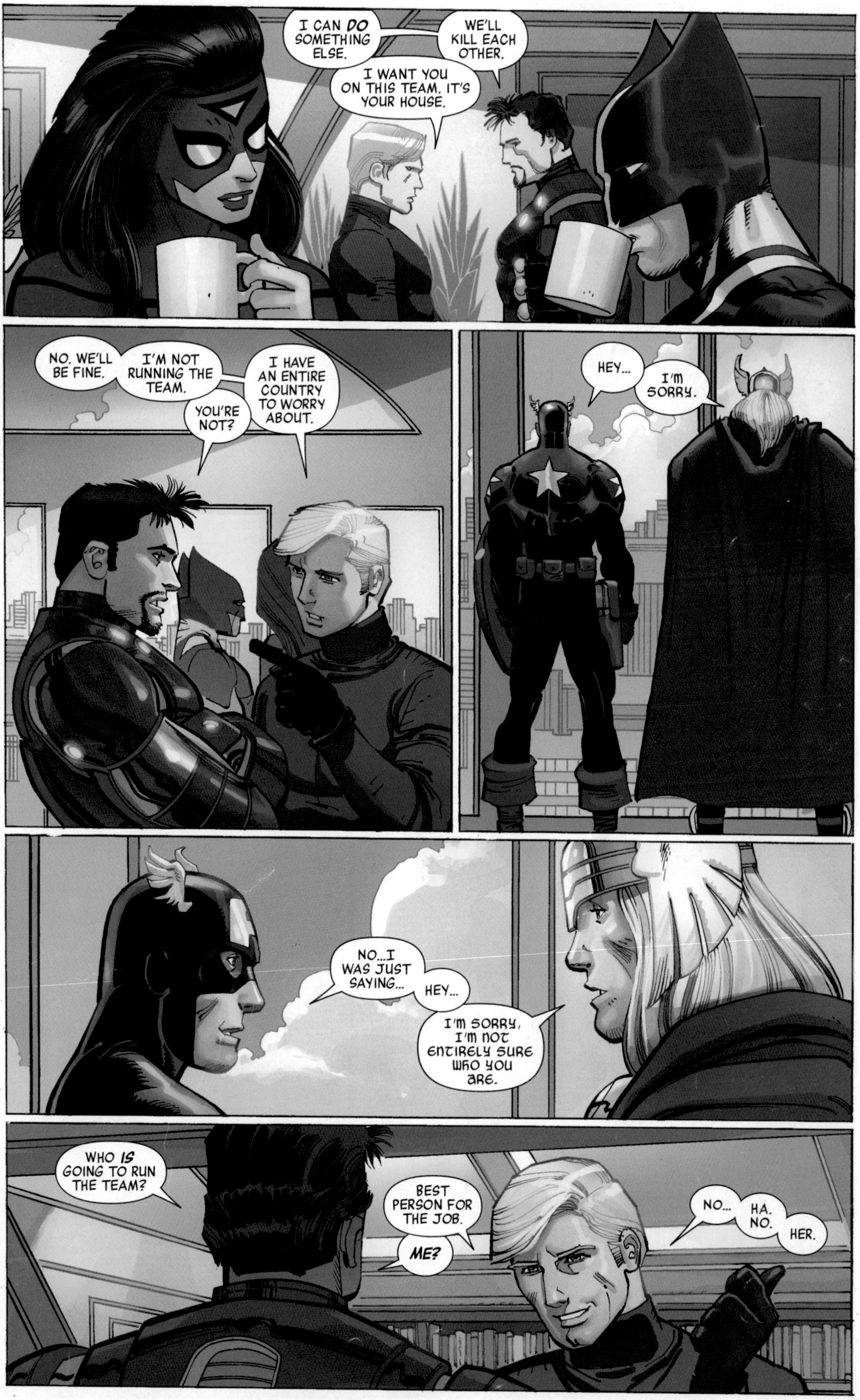
I CAN *DO* SOMETHING ELSE.
WE'LL KILL EACH OTHER.
I WANT YOU ON THIS TEAM. IT'S YOUR HOUSE.
NO. WE'LL BE FINE.
I'M NOT RUNNING THE TEAM.
YOU'RE NOT?
I HAVE AN ENTIRE COUNTRY TO WORRY ABOUT.
HEY...
I'M SORRY.
NO...I WAS JUST SAYING...
HEY...
I'M SORRY, I'M NOT ENTIRELY SURE WHO YOU ARE.
WHO *IS* GOING TO RUN THE TEAM?
BEST PERSON FOR THE JOB.
ME?
NO...
HA. NO.
HER.

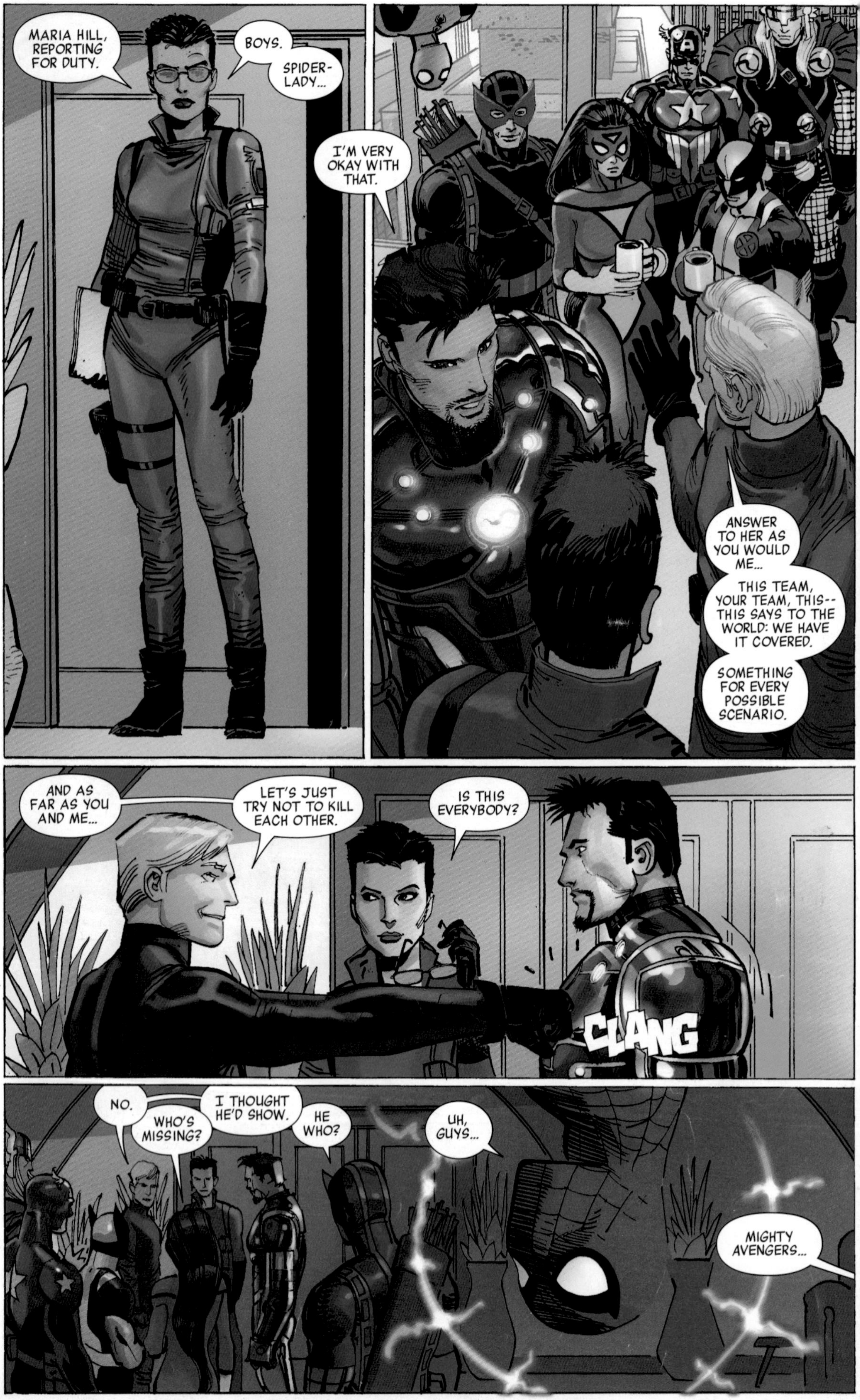
MARIA HILL, REPORTING FOR DUTY.
BOYS.
SPIDER-LADY...
I'M VERY OKAY WITH THAT.
ANSWER TO HER AS YOU WOULD ME...
THIS TEAM, YOUR TEAM, THIS-- THIS SAYS TO THE WORLD: WE HAVE IT COVERED.
SOMETHING FOR EVERY POSSIBLE SCENARIO.
AND AS FAR AS YOU AND ME...
LET'S JUST TRY NOT TO KILL EACH OTHER.
IS THIS EVERYBODY?
CLANG
NO.
WHO'S MISSING?
I THOUGHT HE'D SHOW.
HE WHO?
UH, GUYS...
MIGHTY AVENGERS...

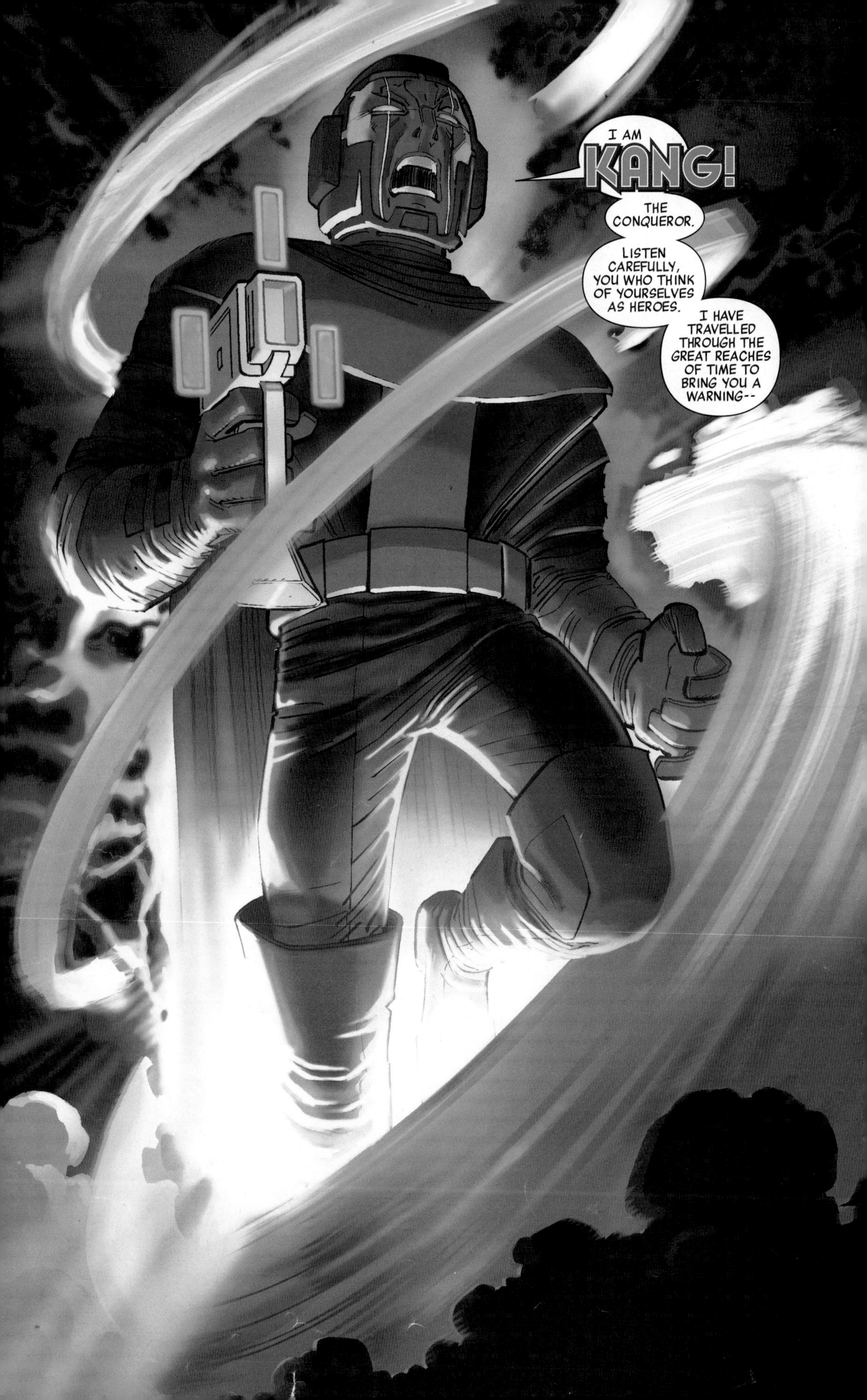
I AM KANG!
THE CONQUEROR.
LISTEN CAREFULLY, YOU WHO THINK OF YOURSELVES AS HEROES.
I HAVE TRAVELLED THROUGH THE GREAT REACHES OF TIME TO BRING YOU A WARNING--

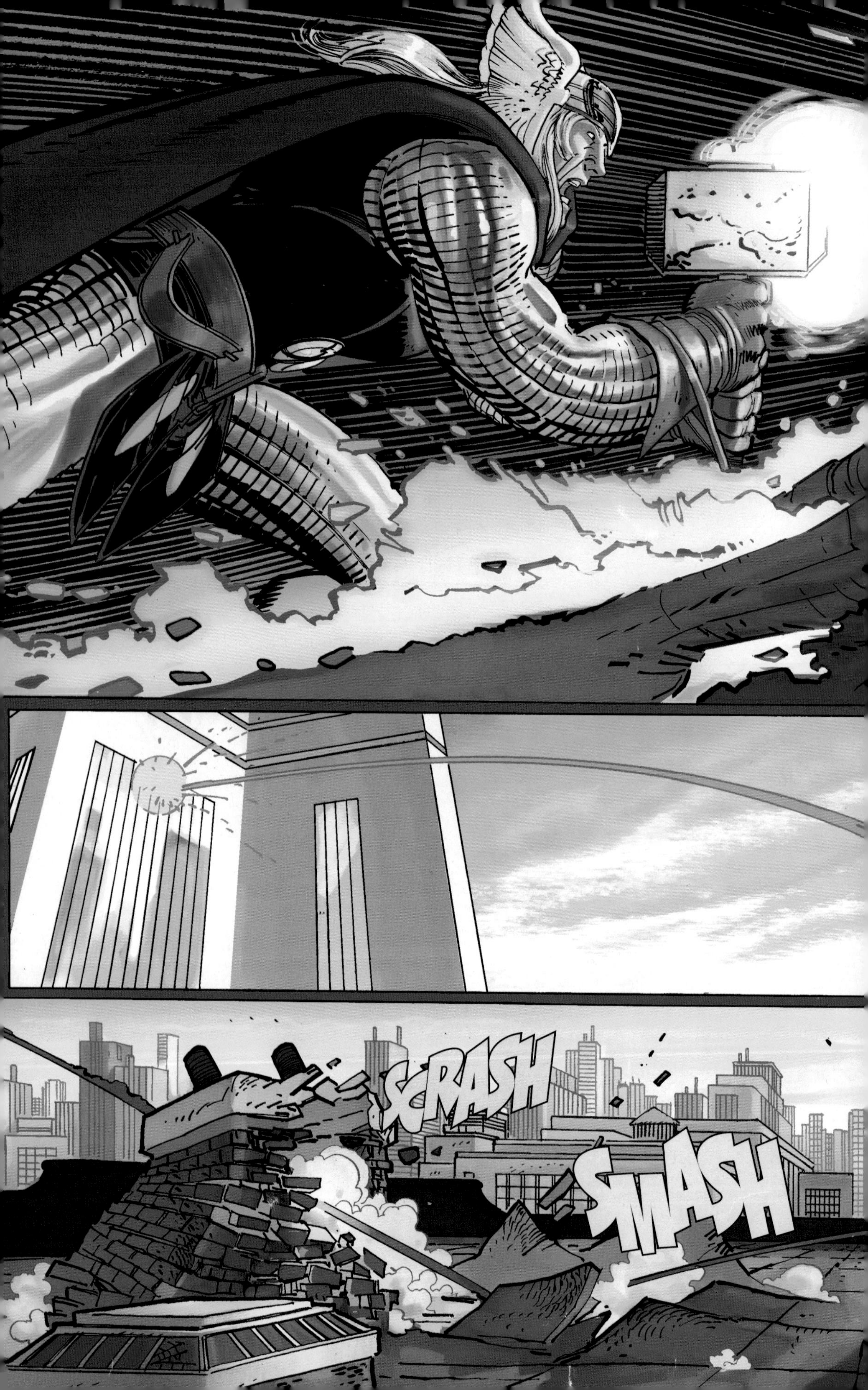
SCRASH
SMASH

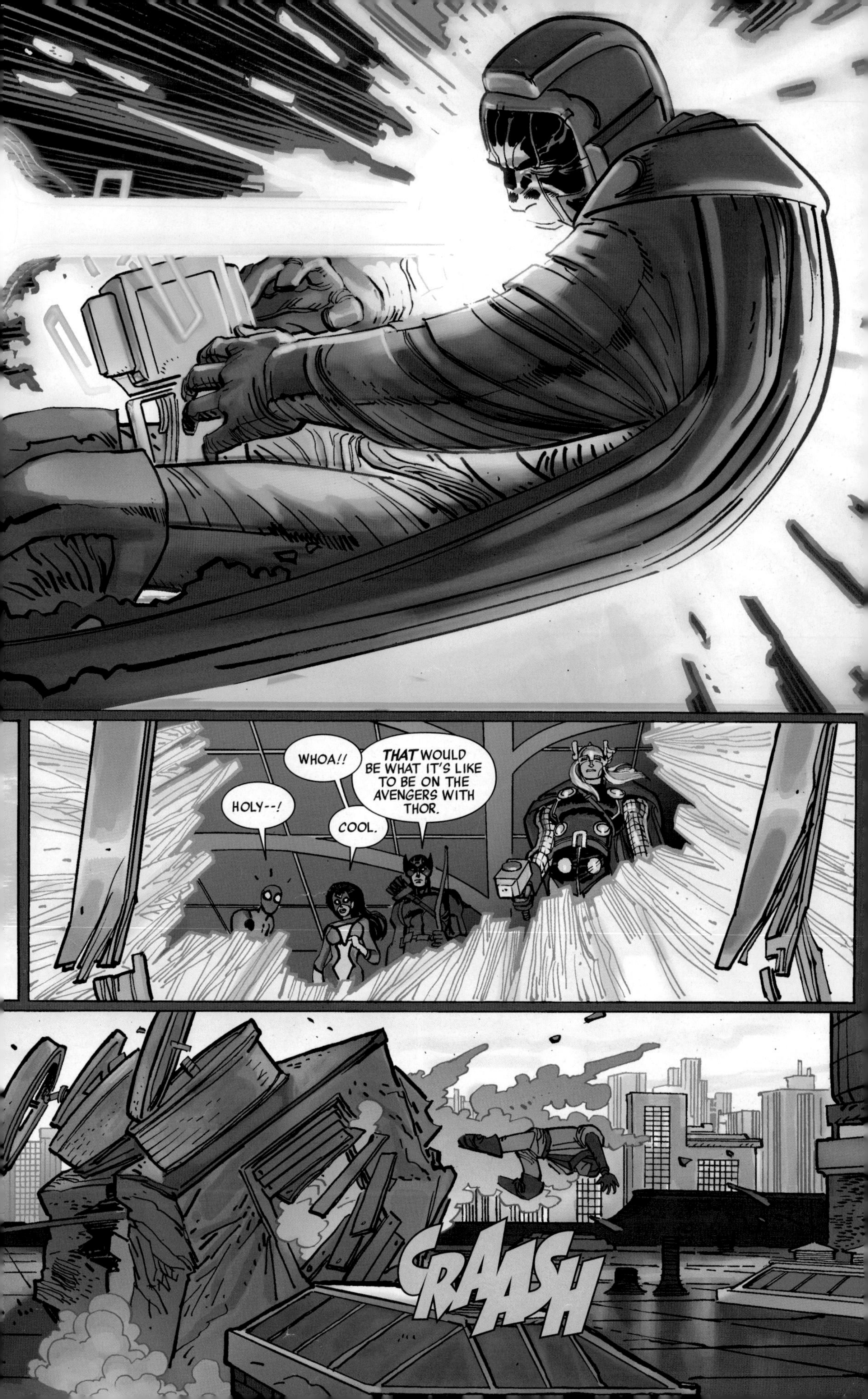
HOLY--!
WHOA!!
COOL.
THAT WOULD BE WHAT IT'S LIKE TO BE ON THE AVENGERS WITH THOR.
CRAASH

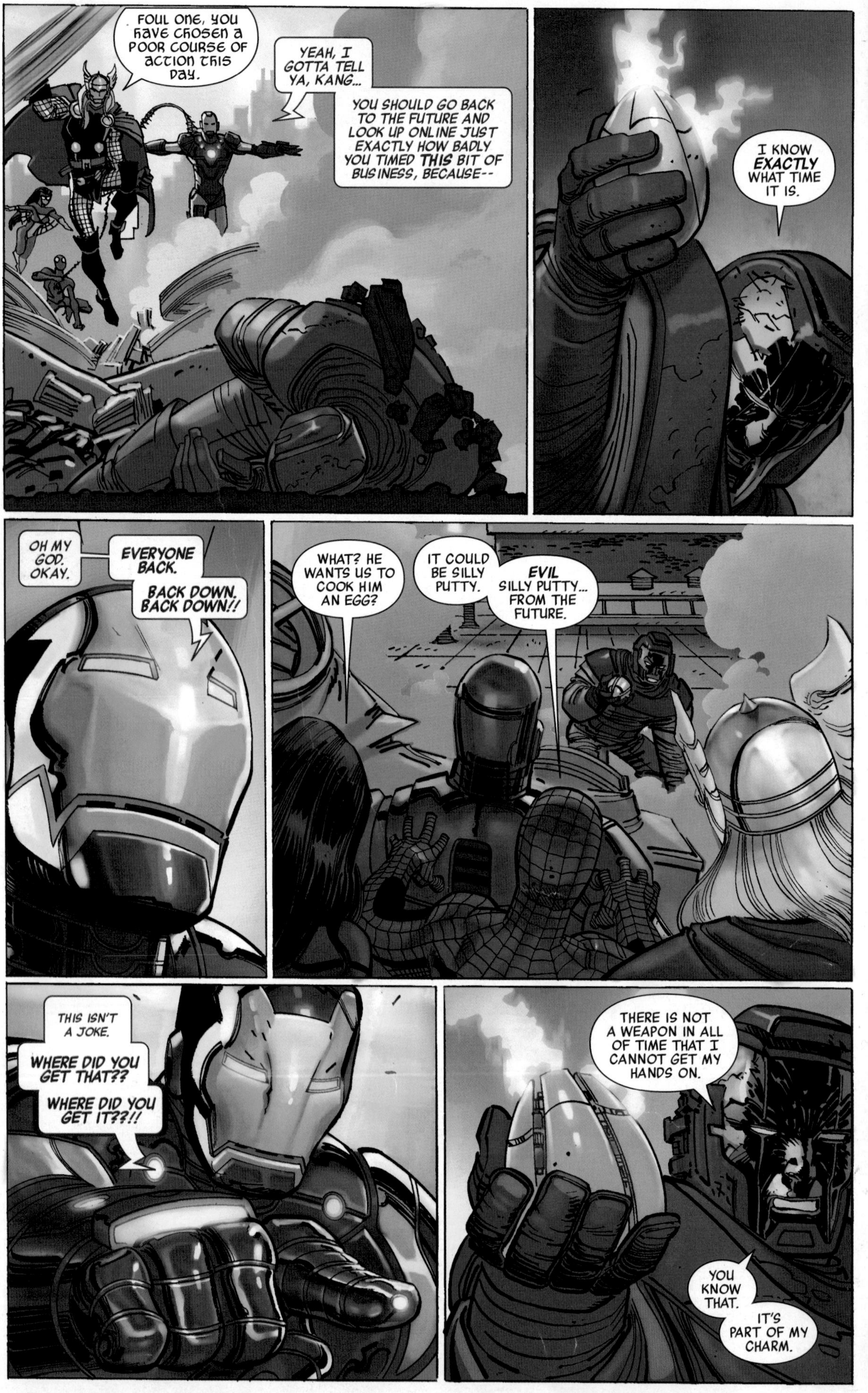
FOUL ONE, YOU HAVE CHOSEN A POOR COURSE OF ACTION THIS DAY.
YEAH, I GOTTA TELL YA, KANG...
YOU SHOULD GO BACK TO THE FUTURE AND LOOK UP ONLINE JUST EXACTLY HOW BADLY YOU TIMED THIS BIT OF BUSINESS, BECAUSE--
I KNOW EXACTLY WHAT TIME IT IS.
OH MY GOD. OKAY.
EVERYONE BACK.
BACK DOWN. BACK DOWN!!
WHAT? HE WANTS US TO COOK HIM AN EGG?
IT COULD BE SILLY PUTTY.
EVIL SILLY PUTTY... FROM THE FUTURE.
THIS ISN'T A JOKE.
WHERE DID YOU GET THAT??
WHERE DID YOU GET IT??!!
THERE IS NOT A WEAPON IN ALL OF TIME THAT I CANNOT GET MY HANDS ON.
YOU KNOW THAT.
IT'S PART OF MY CHARM.

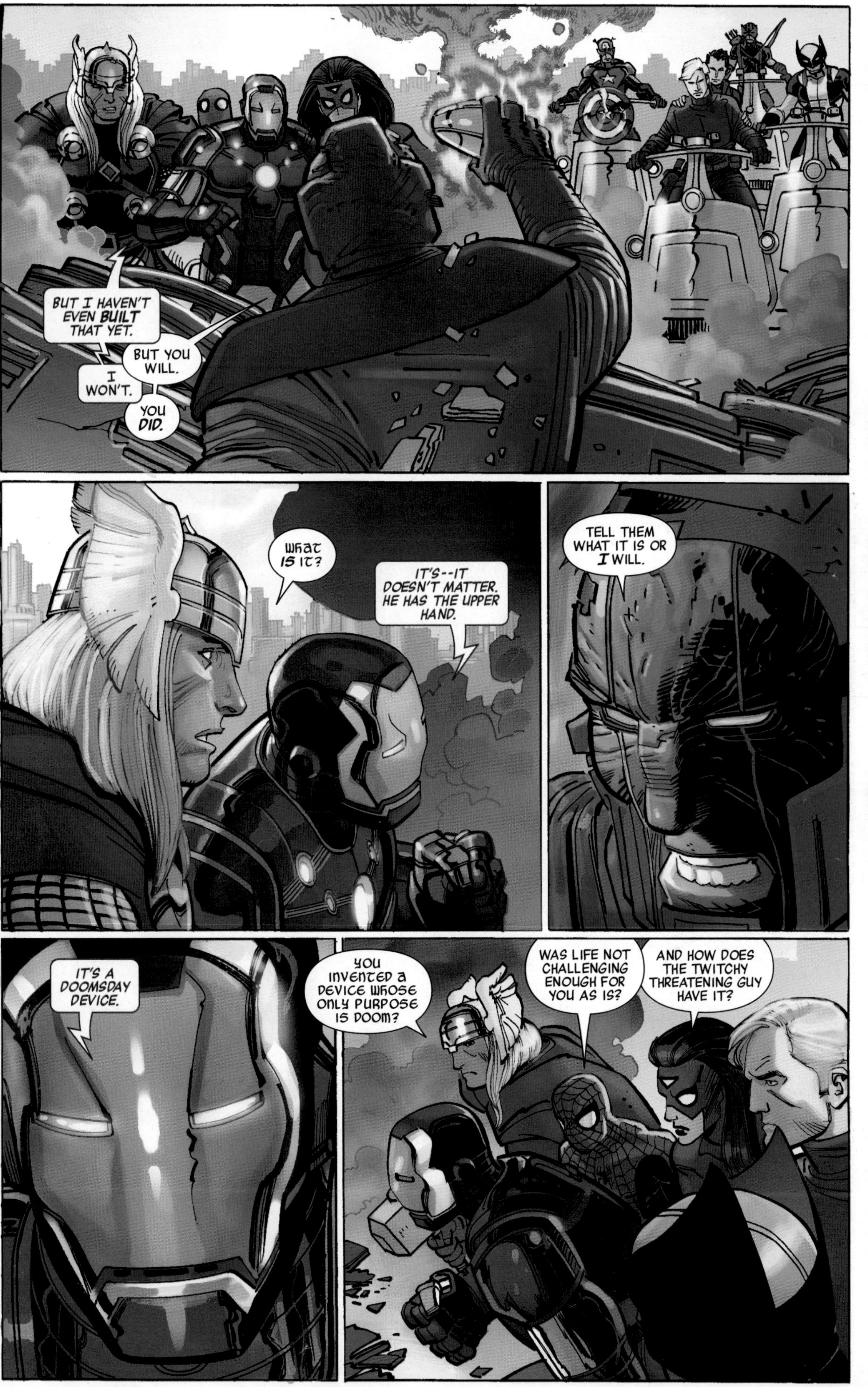

BUT I HAVEN'T EVEN BUILT THAT YET.
BUT YOU WILL.
I WON'T.
YOU DID.
WHAT IS IT?
IT'S--IT DOESN'T MATTER. HE HAS THE UPPER HAND.
TELL THEM WHAT IT IS OR I WILL.
IT'S A DOOMSDAY DEVICE.
YOU INVENTED A DEVICE WHOSE ONLY PURPOSE IS DOOM?
WAS LIFE NOT CHALLENGING ENOUGH FOR YOU AS IS?
AND HOW DOES THE TWITCHY THREATENING GUY HAVE IT?

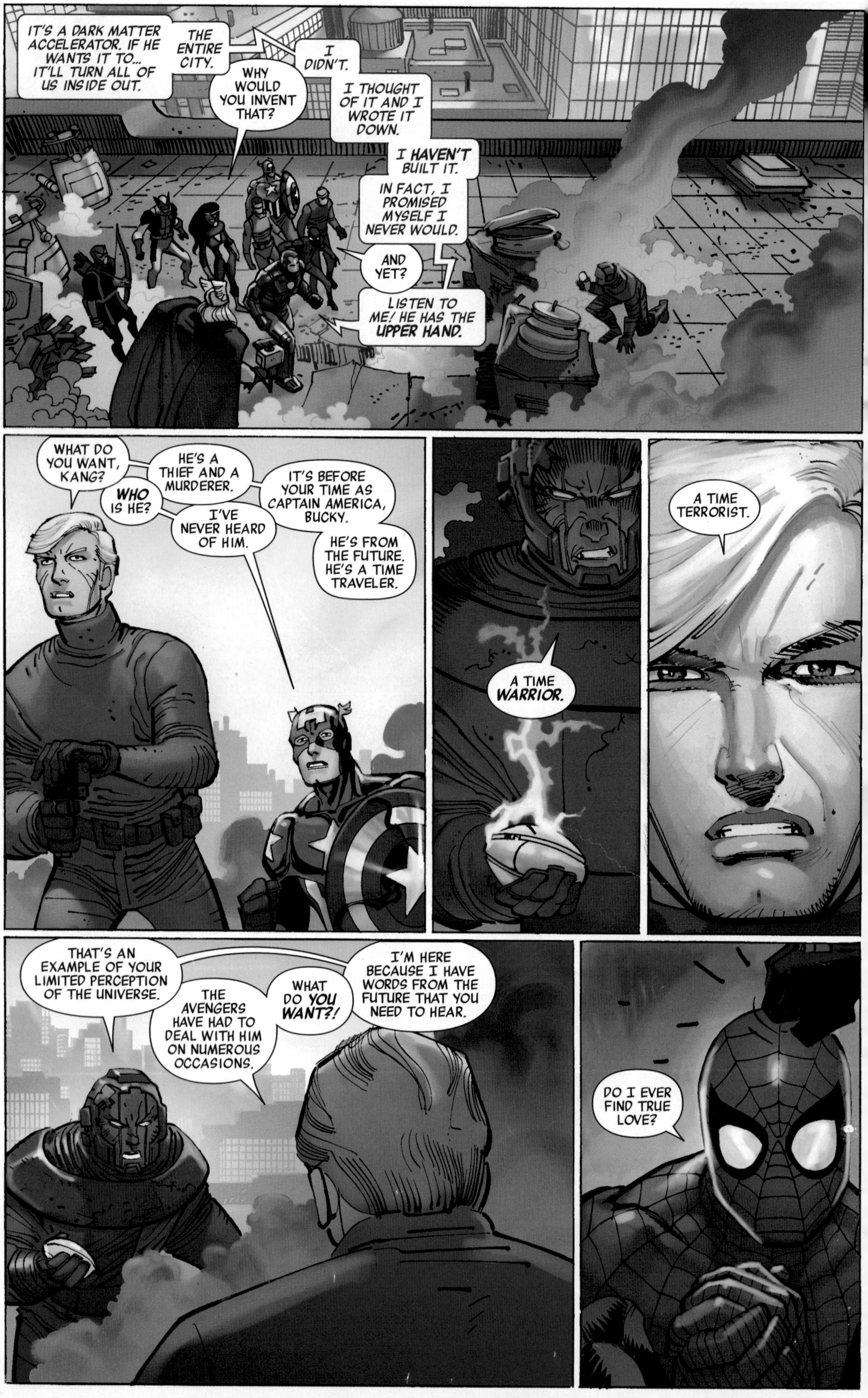
IT'S A DARK MATTER ACCELERATOR. IF HE WANTS IT TO... IT'LL TURN ALL OF US INSIDE OUT.
THE ENTIRE CITY.
WHY WOULD YOU INVENT THAT?
I DIDN'T.
I THOUGHT OF IT AND I WROTE IT DOWN.
I HAVEN'T BUILT IT.
IN FACT, I PROMISED MYSELF I NEVER WOULD.
AND YET?
LISTEN TO ME! HE HAS THE UPPER HAND.
WHAT DO YOU WANT, KANG?
HE'S A THIEF AND A MURDERER.
WHO IS HE?
I'VE NEVER HEARD OF HIM.
IT'S BEFORE YOUR TIME AS CAPTAIN AMERICA, BUCKY.
HE'S FROM THE FUTURE. HE'S A TIME TRAVELER.
A TIME WARRIOR.
A TIME TERRORIST.
THAT'S AN EXAMPLE OF YOUR LIMITED PERCEPTION OF THE UNIVERSE.
THE AVENGERS HAVE HAD TO DEAL WITH HIM ON NUMEROUS OCCASIONS.
WHAT DO YOU WANT?!
I'M HERE BECAUSE I HAVE WORDS FROM THE FUTURE THAT YOU NEED TO HEAR.
DO I EVER FIND TRUE LOVE?

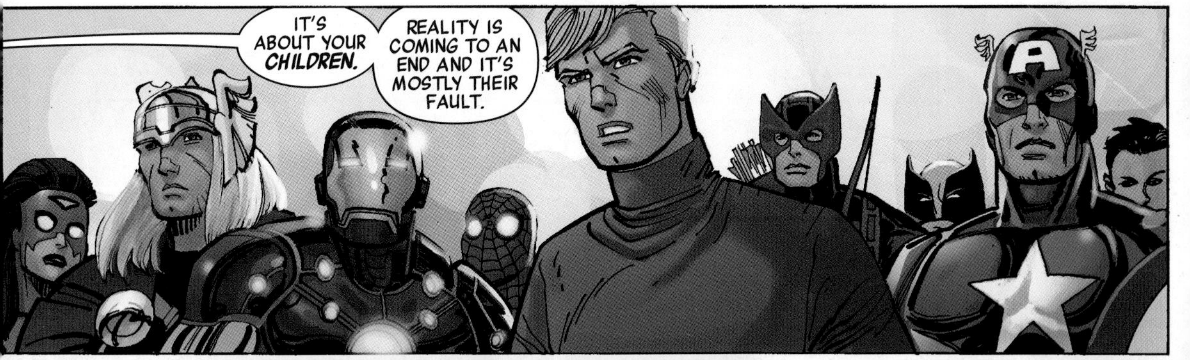

IT'S ABOUT YOUR CHILDREN.
REALITY IS COMING TO AN END AND IT'S MOSTLY THEIR FAULT.

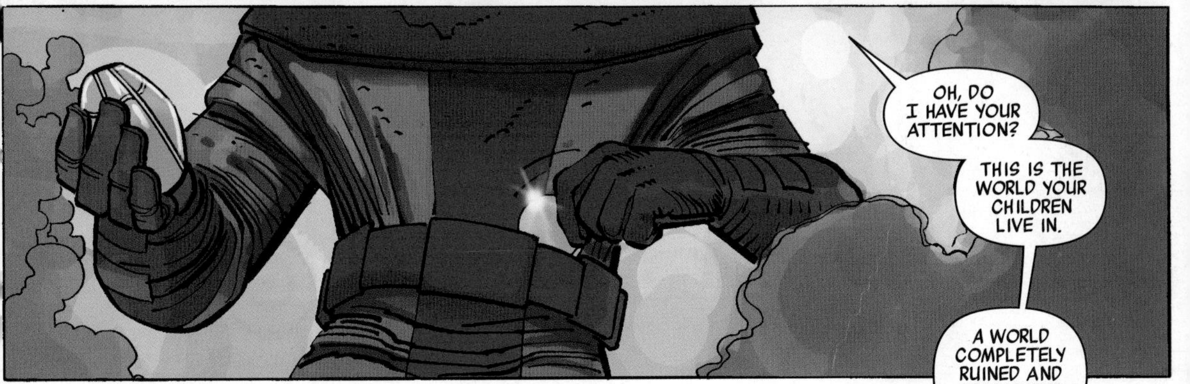

OH, DO I HAVE YOUR ATTENTION?
THIS IS THE WORLD YOUR CHILDREN LIVE IN.
A WORLD COMPLETELY RUINED AND REINVENTED BY ULTRON.

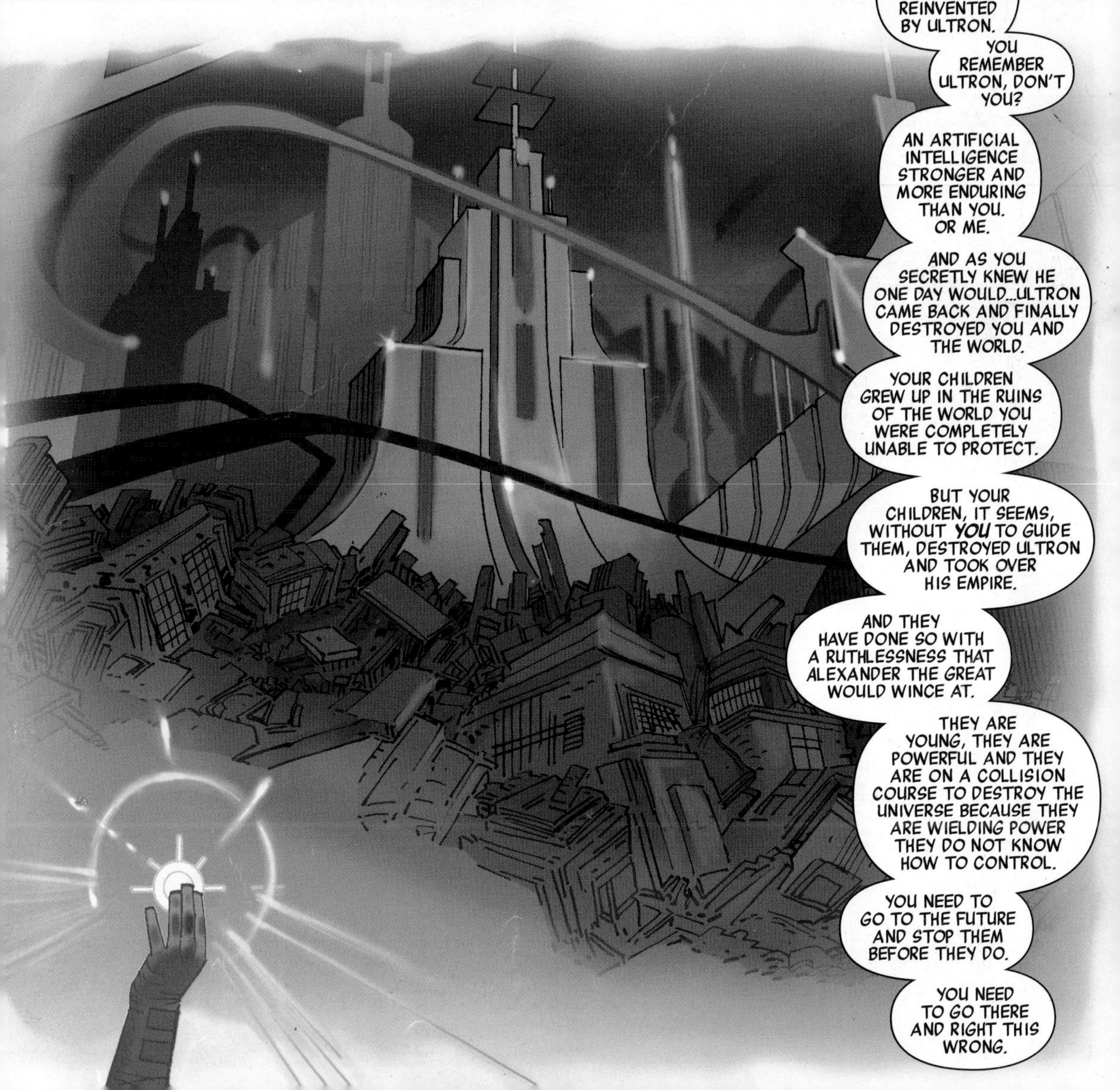

YOU REMEMBER ULTRON, DON'T YOU?
AN ARTIFICIAL INTELLIGENCE STRONGER AND MORE ENDURING THAN YOU. OR ME.
AND AS YOU SECRETLY KNEW HE ONE DAY WOULD...ULTRON CAME BACK AND FINALLY DESTROYED YOU AND THE WORLD.
YOUR CHILDREN GREW UP IN THE RUINS OF THE WORLD YOU WERE COMPLETELY UNABLE TO PROTECT.
BUT YOUR CHILDREN, IT SEEMS, WITHOUT YOU TO GUIDE THEM, DESTROYED ULTRON AND TOOK OVER HIS EMPIRE.
AND THEY HAVE DONE SO WITH A RUTHLESSNESS THAT ALEXANDER THE GREAT WOULD WINCE AT.
THEY ARE YOUNG, THEY ARE POWERFUL AND THEY ARE ON A COLLISION COURSE TO DESTROY THE UNIVERSE BECAUSE THEY ARE WIELDING POWER THEY DO NOT KNOW HOW TO CONTROL.
YOU NEED TO GO TO THE FUTURE AND STOP THEM BEFORE THEY DO.
YOU NEED TO GO THERE AND RIGHT THIS WRONG.

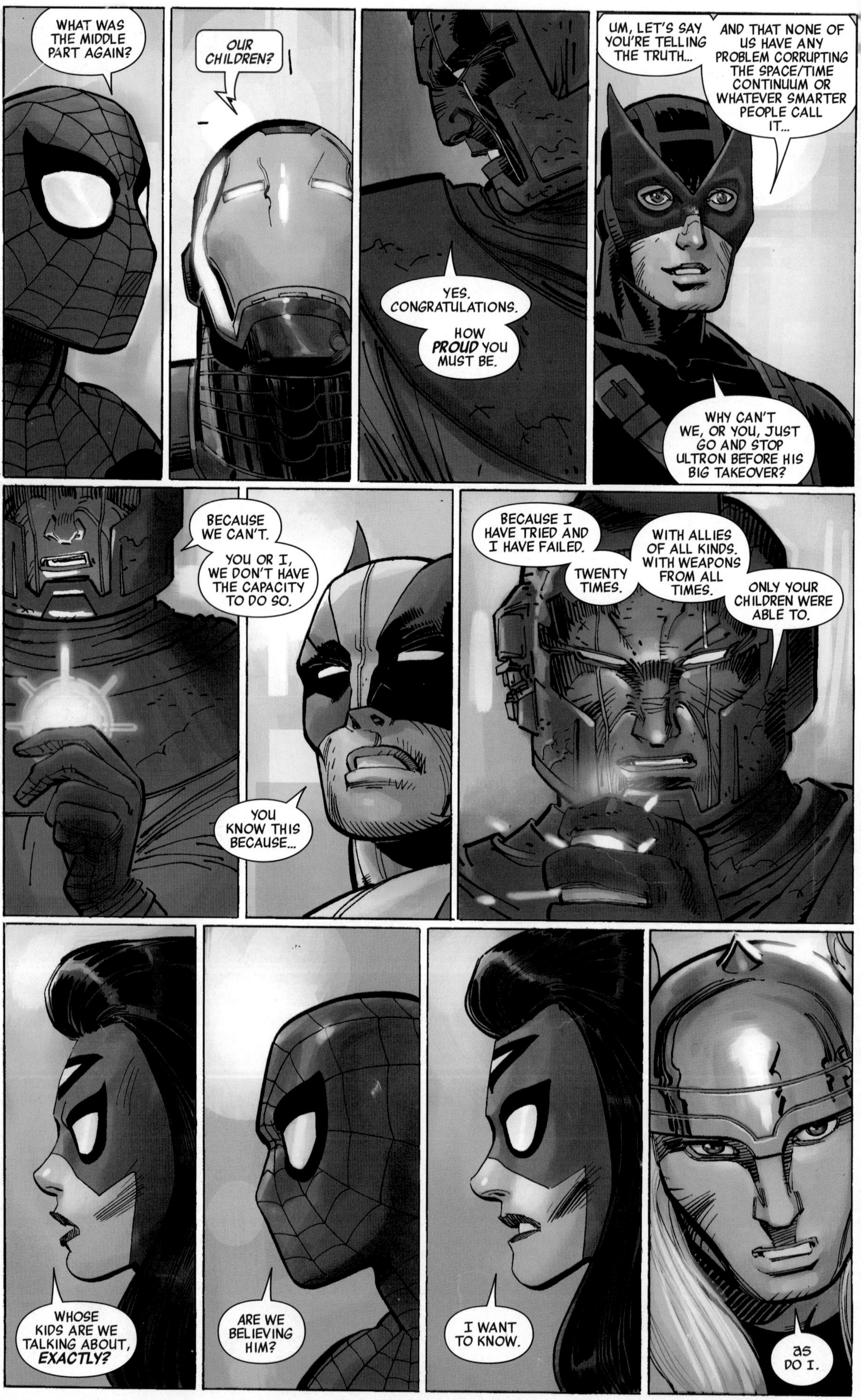
WHAT WAS THE MIDDLE PART AGAIN?
OUR CHILDREN?
YES. CONGRATULATIONS.
HOW PROUD YOU MUST BE.
UM, LET'S SAY YOU'RE TELLING THE TRUTH...
AND THAT NONE OF US HAVE ANY PROBLEM CORRUPTING THE SPACE/TIME CONTINUUM OR WHATEVER SMARTER PEOPLE CALL IT...
WHY CAN'T WE, OR YOU, JUST GO AND STOP ULTRON BEFORE HIS BIG TAKEOVER?
BECAUSE WE CAN'T.
YOU OR I, WE DON'T HAVE THE CAPACITY TO DO SO.
YOU KNOW THIS BECAUSE...
BECAUSE I HAVE TRIED AND I HAVE FAILED.
TWENTY TIMES.
WITH ALLIES OF ALL KINDS. WITH WEAPONS FROM ALL TIMES.
ONLY YOUR CHILDREN WERE ABLE TO.
WHOSE KIDS ARE WE TALKING ABOUT, EXACTLY?
ARE WE BELIEVING HIM?
I WANT TO KNOW.
AS DO I.

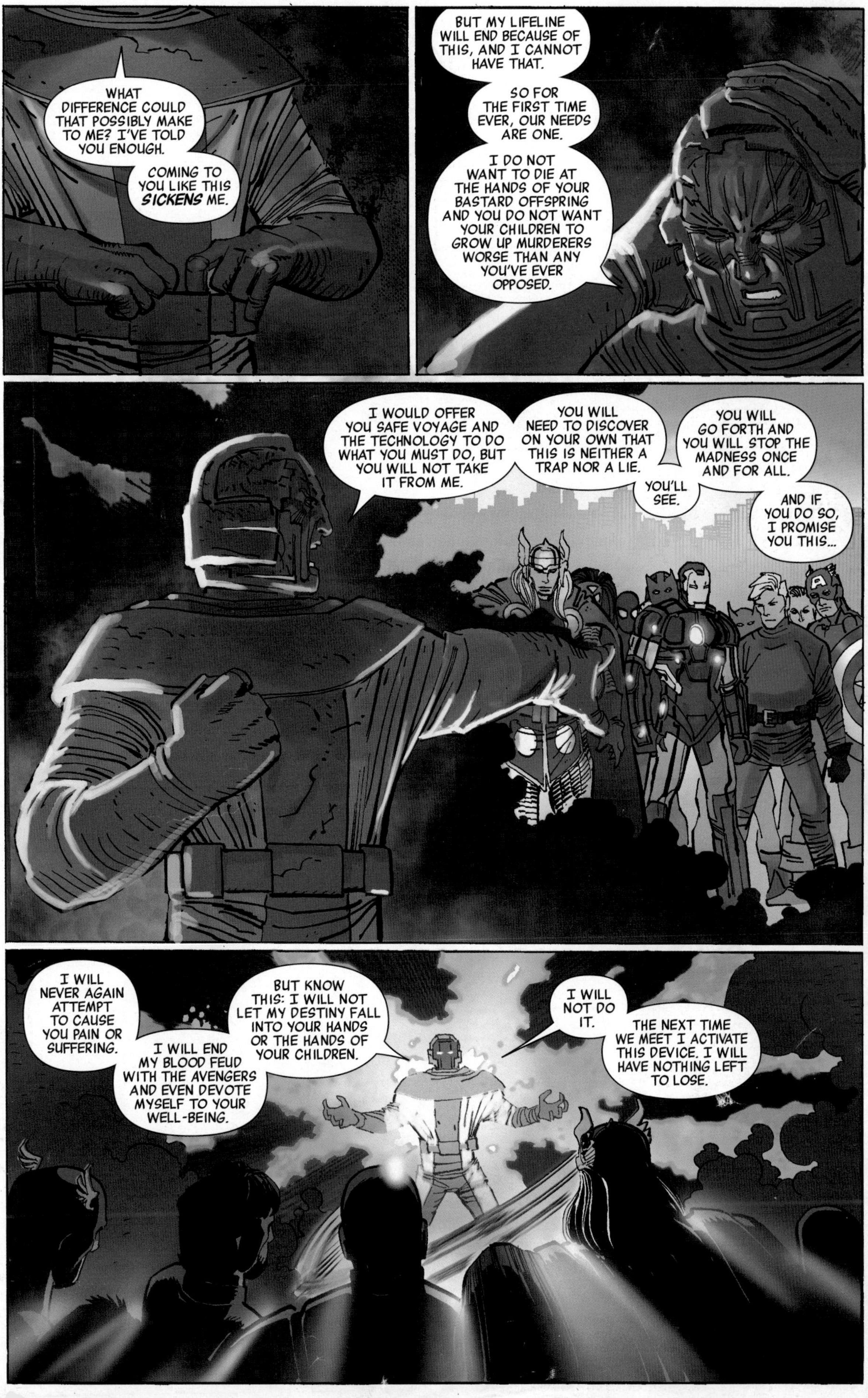
WHAT DIFFERENCE COULD THAT POSSIBLY MAKE TO ME? I'VE TOLD YOU ENOUGH.
COMING TO YOU LIKE THIS SICKENS ME.
BUT MY LIFELINE WILL END BECAUSE OF THIS, AND I CANNOT HAVE THAT.
SO FOR THE FIRST TIME EVER, OUR NEEDS ARE ONE.
I DO NOT WANT TO DIE AT THE HANDS OF YOUR BASTARD OFFSPRING AND YOU DO NOT WANT YOUR CHILDREN TO GROW UP MURDERERS WORSE THAN ANY YOU'VE EVER OPPOSED.
I WOULD OFFER YOU SAFE VOYAGE AND THE TECHNOLOGY TO DO WHAT YOU MUST DO, BUT YOU WILL NOT TAKE IT FROM ME.
YOU WILL NEED TO DISCOVER ON YOUR OWN THAT THIS IS NEITHER A TRAP NOR A LIE.
YOU'LL SEE.
YOU WILL GO FORTH AND YOU WILL STOP THE MADNESS ONCE AND FOR ALL.
AND IF YOU DO SO, I PROMISE YOU THIS...
I WILL NEVER AGAIN ATTEMPT TO CAUSE YOU PAIN OR SUFFERING.
I WILL END MY BLOOD FEUD WITH THE AVENGERS AND EVEN DEVOTE MYSELF TO YOUR WELL-BEING.
BUT KNOW THIS: I WILL NOT LET MY DESTINY FALL INTO YOUR HANDS OR THE HANDS OF YOUR CHILDREN.
I WILL NOT DO IT.
THE NEXT TIME WE MEET I ACTIVATE THIS DEVICE. I WILL HAVE NOTHING LEFT TO LOSE.

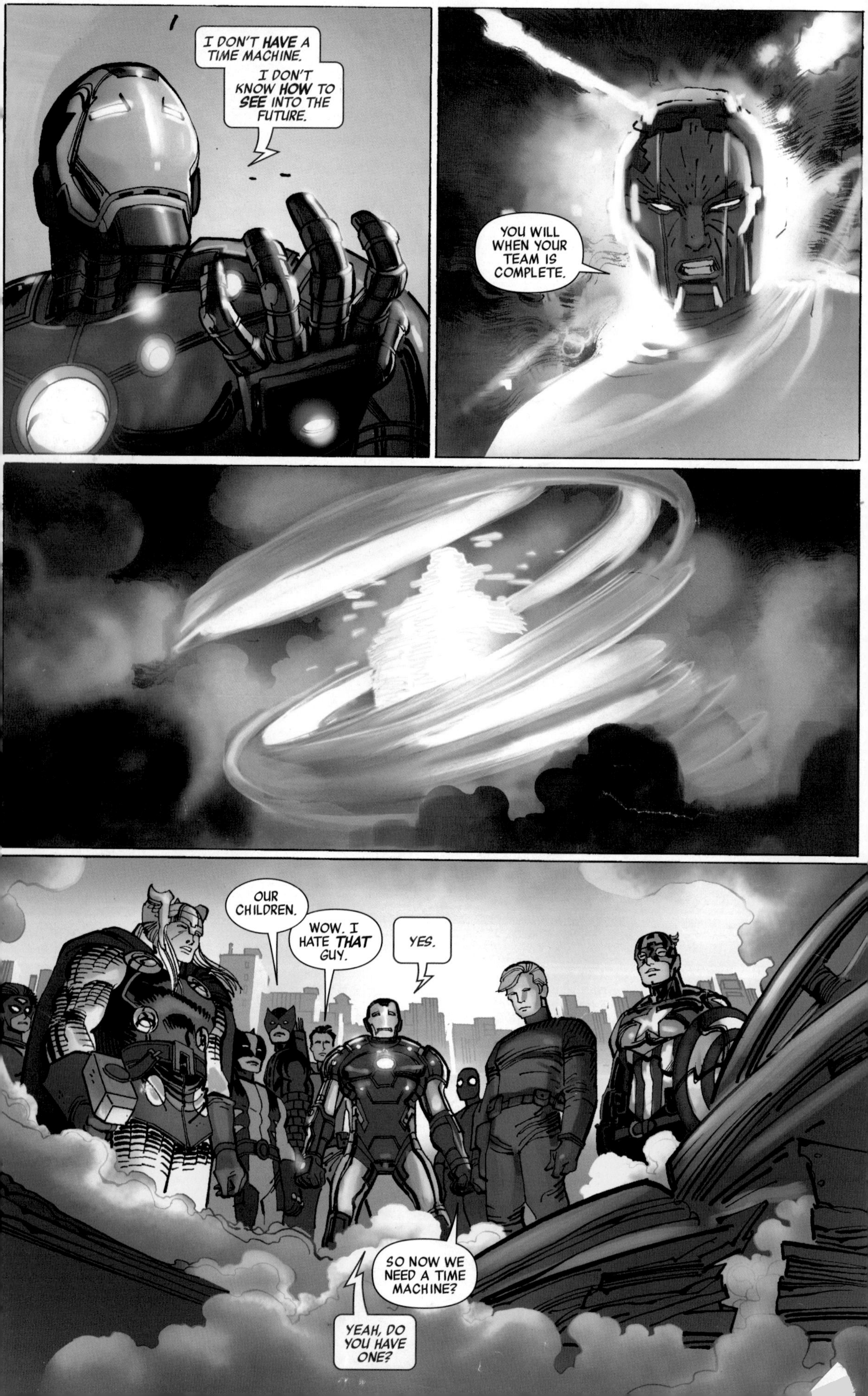
I DON'T HAVE A TIME MACHINE.
I DON'T KNOW HOW TO SEE INTO THE FUTURE.
YOU WILL WHEN YOUR TEAM IS COMPLETE.
OUR CHILDREN.
WOW. I HATE THAT GUY.
YES.
SO NOW WE NEED A TIME MACHINE?
YEAH, DO YOU HAVE ONE?

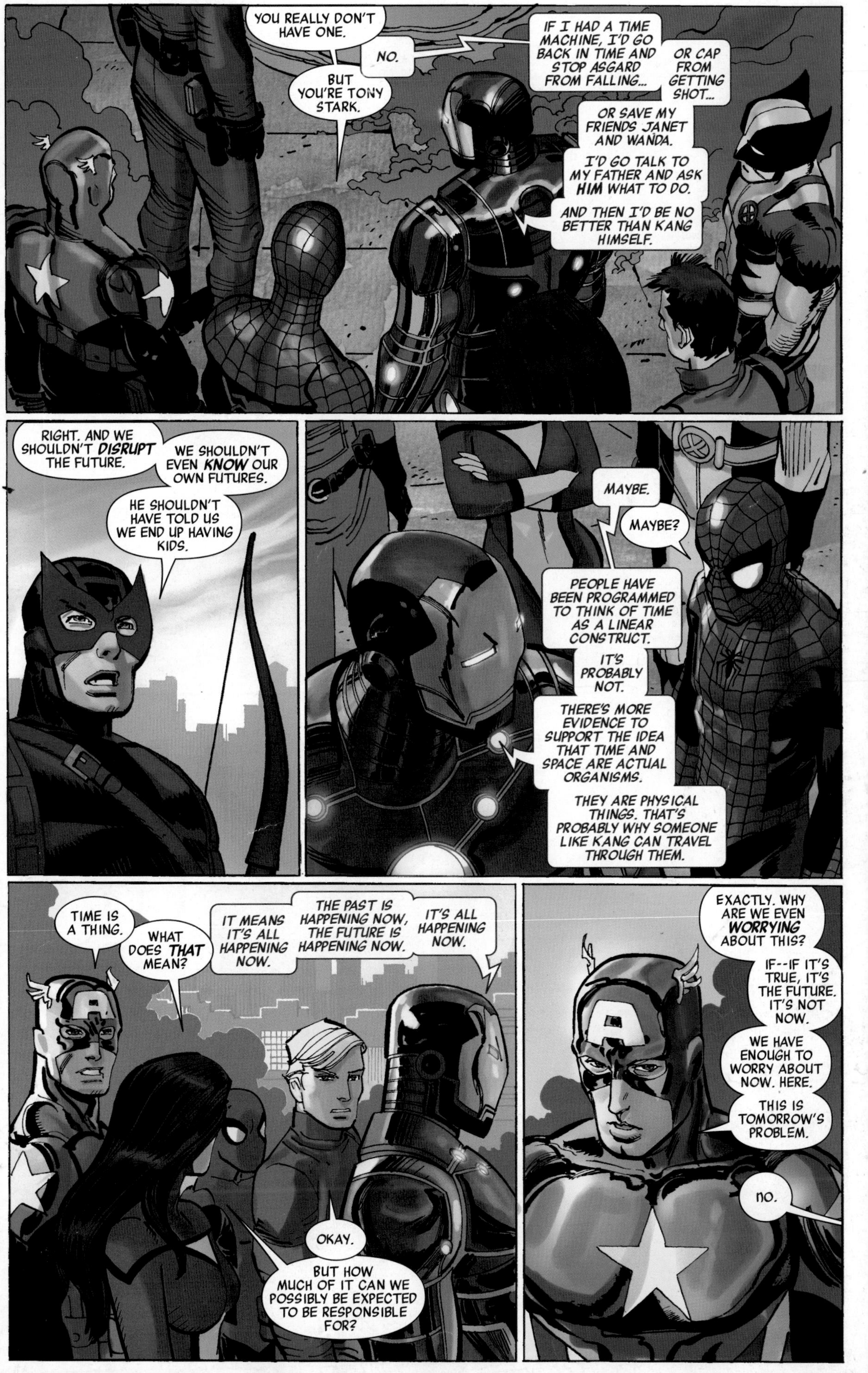
YOU REALLY DON'T HAVE ONE.
NO.
BUT YOU'RE TONY STARK.
IF I HAD A TIME MACHINE, I'D GO BACK IN TIME AND STOP ASGARD FROM FALLING...
OR CAP FROM GETTING SHOT...
OR SAVE MY FRIENDS JANET AND WANDA.
I'D GO TALK TO MY FATHER AND ASK HIM WHAT TO DO.
AND THEN I'D BE NO BETTER THAN KANG HIMSELF.
RIGHT. AND WE SHOULDN'T DISRUPT THE FUTURE.
WE SHOULDN'T EVEN KNOW OUR OWN FUTURES.
HE SHOULDN'T HAVE TOLD US WE END UP HAVING KIDS.
MAYBE.
MAYBE?
PEOPLE HAVE BEEN PROGRAMMED TO THINK OF TIME AS A LINEAR CONSTRUCT.
IT'S PROBABLY NOT.
THERE'S MORE EVIDENCE TO SUPPORT THE IDEA THAT TIME AND SPACE ARE ACTUAL ORGANISMS.
THEY ARE PHYSICAL THINGS. THAT'S PROBABLY WHY SOMEONE LIKE KANG CAN TRAVEL THROUGH THEM.
TIME IS A THING.
WHAT DOES THAT MEAN?
IT MEANS IT'S ALL HAPPENING NOW.
THE PAST IS HAPPENING NOW, THE FUTURE IS HAPPENING NOW.
IT'S ALL HAPPENING NOW.
OKAY.
BUT HOW MUCH OF IT CAN WE POSSIBLY BE EXPECTED TO BE RESPONSIBLE FOR?
EXACTLY. WHY ARE WE EVEN WORRYING ABOUT THIS?
IF--IF IT'S TRUE, IT'S THE FUTURE. IT'S NOT NOW.
WE HAVE ENOUGH TO WORRY ABOUT NOW. HERE.
THIS IS TOMORROW'S PROBLEM.
NO.

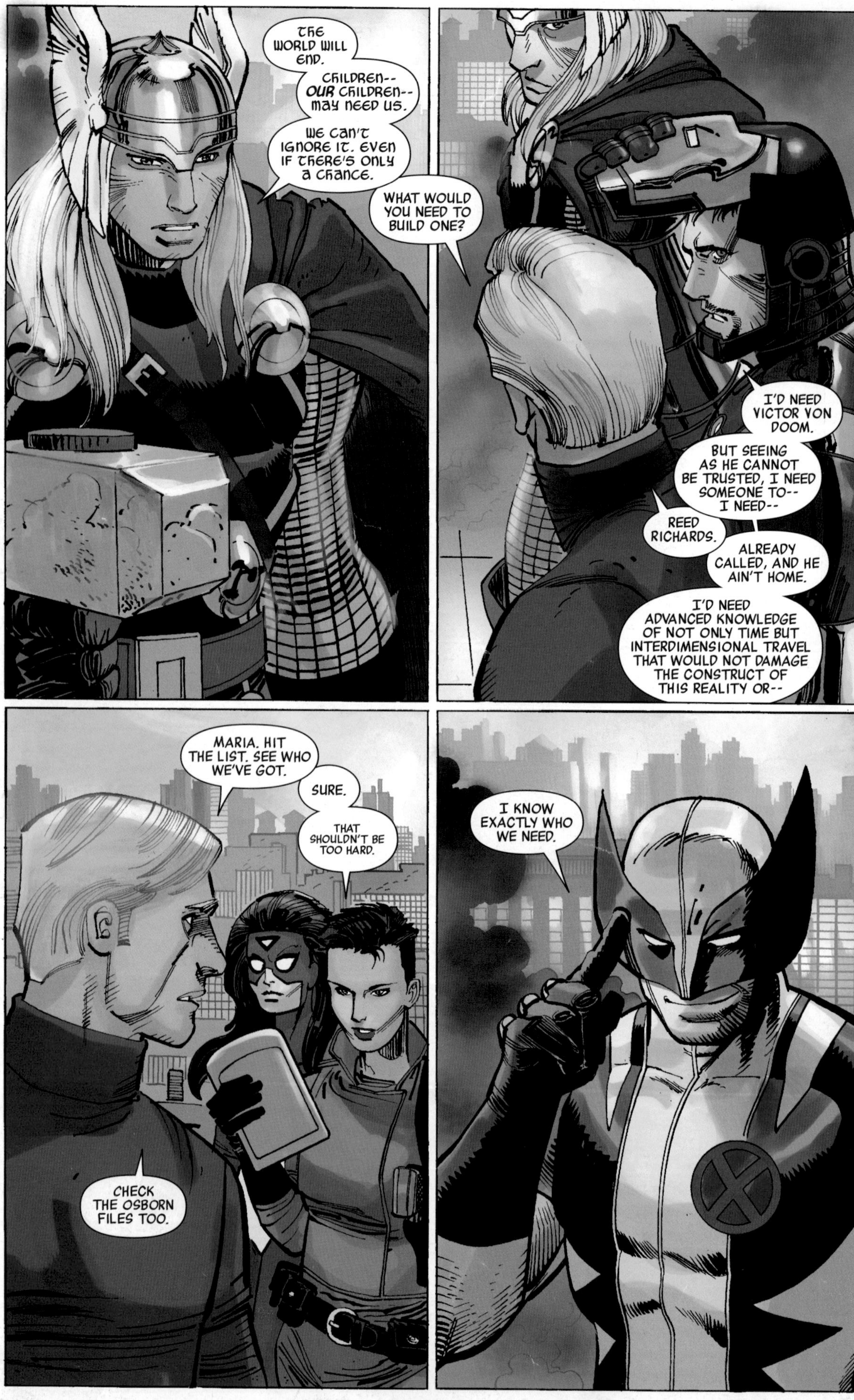
THE WORLD WILL END.
CHILDREN-- OUR CHILDREN-- MAY NEED US.
WE CAN'T IGNORE IT. EVEN IF THERE'S ONLY A CHANCE.
WHAT WOULD YOU NEED TO BUILD ONE?
I'D NEED VICTOR VON DOOM.
BUT SEEING AS HE CANNOT BE TRUSTED, I NEED SOMEONE TO-- I NEED--
REED RICHARDS.
ALREADY CALLED, AND HE AIN'T HOME.
I'D NEED ADVANCED KNOWLEDGE OF NOT ONLY TIME BUT INTERDIMENSIONAL TRAVEL THAT WOULD NOT DAMAGE THE CONSTRUCT OF THIS REALITY OR--
MARIA. HIT THE LIST. SEE WHO WE'VE GOT.
SURE.
THAT SHOULDN'T BE TOO HARD.
CHECK THE OSBORN FILES TOO.
I KNOW EXACTLY WHO WE NEED.

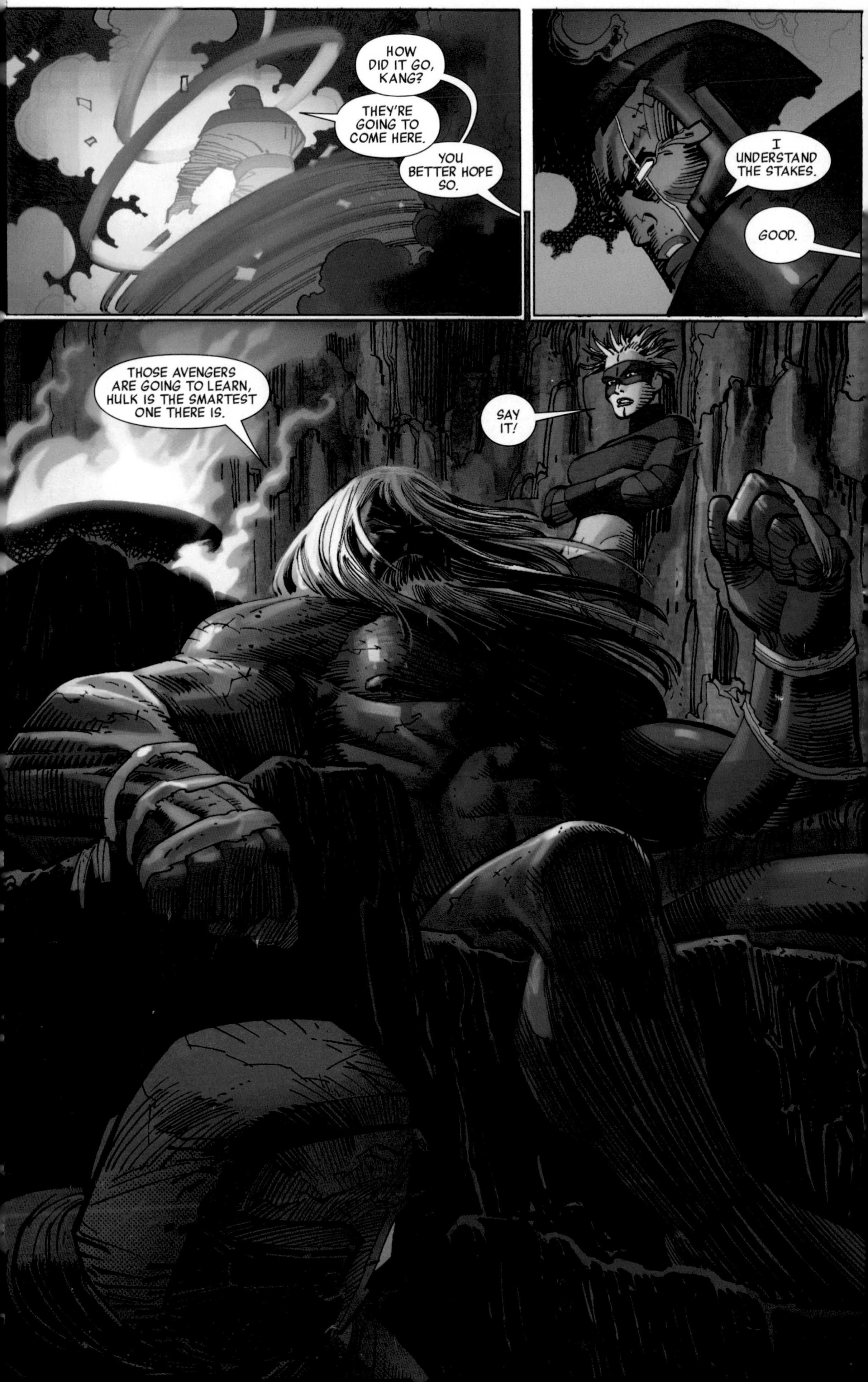
HOW DID IT GO, KANG?
THEY'RE GOING TO COME HERE.
YOU BETTER HOPE SO.
I UNDERSTAND THE STAKES.
GOOD.
THOSE AVENGERS ARE GOING TO LEARN, HULK IS THE SMARTEST ONE THERE IS.
SAY IT!

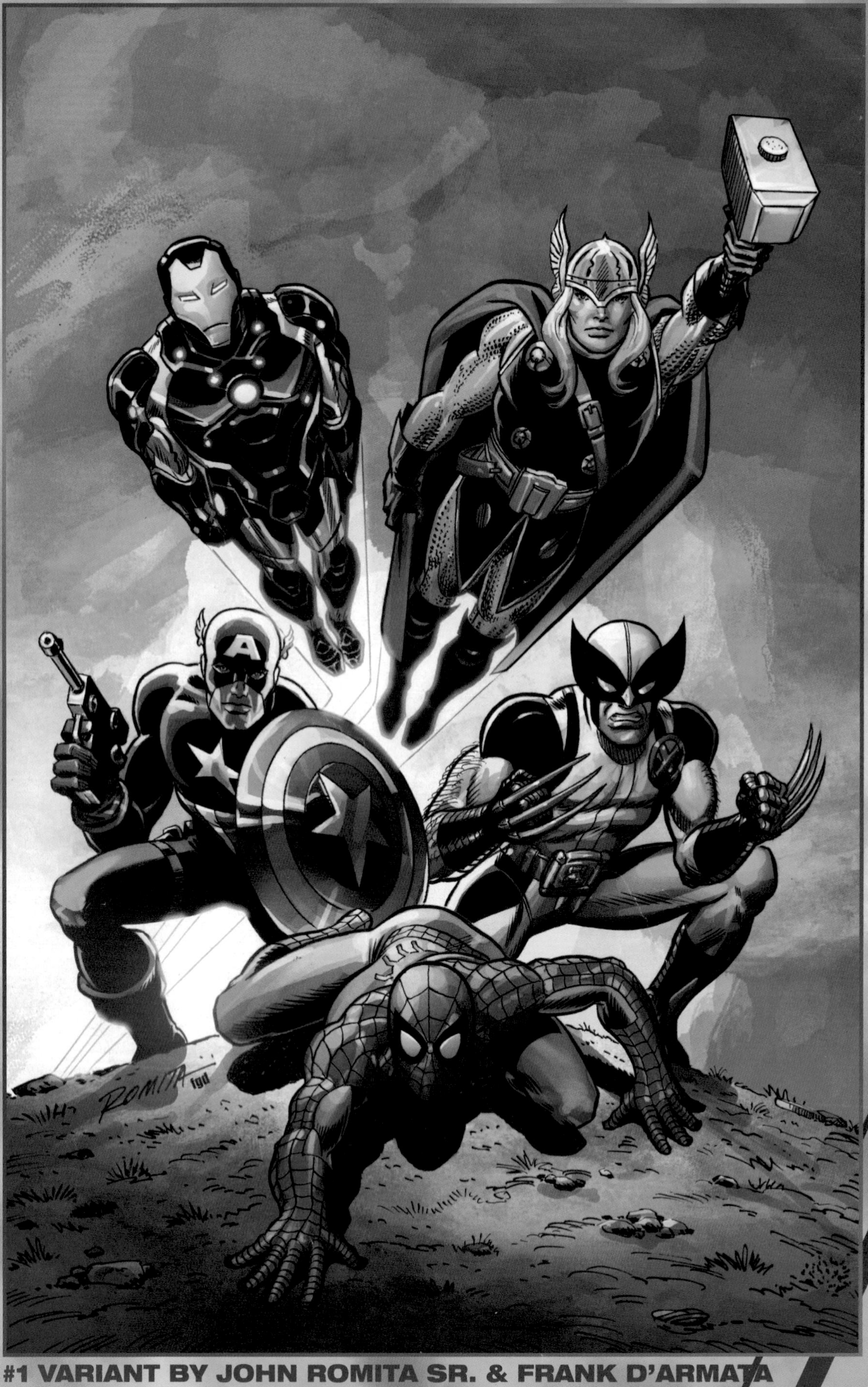
ROMITA
fgd

#1 VARIANT BY JOHN ROMITA SR. & FRANK D'ARMATA

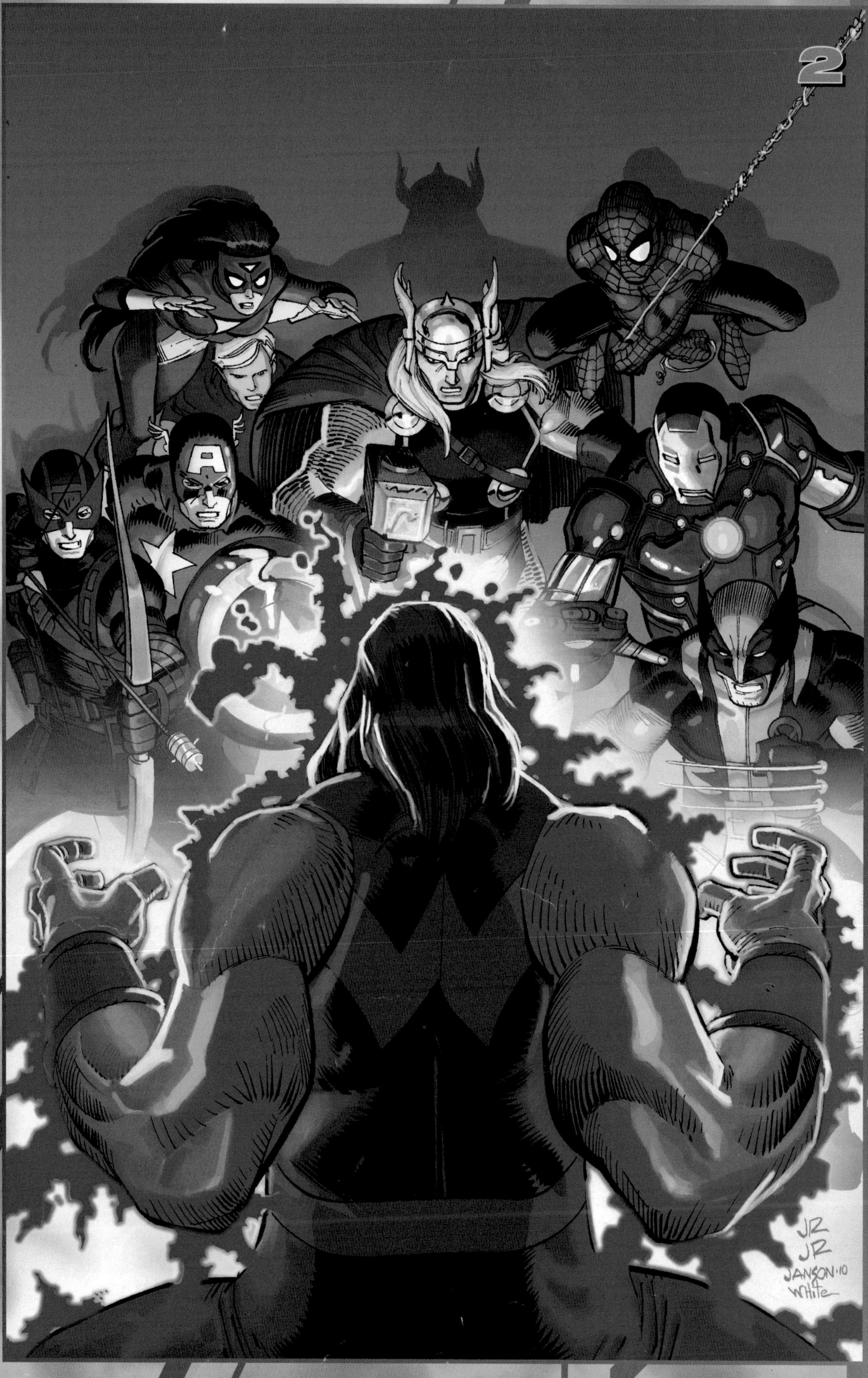
2
JR
JR
JANSON·10
White

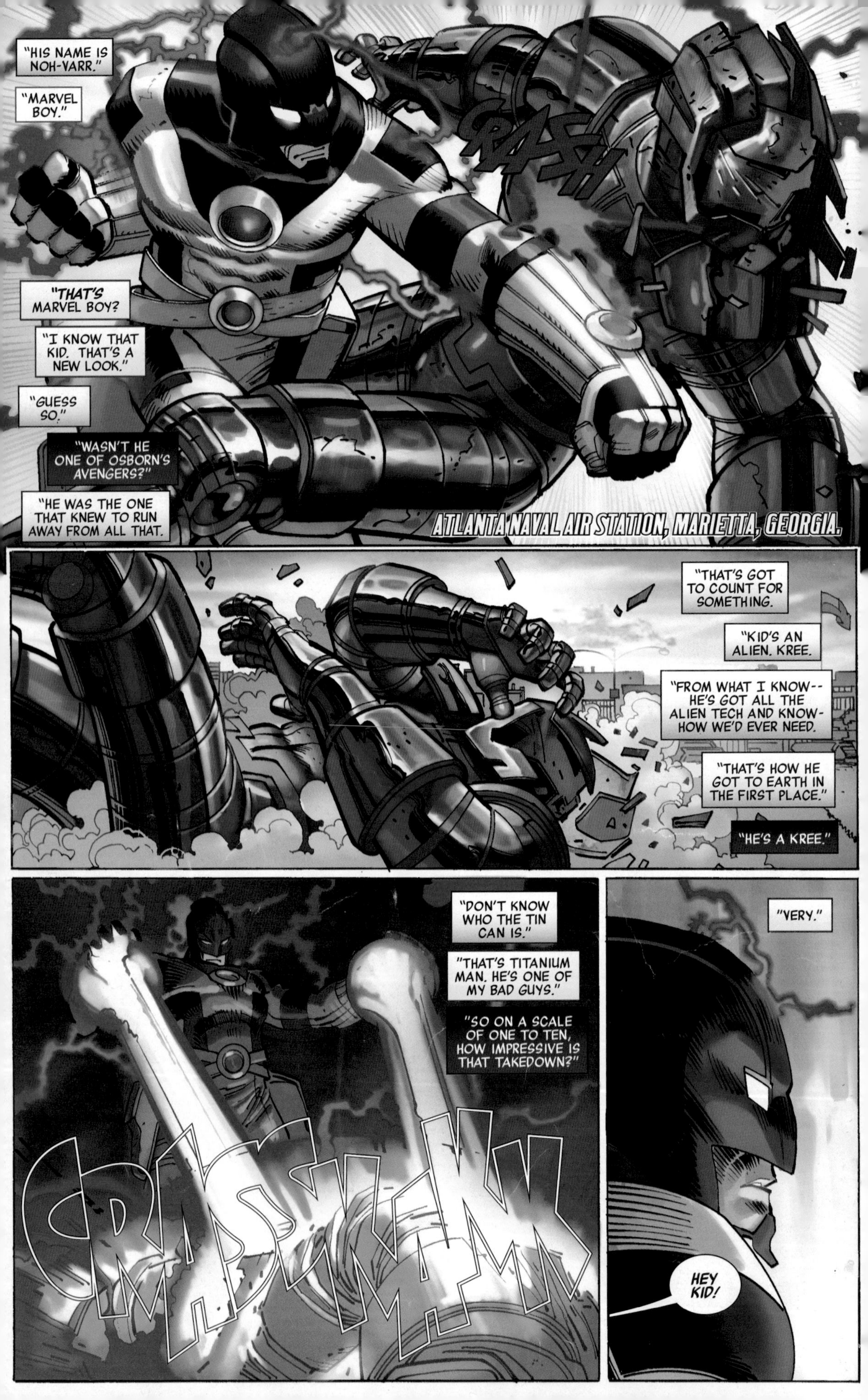
"HIS NAME IS NOH-VARR."
"MARVEL BOY."
CRASH
"THAT'S MARVEL BOY?
"I KNOW THAT KID. THAT'S A NEW LOOK."
"GUESS SO."
"WASN'T HE ONE OF OSBORN'S AVENGERS?"
"HE WAS THE ONE THAT KNEW TO RUN AWAY FROM ALL THAT.
ATLANTA NAVAL AIR STATION, MARIETTA, GEORGIA.
"THAT'S GOT TO COUNT FOR SOMETHING.
"KID'S AN ALIEN. KREE.
"FROM WHAT I KNOW-- HE'S GOT ALL THE ALIEN TECH AND KNOW-HOW WE'D EVER NEED.
"THAT'S HOW HE GOT TO EARTH IN THE FIRST PLACE."
"HE'S A KREE."
"DON'T KNOW WHO THE TIN CAN IS."
"THAT'S TITANIUM MAN. HE'S ONE OF MY BAD GUYS."
"SO ON A SCALE OF ONE TO TEN, HOW IMPRESSIVE IS THAT TAKEDOWN?"
"VERY."
HEY KID!

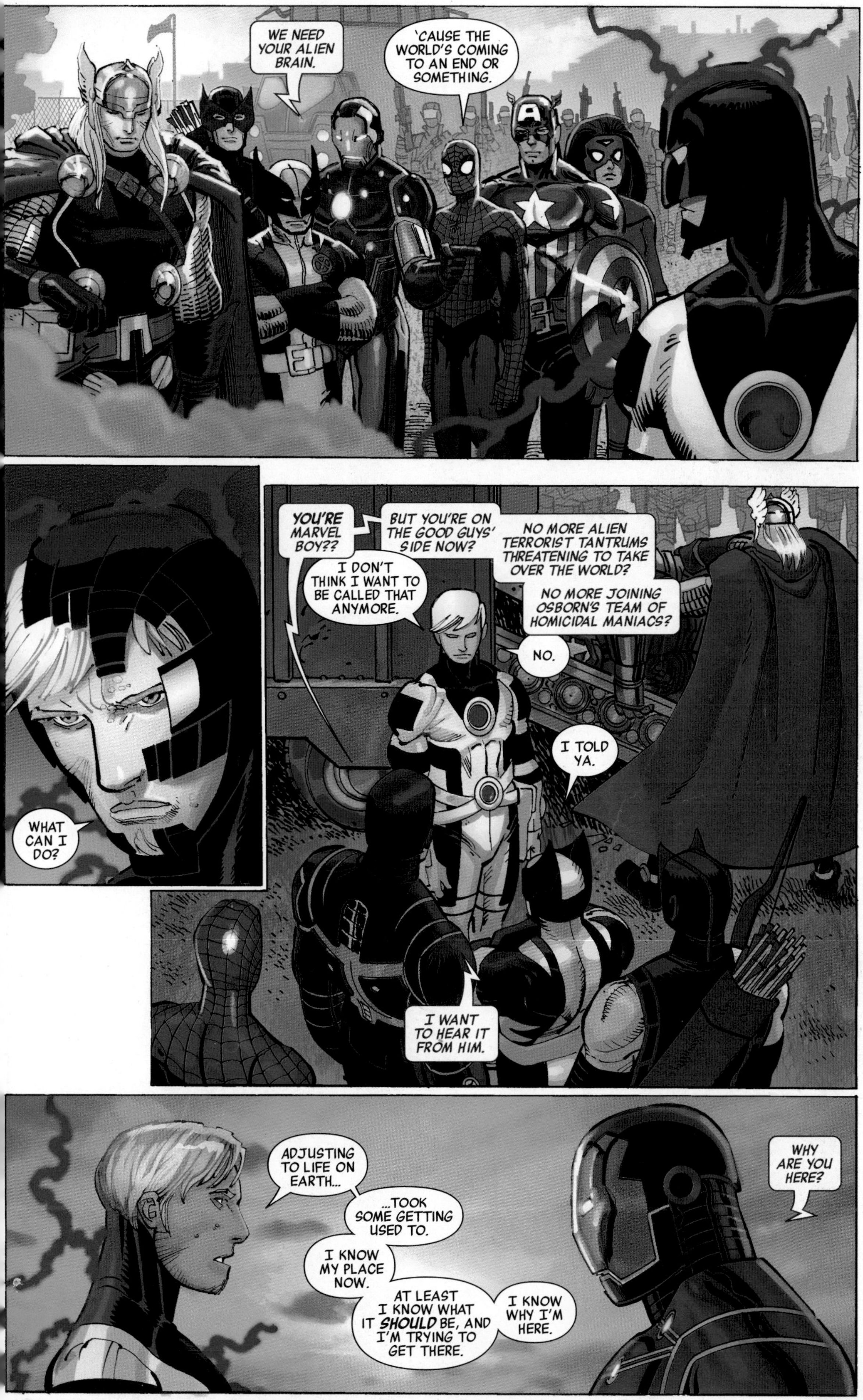
WE NEED YOUR ALIEN BRAIN.
'CAUSE THE WORLD'S COMING TO AN END OR SOMETHING.
WHAT CAN I DO?
YOU'RE MARVEL BOY??
BUT YOU'RE ON THE GOOD GUYS' SIDE NOW?
I DON'T THINK I WANT TO BE CALLED THAT ANYMORE.
NO MORE ALIEN TERRORIST TANTRUMS THREATENING TO TAKE OVER THE WORLD?
NO MORE JOINING OSBORN'S TEAM OF HOMICIDAL MANIACS?
NO.
I TOLD YA.
I WANT TO HEAR IT FROM HIM.
WHY ARE YOU HERE?
ADJUSTING TO LIFE ON EARTH...
...TOOK SOME GETTING USED TO.
I KNOW MY PLACE NOW.
AT LEAST I KNOW WHAT IT SHOULD BE, AND I'M TRYING TO GET THERE.
I KNOW WHY I'M HERE.

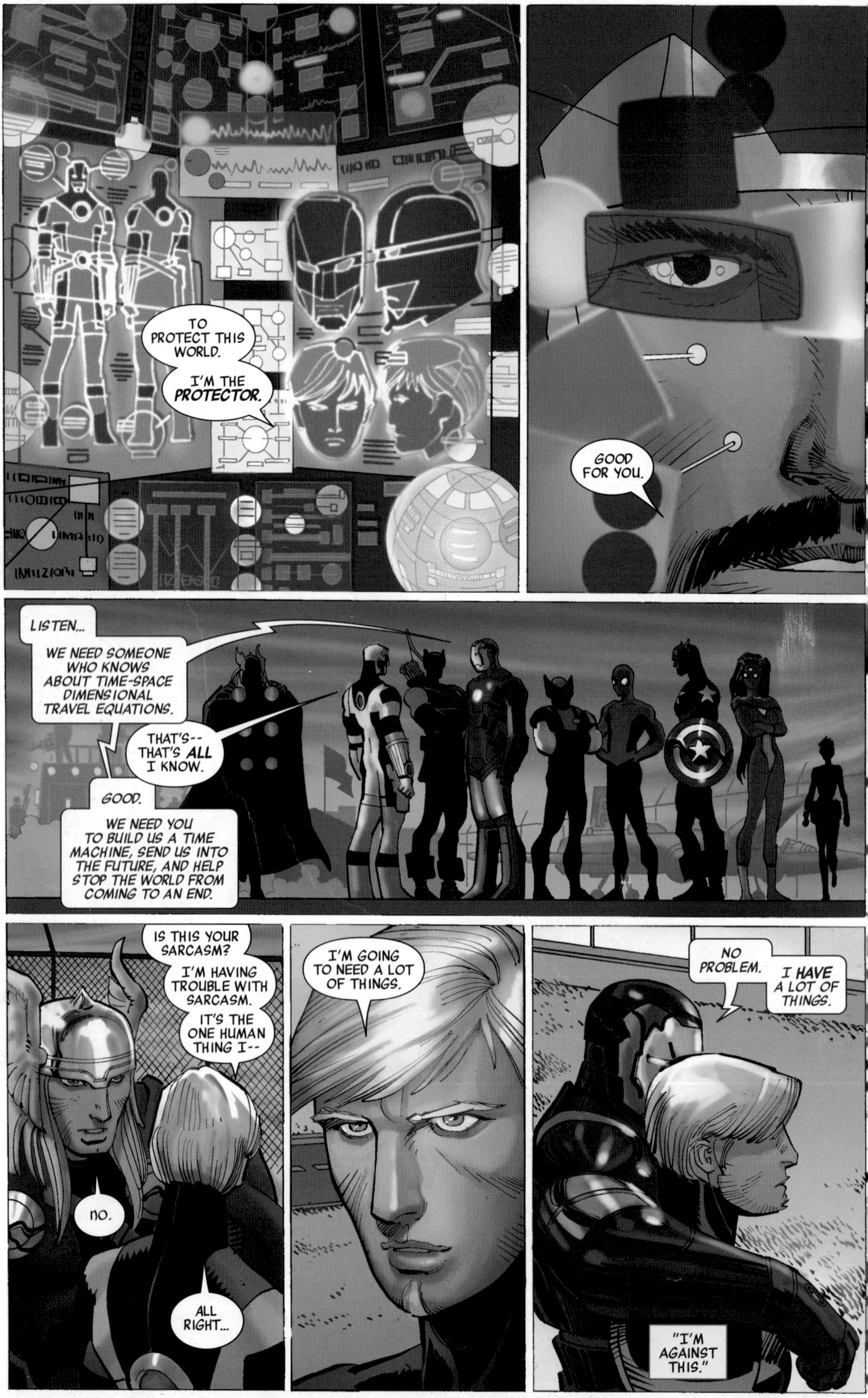
TO PROTECT THIS WORLD.
I'M THE PROTECTOR.
GOOD FOR YOU.
LISTEN...
WE NEED SOMEONE WHO KNOWS ABOUT TIME-SPACE DIMENSIONAL TRAVEL EQUATIONS.
THAT'S-- THAT'S ALL I KNOW.
GOOD.
WE NEED YOU TO BUILD US A TIME MACHINE, SEND US INTO THE FUTURE, AND HELP STOP THE WORLD FROM COMING TO AN END.
IS THIS YOUR SARCASM?
I'M HAVING TROUBLE WITH SARCASM.
IT'S THE ONE HUMAN THING I--
no.
ALL RIGHT...
I'M GOING TO NEED A LOT OF THINGS.
NO PROBLEM.
I HAVE A LOT OF THINGS.
"I'M AGAINST THIS."

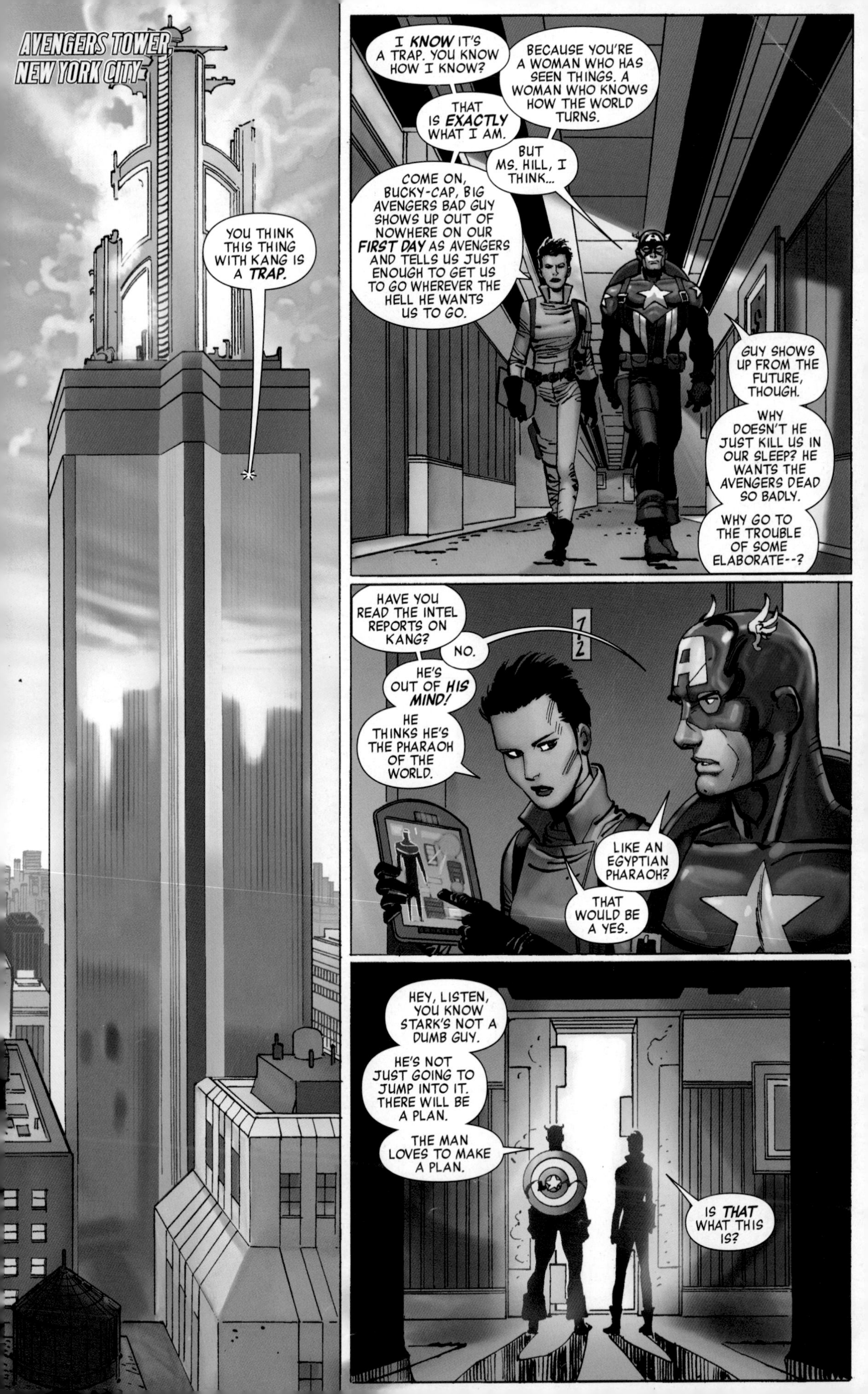
AVENGERS TOWER, NEW YORK CITY
YOU THINK THIS THING WITH KANG IS A TRAP.
I KNOW IT'S A TRAP. YOU KNOW HOW I KNOW?
BECAUSE YOU'RE A WOMAN WHO HAS SEEN THINGS. A WOMAN WHO KNOWS HOW THE WORLD TURNS.
THAT IS EXACTLY WHAT I AM.
BUT MS. HILL, I THINK...
COME ON, BUCKY-CAP, BIG AVENGERS BAD GUY SHOWS UP OUT OF NOWHERE ON OUR FIRST DAY AS AVENGERS AND TELLS US JUST ENOUGH TO GET US TO GO WHEREVER THE HELL HE WANTS US TO GO.
GUY SHOWS UP FROM THE FUTURE, THOUGH.
WHY DOESN'T HE JUST KILL US IN OUR SLEEP? HE WANTS THE AVENGERS DEAD SO BADLY.
WHY GO TO THE TROUBLE OF SOME ELABORATE--?
HAVE YOU READ THE INTEL REPORTS ON KANG?
NO.
HE'S OUT OF HIS MIND!
HE THINKS HE'S THE PHARAOH OF THE WORLD.
LIKE AN EGYPTIAN PHARAOH?
THAT WOULD BE A YES.
HEY, LISTEN, YOU KNOW STARK'S NOT A DUMB GUY.
HE'S NOT JUST GOING TO JUMP INTO IT. THERE WILL BE A PLAN.
THE MAN LOVES TO MAKE A PLAN.
IS THAT WHAT THIS IS?

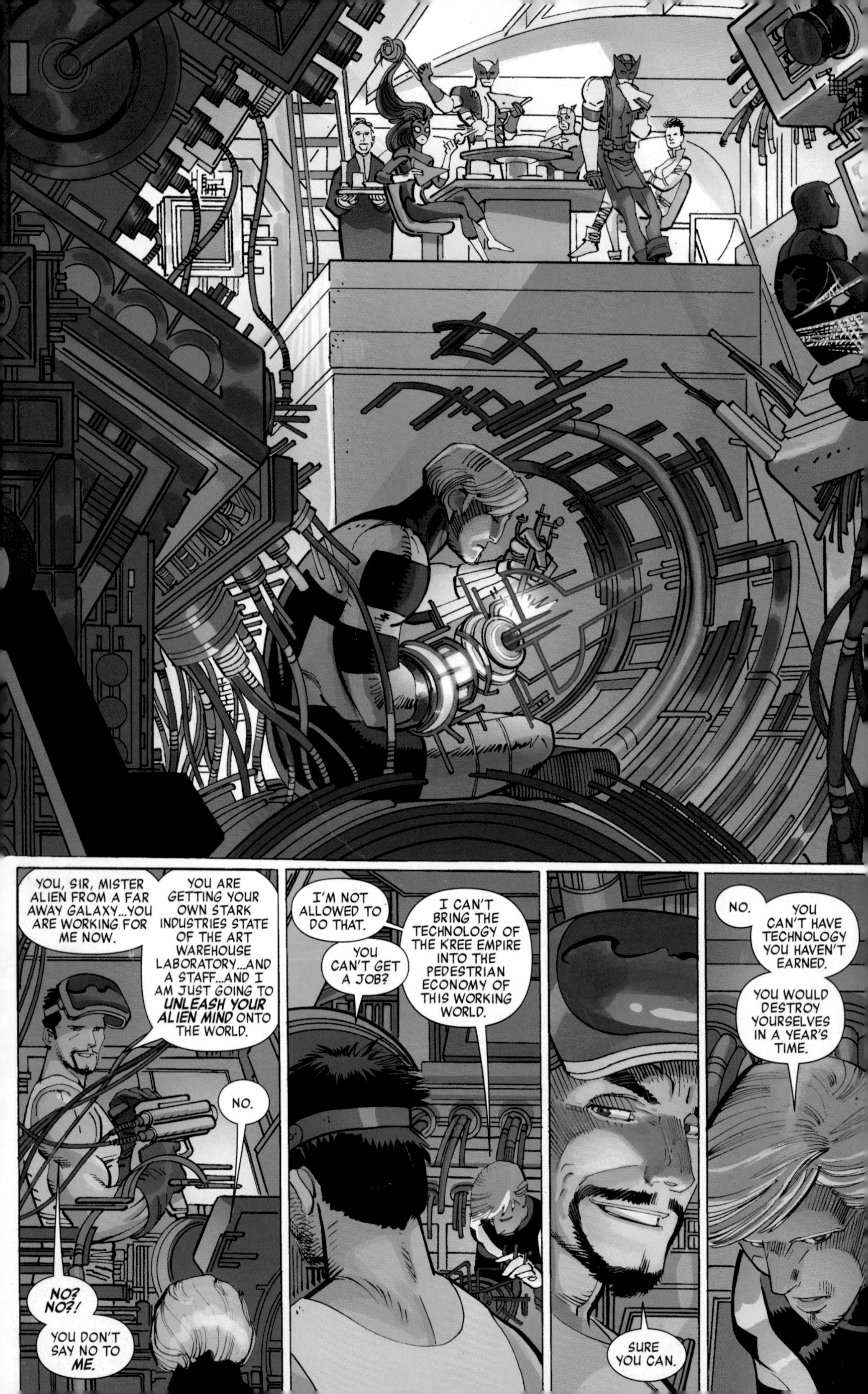
YOU, SIR, MISTER ALIEN FROM A FAR AWAY GALAXY...YOU ARE WORKING FOR ME NOW.
YOU ARE GETTING YOUR OWN STARK INDUSTRIES STATE OF THE ART WAREHOUSE LABORATORY...AND A STAFF...AND I AM JUST GOING TO **UNLEASH YOUR ALIEN MIND** ONTO THE WORLD.
NO.
NO? NO?!
YOU DON'T SAY NO TO *ME.*
I'M NOT ALLOWED TO DO THAT.
I CAN'T BRING THE TECHNOLOGY OF THE KREE EMPIRE INTO THE PEDESTRIAN ECONOMY OF THIS WORKING WORLD.
YOU CAN'T GET A JOB?
NO.
YOU CAN'T HAVE TECHNOLOGY YOU HAVEN'T EARNED.
YOU WOULD DESTROY YOURSELVES IN A YEAR'S TIME.
SURE YOU CAN.

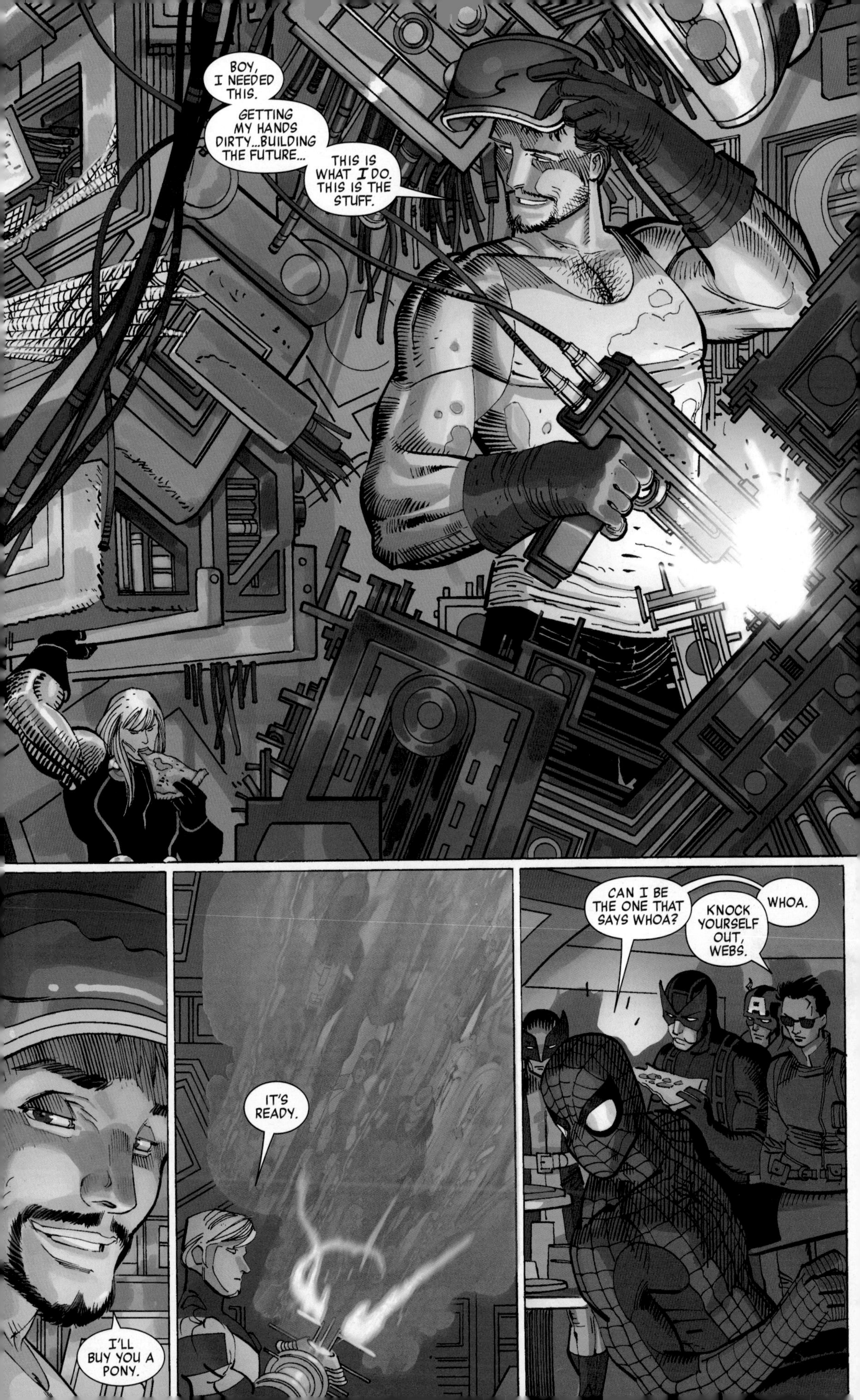
BOY, I NEEDED THIS.
GETTING MY HANDS DIRTY...BUILDING THE FUTURE...
THIS IS WHAT I DO. THIS IS THE STUFF.
I'LL BUY YOU A PONY.
IT'S READY.
CAN I BE THE ONE THAT SAYS WHOA?
KNOCK YOURSELF OUT, WEBS.
WHOA.

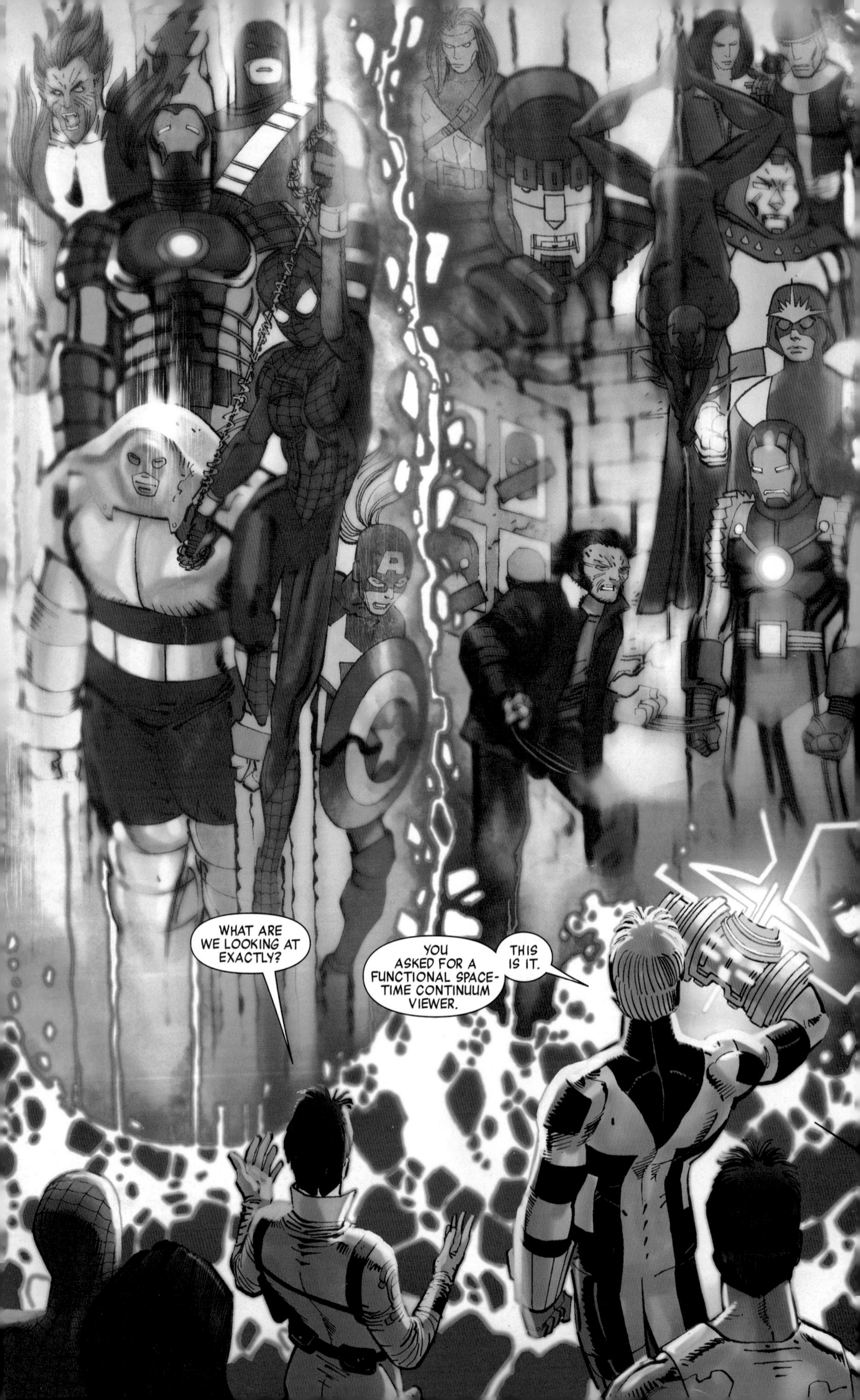
WHAT ARE WE LOOKING AT EXACTLY?
YOU ASKED FOR A FUNCTIONAL SPACE-TIME CONTINUUM VIEWER.
THIS IS IT.

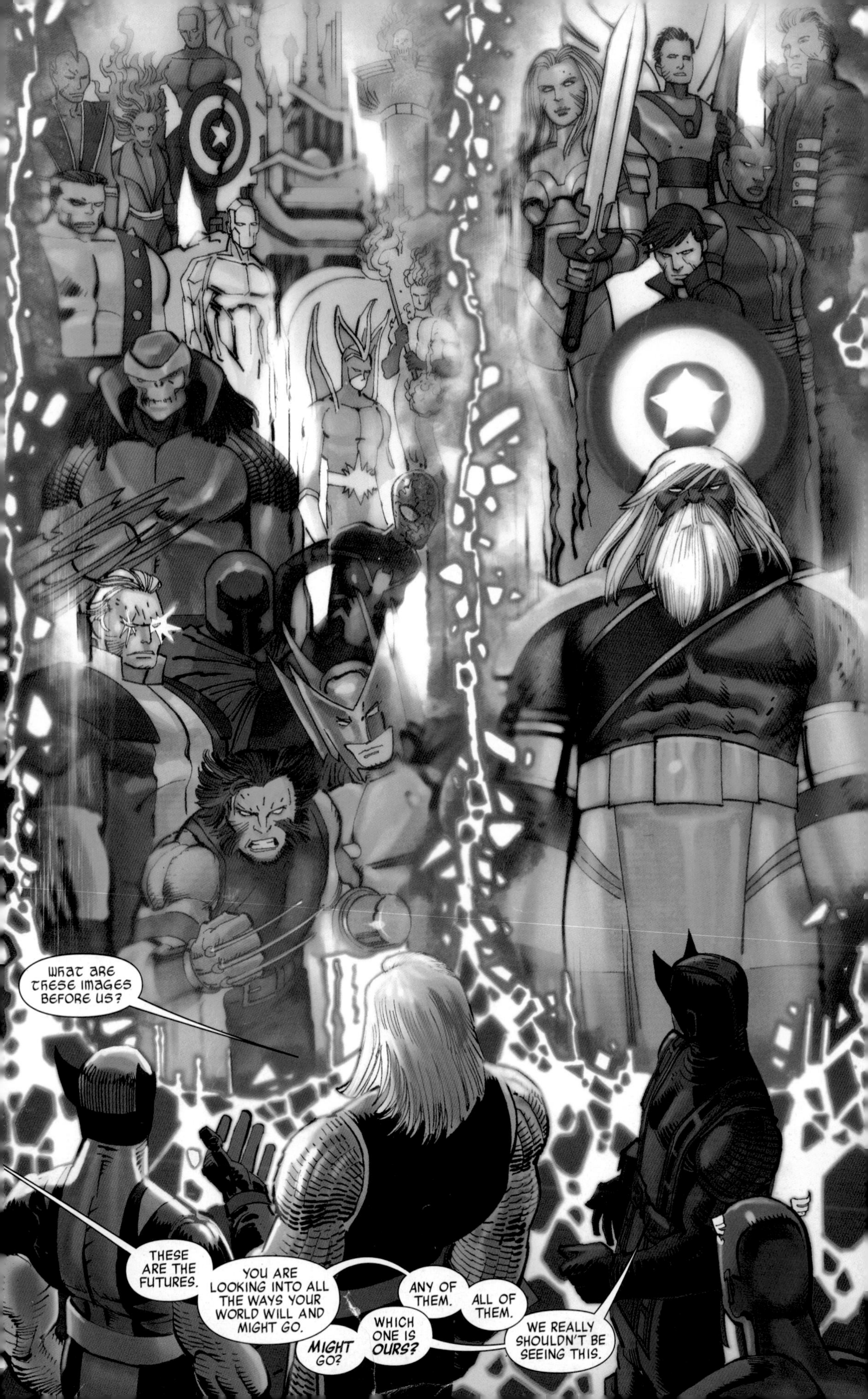
WHAT ARE THESE IMAGES BEFORE US?
THESE ARE THE FUTURES.
YOU ARE LOOKING INTO ALL THE WAYS YOUR WORLD WILL AND MIGHT GO.
MIGHT GO?
ANY OF THEM.
ALL OF THEM.
WHICH ONE IS OURS?
WE REALLY SHOULDN'T BE SEEING THIS.

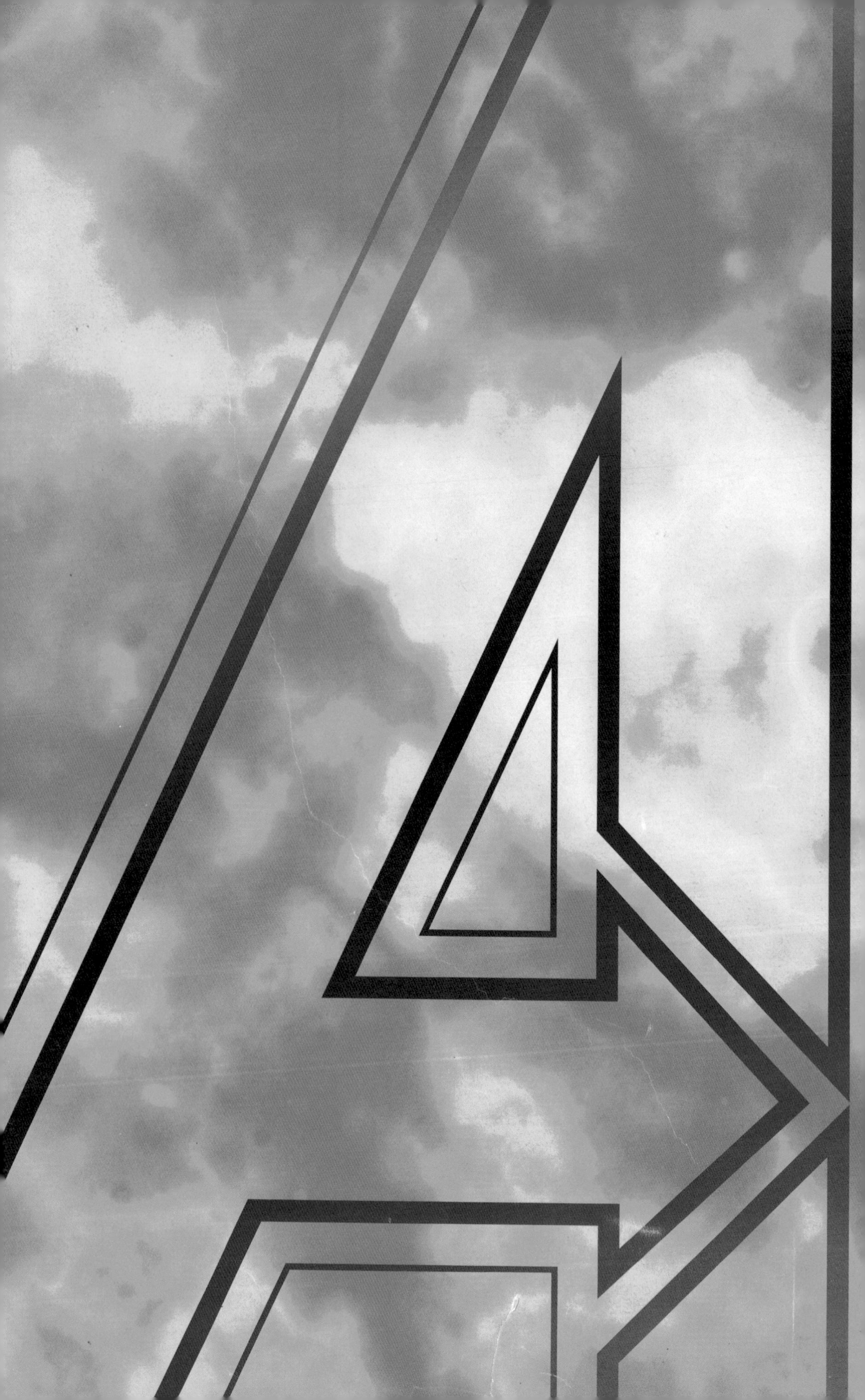

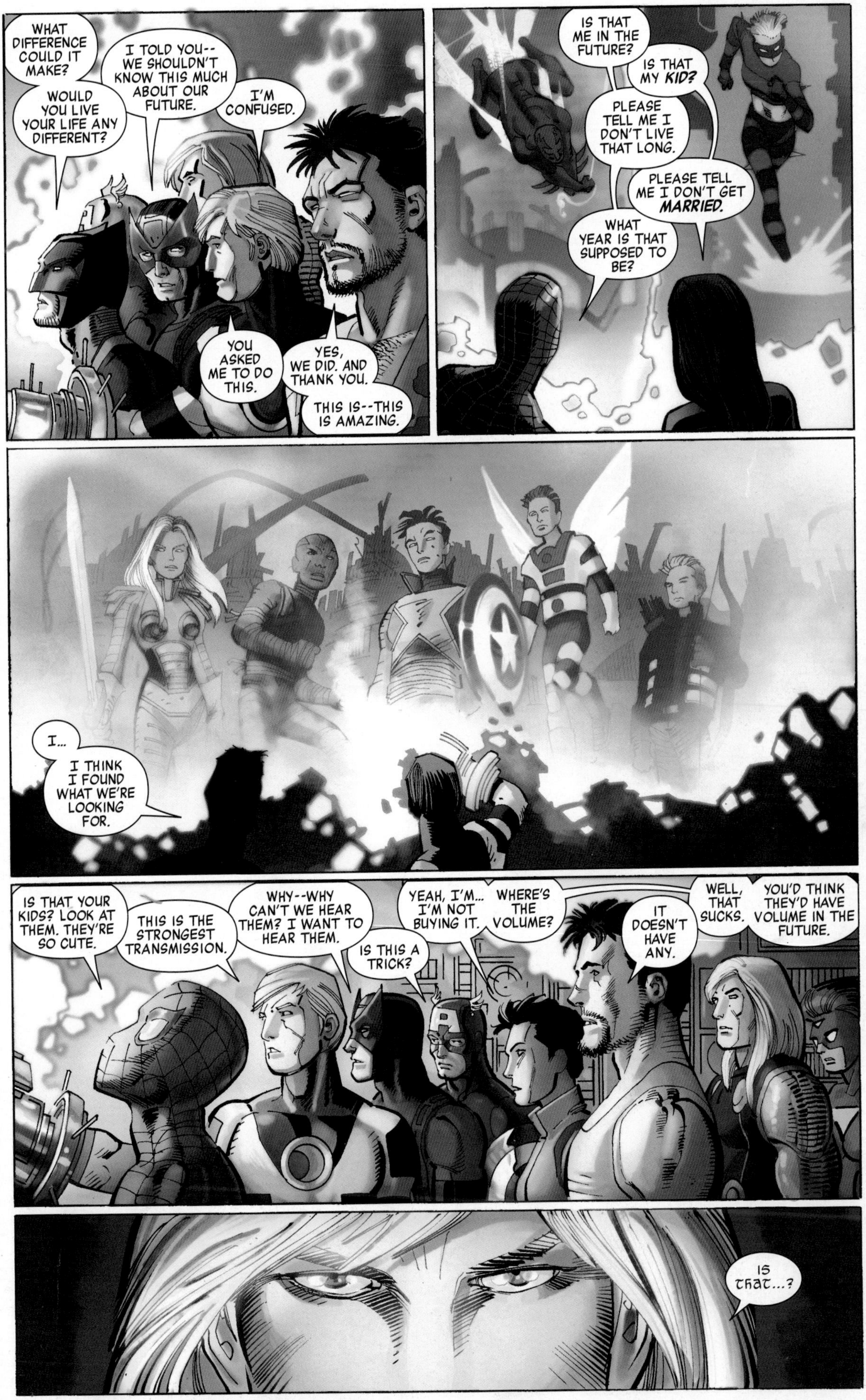
WHAT DIFFERENCE COULD IT MAKE?
WOULD YOU LIVE YOUR LIFE ANY DIFFERENT?
I TOLD YOU-- WE SHOULDN'T KNOW THIS MUCH ABOUT OUR FUTURE.
I'M CONFUSED.
YOU ASKED ME TO DO THIS.
YES, WE DID. AND THANK YOU.
THIS IS--THIS IS AMAZING.
IS THAT ME IN THE FUTURE?
IS THAT MY *KID?*
PLEASE TELL ME I DON'T LIVE THAT LONG.
PLEASE TELL ME I DON'T GET ***MARRIED.***
WHAT YEAR IS THAT SUPPOSED TO BE?
I... I THINK I FOUND WHAT WE'RE LOOKING FOR.
IS THAT YOUR KIDS? LOOK AT THEM. THEY'RE SO CUTE.
THIS IS THE STRONGEST TRANSMISSION.
WHY--WHY CAN'T WE HEAR THEM? I WANT TO HEAR THEM.
YEAH, I'M... I'M NOT BUYING IT.
IS THIS A TRICK?
WHERE'S THE VOLUME?
IT DOESN'T HAVE ANY.
WELL, THAT SUCKS.
YOU'D THINK THEY'D HAVE VOLUME IN THE FUTURE.
IS THAT...?

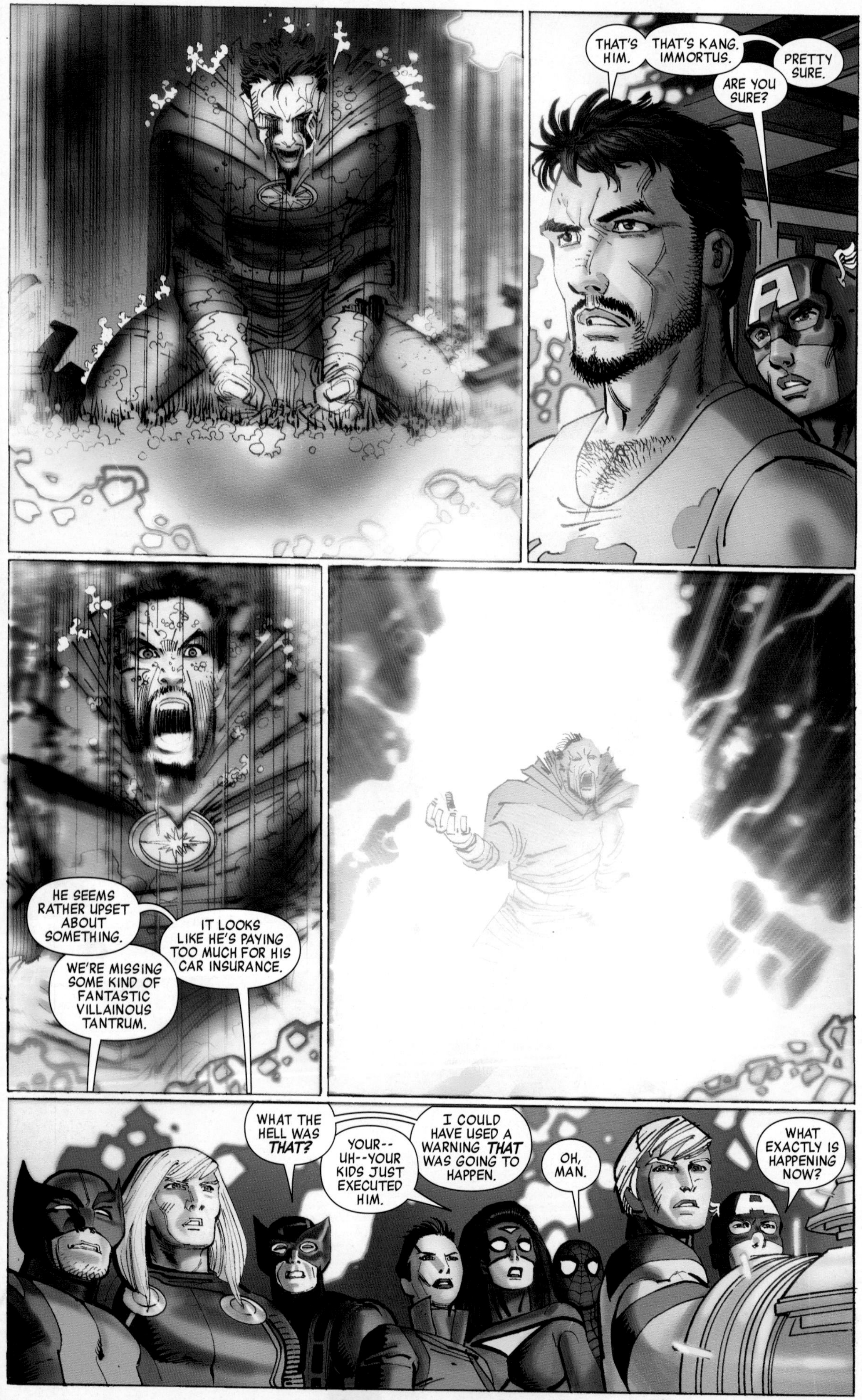
THAT'S HIM.
THAT'S KANG. IMMORTUS.
ARE YOU SURE?
PRETTY SURE.
HE SEEMS RATHER UPSET ABOUT SOMETHING.
IT LOOKS LIKE HE'S PAYING TOO MUCH FOR HIS CAR INSURANCE.
WE'RE MISSING SOME KIND OF FANTASTIC VILLAINOUS TANTRUM.
WHAT THE HELL WAS *THAT?*
YOUR-- UH--YOUR KIDS JUST EXECUTED HIM.
I COULD HAVE USED A WARNING *THAT* WAS GOING TO HAPPEN.
OH, MAN.
WHAT EXACTLY IS HAPPENING NOW?

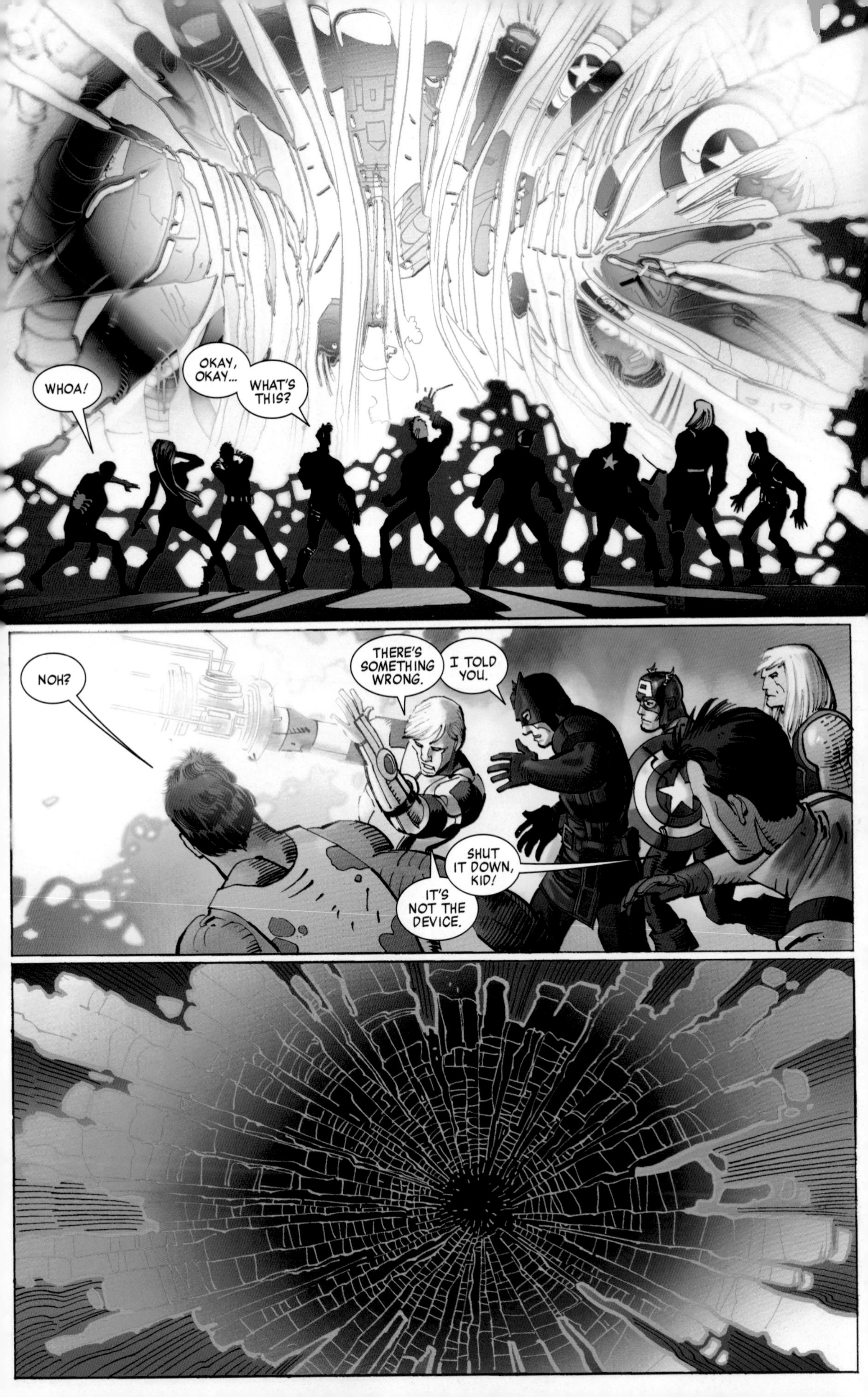
WHOA!
OKAY, OKAY...
WHAT'S THIS?
NOH?
THERE'S SOMETHING WRONG.
I TOLD YOU.
SHUT IT DOWN, KID!
IT'S NOT THE DEVICE.

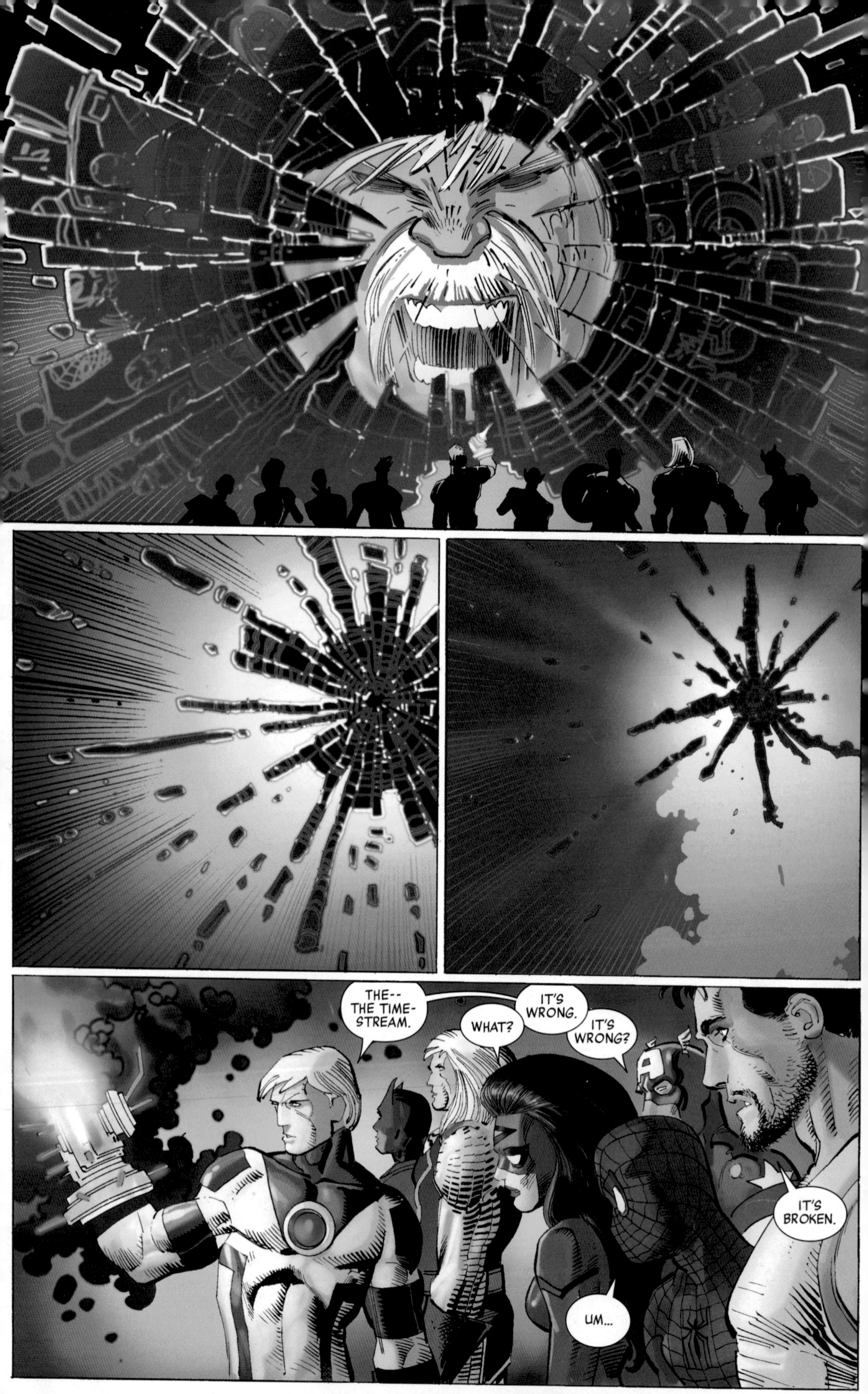
THE-- THE TIME-STREAM.
WHAT?
IT'S WRONG.
IT'S WRONG?
IT'S BROKEN.
UM...

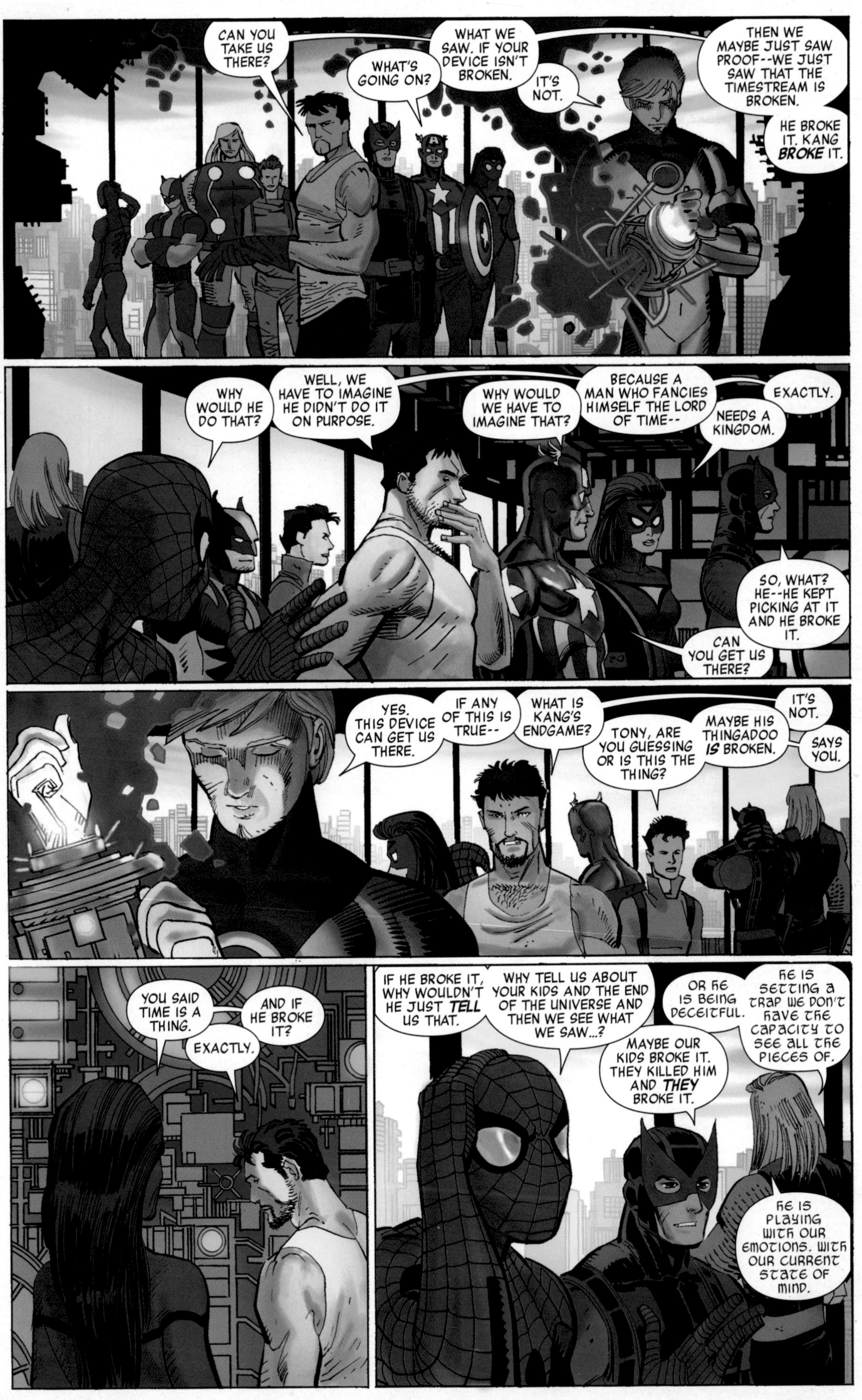
CAN YOU TAKE US THERE?
WHAT'S GOING ON?
WHAT WE SAW. IF YOUR DEVICE ISN'T BROKEN.
IT'S NOT.
THEN WE MAYBE JUST SAW PROOF--WE JUST SAW THAT THE TIMESTREAM IS BROKEN.
HE BROKE IT. KANG BROKE IT.
WHY WOULD HE DO THAT?
WELL, WE HAVE TO IMAGINE HE DIDN'T DO IT ON PURPOSE.
WHY WOULD WE HAVE TO IMAGINE THAT?
BECAUSE A MAN WHO FANCIES HIMSELF THE LORD OF TIME--
EXACTLY.
NEEDS A KINGDOM.
SO, WHAT? HE--HE KEPT PICKING AT IT AND HE BROKE IT.
CAN YOU GET US THERE?
YES. THIS DEVICE CAN GET US THERE.
IF ANY OF THIS IS TRUE--
WHAT IS KANG'S ENDGAME?
TONY, ARE YOU GUESSING OR IS THIS THE THING?
MAYBE HIS THINGADOO IS BROKEN.
IT'S NOT.
SAYS YOU.
YOU SAID TIME IS A THING.
AND IF HE BROKE IT?
EXACTLY.
IF HE BROKE IT, WHY WOULDN'T HE JUST TELL US THAT.
WHY TELL US ABOUT YOUR KIDS AND THE END OF THE UNIVERSE AND THEN WE SEE WHAT WE SAW...?
MAYBE OUR KIDS BROKE IT. THEY KILLED HIM AND THEY BROKE IT.
OR HE IS BEING DECEITFUL.
HE IS SETTING A TRAP WE DON'T HAVE THE CAPACITY TO SEE ALL THE PIECES OF.
HE IS PLAYING WITH OUR EMOTIONS. WITH OUR CURRENT STATE OF MIND.

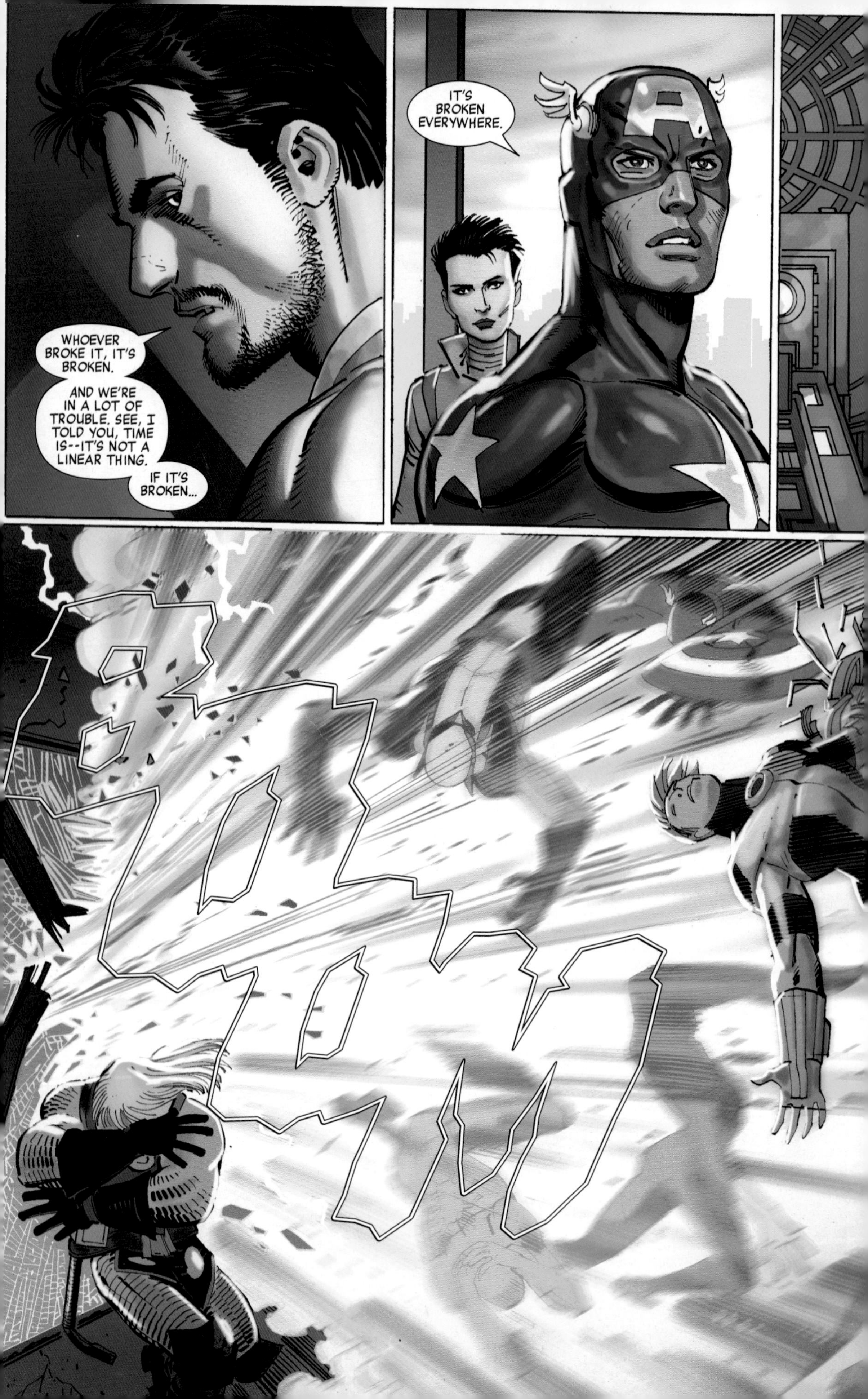
WHOEVER BROKE IT, IT'S BROKEN.
AND WE'RE IN A LOT OF TROUBLE. SEE, I TOLD YOU, TIME IS--IT'S NOT A LINEAR THING.
IF IT'S BROKEN...
IT'S BROKEN EVERYWHERE.

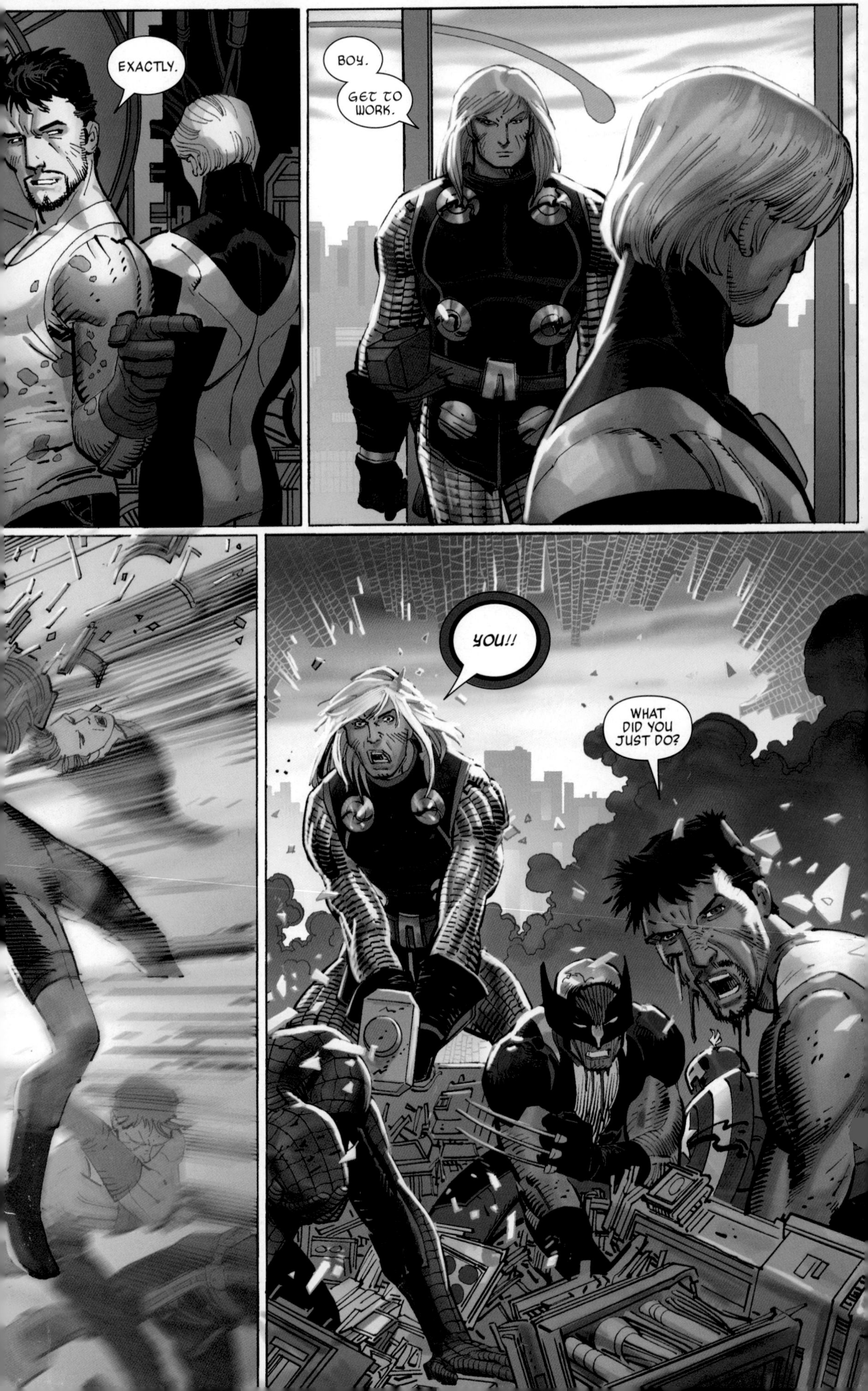
EXACTLY.
BOY.
GET TO WORK.
YOU!!
WHAT DID YOU JUST DO?

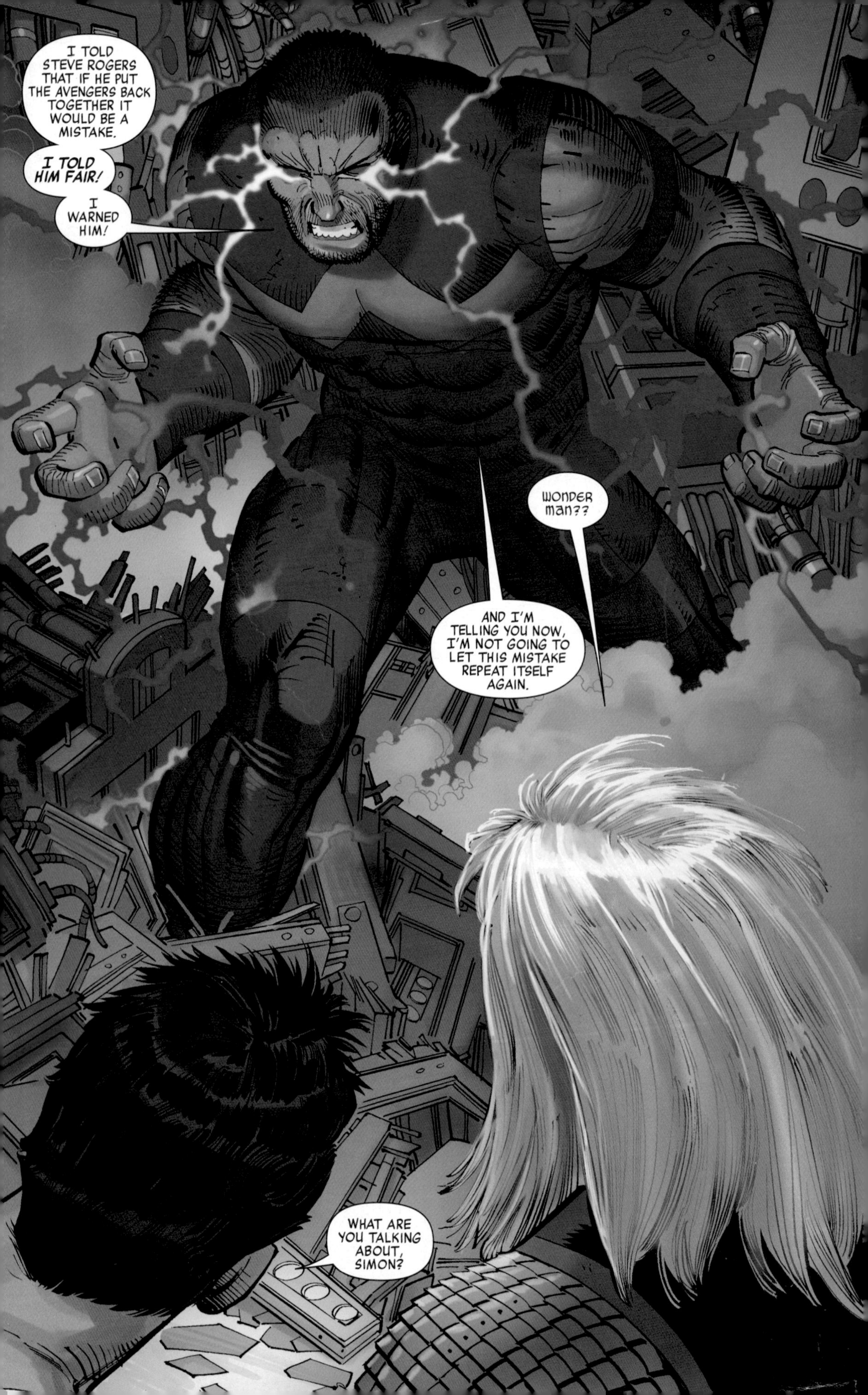
I TOLD STEVE ROGERS THAT IF HE PUT THE AVENGERS BACK TOGETHER IT WOULD BE A MISTAKE.
I TOLD HIM FAIR!
I WARNED HIM!
AND I'M TELLING YOU NOW, I'M NOT GOING TO LET THIS MISTAKE REPEAT ITSELF AGAIN.
WONDER MAN??
WHAT ARE YOU TALKING ABOUT, SIMON?

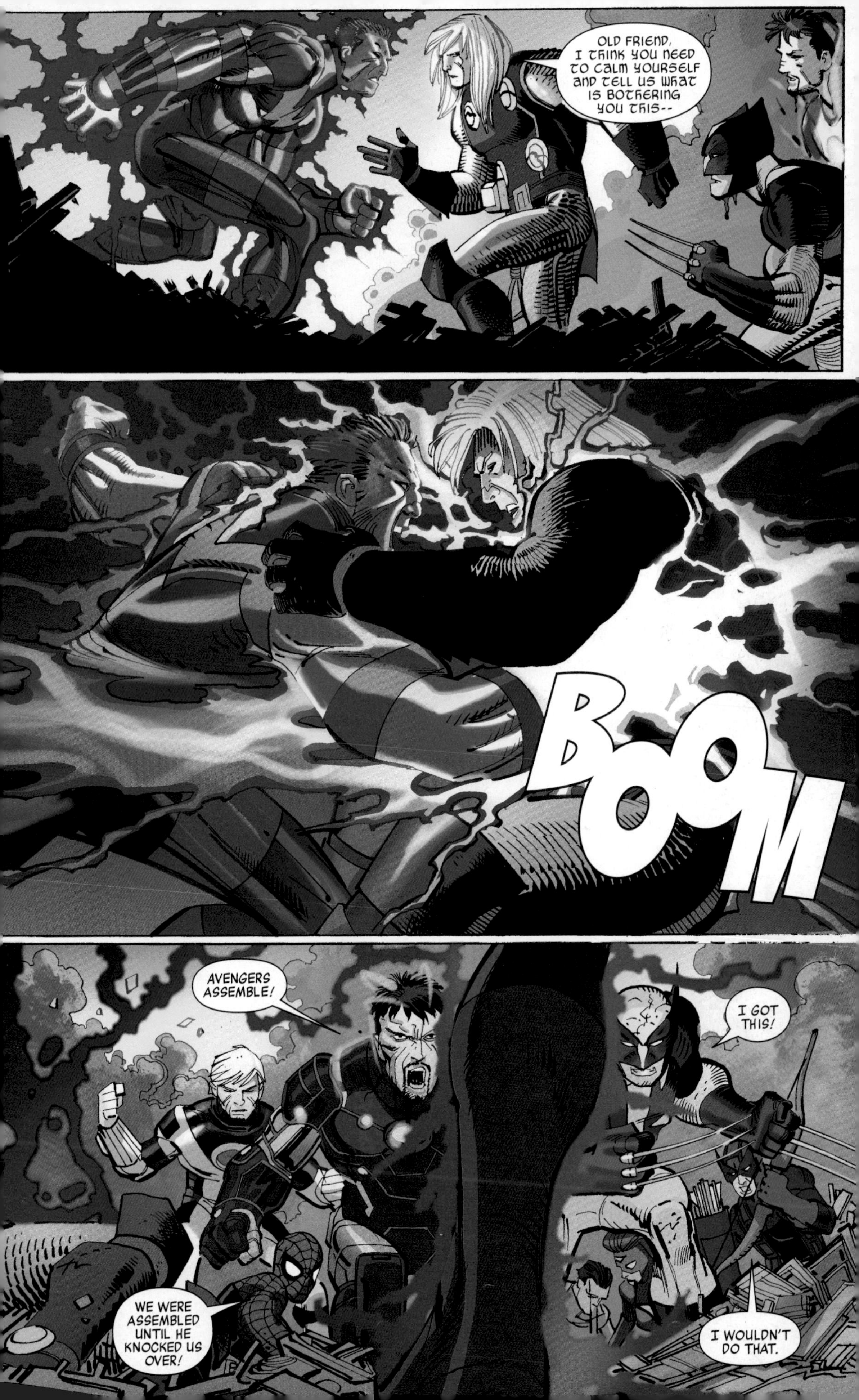
OLD FRIEND, I THINK YOU NEED TO CALM YOURSELF AND TELL US WHAT IS BOTHERING YOU THIS--
BOOM
AVENGERS ASSEMBLE!
I GOT THIS!
WE WERE ASSEMBLED UNTIL HE KNOCKED US OVER!
I WOULDN'T DO THAT.

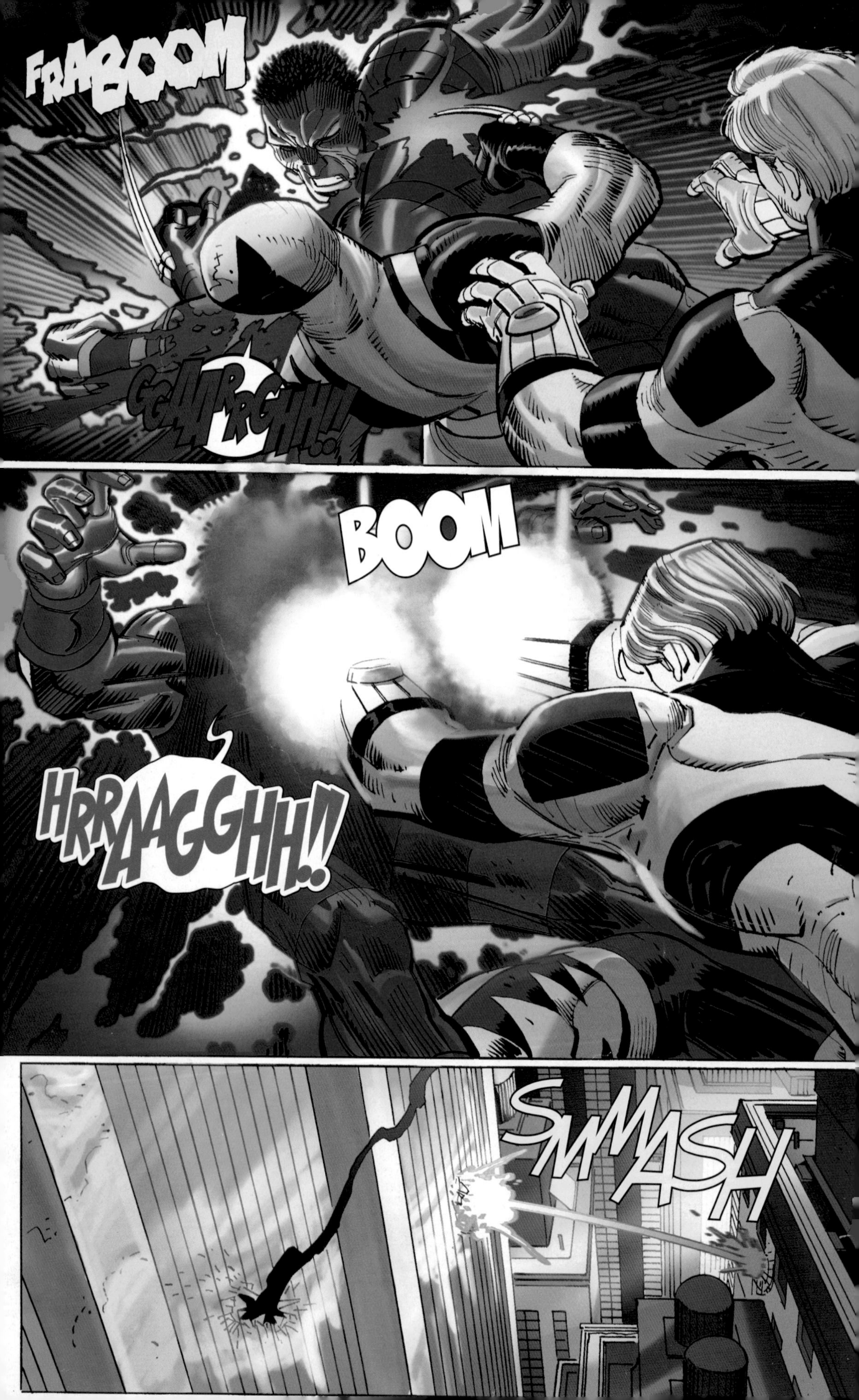

FRABOOM
GGAARRGHH!!
BOOM
HRRAAGGHH!!
SMMASH

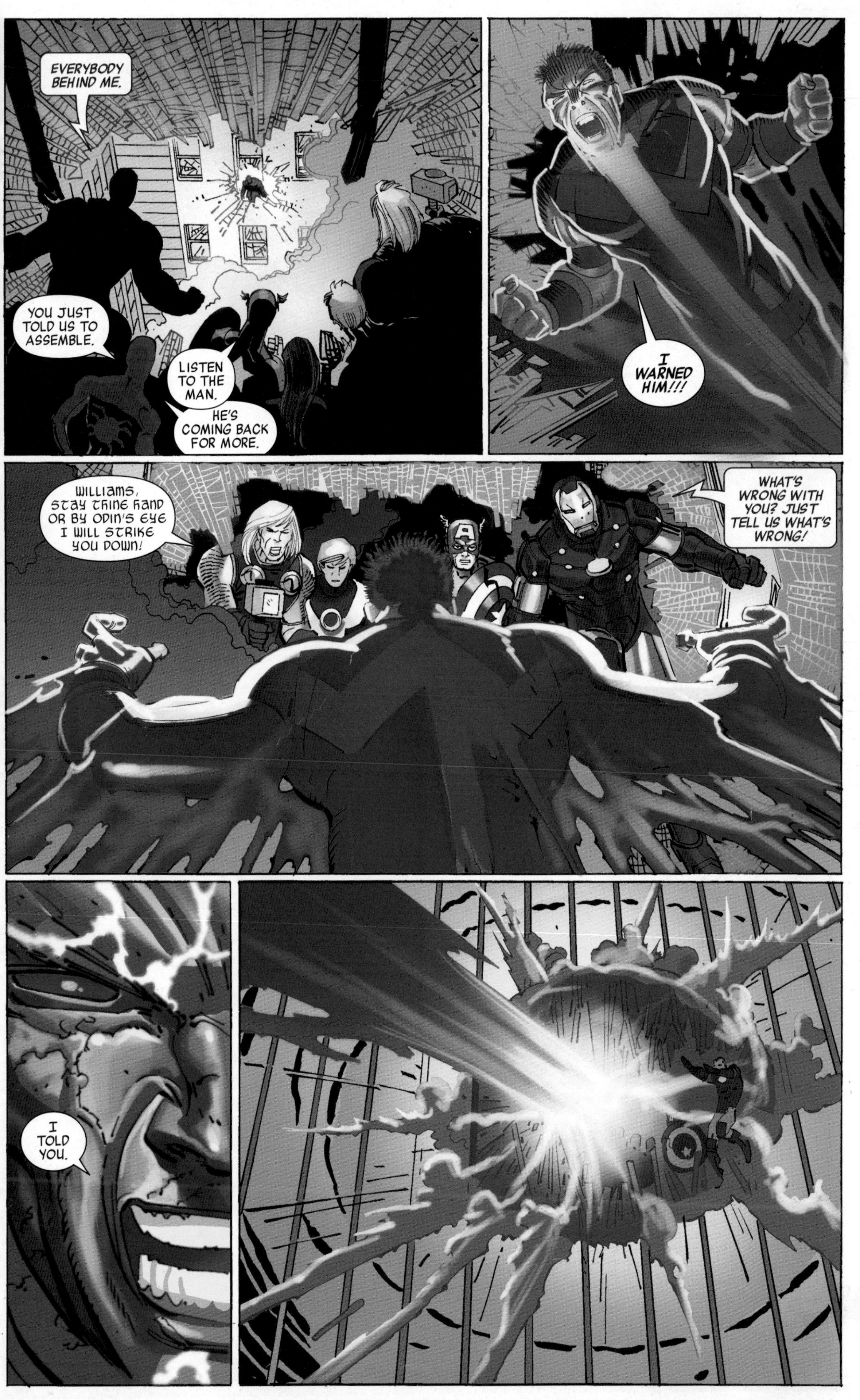
EVERYBODY BEHIND ME.
YOU JUST TOLD US TO ASSEMBLE.
LISTEN TO THE MAN.
HE'S COMING BACK FOR MORE.
I WARNED HIM!!!
WILLIAMS, STAY THINE HAND OR BY ODIN'S EYE I WILL STRIKE YOU DOWN!
WHAT'S WRONG WITH YOU? JUST TELL US WHAT'S WRONG!
I TOLD YOU.

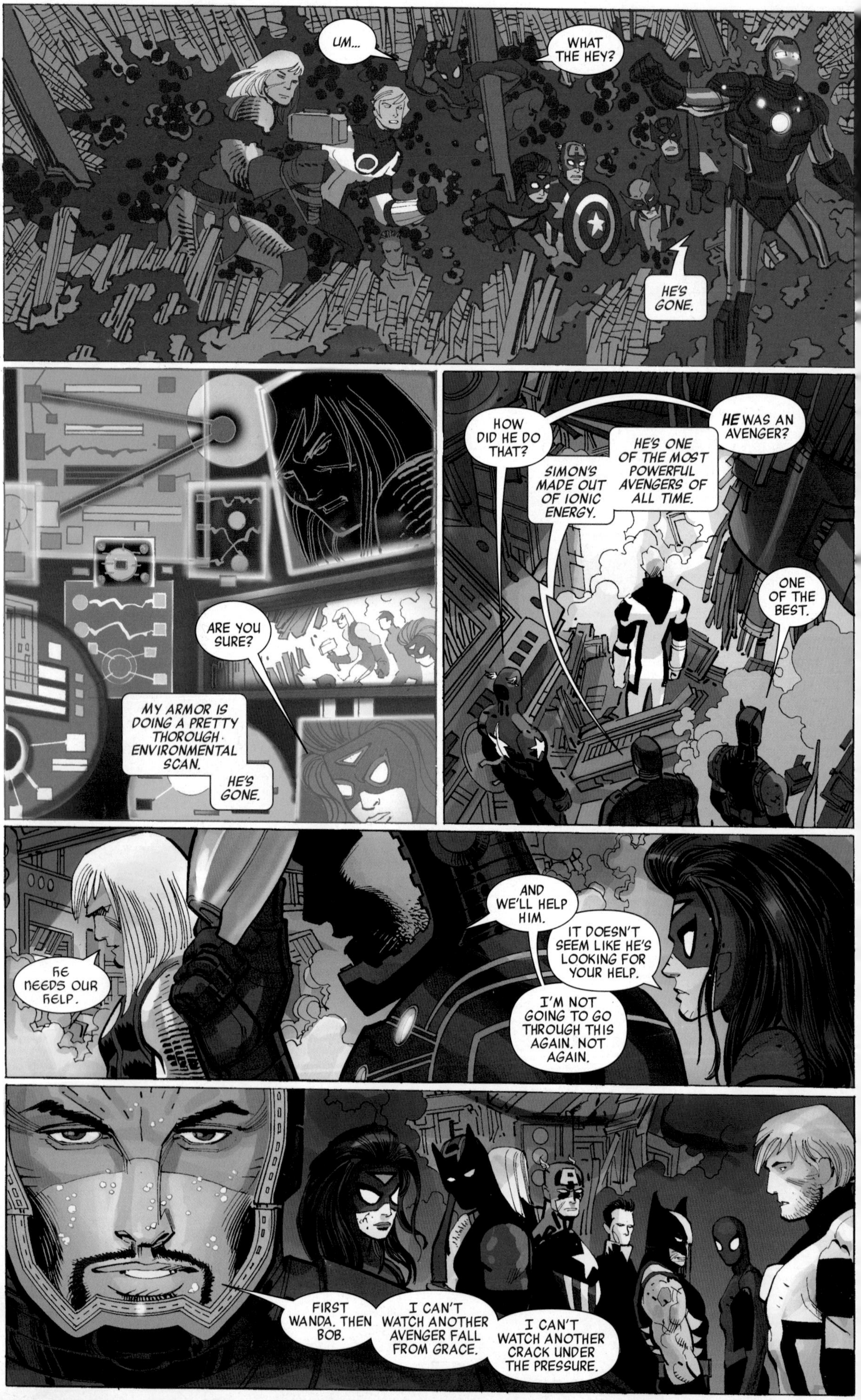
UM...
WHAT THE HEY?
HE'S GONE.
ARE YOU SURE?
MY ARMOR IS DOING A PRETTY THOROUGH ENVIRONMENTAL SCAN.
HE'S GONE.
HOW DID HE DO THAT?
SIMON'S MADE OUT OF IONIC ENERGY.
HE'S ONE OF THE MOST POWERFUL AVENGERS OF ALL TIME.
HE WAS AN AVENGER?
ONE OF THE BEST.
HE NEEDS OUR HELP.
AND WE'LL HELP HIM.
IT DOESN'T SEEM LIKE HE'S LOOKING FOR YOUR HELP.
I'M NOT GOING TO GO THROUGH THIS AGAIN. NOT AGAIN.
FIRST WANDA. THEN BOB.
I CAN'T WATCH ANOTHER AVENGER FALL FROM GRACE.
I CAN'T WATCH ANOTHER CRACK UNDER THE PRESSURE.

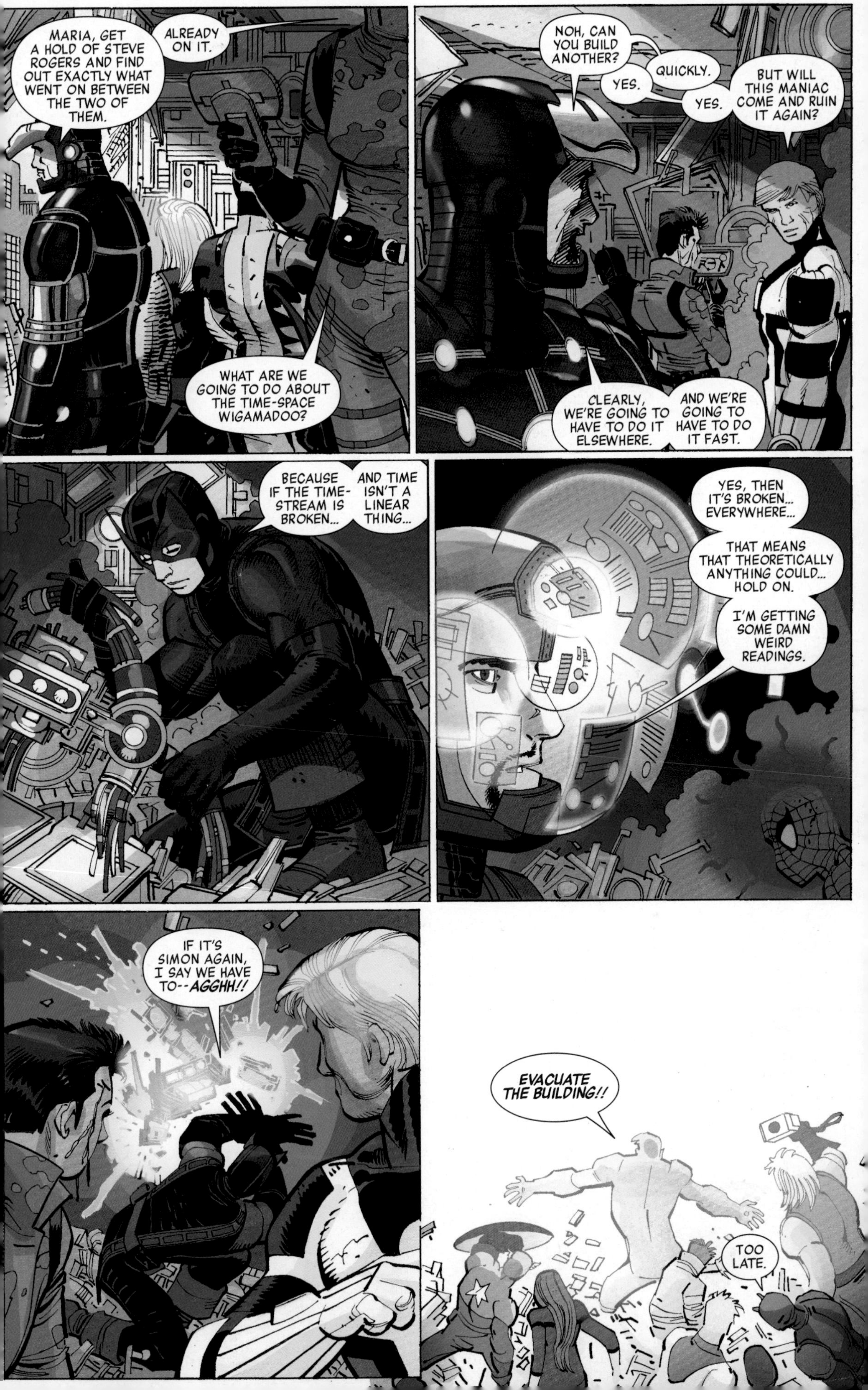
MARIA, GET A HOLD OF STEVE ROGERS AND FIND OUT EXACTLY WHAT WENT ON BETWEEN THE TWO OF THEM.
ALREADY ON IT.
WHAT ARE WE GOING TO DO ABOUT THE TIME-SPACE WIGAMADOO?
NOH, CAN YOU BUILD ANOTHER?
YES.
QUICKLY.
YES.
BUT WILL THIS MANIAC COME AND RUIN IT AGAIN?
CLEARLY, WE'RE GOING TO HAVE TO DO IT ELSEWHERE.
AND WE'RE GOING TO HAVE TO DO IT FAST.
BECAUSE IF THE TIME-STREAM IS BROKEN...
AND TIME ISN'T A LINEAR THING...
YES, THEN IT'S BROKEN... EVERYWHERE...
THAT MEANS THAT THEORETICALLY ANYTHING COULD... HOLD ON.
I'M GETTING SOME DAMN WEIRD READINGS.
IF IT'S SIMON AGAIN, I SAY WE HAVE TO--AGGHH!!
EVACUATE THE BUILDING!!
TOO LATE.

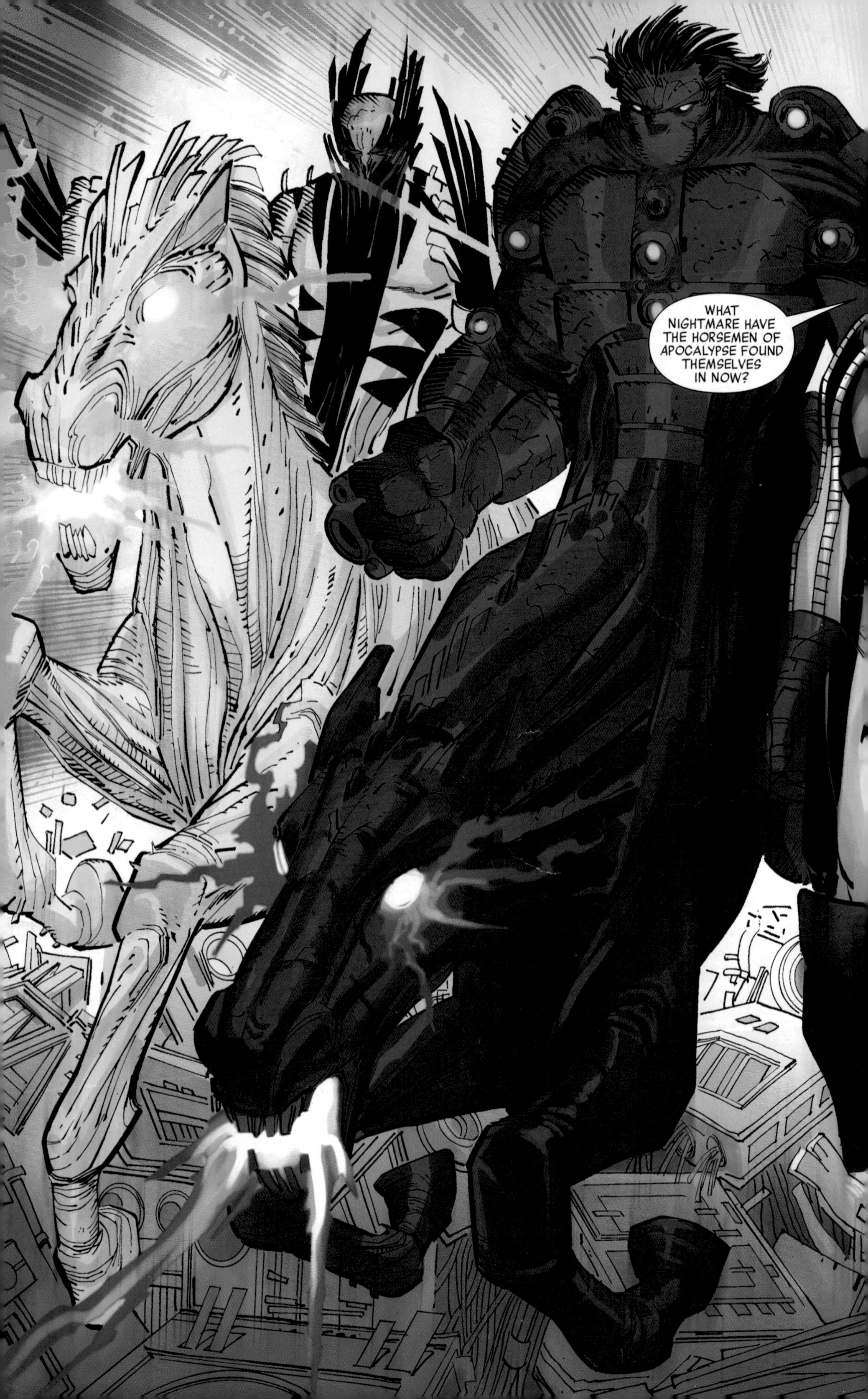
WHAT NIGHTMARE HAVE THE HORSEMEN OF APOCALYPSE FOUND THEMSELVES IN NOW?

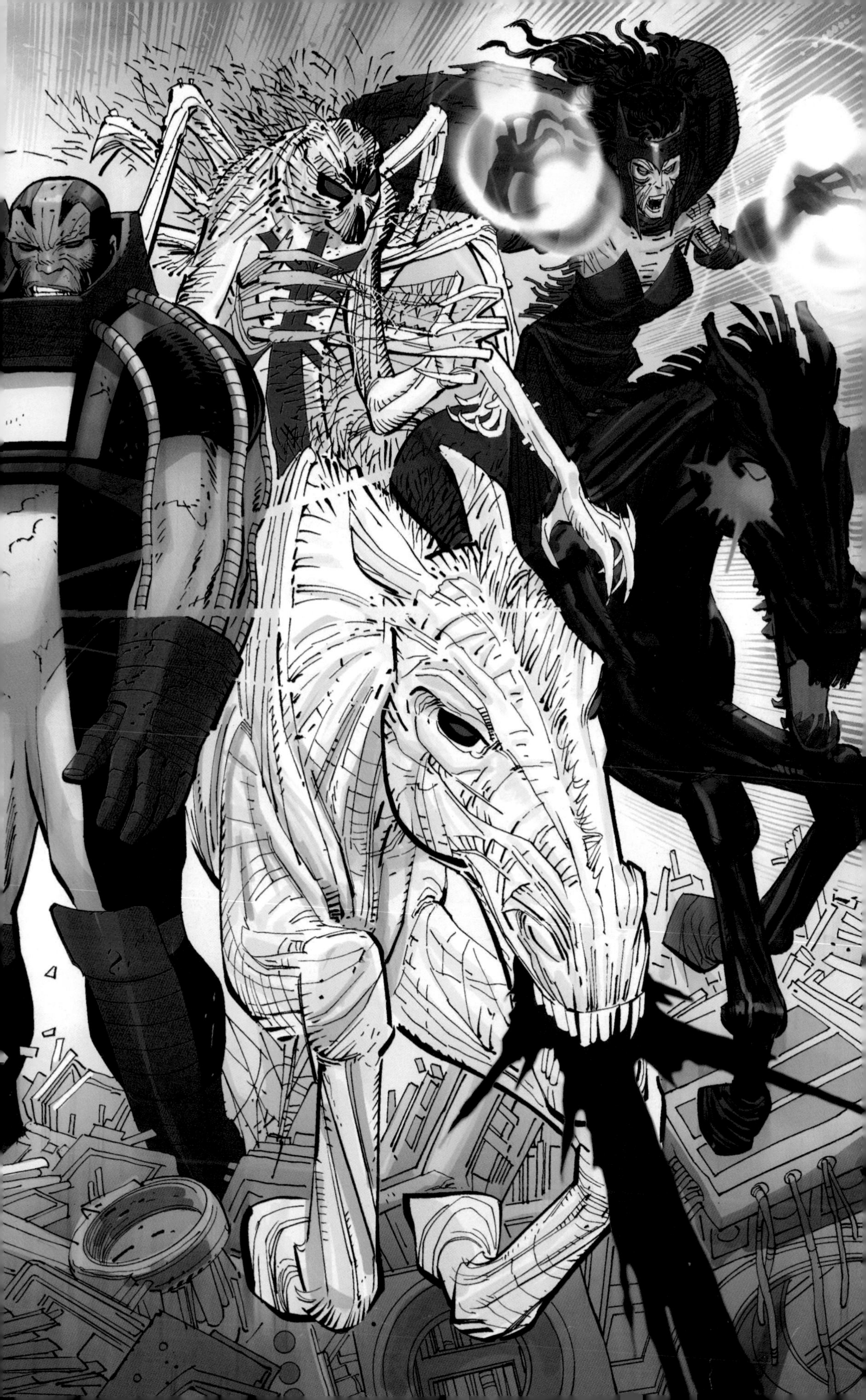

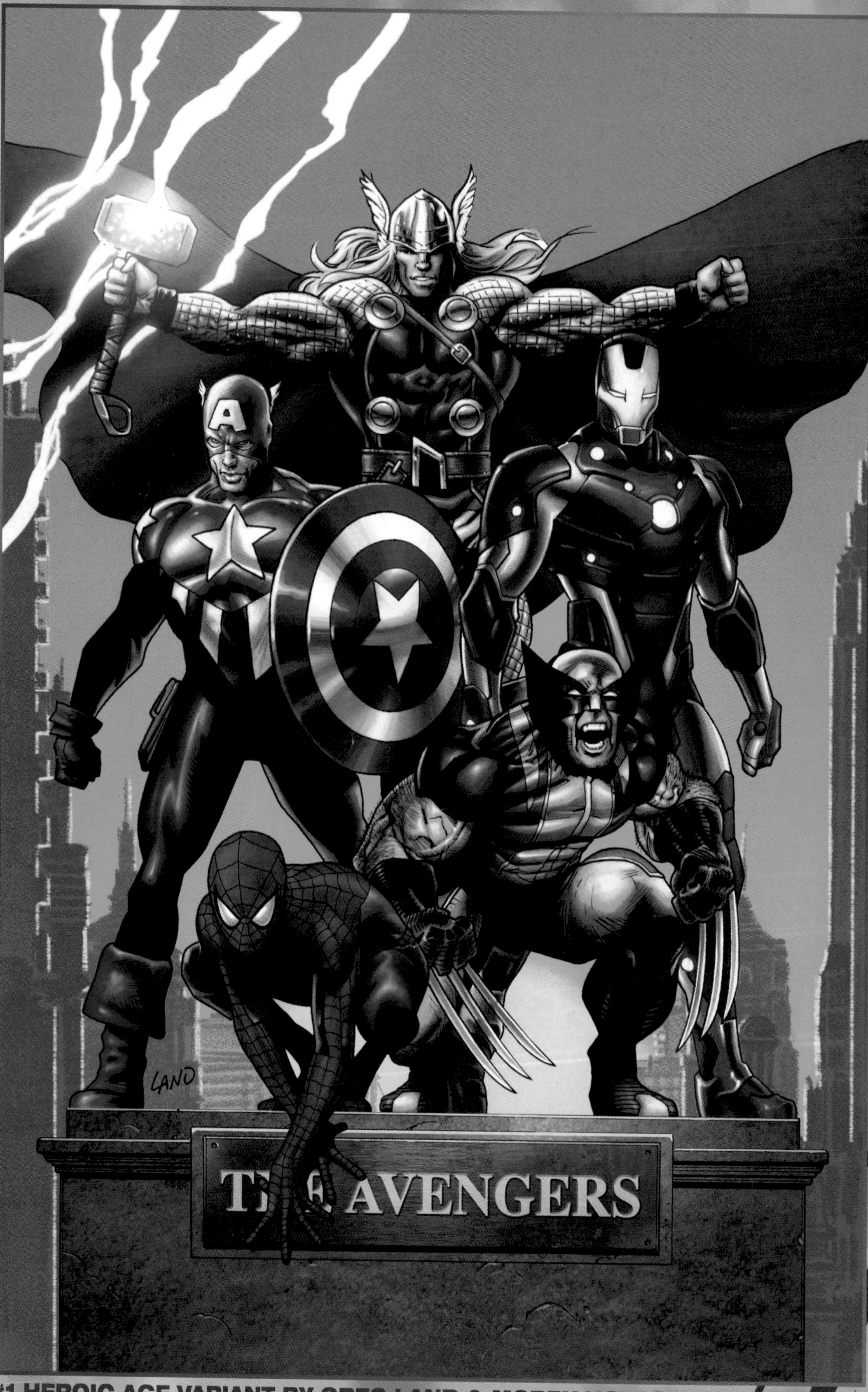
LAND
AVENGERS

#1 HEROIC AGE VARIANT BY GREG LAND & MORRY HOLLOWELL

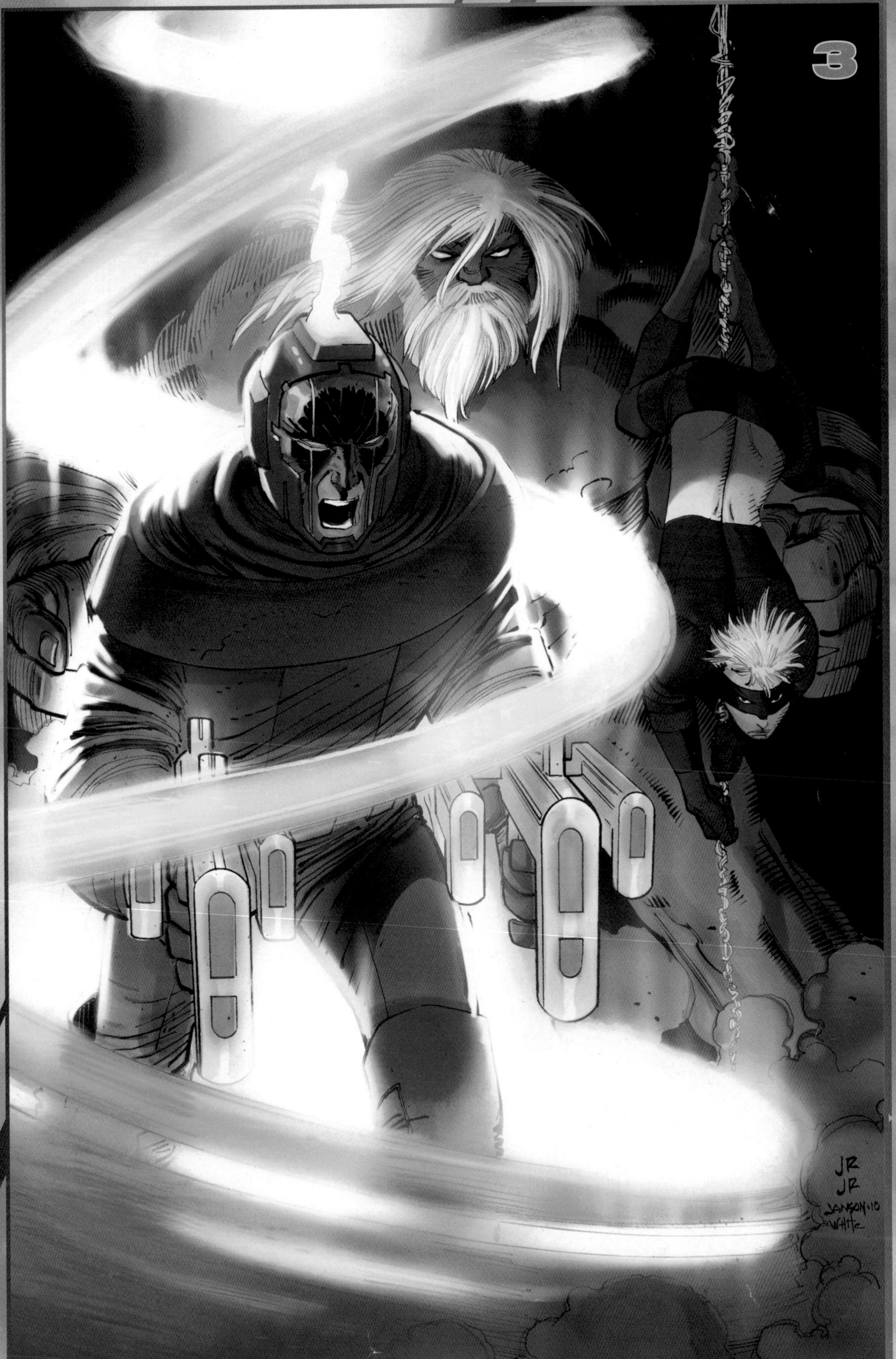
3
JR JR
JANSON '10
WHITE

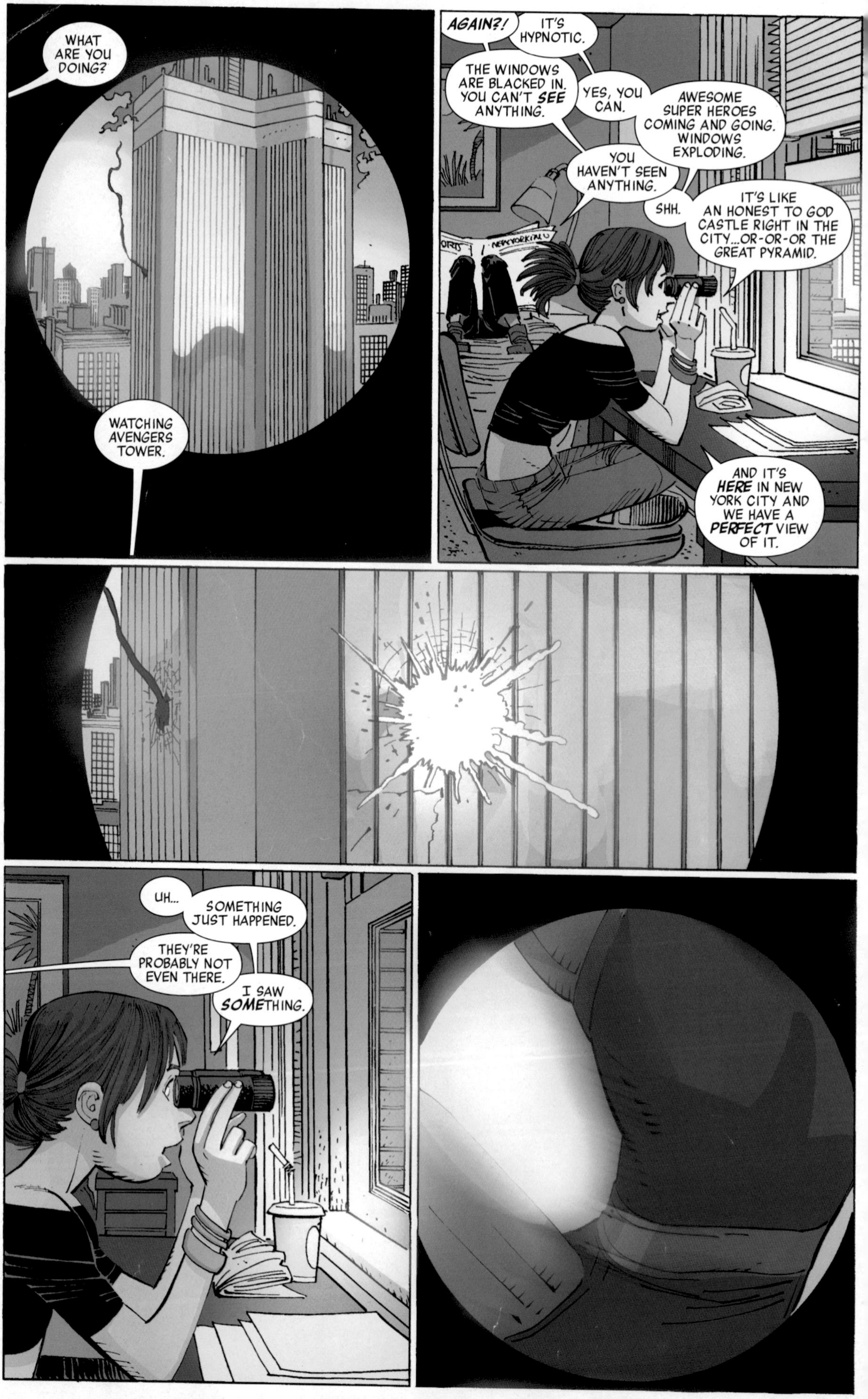

WHAT ARE YOU DOING?
WATCHING AVENGERS TOWER.
AGAIN?!
IT'S HYPNOTIC.
THE WINDOWS ARE BLACKED IN. YOU CAN'T SEE ANYTHING.
YES, YOU CAN.
AWESOME SUPER HEROES COMING AND GOING. WINDOWS EXPLODING.
YOU HAVEN'T SEEN ANYTHING.
SHH.
IT'S LIKE AN HONEST TO GOD CASTLE RIGHT IN THE CITY...OR-OR-OR THE GREAT PYRAMID.
AND IT'S HERE IN NEW YORK CITY AND WE HAVE A PERFECT VIEW OF IT.
UH...
SOMETHING JUST HAPPENED.
THEY'RE PROBABLY NOT EVEN THERE.
I SAW SOMETHING.

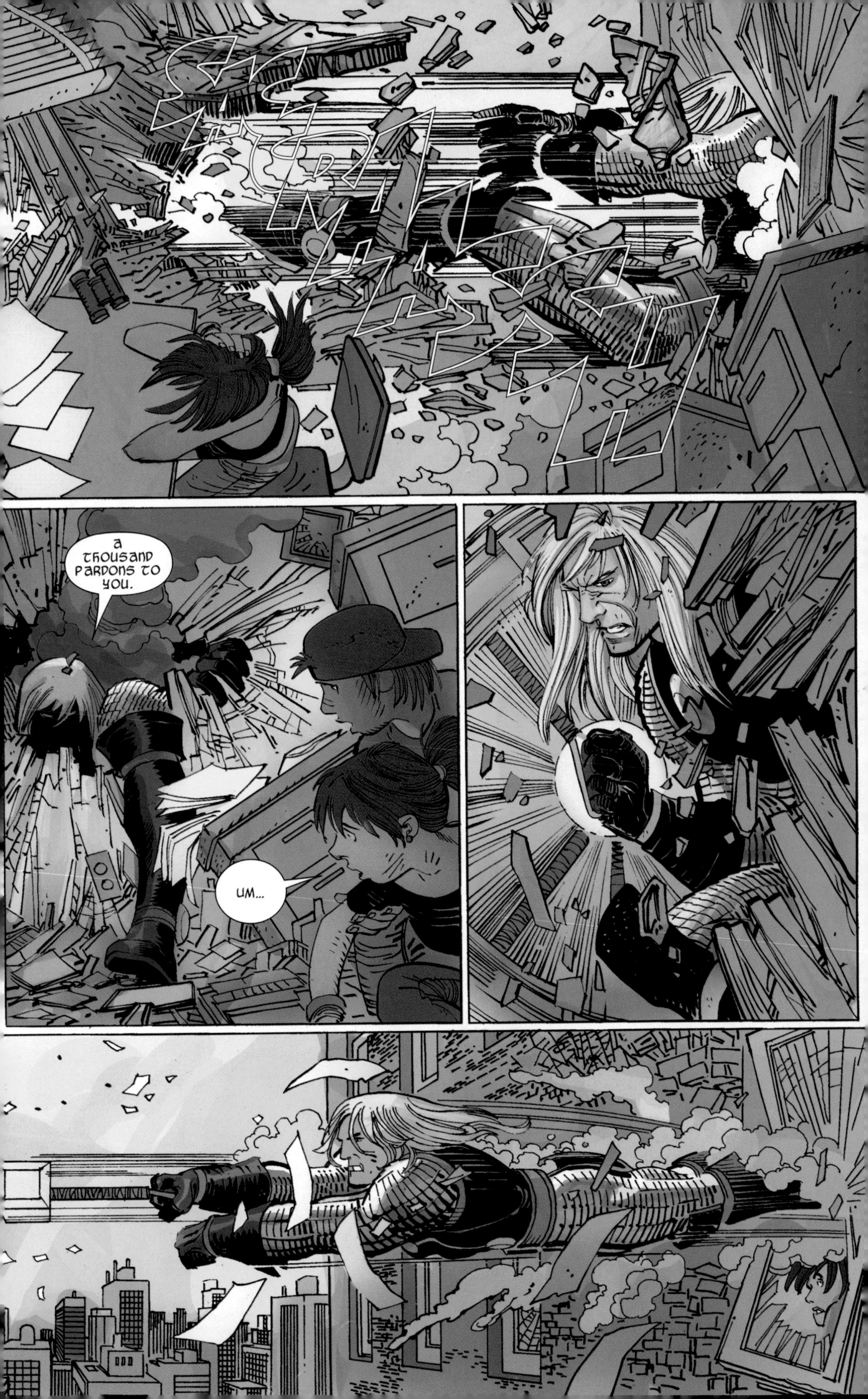
A THOUSAND PARDONS TO YOU.
UM...

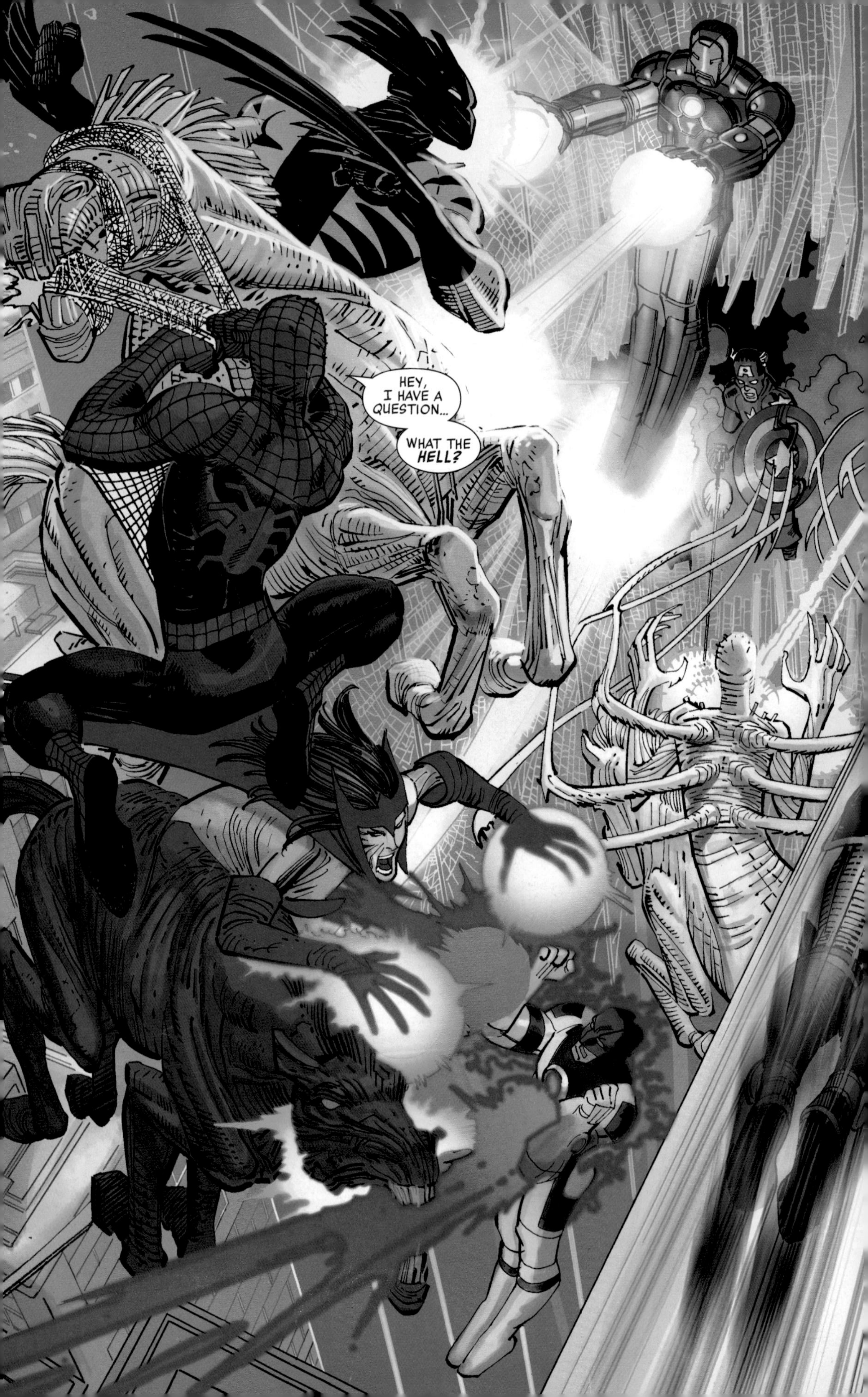
HEY, I HAVE A QUESTION...
WHAT THE **HELL?**

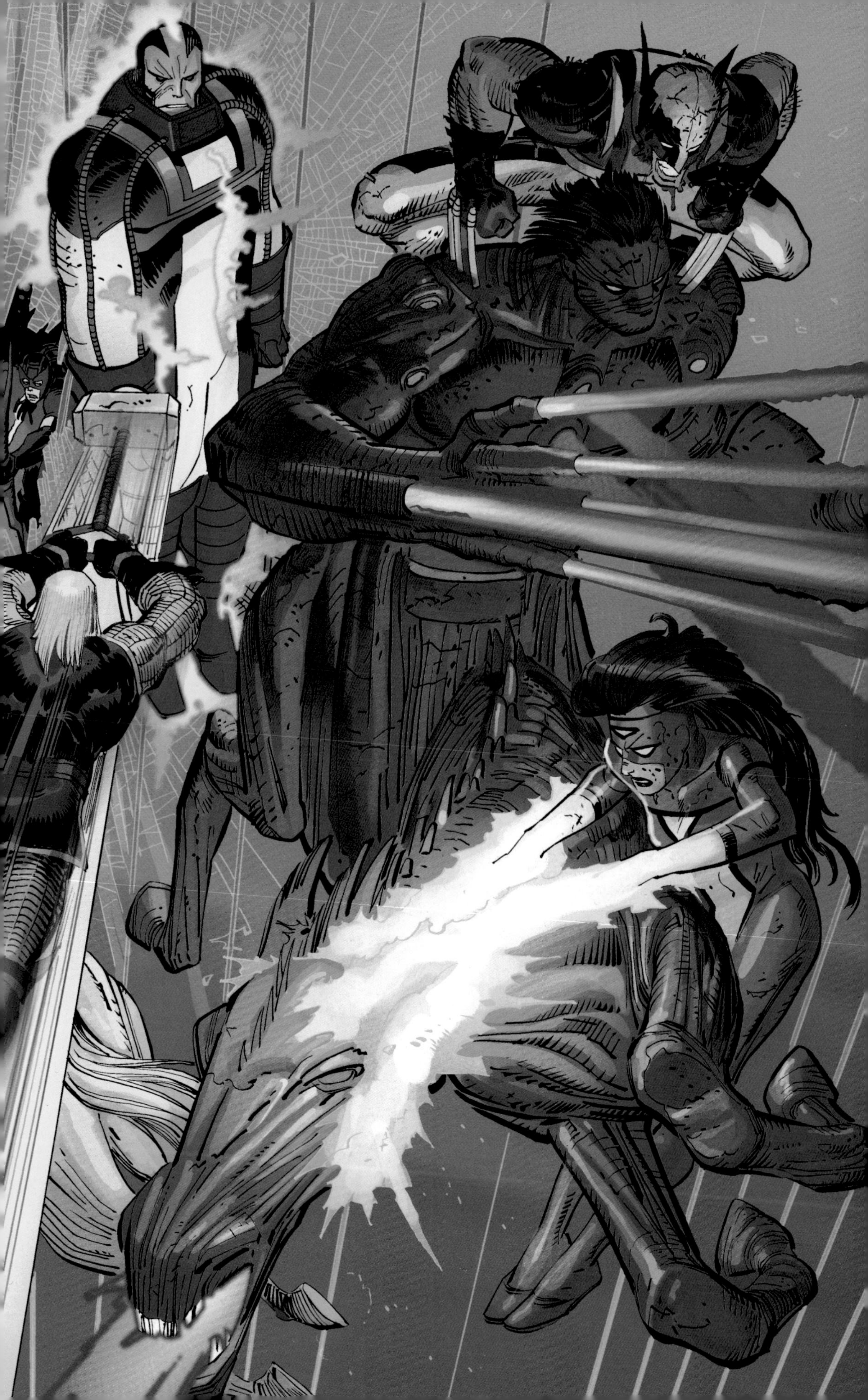

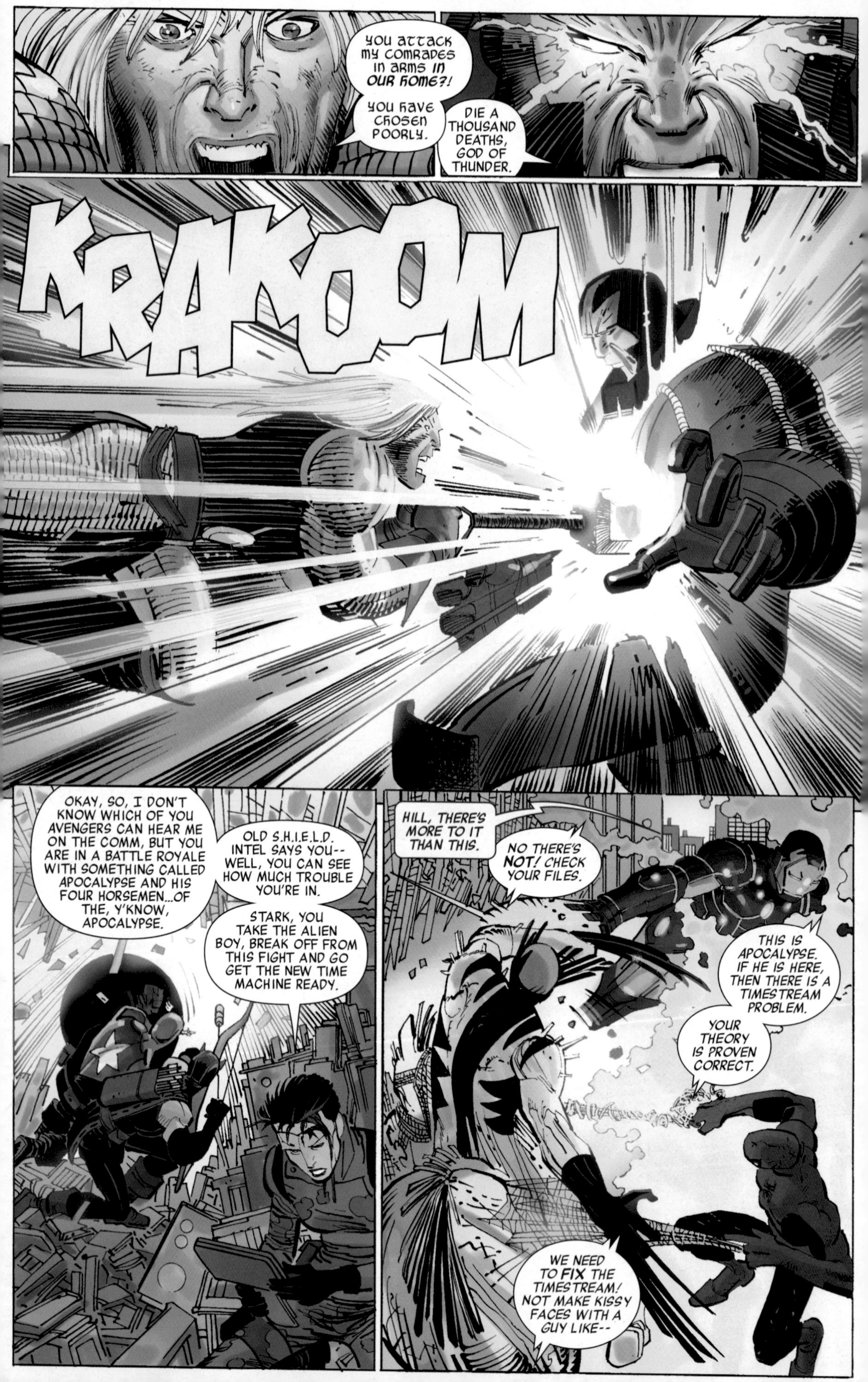
YOU ATTACK MY COMRADES IN ARMS IN OUR HOME?!
YOU HAVE CHOSEN POORLY.
DIE A THOUSAND DEATHS, GOD OF THUNDER.
KRAKOOM
OKAY, SO, I DON'T KNOW WHICH OF YOU AVENGERS CAN HEAR ME ON THE COMM, BUT YOU ARE IN A BATTLE ROYALE WITH SOMETHING CALLED APOCALYPSE AND HIS FOUR HORSEMEN...OF THE, Y'KNOW, APOCALYPSE.
OLD S.H.I.E.L.D. INTEL SAYS YOU-- WELL, YOU CAN SEE HOW MUCH TROUBLE YOU'RE IN.
STARK, YOU TAKE THE ALIEN BOY, BREAK OFF FROM THIS FIGHT AND GO GET THE NEW TIME MACHINE READY.
HILL, THERE'S MORE TO IT THAN THIS.
NO THERE'S NOT! CHECK YOUR FILES.
THIS IS APOCALYPSE. IF HE IS HERE, THEN THERE IS A TIMESTREAM PROBLEM.
YOUR THEORY IS PROVEN CORRECT.
WE NEED TO FIX THE TIMESTREAM! NOT MAKE KISSY FACES WITH A GUY LIKE--

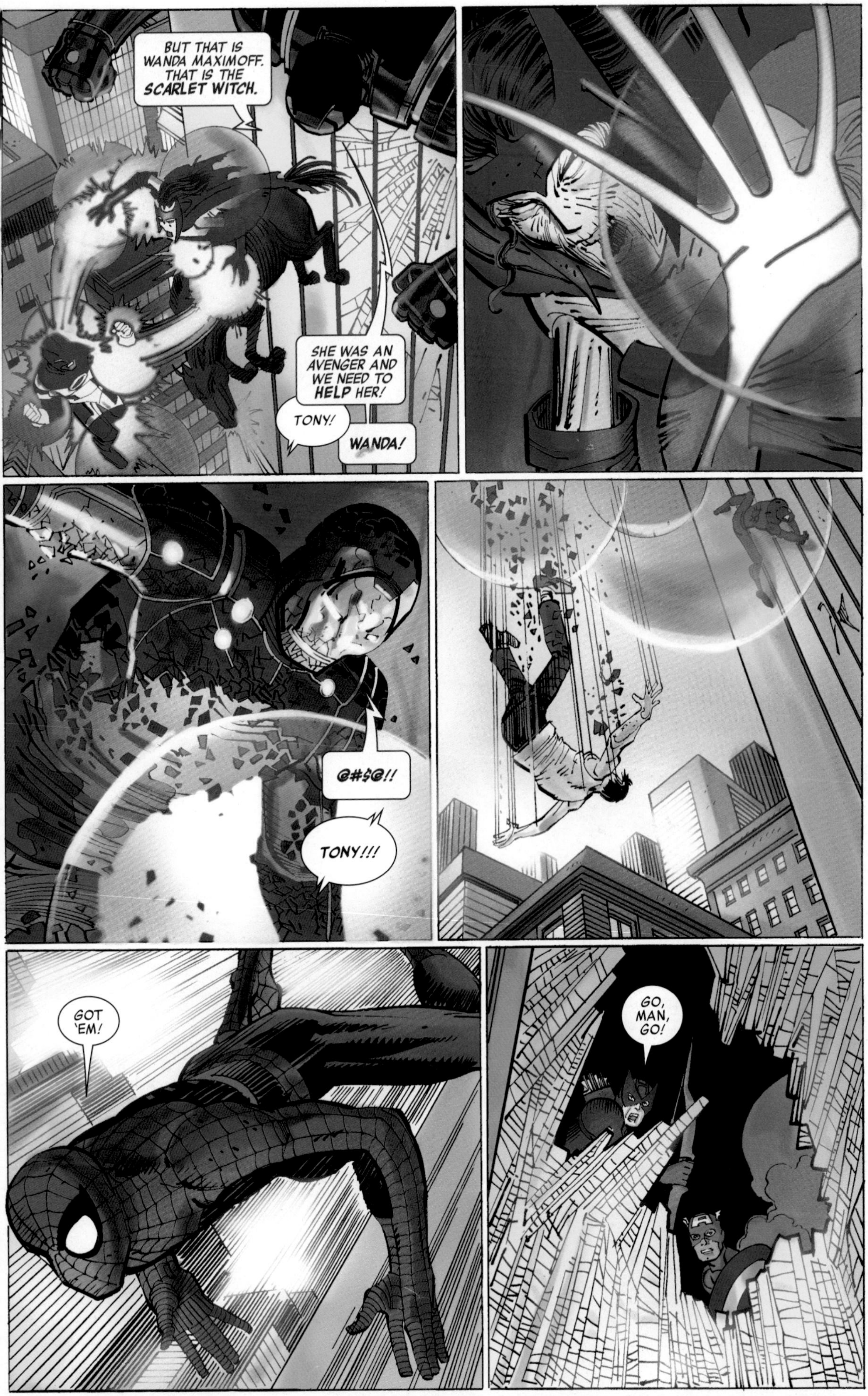

BUT THAT IS WANDA MAXIMOFF. THAT IS THE SCARLET WITCH.
SHE WAS AN AVENGER AND WE NEED TO HELP HER!
TONY!
WANDA!
@#$@!!
TONY!!!
GOT 'EM!
GO, MAN, GO!

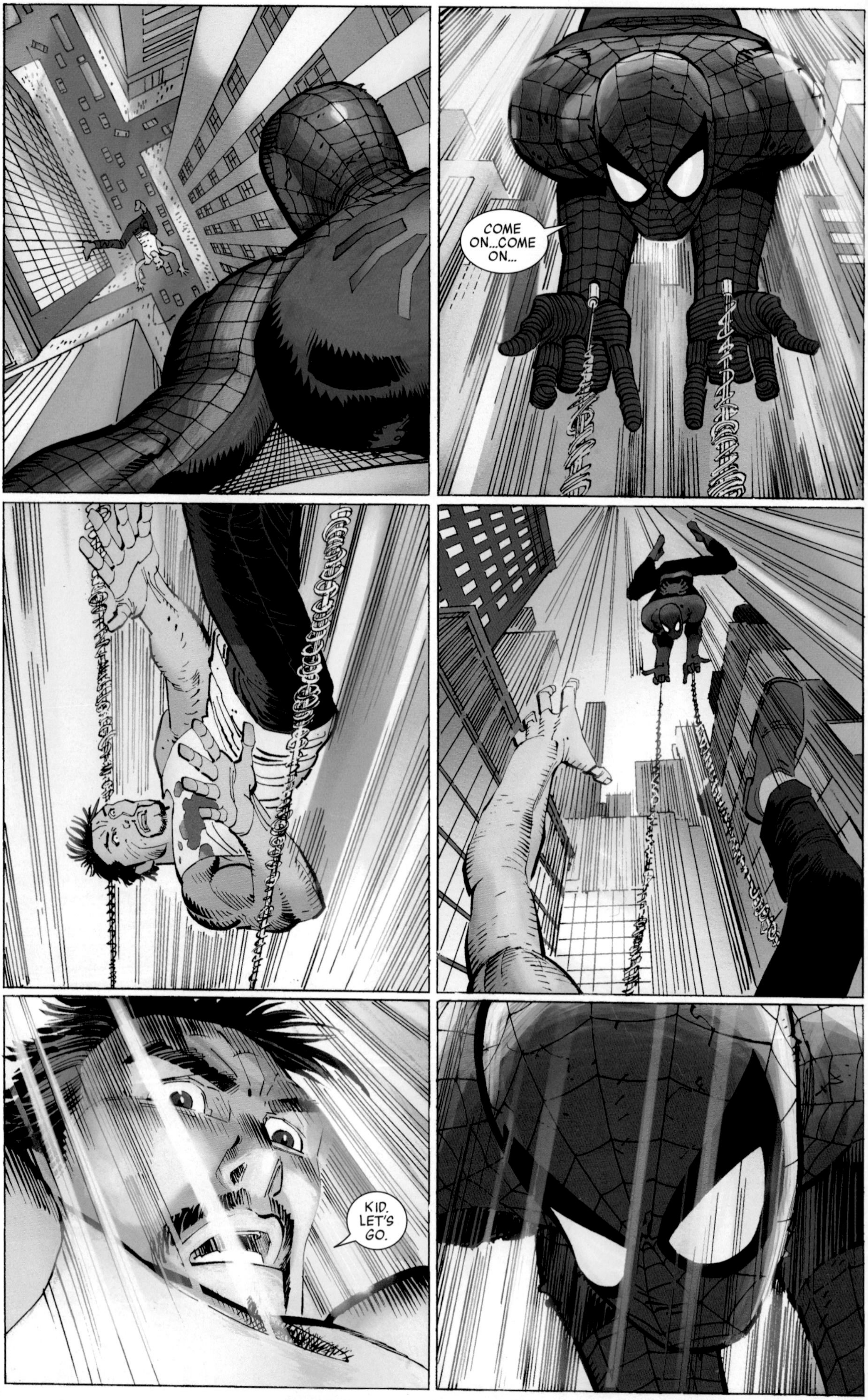
COME ON...COME ON...
KID. LET'S GO.

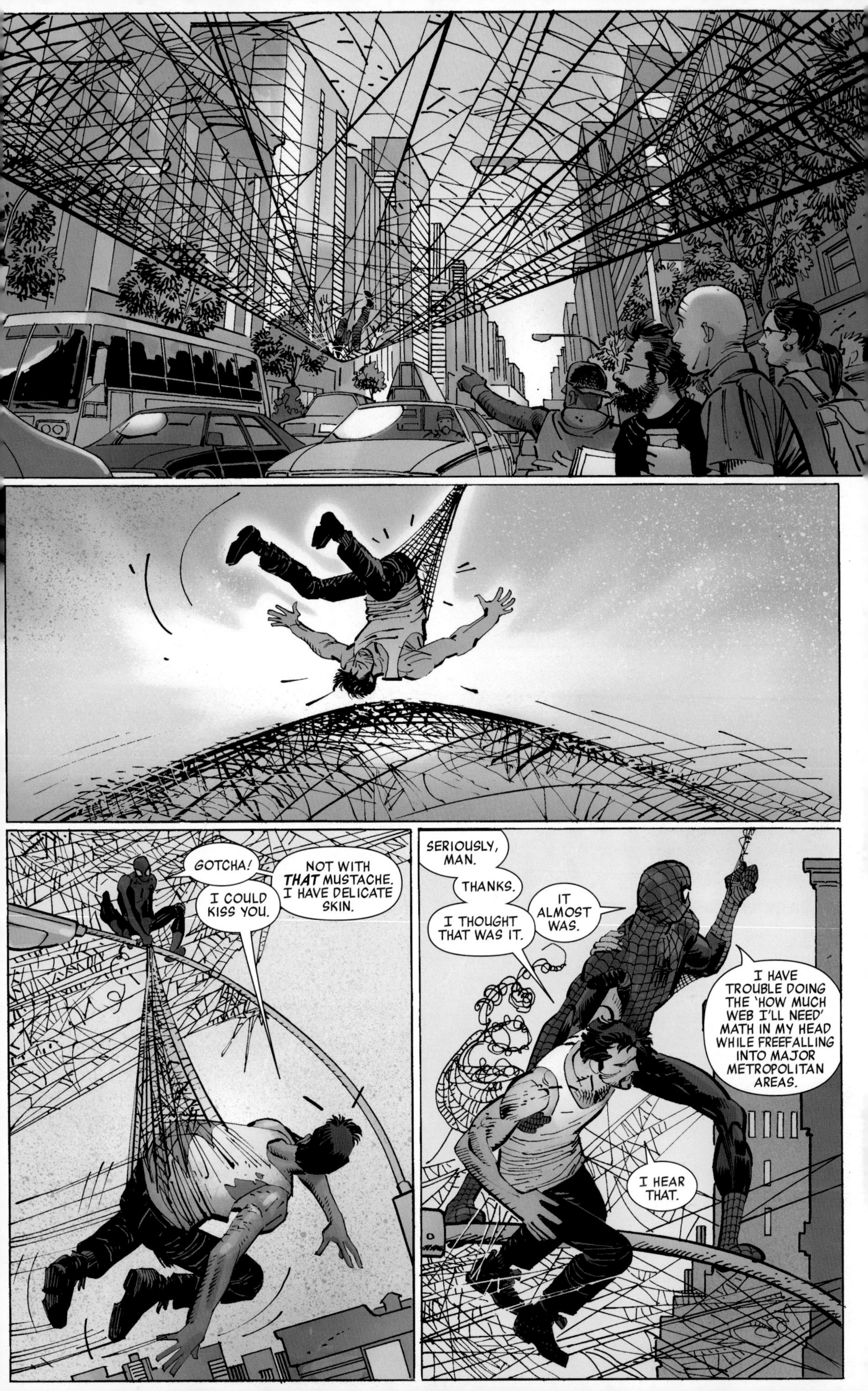
GOTCHA!
I COULD KISS YOU.
NOT WITH THAT MUSTACHE. I HAVE DELICATE SKIN.
SERIOUSLY, MAN.
THANKS.
I THOUGHT THAT WAS IT.
IT ALMOST WAS.
I HAVE TROUBLE DOING THE 'HOW MUCH WEB I'LL NEED' MATH IN MY HEAD WHILE FREEFALLING INTO MAJOR METROPOLITAN AREAS.
I HEAR THAT.

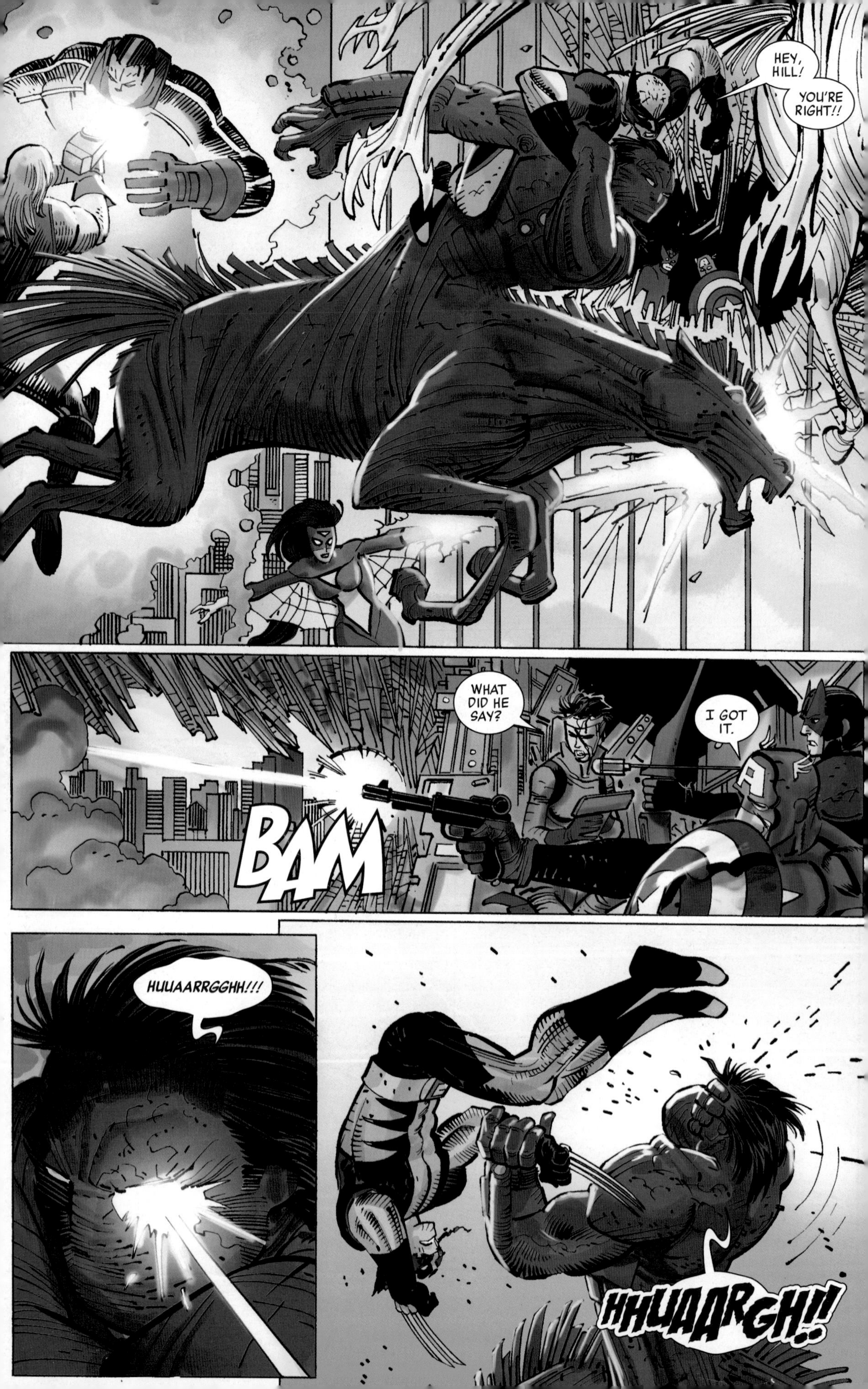
HEY, HILL!
YOU'RE RIGHT!!
WHAT DID HE SAY?
I GOT IT.
BAM
HUUAARRGGHH!!!
HHUAARGH!!

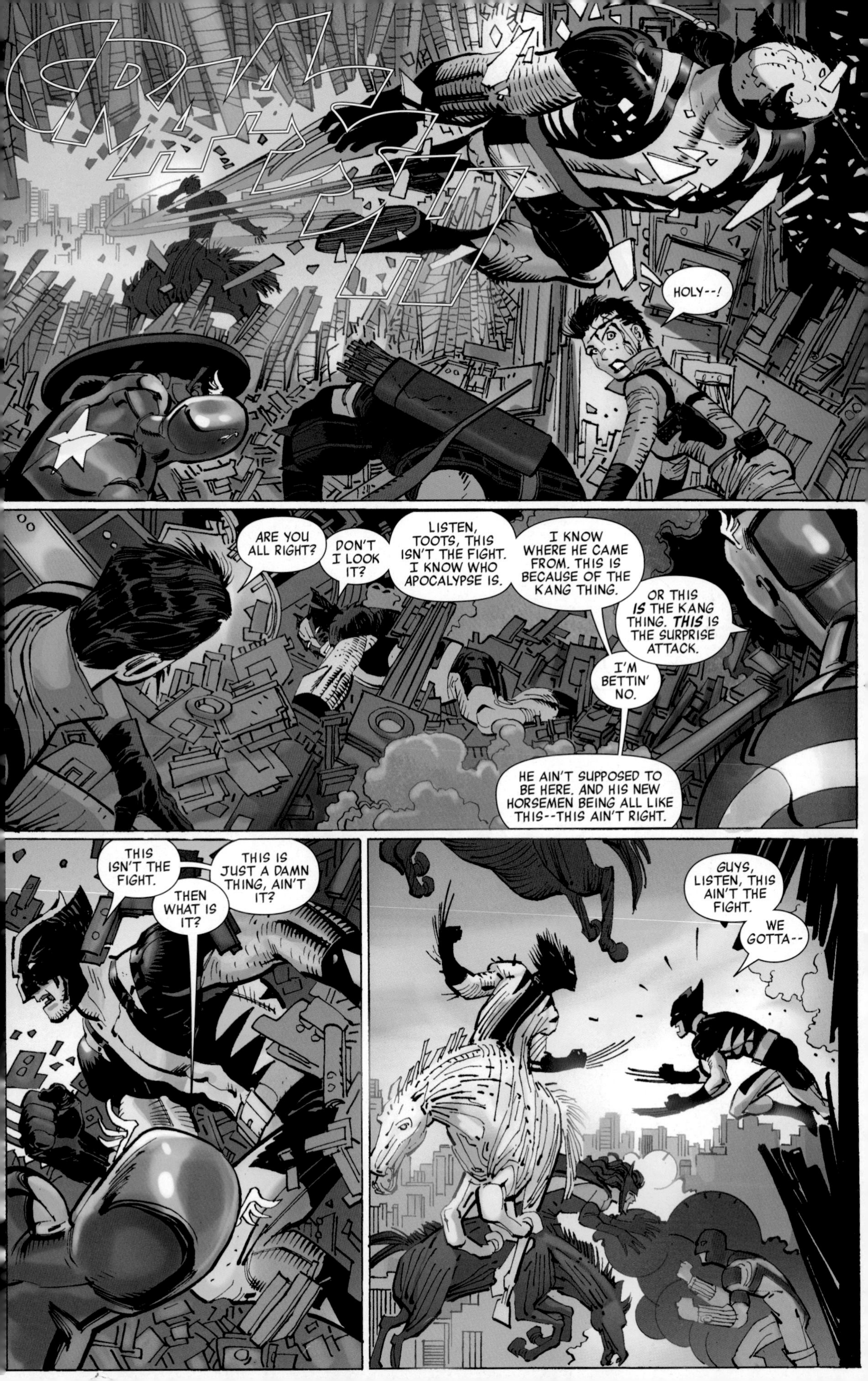

HOLY--!
ARE YOU ALL RIGHT?
DON'T I LOOK IT?
LISTEN, TOOTS, THIS ISN'T THE FIGHT. I KNOW WHO APOCALYPSE IS.
I KNOW WHERE HE CAME FROM. THIS IS BECAUSE OF THE KANG THING.
OR THIS *IS* THE KANG THING. *THIS* IS THE SURPRISE ATTACK.
I'M BETTIN' NO.
HE AIN'T SUPPOSED TO BE HERE. AND HIS NEW HORSEMEN BEING ALL LIKE THIS--THIS AIN'T RIGHT.
THIS ISN'T THE FIGHT.
THIS IS JUST A DAMN THING, AIN'T IT?
THEN WHAT IS IT?
GUYS, LISTEN, THIS AIN'T THE FIGHT.
WE GOTTA--

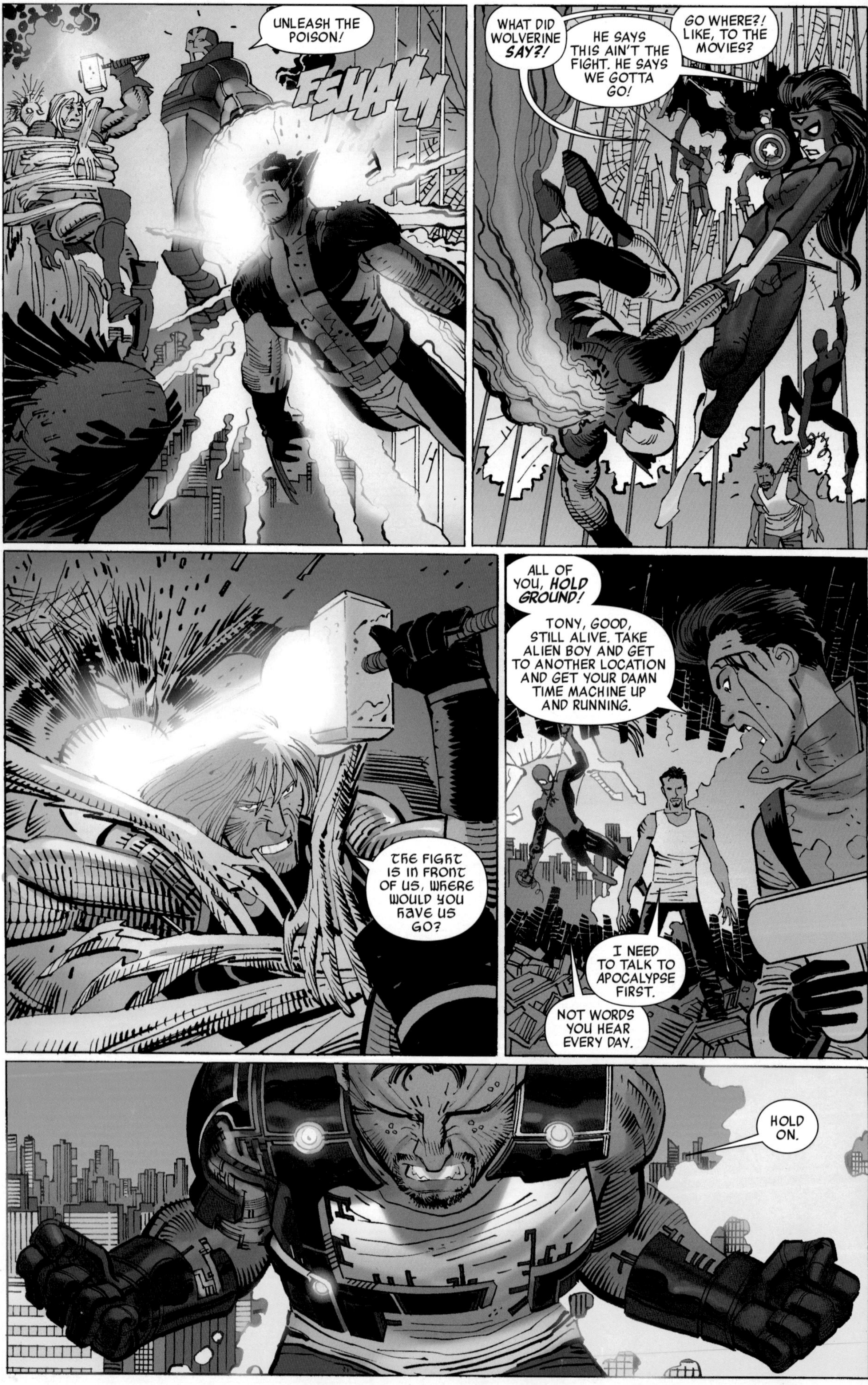
UNLEASH THE POISON!
FSHAMM
WHAT DID WOLVERINE SAY?!
HE SAYS THIS AIN'T THE FIGHT. HE SAYS WE GOTTA GO!
GO WHERE?! LIKE, TO THE MOVIES?
THE FIGHT IS IN FRONT OF US, WHERE WOULD YOU HAVE US GO?
ALL OF YOU, HOLD GROUND!
TONY, GOOD, STILL ALIVE. TAKE ALIEN BOY AND GET TO ANOTHER LOCATION AND GET YOUR DAMN TIME MACHINE UP AND RUNNING.
I NEED TO TALK TO APOCALYPSE FIRST.
NOT WORDS YOU HEAR EVERY DAY.
HOLD ON.

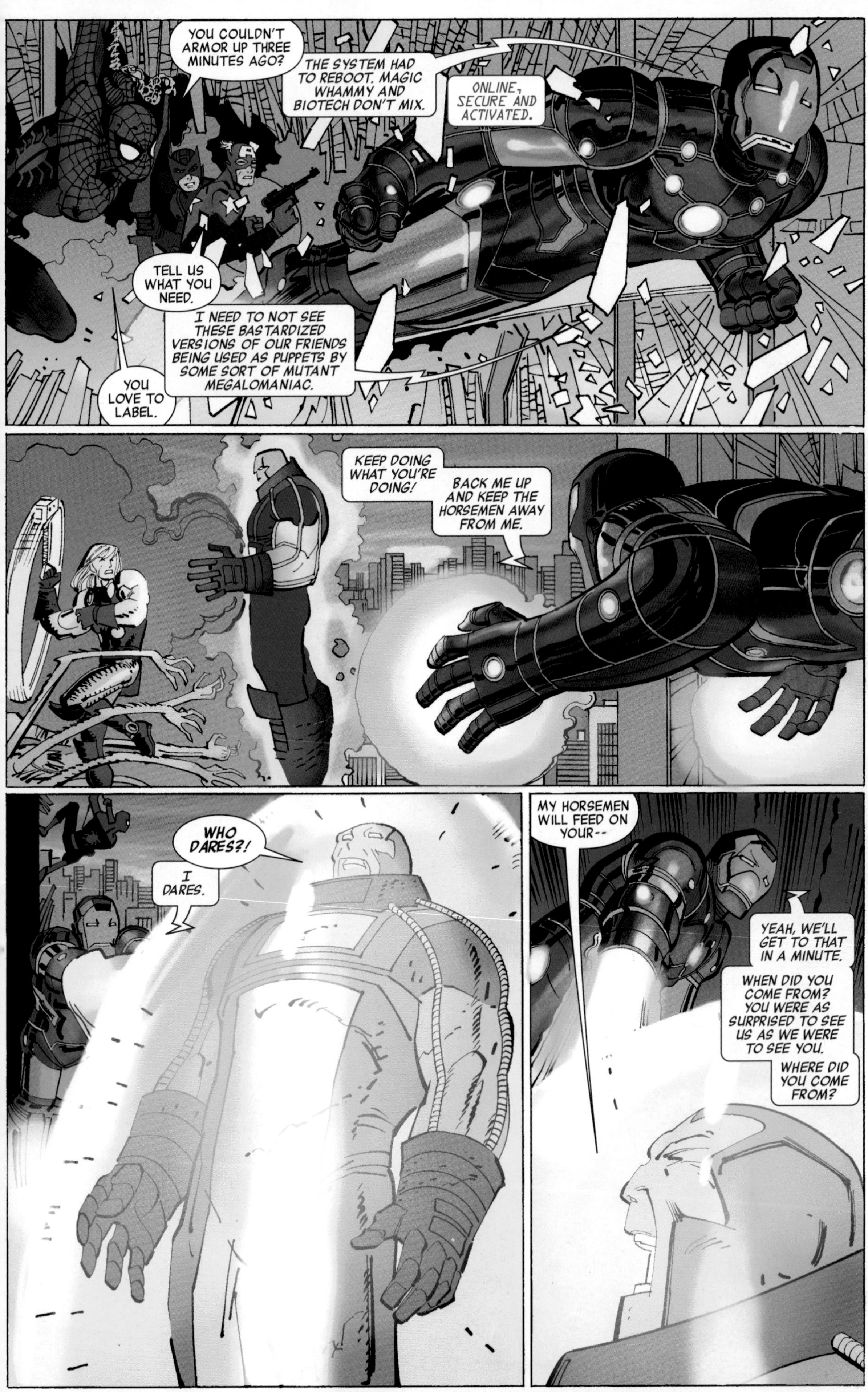
YOU COULDN'T ARMOR UP THREE MINUTES AGO?
THE SYSTEM HAD TO REBOOT. MAGIC WHAMMY AND BIOTECH DON'T MIX.
ONLINE, SECURE AND ACTIVATED.
TELL US WHAT YOU NEED.
I NEED TO NOT SEE THESE BASTARDIZED VERSIONS OF OUR FRIENDS BEING USED AS PUPPETS BY SOME SORT OF MUTANT MEGALOMANIAC.
YOU LOVE TO LABEL.
KEEP DOING WHAT YOU'RE DOING!
BACK ME UP AND KEEP THE HORSEMEN AWAY FROM ME.
WHO DARES?!
I DARES.
MY HORSEMEN WILL FEED ON YOUR--
YEAH, WE'LL GET TO THAT IN A MINUTE.
WHEN DID YOU COME FROM? YOU WERE AS SURPRISED TO SEE US AS WE WERE TO SEE YOU.
WHERE DID YOU COME FROM?

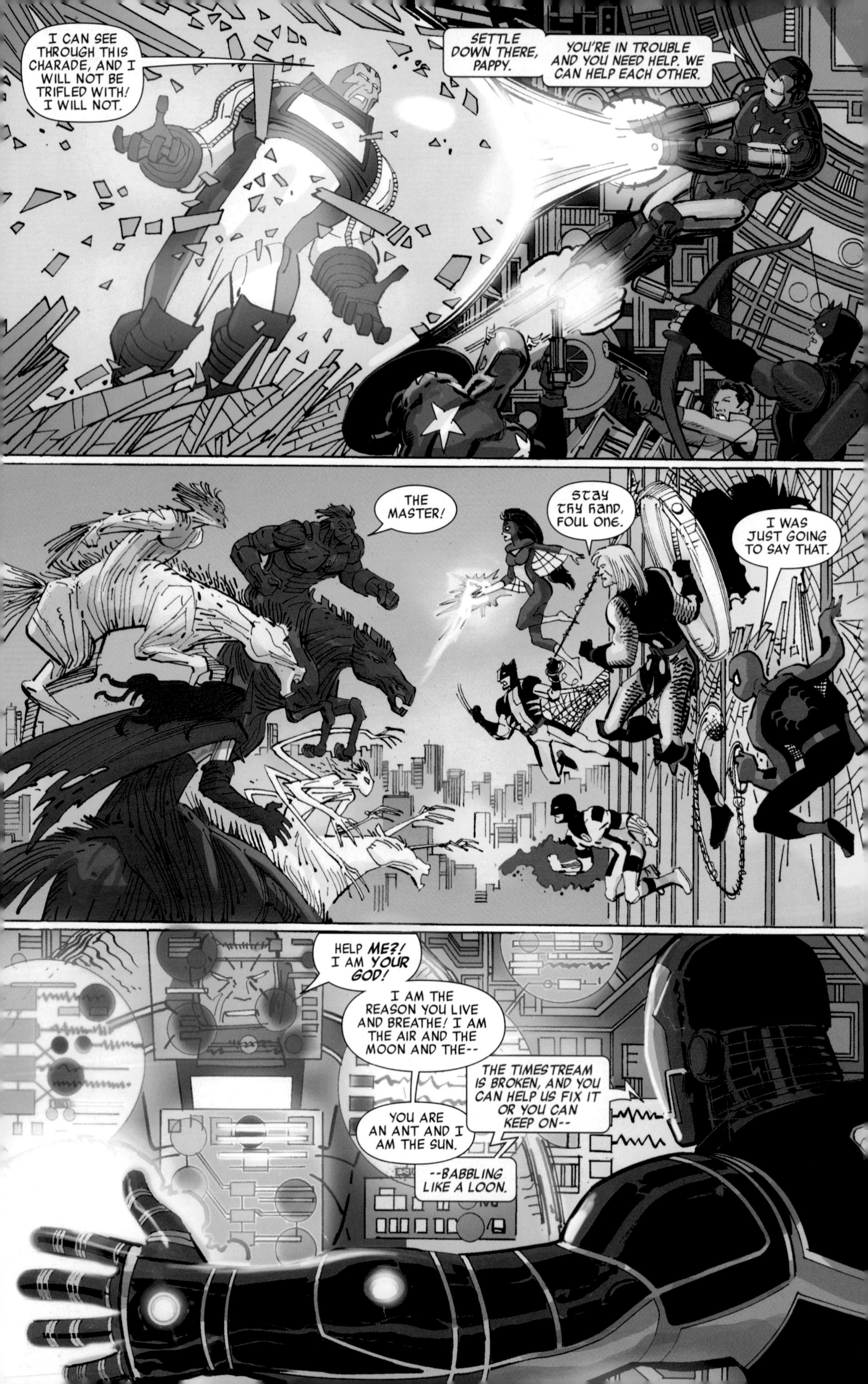
I CAN SEE THROUGH THIS CHARADE, AND I WILL NOT BE TRIFLED WITH! I WILL NOT.
SETTLE DOWN THERE, PAPPY.
YOU'RE IN TROUBLE AND YOU NEED HELP. WE CAN HELP EACH OTHER.
THE MASTER!
STAY THY HAND, FOUL ONE.
I WAS JUST GOING TO SAY THAT.
HELP ME?! I AM YOUR GOD!
I AM THE REASON YOU LIVE AND BREATHE! I AM THE AIR AND THE MOON AND THE--
YOU ARE AN ANT AND I AM THE SUN.
THE TIMESTREAM IS BROKEN, AND YOU CAN HELP US FIX IT OR YOU CAN KEEP ON--
--BABBLING LIKE A LOON.

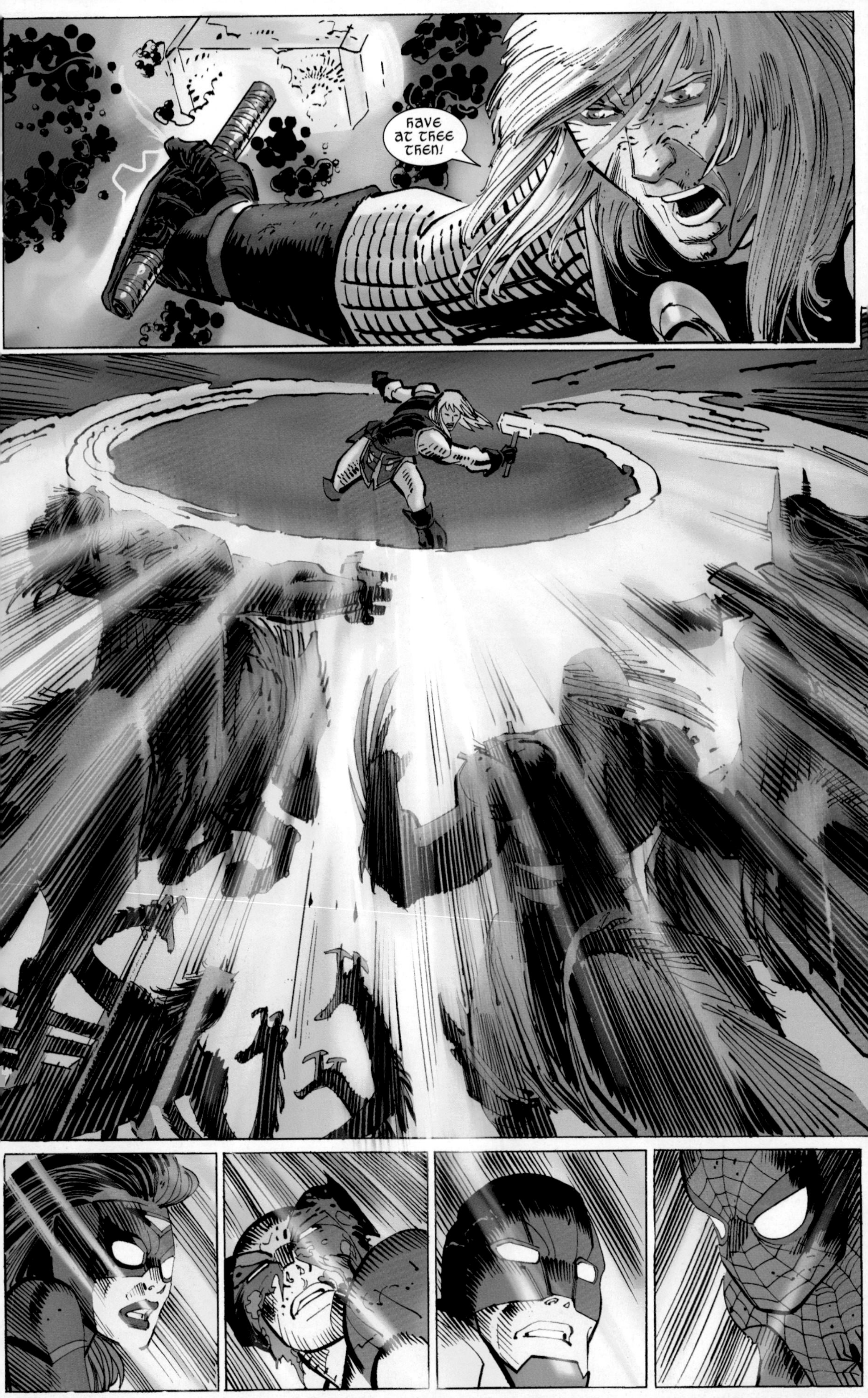
HAVE AT THEE THEN!

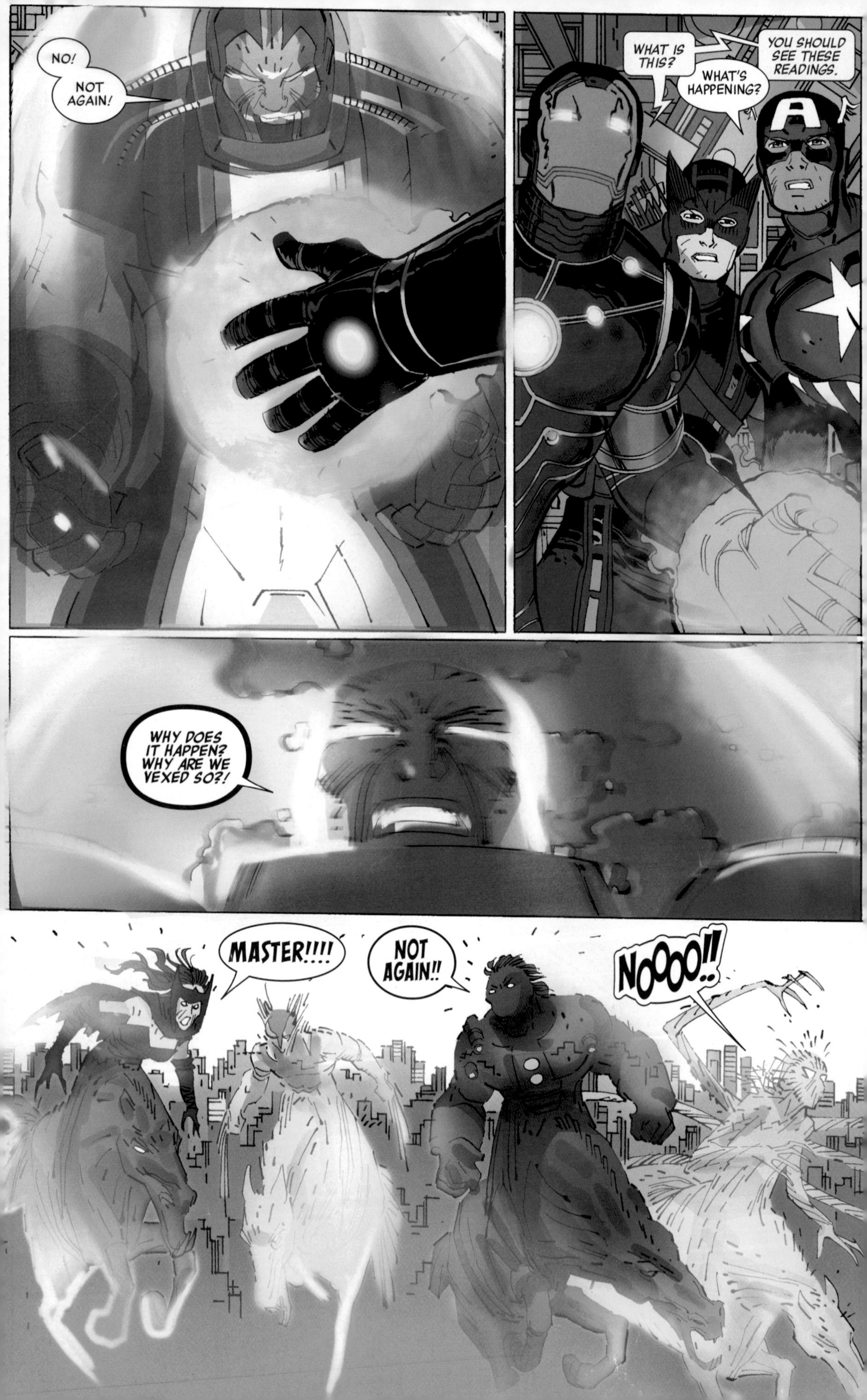
NO!
NOT AGAIN!
WHAT IS THIS?
YOU SHOULD SEE THESE READINGS.
WHAT'S HAPPENING?
WHY DOES IT HAPPEN? WHY ARE WE VEXED SO?!
MASTER!!!!
NOT AGAIN!!
NOOOO!!

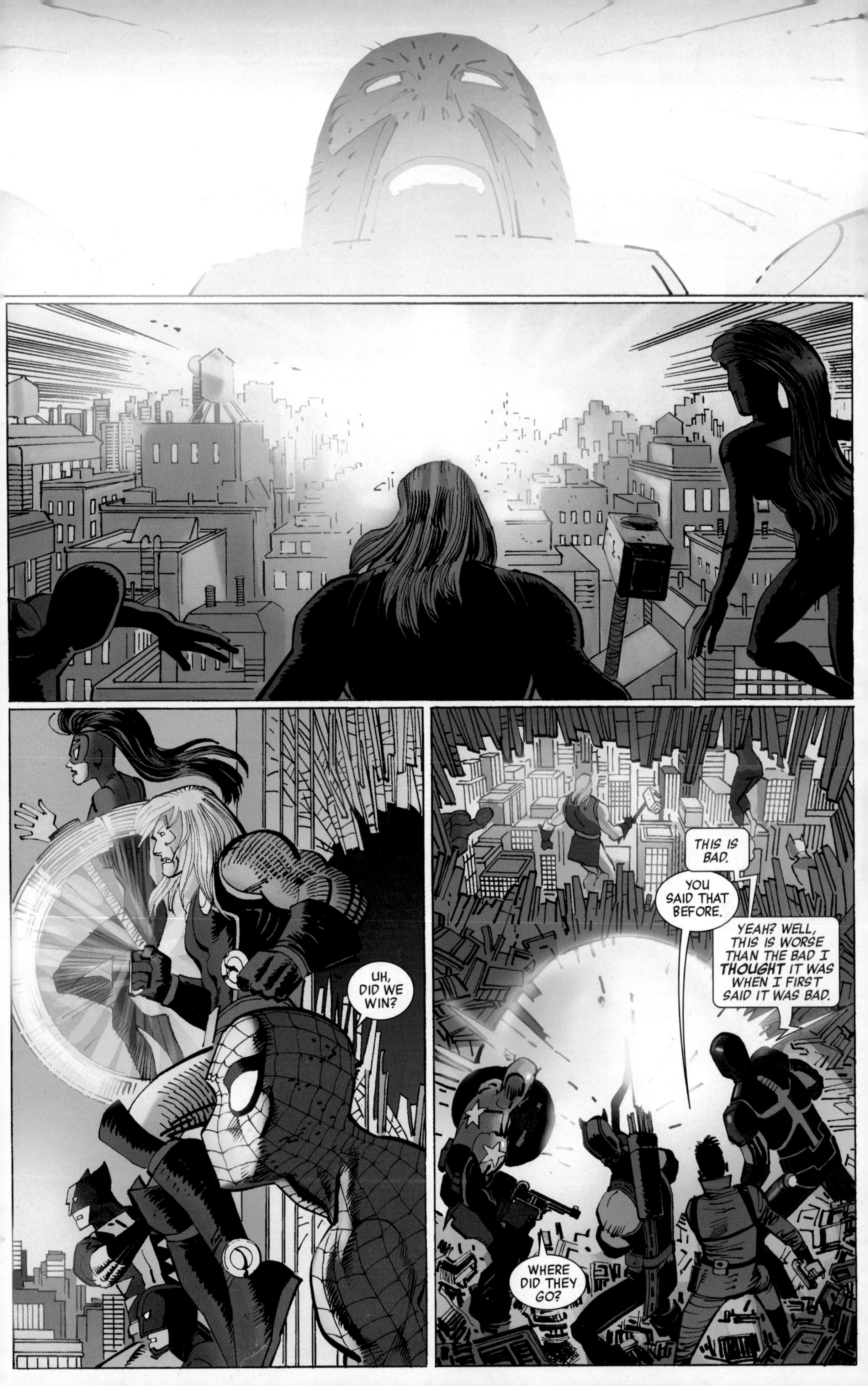
UH, DID WE WIN?
THIS IS BAD.
YOU SAID THAT BEFORE.
YEAH? WELL, THIS IS WORSE THAN THE BAD I THOUGHT IT WAS WHEN I FIRST SAID IT WAS BAD.
WHERE DID THEY GO?

APOCALYPSE AND HIS MERRY MEN ARE TRAPPED IN THE TIME-STREAM HELL KANG CREATED.

AND YOU KNOW THIS BECAUSE...

HE HAD NO IDEA WHERE HE WAS OR HOW HE GOT HERE. HE WAS REACTING LIKE A CAGED ANIMAL.

AND BECAUSE OF ALL THAT, I DIDN'T ACTUALLY THINK HE WOULD HELP ME FIGURE THIS WHOLE THING OUT. I WAS JUST TRYING TO STALL HIM--

SO YOU COULD--

--SCAN EVERY MOLECULE AND PARTICLE ON HIM.

WHAT ARE **WE** DOING OUT HERE?

RECON.

MAKING SURE THE BAD GUYS DON'T COME BACK?

LIKE SMART PEOPLE DO.

I FORGOT WHAT THAT FELT LIKE.

WHAT DID YOU FIND?

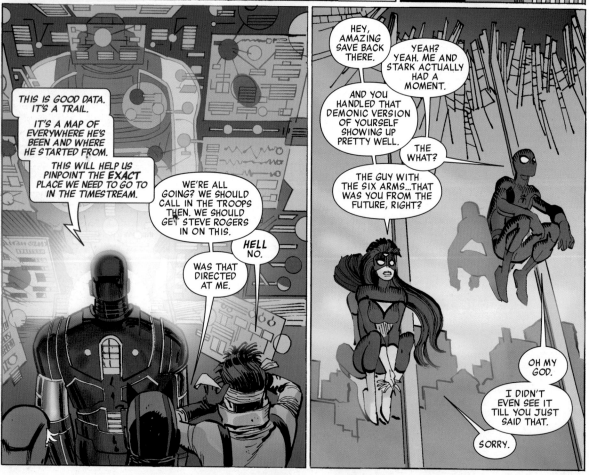

THIS IS GOOD DATA. IT'S A TRAIL.

IT'S A MAP OF EVERYWHERE HE'S BEEN AND WHERE HE STARTED FROM.

THIS WILL HELP US PINPOINT THE **EXACT** PLACE WE NEED TO GO TO IN THE TIMESTREAM.

WE'RE ALL GOING? WE SHOULD CALL IN THE TROOPS THEN. WE SHOULD GET STEVE ROGERS IN ON THIS.

HELL NO.

WAS THAT DIRECTED AT ME.

HEY, AMAZING SAVE BACK THERE.

YEAH? YEAH. ME AND STARK ACTUALLY HAD A MOMENT.

AND YOU HANDLED THAT DEMONIC VERSION OF YOURSELF SHOWING UP PRETTY WELL.

THE WHAT?

THE GUY WITH THE SIX ARMS...THAT WAS YOU FROM THE FUTURE, RIGHT?

OH MY GOD.

I DIDN'T EVEN SEE IT TILL YOU JUST SAID THAT.

SORRY.

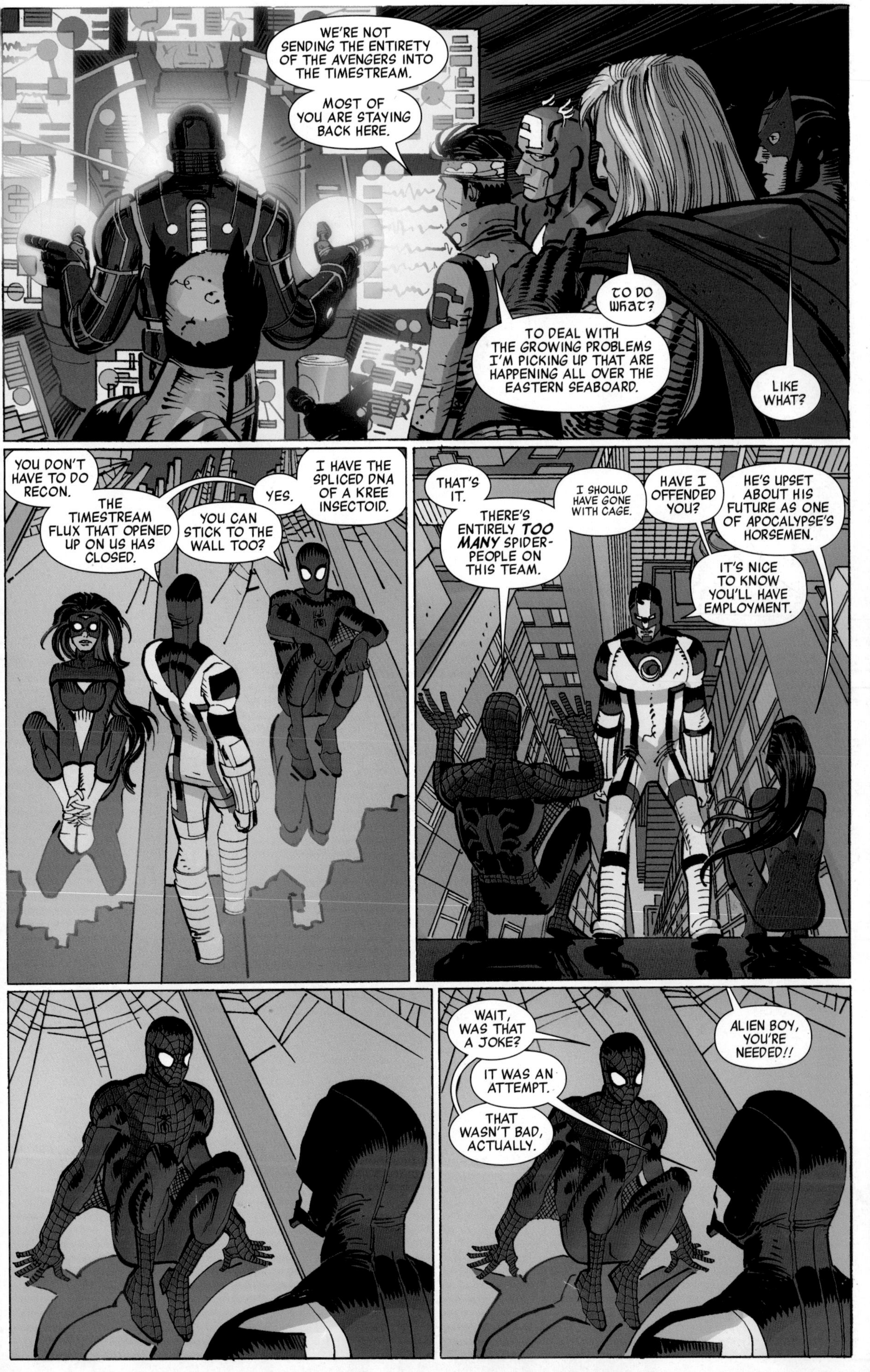
WE'RE NOT SENDING THE ENTIRETY OF THE AVENGERS INTO THE TIMESTREAM.
MOST OF YOU ARE STAYING BACK HERE.
TO DO WHAT?
TO DEAL WITH THE GROWING PROBLEMS I'M PICKING UP THAT ARE HAPPENING ALL OVER THE EASTERN SEABOARD.
LIKE WHAT?
YOU DON'T HAVE TO DO RECON.
THE TIMESTREAM FLUX THAT OPENED UP ON US HAS CLOSED.
YOU CAN STICK TO THE WALL TOO?
YES.
I HAVE THE SPLICED DNA OF A KREE INSECTOID.
THAT'S IT.
THERE'S ENTIRELY TOO MANY SPIDER-PEOPLE ON THIS TEAM.
I SHOULD HAVE GONE WITH CAGE.
HAVE I OFFENDED YOU?
HE'S UPSET ABOUT HIS FUTURE AS ONE OF APOCALYPSE'S HORSEMEN.
IT'S NICE TO KNOW YOU'LL HAVE EMPLOYMENT.
WAIT, WAS THAT A JOKE?
IT WAS AN ATTEMPT.
THAT WASN'T BAD, ACTUALLY.
ALIEN BOY, YOU'RE NEEDED!!

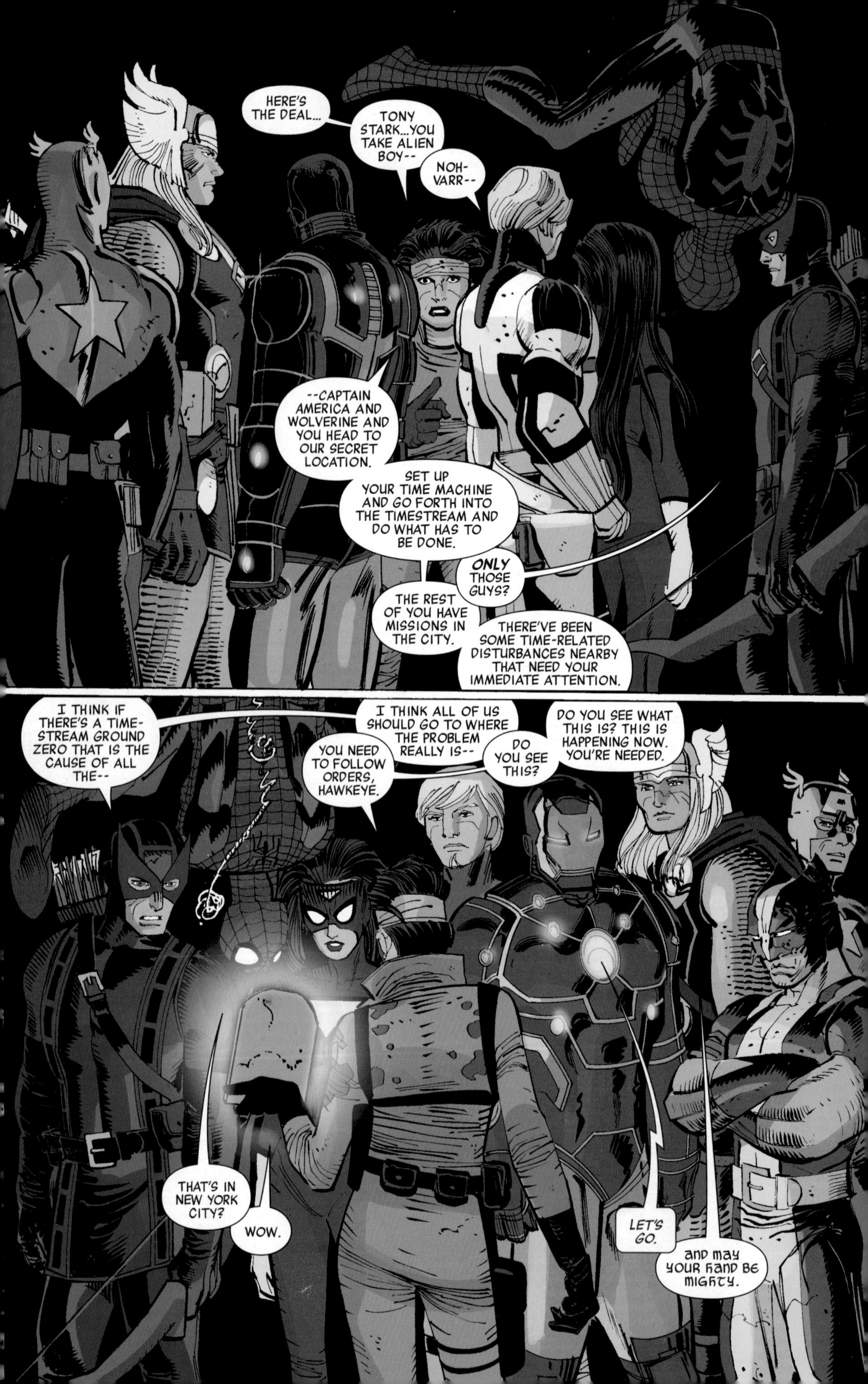
HERE'S THE DEAL...
TONY STARK...YOU TAKE ALIEN BOY--
NOH-VARR--
--CAPTAIN AMERICA AND WOLVERINE AND YOU HEAD TO OUR SECRET LOCATION.
SET UP YOUR TIME MACHINE AND GO FORTH INTO THE TIMESTREAM AND DO WHAT HAS TO BE DONE.
ONLY THOSE GUYS?
THE REST OF YOU HAVE MISSIONS IN THE CITY.
THERE'VE BEEN SOME TIME-RELATED DISTURBANCES NEARBY THAT NEED YOUR IMMEDIATE ATTENTION.
I THINK IF THERE'S A TIME-STREAM GROUND ZERO THAT IS THE CAUSE OF ALL THE--
I THINK ALL OF US SHOULD GO TO WHERE THE PROBLEM REALLY IS--
YOU NEED TO FOLLOW ORDERS, HAWKEYE.
DO YOU SEE THIS?
DO YOU SEE WHAT THIS IS? THIS IS HAPPENING NOW. YOU'RE NEEDED.
THAT'S IN NEW YORK CITY?
WOW.
LET'S GO.
AND MAY YOUR HAND BE MIGHTY.

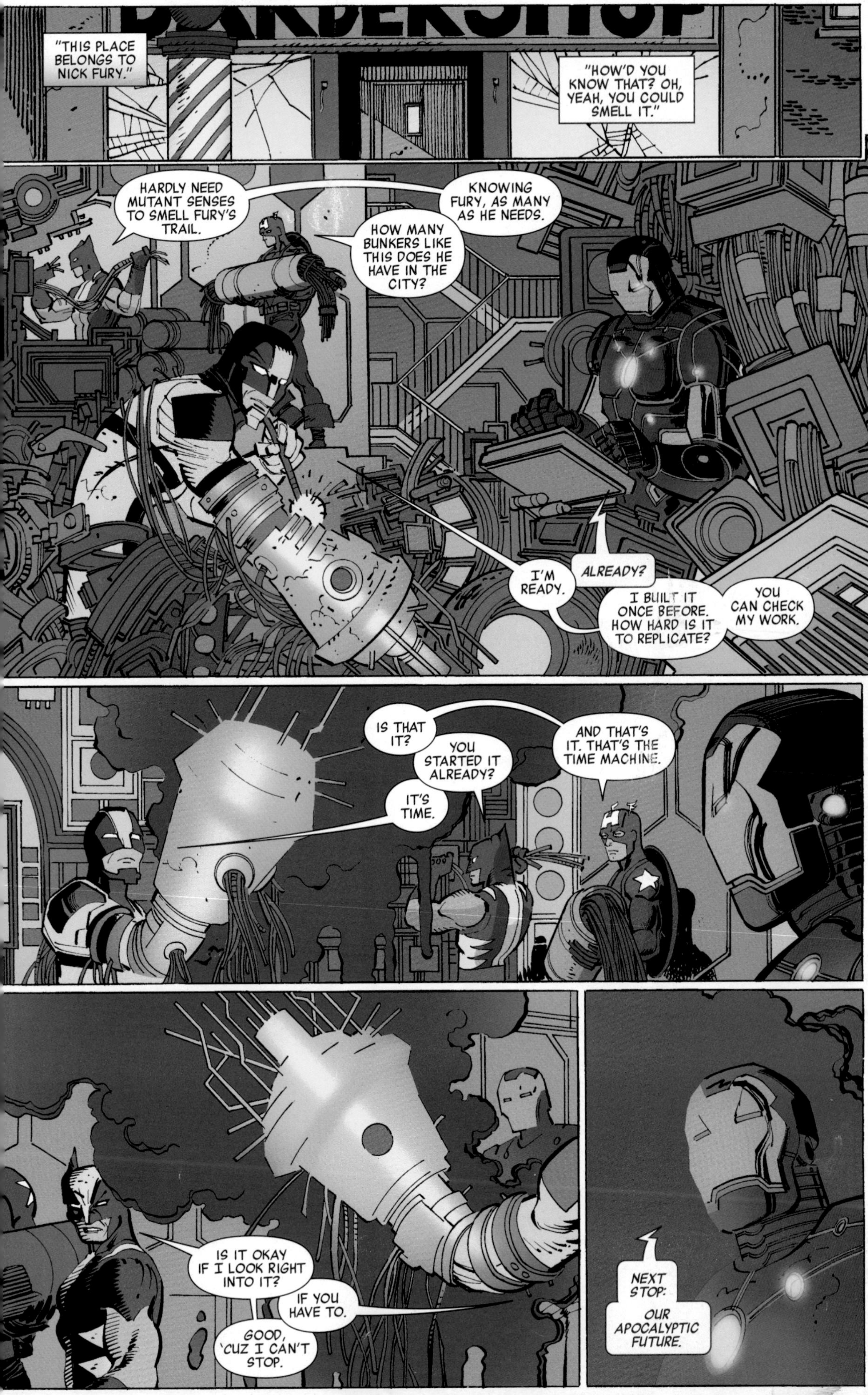

"THIS PLACE BELONGS TO NICK FURY."
"HOW'D YOU KNOW THAT? OH, YEAH, YOU COULD SMELL IT."
HARDLY NEED MUTANT SENSES TO SMELL FURY'S TRAIL.
KNOWING FURY, AS MANY AS HE NEEDS.
HOW MANY BUNKERS LIKE THIS DOES HE HAVE IN THE CITY?
I'M READY.
ALREADY?
I BUILT IT ONCE BEFORE. HOW HARD IS IT TO REPLICATE?
YOU CAN CHECK MY WORK.
IS THAT IT?
YOU STARTED IT ALREADY?
IT'S TIME.
AND THAT'S IT. THAT'S THE TIME MACHINE.
IS IT OKAY IF I LOOK RIGHT INTO IT?
IF YOU HAVE TO.
GOOD, 'CUZ I CAN'T STOP.
NEXT STOP:
OUR APOCALYPTIC FUTURE.

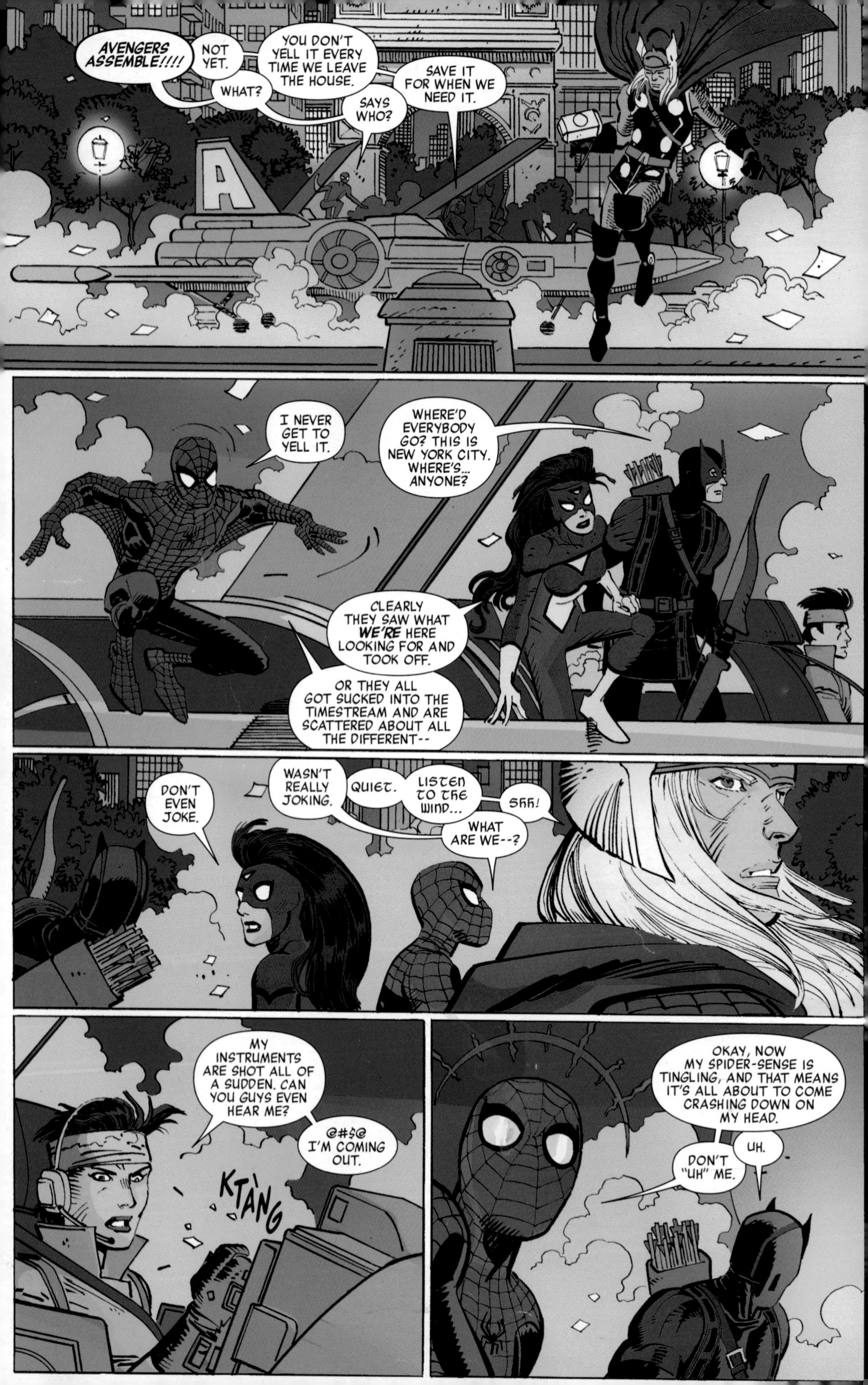
AVENGERS ASSEMBLE!!!!
NOT YET.
WHAT?
YOU DON'T YELL IT EVERY TIME WE LEAVE THE HOUSE.
SAYS WHO?
SAVE IT FOR WHEN WE NEED IT.
I NEVER GET TO YELL IT.
WHERE'D EVERYBODY GO? THIS IS NEW YORK CITY. WHERE'S... ANYONE?
CLEARLY THEY SAW WHAT WE'RE HERE LOOKING FOR AND TOOK OFF.
OR THEY ALL GOT SUCKED INTO THE TIMESTREAM AND ARE SCATTERED ABOUT ALL THE DIFFERENT--
DON'T EVEN JOKE.
WASN'T REALLY JOKING.
QUIET.
LISTEN TO THE WIND...
WHAT ARE WE--?
SHH!
MY INSTRUMENTS ARE SHOT ALL OF A SUDDEN. CAN YOU GUYS EVEN HEAR ME?
@#$@ I'M COMING OUT.
KTANG
OKAY, NOW MY SPIDER-SENSE IS TINGLING, AND THAT MEANS IT'S ALL ABOUT TO COME CRASHING DOWN ON MY HEAD.
UH.
DON'T "UH" ME.

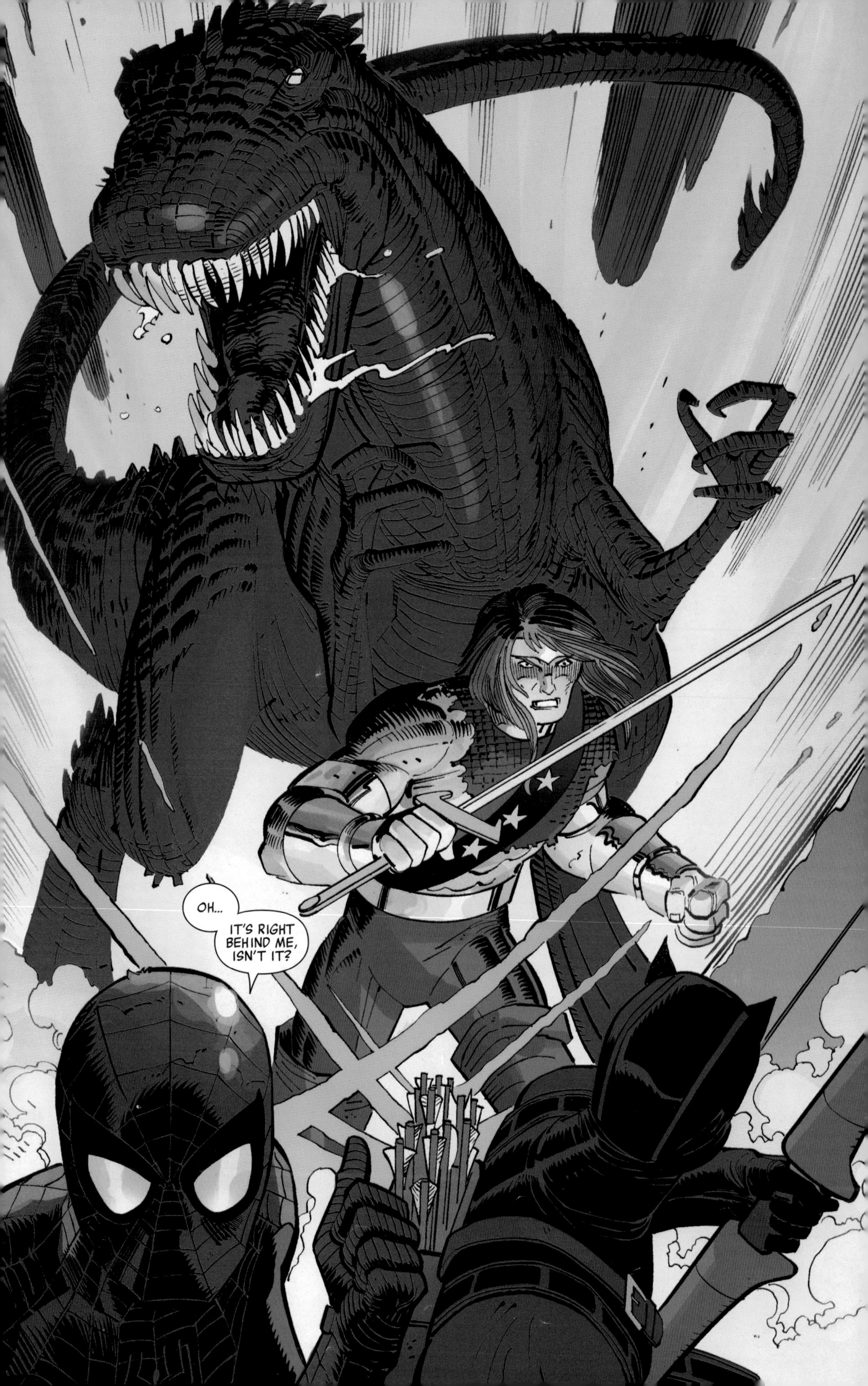
OH...
IT'S RIGHT BEHIND ME, ISN'T IT?

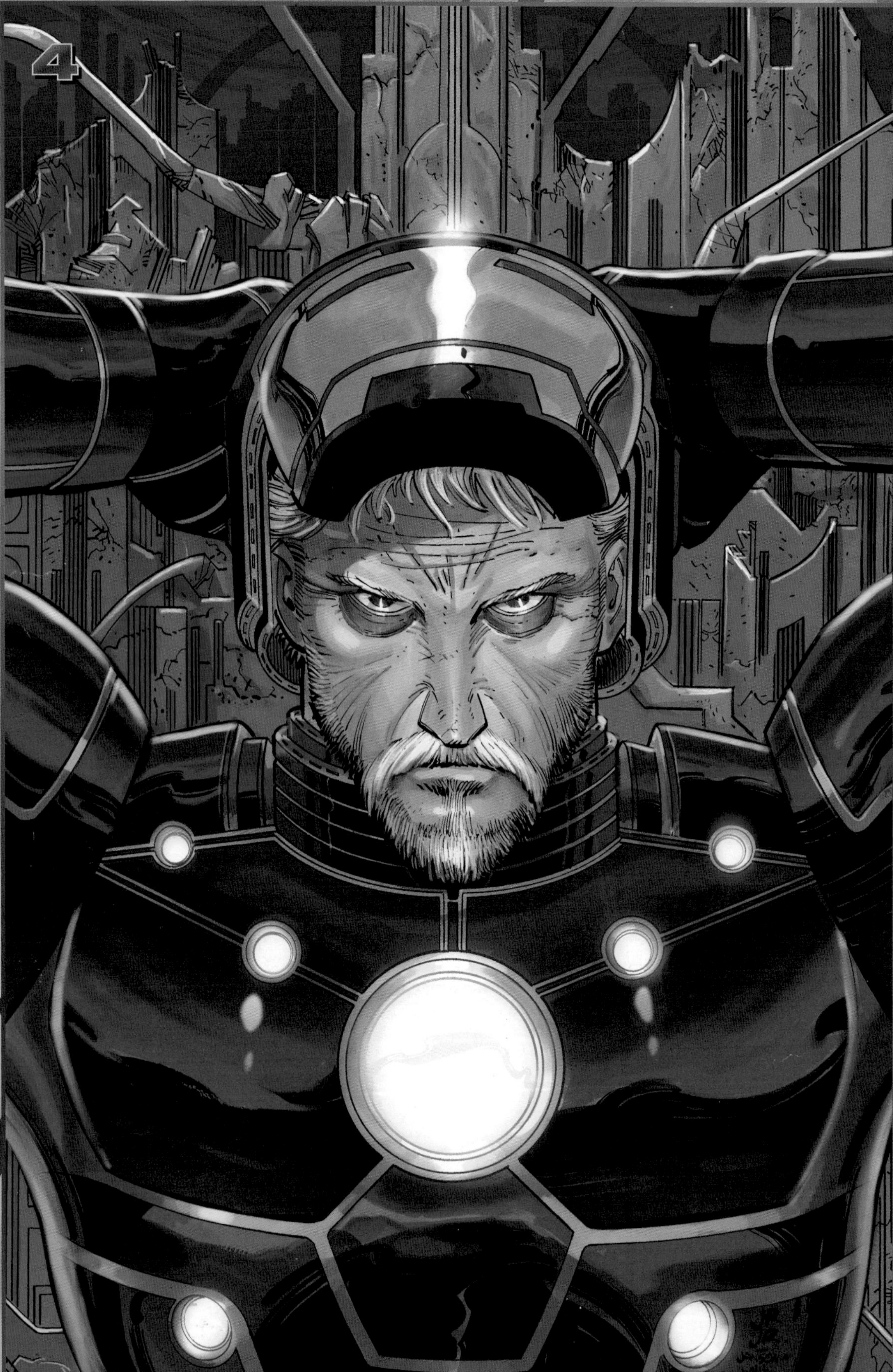
4

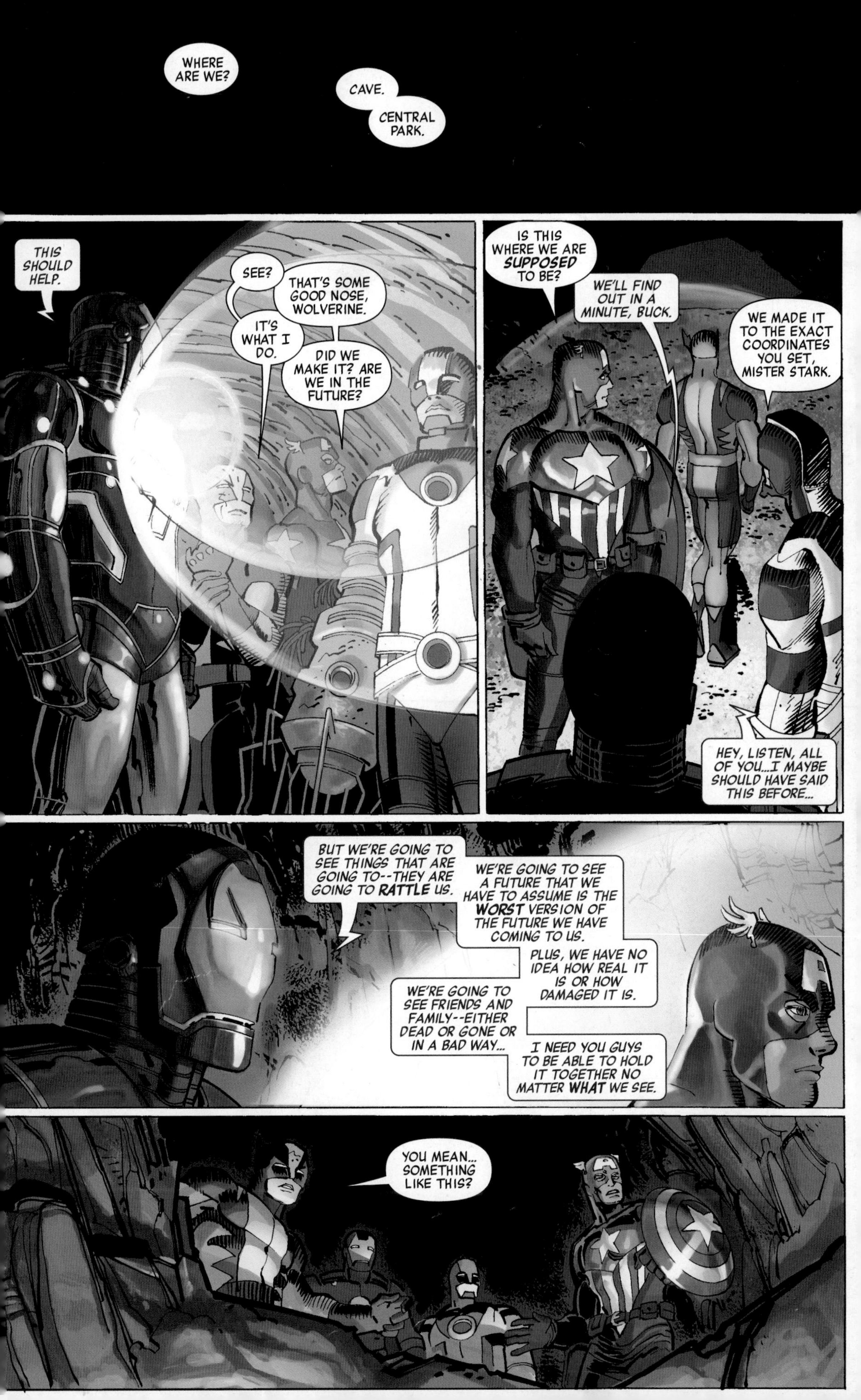
WHERE ARE WE?
CAVE.
CENTRAL PARK.
THIS SHOULD HELP.
SEE?
THAT'S SOME GOOD NOSE, WOLVERINE.
IT'S WHAT I DO.
DID WE MAKE IT? ARE WE IN THE FUTURE?
IS THIS WHERE WE ARE SUPPOSED TO BE?
WE'LL FIND OUT IN A MINUTE, BUCK.
WE MADE IT TO THE EXACT COORDINATES YOU SET, MISTER STARK.
HEY, LISTEN, ALL OF YOU...I MAYBE SHOULD HAVE SAID THIS BEFORE...
BUT WE'RE GOING TO SEE THINGS THAT ARE GOING TO--THEY ARE GOING TO RATTLE US.
WE'RE GOING TO SEE A FUTURE THAT WE HAVE TO ASSUME IS THE WORST VERSION OF THE FUTURE WE HAVE COMING TO US.
PLUS, WE HAVE NO IDEA HOW REAL IT IS OR HOW DAMAGED IT IS.
WE'RE GOING TO SEE FRIENDS AND FAMILY--EITHER DEAD OR GONE OR IN A BAD WAY...
I NEED YOU GUYS TO BE ABLE TO HOLD IT TOGETHER NO MATTER WHAT WE SEE.
YOU MEAN... SOMETHING LIKE THIS?

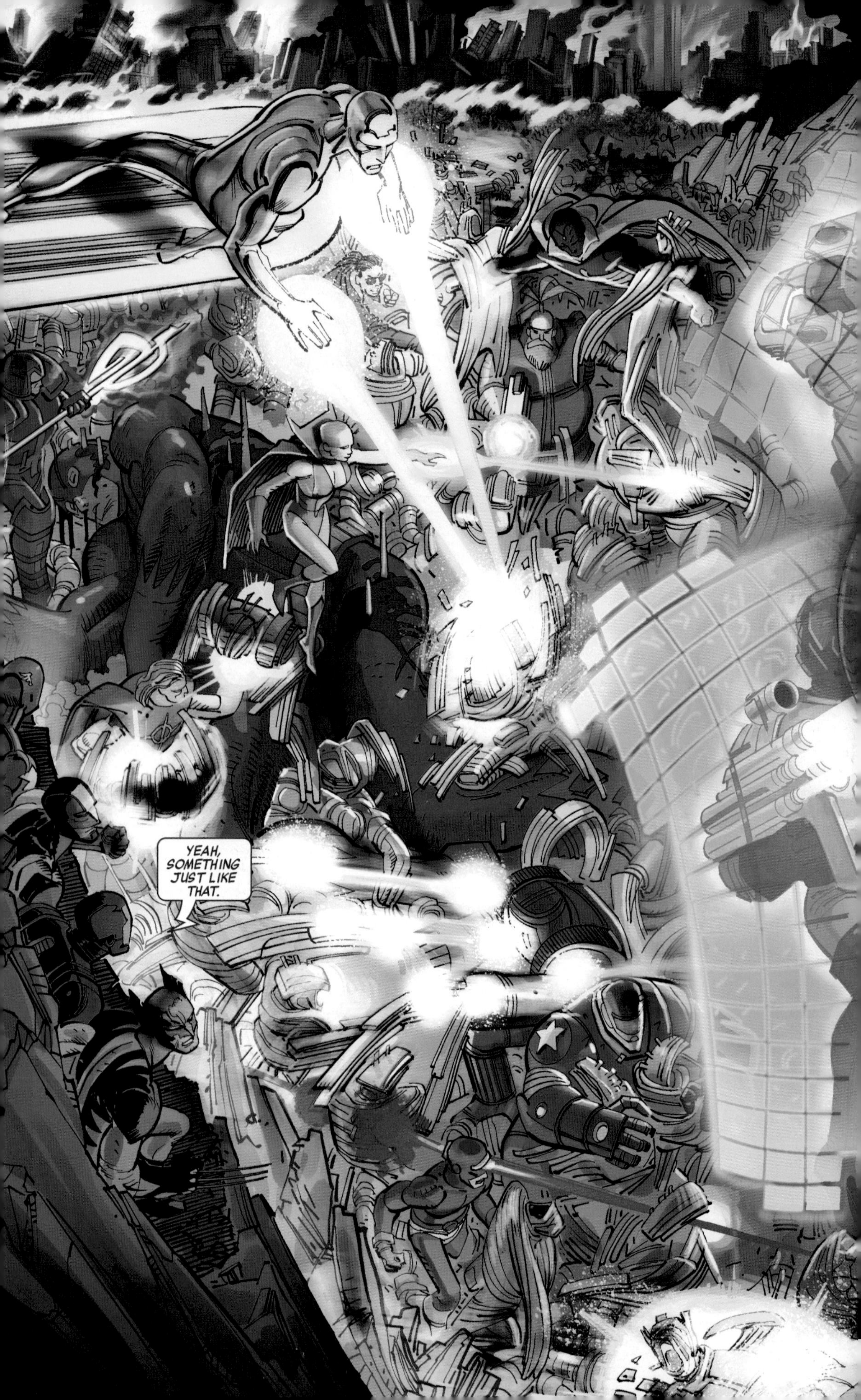
YEAH, SOMETHING JUST LIKE THAT.

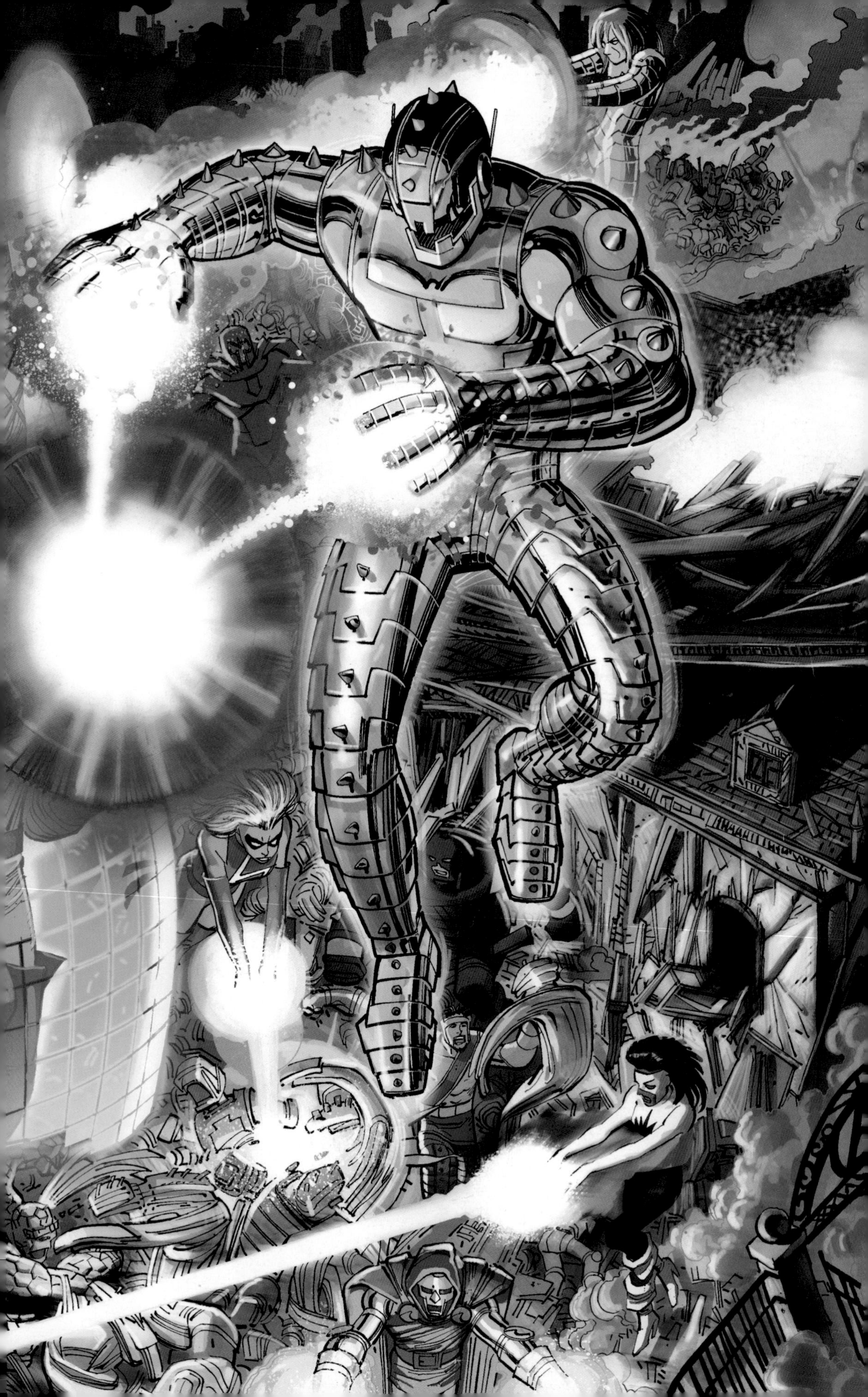

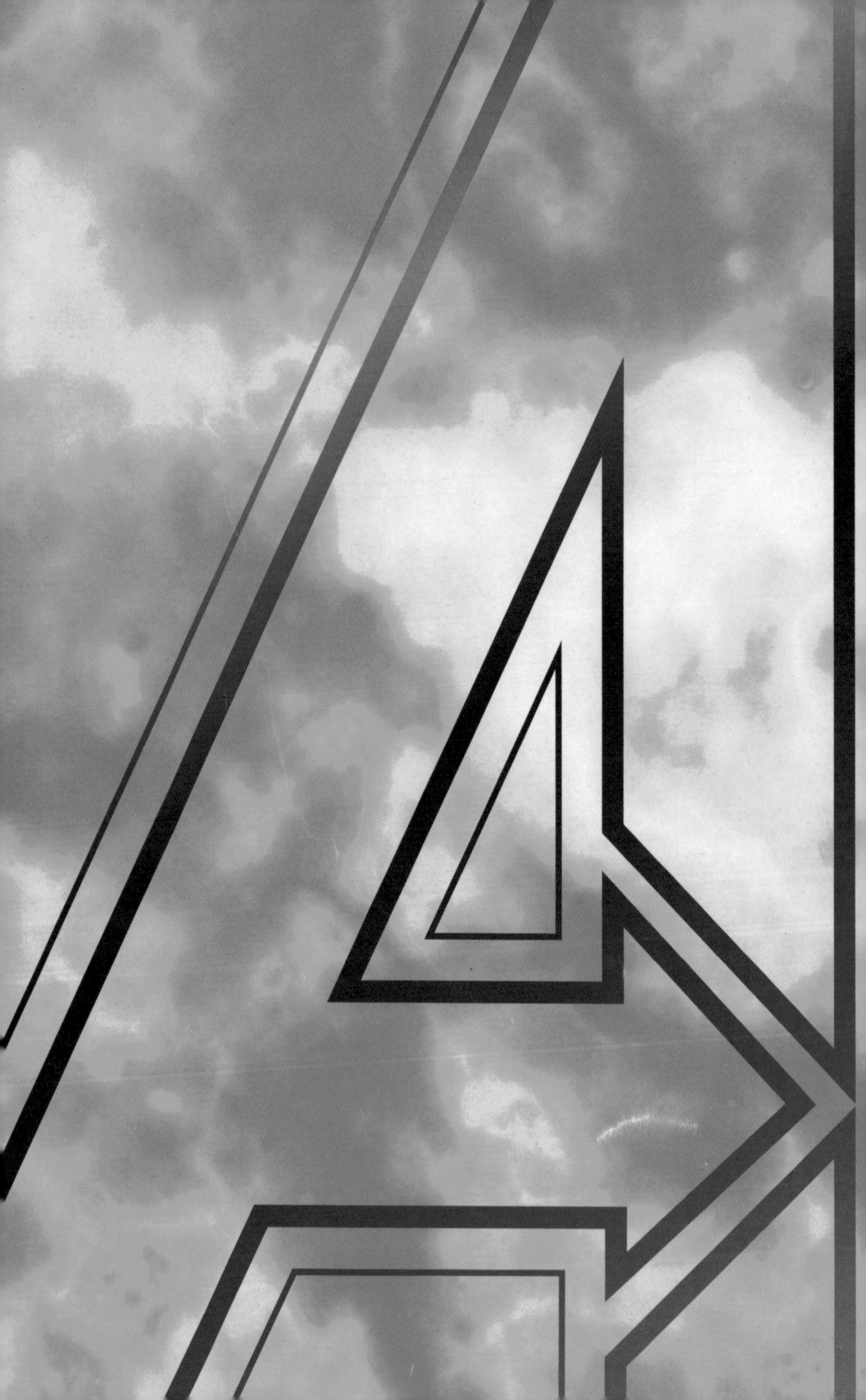

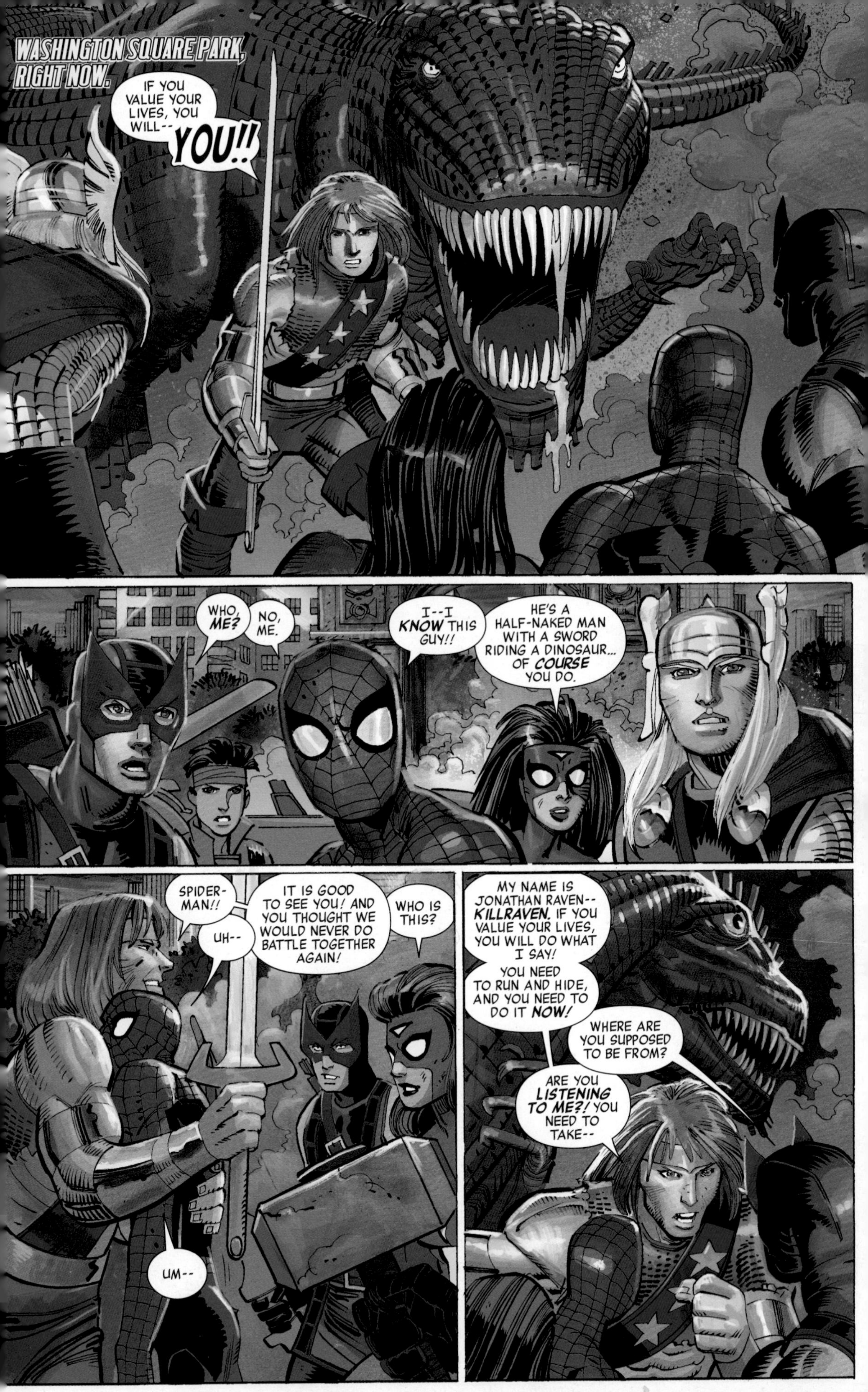
WASHINGTON SQUARE PARK, RIGHT NOW.
IF YOU VALUE YOUR LIVES, YOU WILL-- YOU!!
WHO, ME?
NO, ME.
I--I KNOW THIS GUY!!
HE'S A HALF-NAKED MAN WITH A SWORD RIDING A DINOSAUR... OF COURSE YOU DO.
SPIDER-MAN!!
UH--
IT IS GOOD TO SEE YOU! AND YOU THOUGHT WE WOULD NEVER DO BATTLE TOGETHER AGAIN!
WHO IS THIS?
UM--
MY NAME IS JONATHAN RAVEN-- KILLRAVEN. IF YOU VALUE YOUR LIVES, YOU WILL DO WHAT I SAY!
YOU NEED TO RUN AND HIDE, AND YOU NEED TO DO IT NOW!
WHERE ARE YOU SUPPOSED TO BE FROM?
ARE YOU LISTENING TO ME?! YOU NEED TO TAKE--

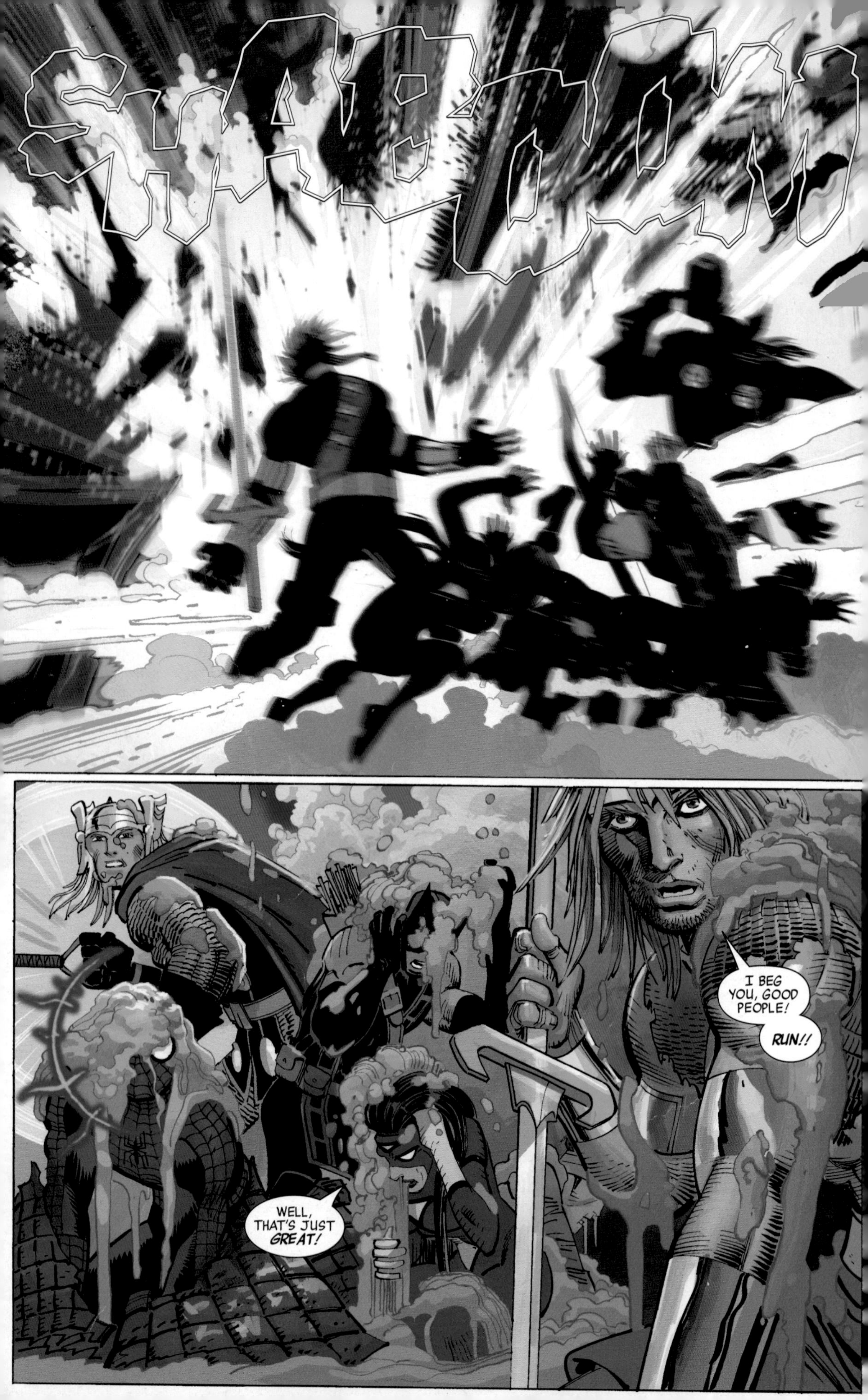
I BEG YOU, GOOD PEOPLE!
RUN!!
WELL, THAT'S JUST GREAT!

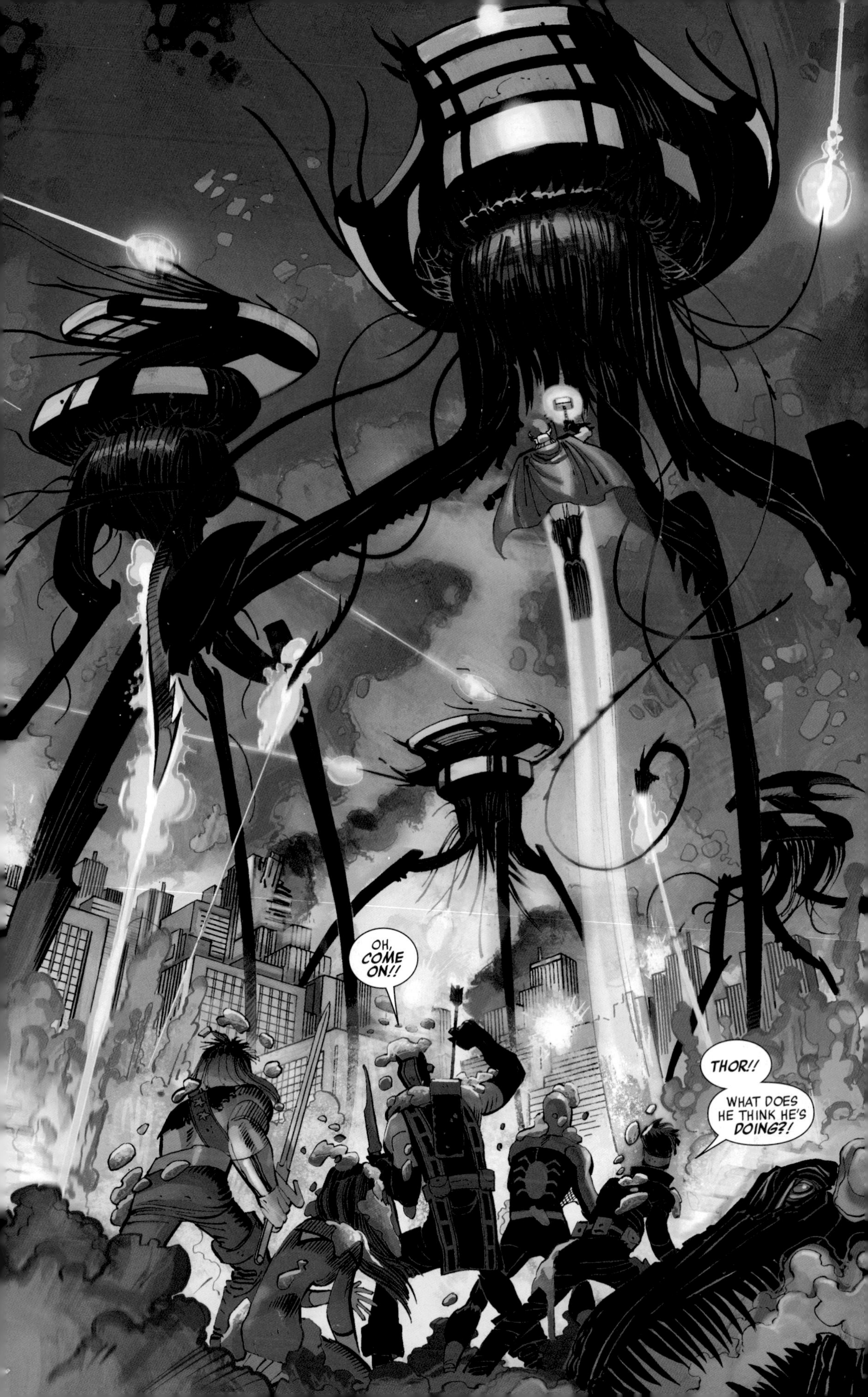
OH, COME ON!!
THOR!!
WHAT DOES HE THINK HE'S DOING?!

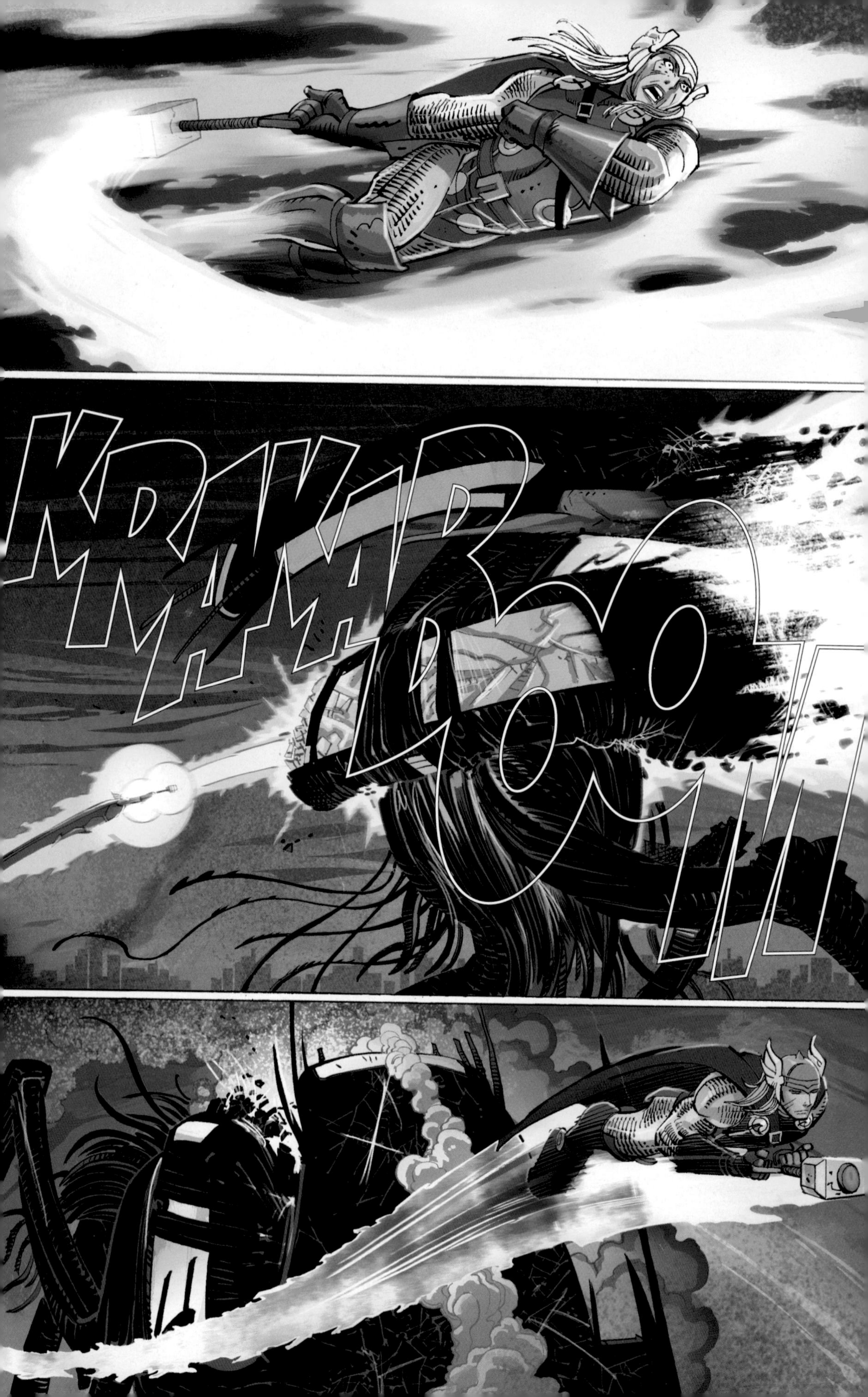
KRAKABOOOM

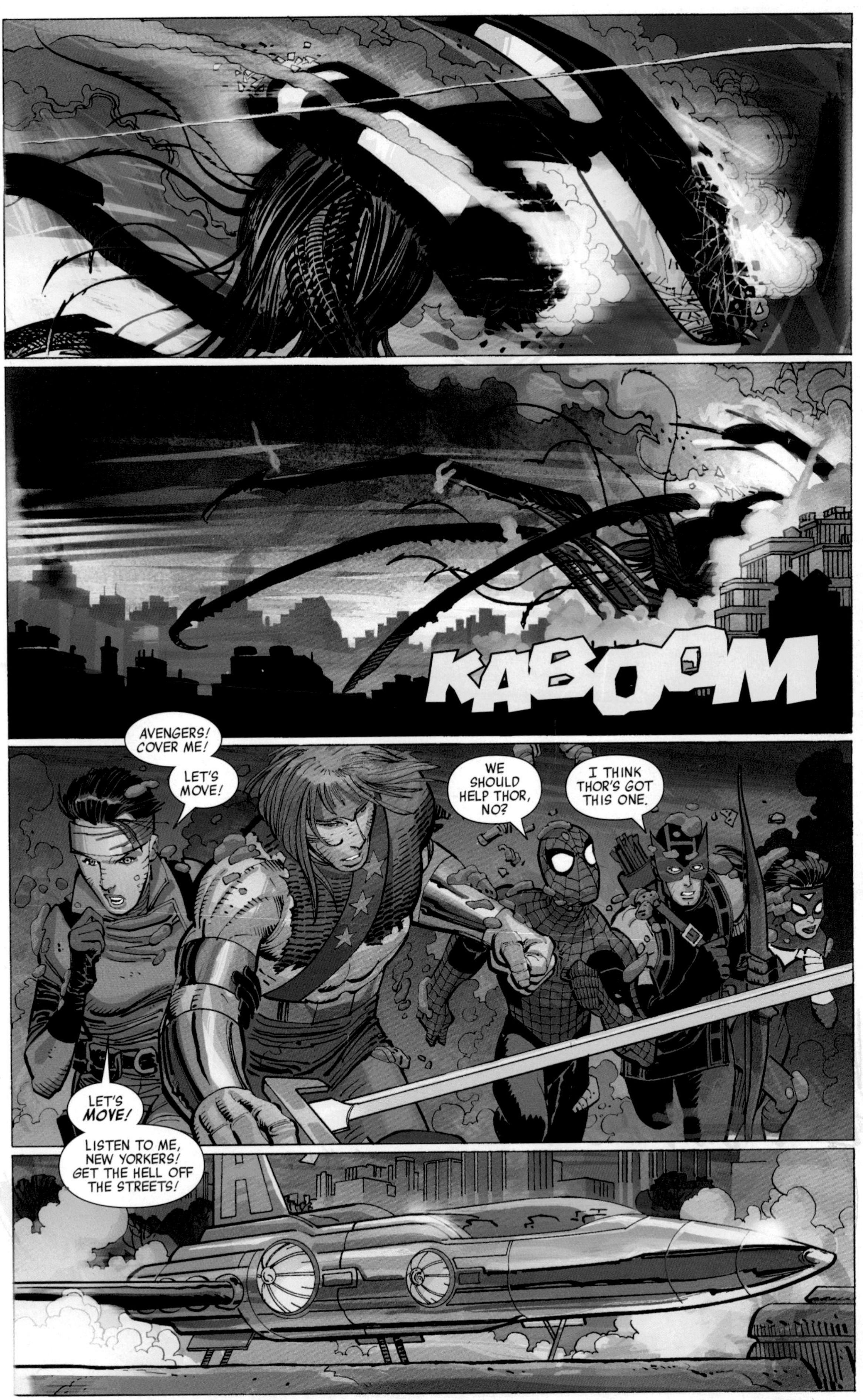
KABOOM
AVENGERS! COVER ME!
LET'S MOVE!
WE SHOULD HELP THOR, NO?
I THINK THOR'S GOT THIS ONE.
LET'S MOVE!
LISTEN TO ME, NEW YORKERS! GET THE HELL OFF THE STREETS!

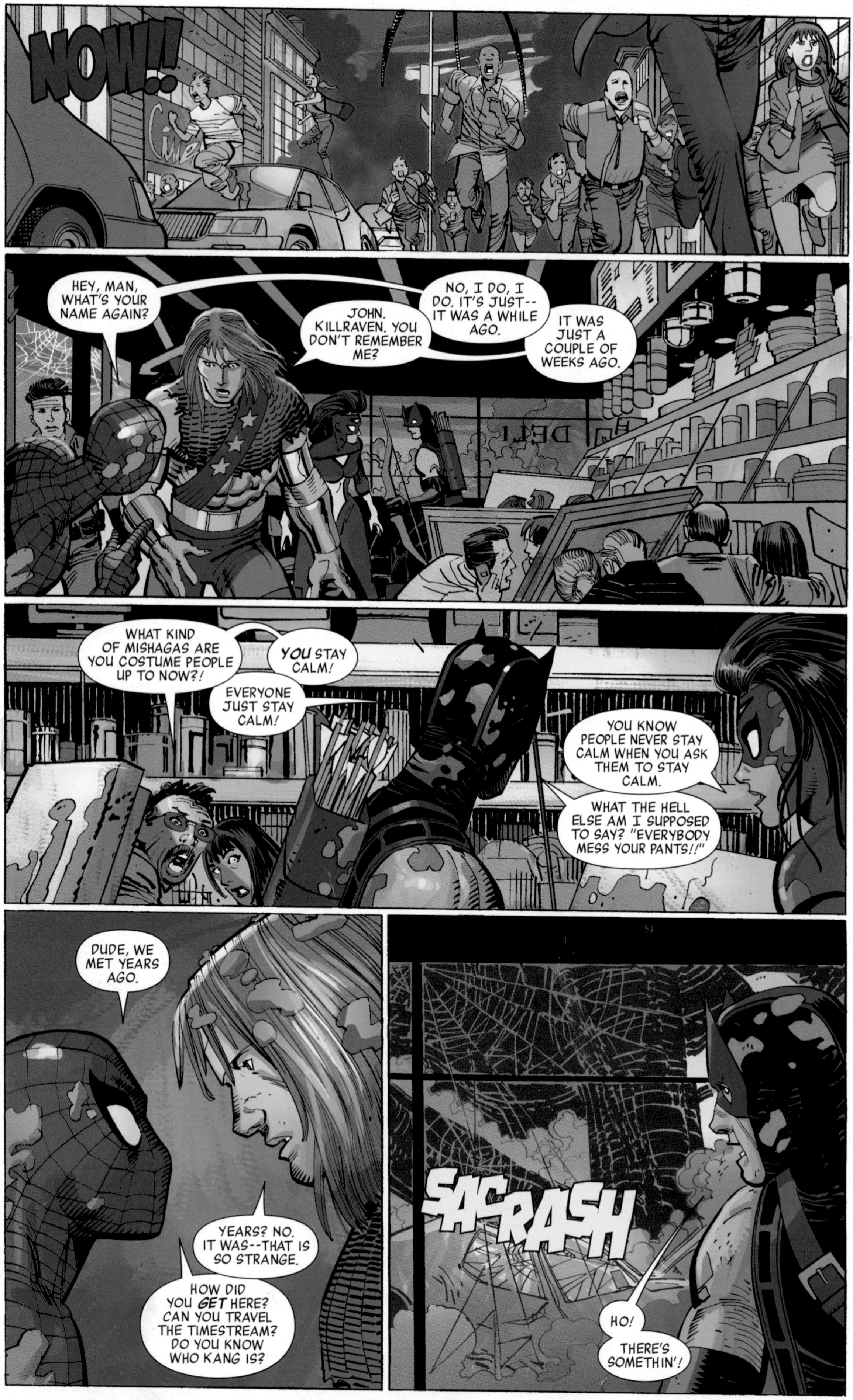
NOW!!
HEY, MAN, WHAT'S YOUR NAME AGAIN?
JOHN. KILLRAVEN. YOU DON'T REMEMBER ME?
NO, I DO, I DO. IT'S JUST-- IT WAS A WHILE AGO.
IT WAS JUST A COUPLE OF WEEKS AGO.
DELI
WHAT KIND OF MISHAGAS ARE YOU COSTUME PEOPLE UP TO NOW?!
YOU STAY CALM!
EVERYONE JUST STAY CALM!
YOU KNOW PEOPLE NEVER STAY CALM WHEN YOU ASK THEM TO STAY CALM.
WHAT THE HELL ELSE AM I SUPPOSED TO SAY? "EVERYBODY MESS YOUR PANTS!!"
DUDE, WE MET YEARS AGO.
YEARS? NO. IT WAS--THAT IS SO STRANGE.
HOW DID YOU GET HERE? CAN YOU TRAVEL THE TIMESTREAM? DO YOU KNOW WHO KANG IS?
SKRASH
HO!
THERE'S SOMETHIN'!

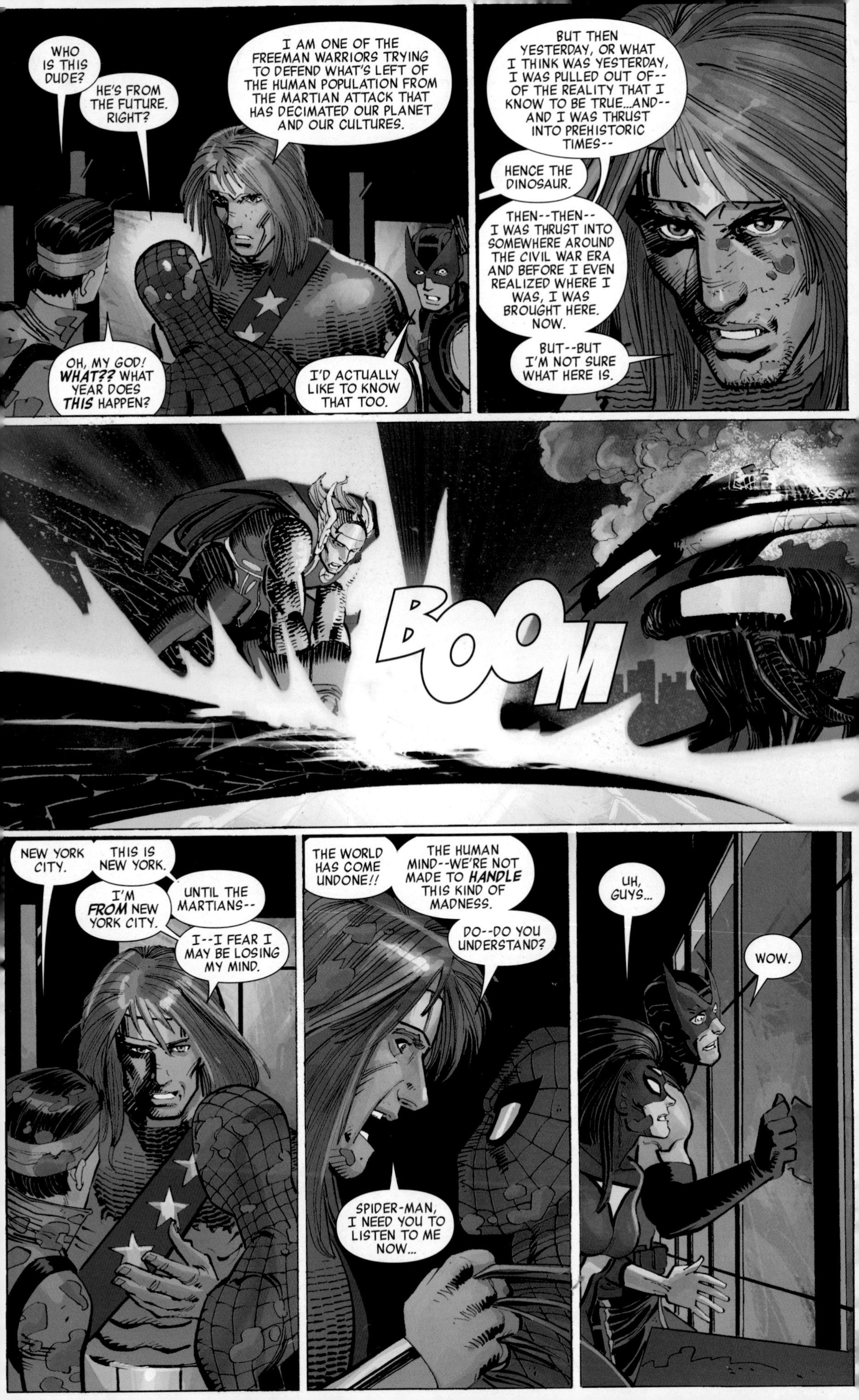
WHO IS THIS DUDE?
HE'S FROM THE FUTURE. RIGHT?
I AM ONE OF THE FREEMAN WARRIORS TRYING TO DEFEND WHAT'S LEFT OF THE HUMAN POPULATION FROM THE MARTIAN ATTACK THAT HAS DECIMATED OUR PLANET AND OUR CULTURES.
OH, MY GOD! **WHAT??** WHAT YEAR DOES **THIS** HAPPEN?
I'D ACTUALLY LIKE TO KNOW THAT TOO.
BUT THEN YESTERDAY, OR WHAT I THINK WAS YESTERDAY, I WAS PULLED OUT OF-- OF THE REALITY THAT I KNOW TO BE TRUE...AND-- AND I WAS THRUST INTO PREHISTORIC TIMES--
HENCE THE DINOSAUR.
THEN--THEN-- I WAS THRUST INTO SOMEWHERE AROUND THE CIVIL WAR ERA AND BEFORE I EVEN REALIZED WHERE I WAS, I WAS BROUGHT HERE. NOW.
BUT--BUT I'M NOT SURE WHAT HERE IS.
BOOM
NEW YORK CITY.
THIS IS NEW YORK.
I'M **FROM** NEW YORK CITY.
UNTIL THE MARTIANS--
I--I FEAR I MAY BE LOSING MY MIND.
THE WORLD HAS COME UNDONE!!
THE HUMAN MIND--WE'RE NOT MADE TO **HANDLE** THIS KIND OF MADNESS.
DO--DO YOU UNDERSTAND?
SPIDER-MAN, I NEED YOU TO LISTEN TO ME NOW...
UH, GUYS...
WOW.

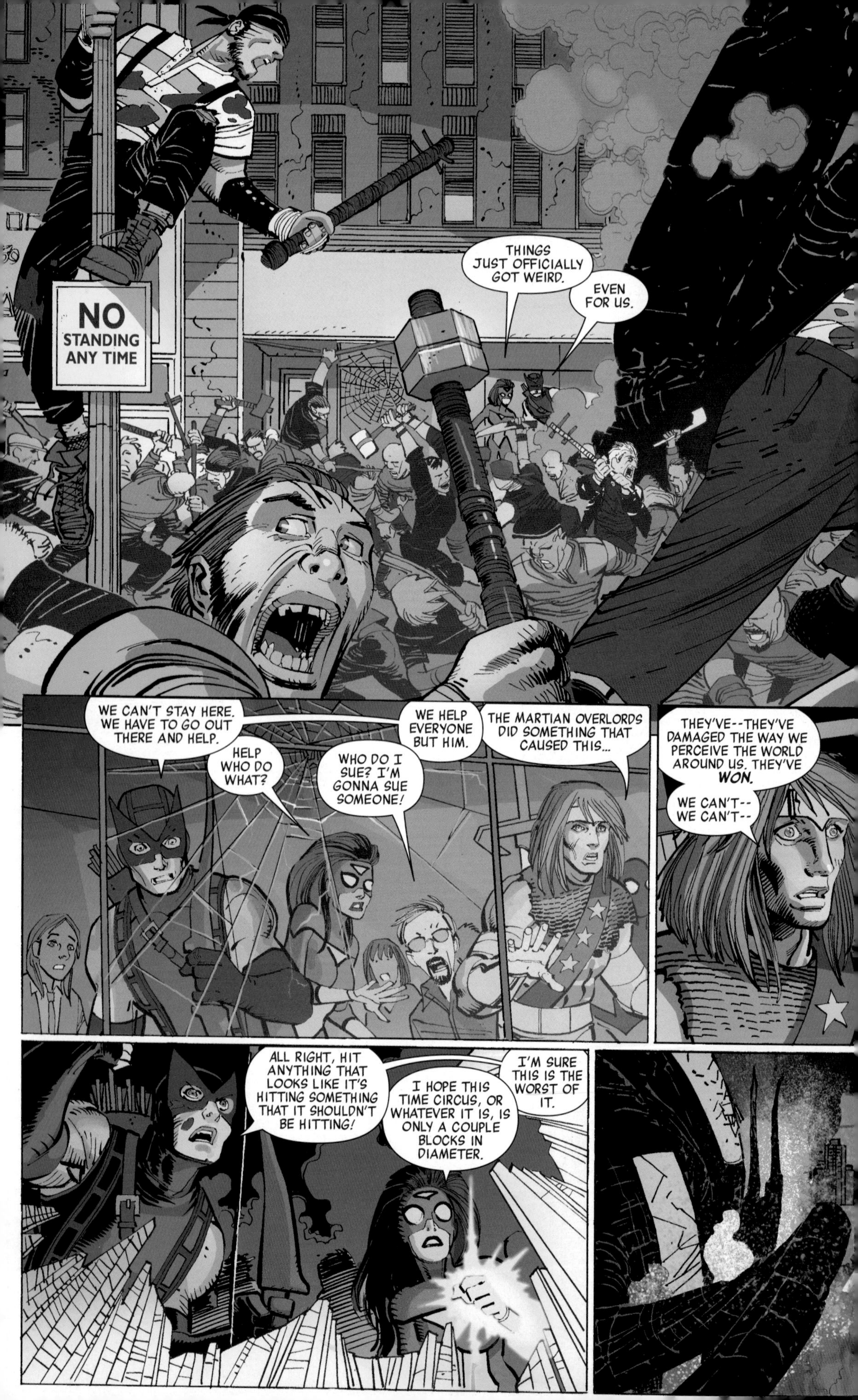
NO STANDING ANY TIME
THINGS JUST OFFICIALLY GOT WEIRD.
EVEN FOR US.
WE CAN'T STAY HERE. WE HAVE TO GO OUT THERE AND HELP.
HELP WHO DO WHAT?
WE HELP EVERYONE BUT HIM.
WHO DO I SUE? I'M GONNA SUE SOMEONE!
THE MARTIAN OVERLORDS DID SOMETHING THAT CAUSED THIS...
THEY'VE--THEY'VE DAMAGED THE WAY WE PERCEIVE THE WORLD AROUND US. THEY'VE **WON.**
WE CAN'T-- WE CAN'T--
ALL RIGHT, HIT ANYTHING THAT LOOKS LIKE IT'S HITTING SOMETHING THAT IT SHOULDN'T BE HITTING!
I'M SURE THIS IS THE WORST OF IT.
I HOPE THIS TIME CIRCUS, OR WHATEVER IT IS, IS ONLY A COUPLE BLOCKS IN DIAMETER.

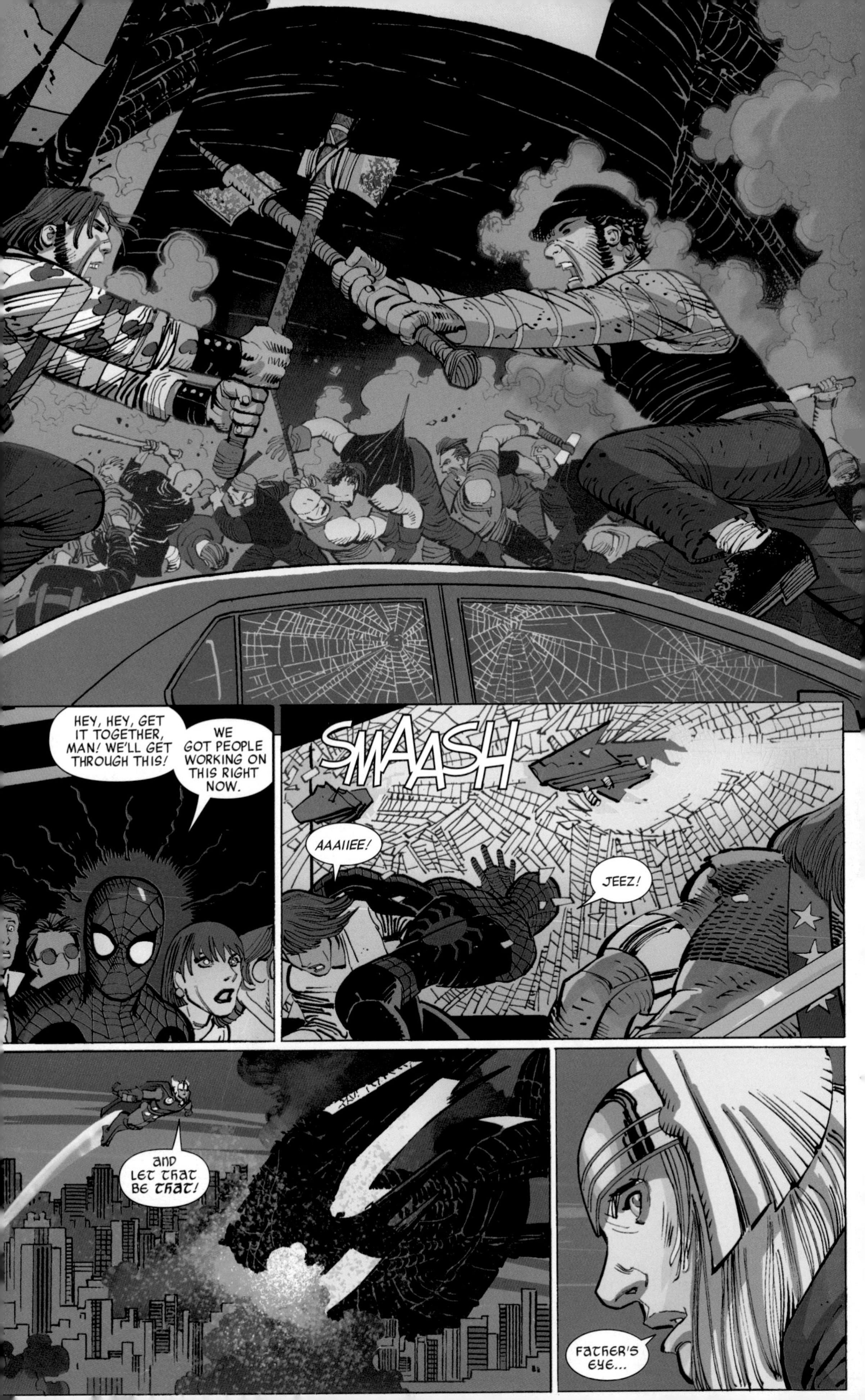
HEY, HEY, GET IT TOGETHER, MAN! WE'LL GET THROUGH THIS!
WE GOT PEOPLE WORKING ON THIS RIGHT NOW.
SMAASH
AAAIIEE!
JEEZ!
AND LET THAT BE THAT!
FATHER'S EYE...

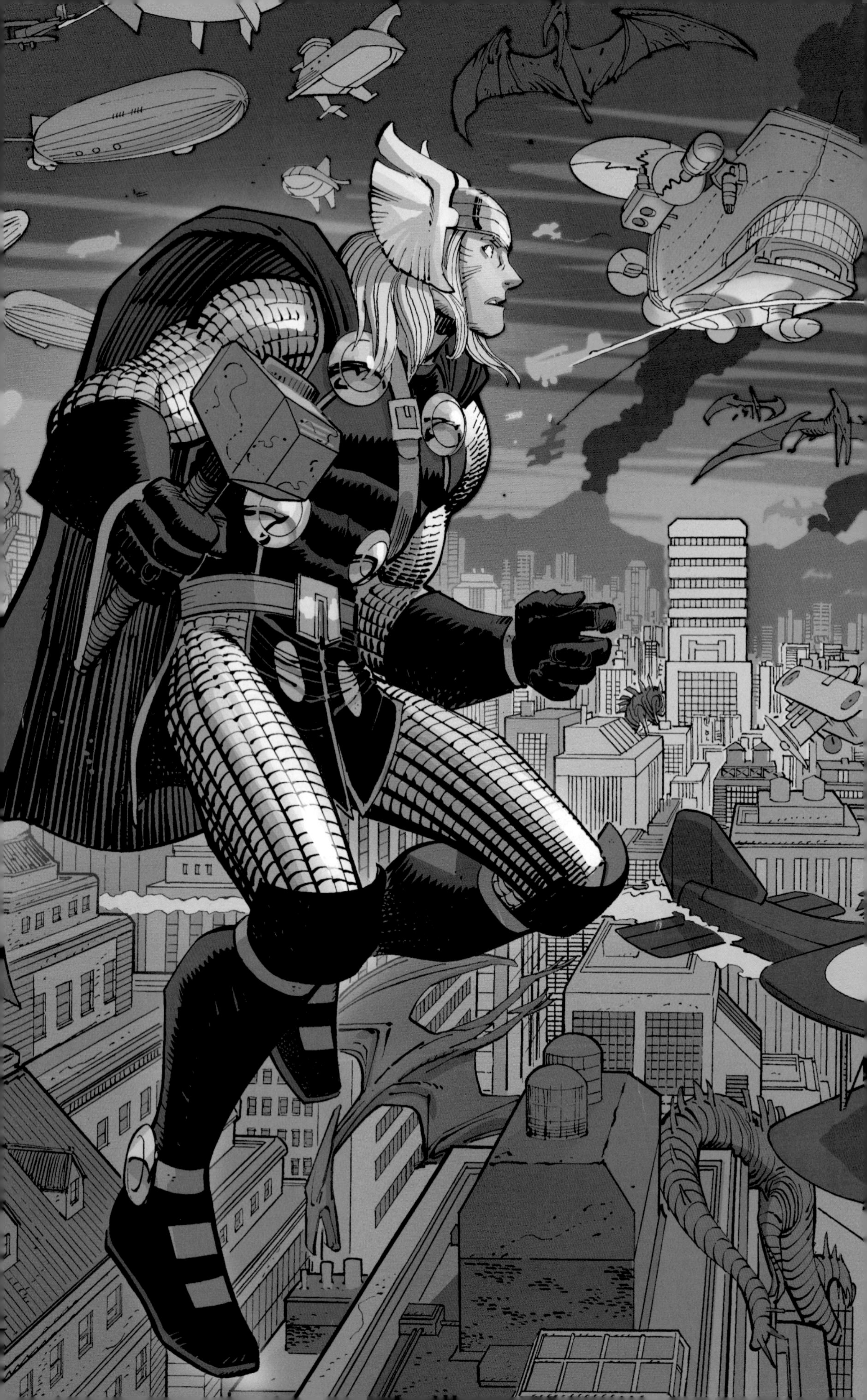

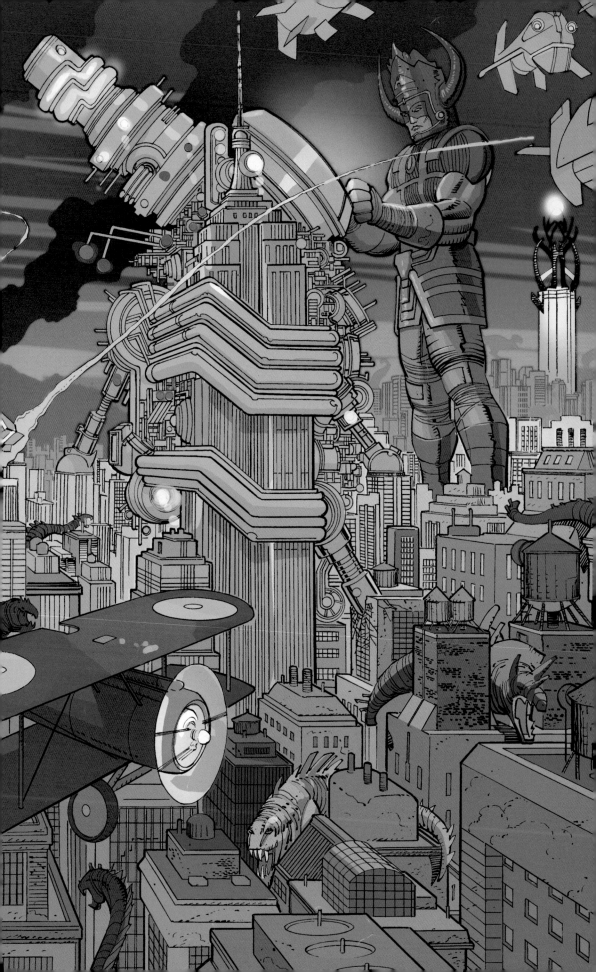

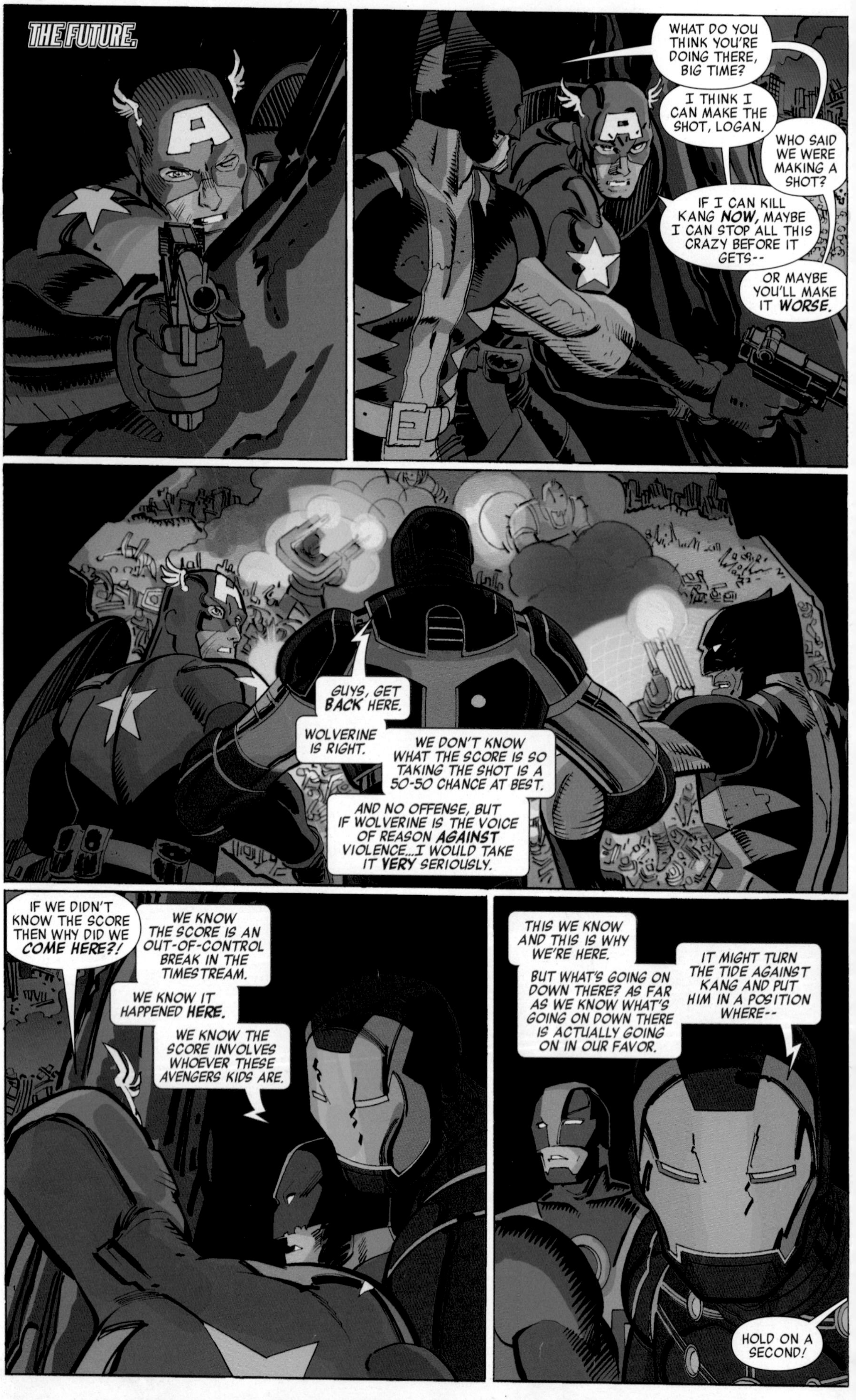
THE FUTURE.
WHAT DO YOU THINK YOU'RE DOING THERE, BIG TIME?
I THINK I CAN MAKE THE SHOT, LOGAN.
WHO SAID WE WERE MAKING A SHOT?
IF I CAN KILL KANG NOW, MAYBE I CAN STOP ALL THIS CRAZY BEFORE IT GETS--
OR MAYBE YOU'LL MAKE IT WORSE.
GUYS, GET BACK HERE.
WOLVERINE IS RIGHT.
WE DON'T KNOW WHAT THE SCORE IS SO TAKING THE SHOT IS A 50-50 CHANCE AT BEST.
AND NO OFFENSE, BUT IF WOLVERINE IS THE VOICE OF REASON AGAINST VIOLENCE...I WOULD TAKE IT VERY SERIOUSLY.
IF WE DIDN'T KNOW THE SCORE THEN WHY DID WE COME HERE?!
WE KNOW THE SCORE IS AN OUT-OF-CONTROL BREAK IN THE TIMESTREAM.
WE KNOW IT HAPPENED HERE.
WE KNOW THE SCORE INVOLVES WHOEVER THESE AVENGERS KIDS ARE.
THIS WE KNOW AND THIS IS WHY WE'RE HERE.
BUT WHAT'S GOING ON DOWN THERE? AS FAR AS WE KNOW WHAT'S GOING ON DOWN THERE IS ACTUALLY GOING ON IN OUR FAVOR.
IT MIGHT TURN THE TIDE AGAINST KANG AND PUT HIM IN A POSITION WHERE--
HOLD ON A SECOND!

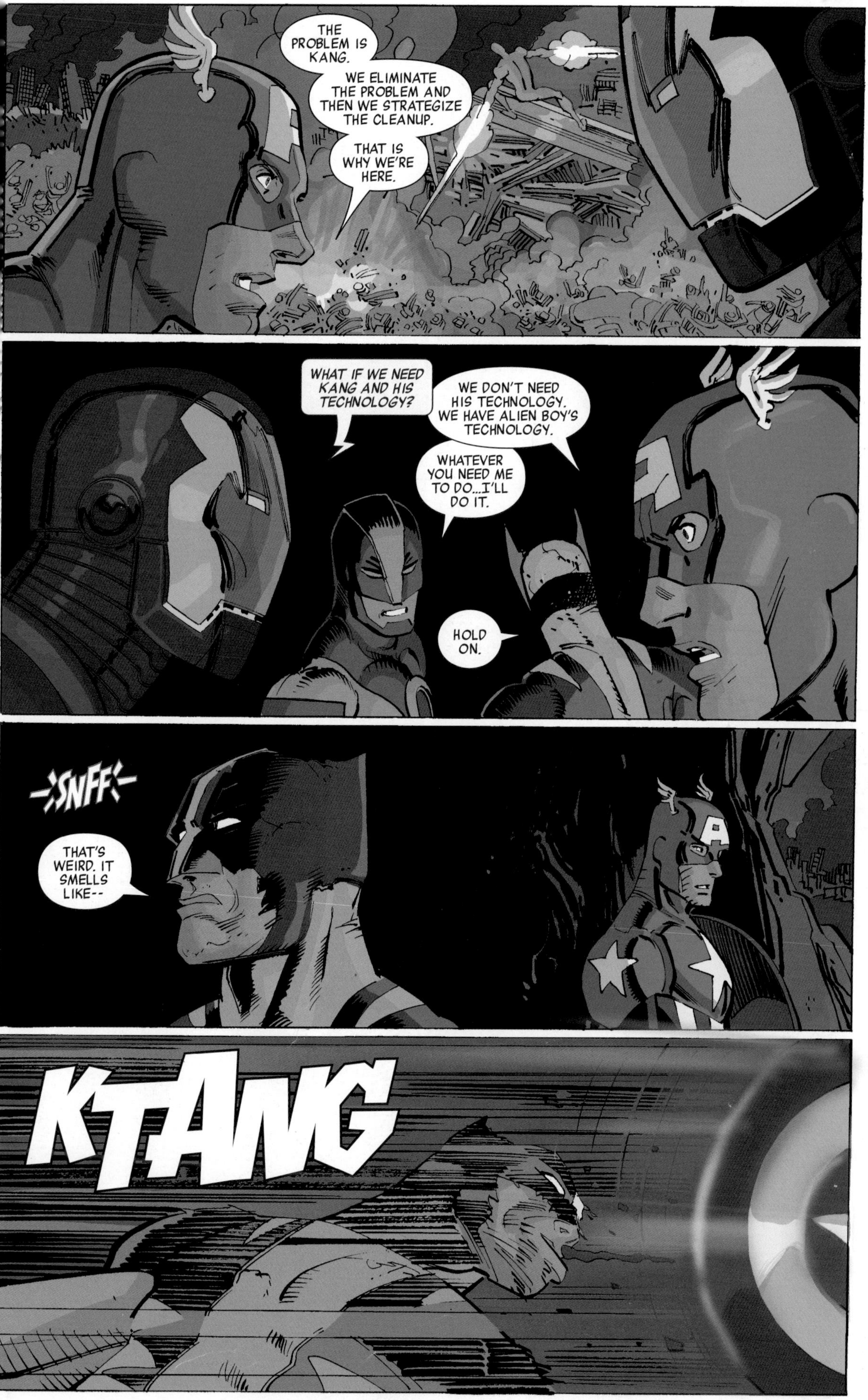
THE PROBLEM IS KANG.
WE ELIMINATE THE PROBLEM AND THEN WE STRATEGIZE THE CLEANUP.
THAT IS WHY WE'RE HERE.
WHAT IF WE NEED KANG AND HIS TECHNOLOGY?
WE DON'T NEED HIS TECHNOLOGY. WE HAVE ALIEN BOY'S TECHNOLOGY.
WHATEVER YOU NEED ME TO DO...I'LL DO IT.
HOLD ON.
SNFF
THAT'S WEIRD. IT SMELLS LIKE--
KTANG

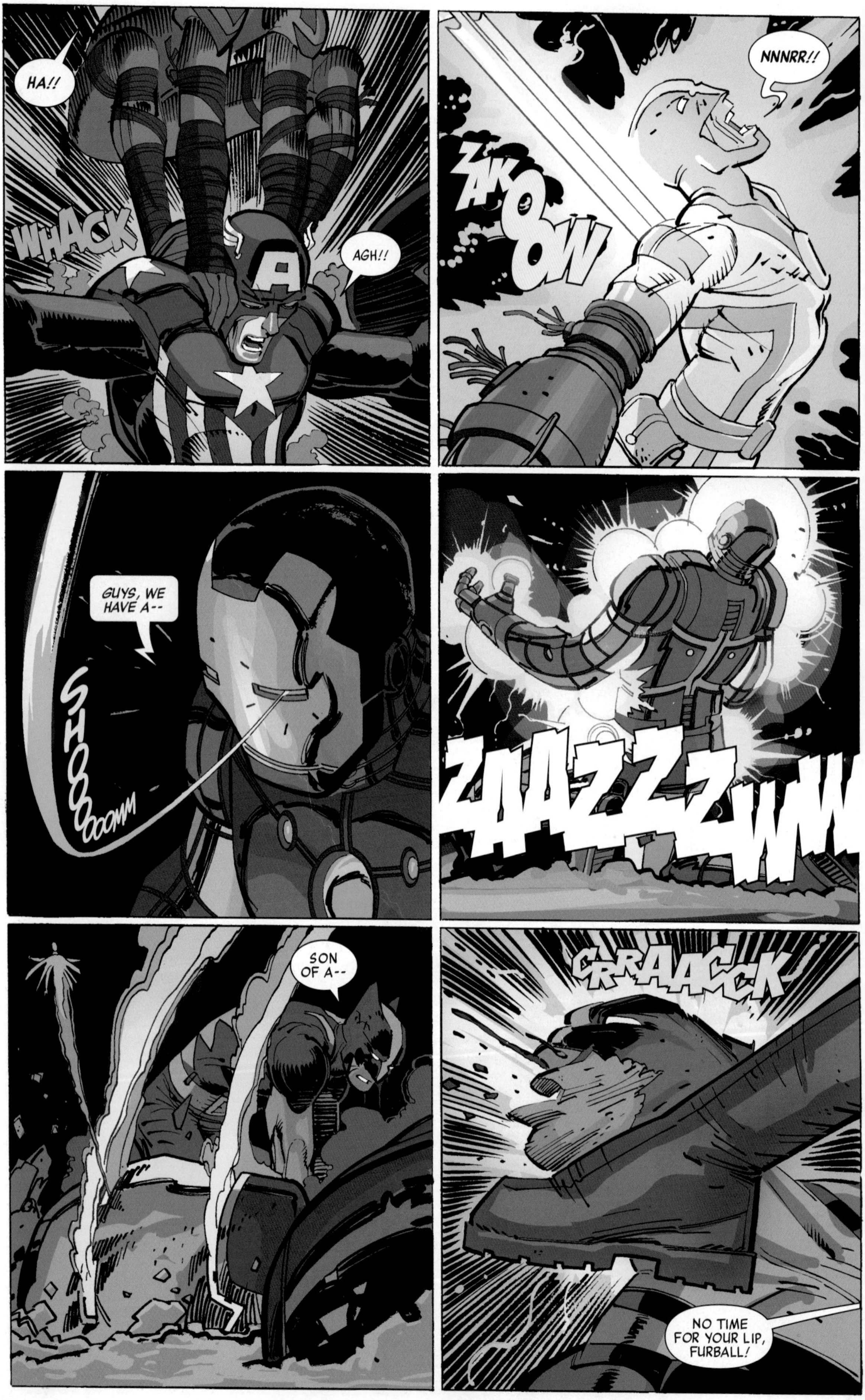
HA!!
WHACK
AGH!!
NNNRR!!
ZAKOOW
GUYS, WE HAVE A--
SHOOOOOOMM
ZAAZZZWW
SON OF A--
CRRAACCK
NO TIME FOR YOUR LIP, FURBALL!

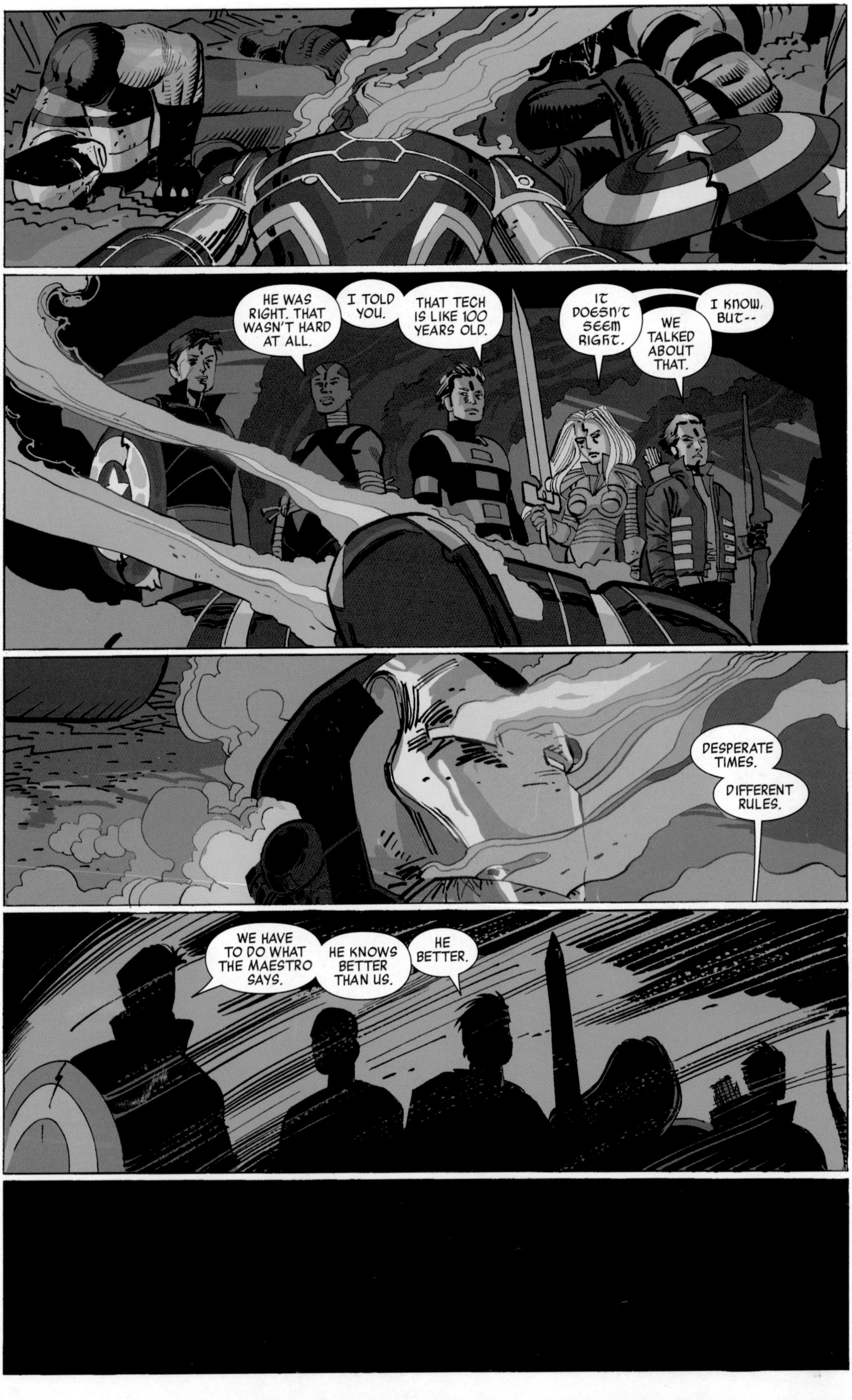
HE WAS RIGHT. THAT WASN'T HARD AT ALL.
I TOLD YOU.
THAT TECH IS LIKE 100 YEARS OLD.
IT DOESN'T SEEM RIGHT.
I KNOW, BUT--
WE TALKED ABOUT THAT.
DESPERATE TIMES.
DIFFERENT RULES.
WE HAVE TO DO WHAT THE MAESTRO SAYS.
HE KNOWS BETTER THAN US.
HE BETTER.

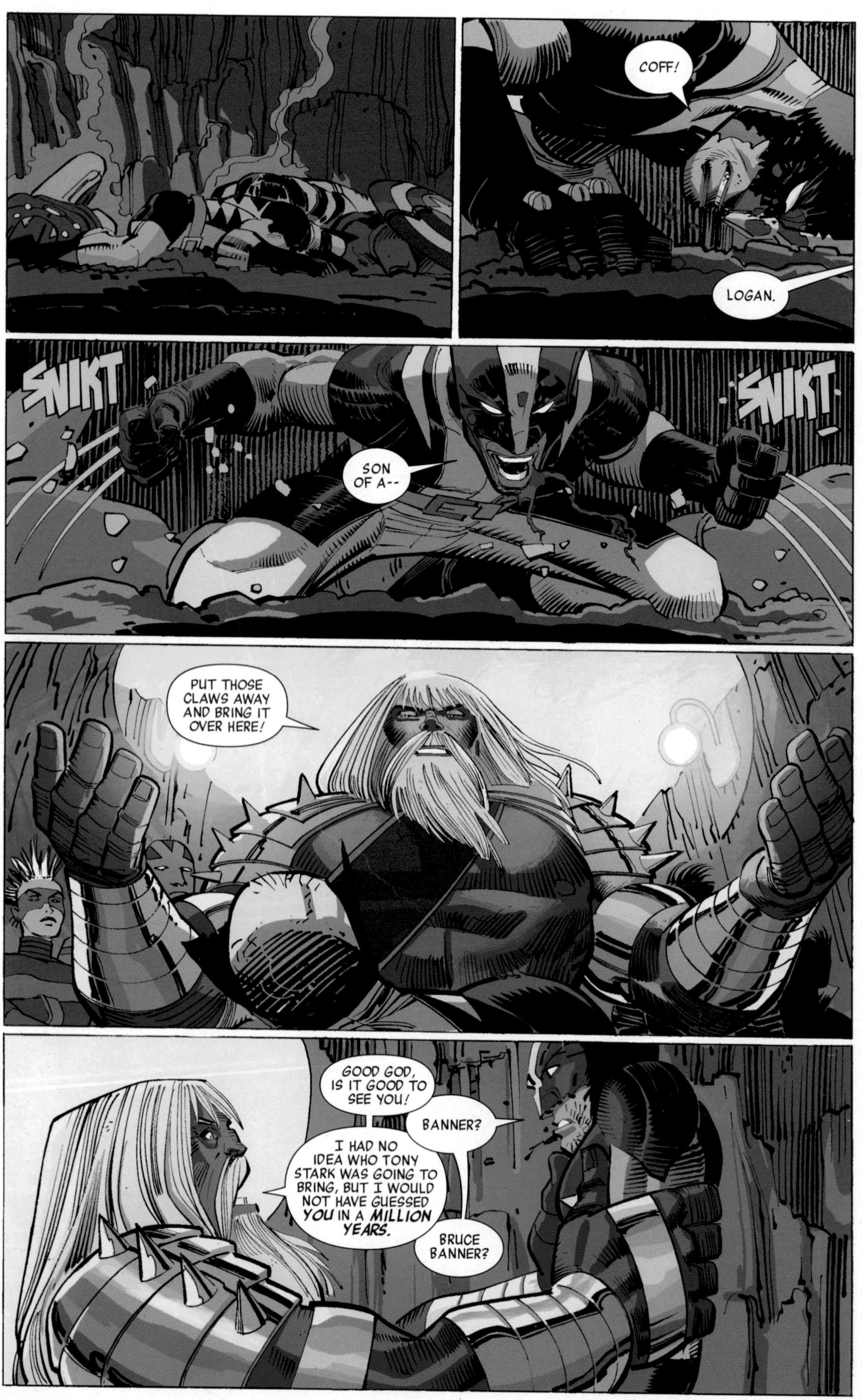
COFF!
LOGAN.
SNIKT
SNIKT
SON OF A--
PUT THOSE CLAWS AWAY AND BRING IT OVER HERE!
GOOD GOD, IS IT GOOD TO SEE YOU!
BANNER?
I HAD NO IDEA WHO TONY STARK WAS GOING TO BRING, BUT I WOULD NOT HAVE GUESSED YOU IN A MILLION YEARS.
BRUCE BANNER?

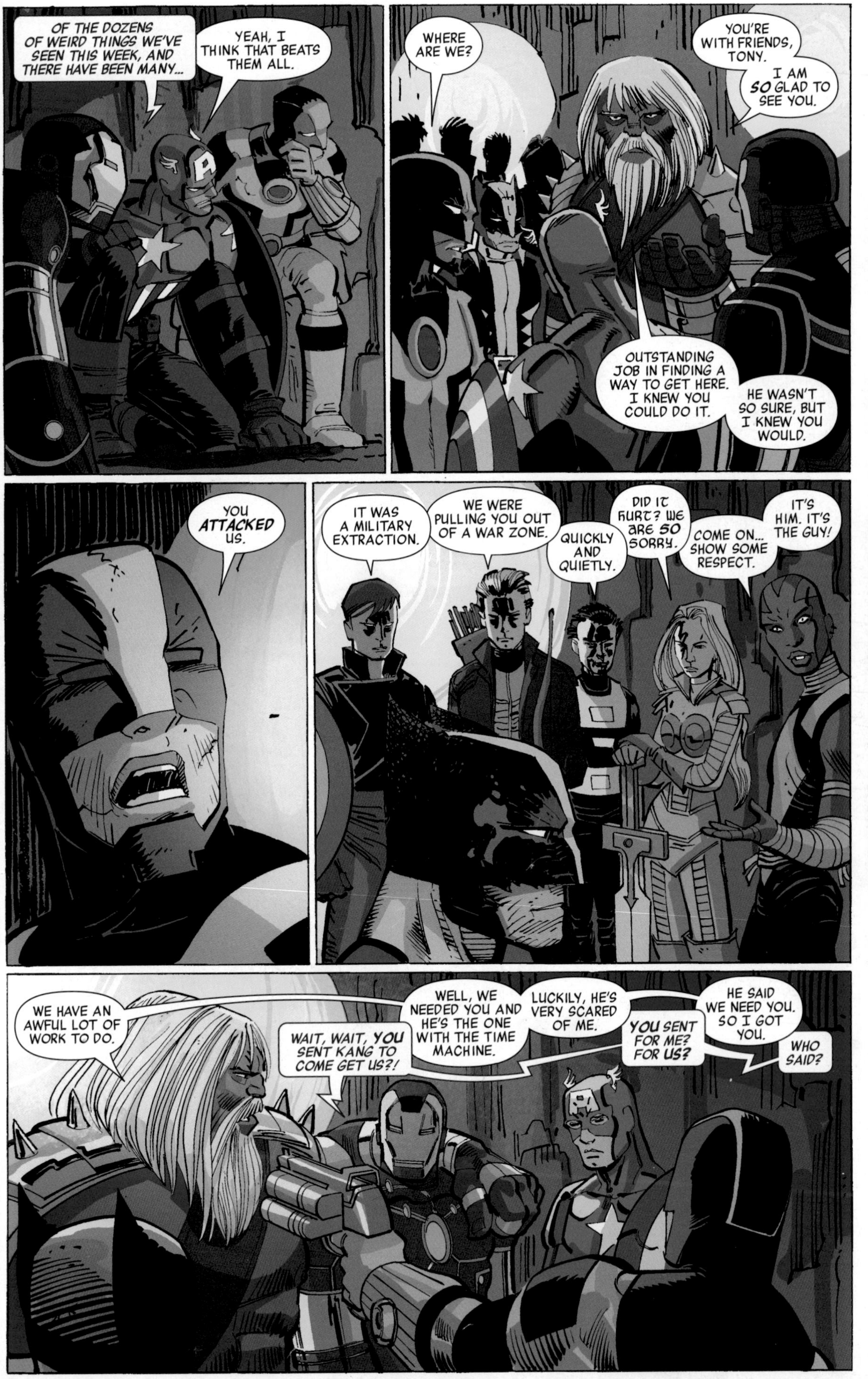

OF THE DOZENS OF WEIRD THINGS WE'VE SEEN THIS WEEK, AND THERE HAVE BEEN MANY...
YEAH, I THINK THAT BEATS THEM ALL.
WHERE ARE WE?
YOU'RE WITH FRIENDS, TONY.
I AM SO GLAD TO SEE YOU.
OUTSTANDING JOB IN FINDING A WAY TO GET HERE. I KNEW YOU COULD DO IT.
HE WASN'T SO SURE, BUT I KNEW YOU WOULD.
YOU ATTACKED US.
IT WAS A MILITARY EXTRACTION.
WE WERE PULLING YOU OUT OF A WAR ZONE.
QUICKLY AND QUIETLY.
DID IT HURT? WE ARE SO SORRY.
COME ON... SHOW SOME RESPECT.
IT'S HIM. IT'S THE GUY!
WE HAVE AN AWFUL LOT OF WORK TO DO.
WAIT, WAIT, YOU SENT KANG TO COME GET US?!
WELL, WE NEEDED YOU AND HE'S THE ONE WITH THE TIME MACHINE.
LUCKILY, HE'S VERY SCARED OF ME.
YOU SENT FOR ME? FOR US?
HE SAID WE NEED YOU. SO I GOT YOU.
WHO SAID?

HIM.

HELLO, TONY.

YEAH, THIS IS AS WEIRD AS I THOUGHT IT WAS GOING TO BE.

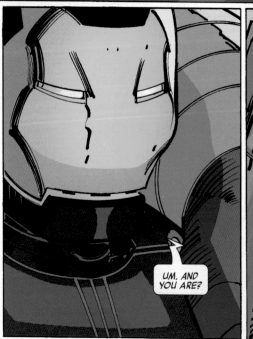

UM. AND YOU ARE?

IT'S ME, TONY.

IT'S YOU.

AND YOU KNOW BETTER THAN ANYONE ON THE PLANET THAT IF I HAD TO RESORT TO ALL OF THIS...I HAD NO OTHER CHOICE.

BANNER, HOLD HIM.

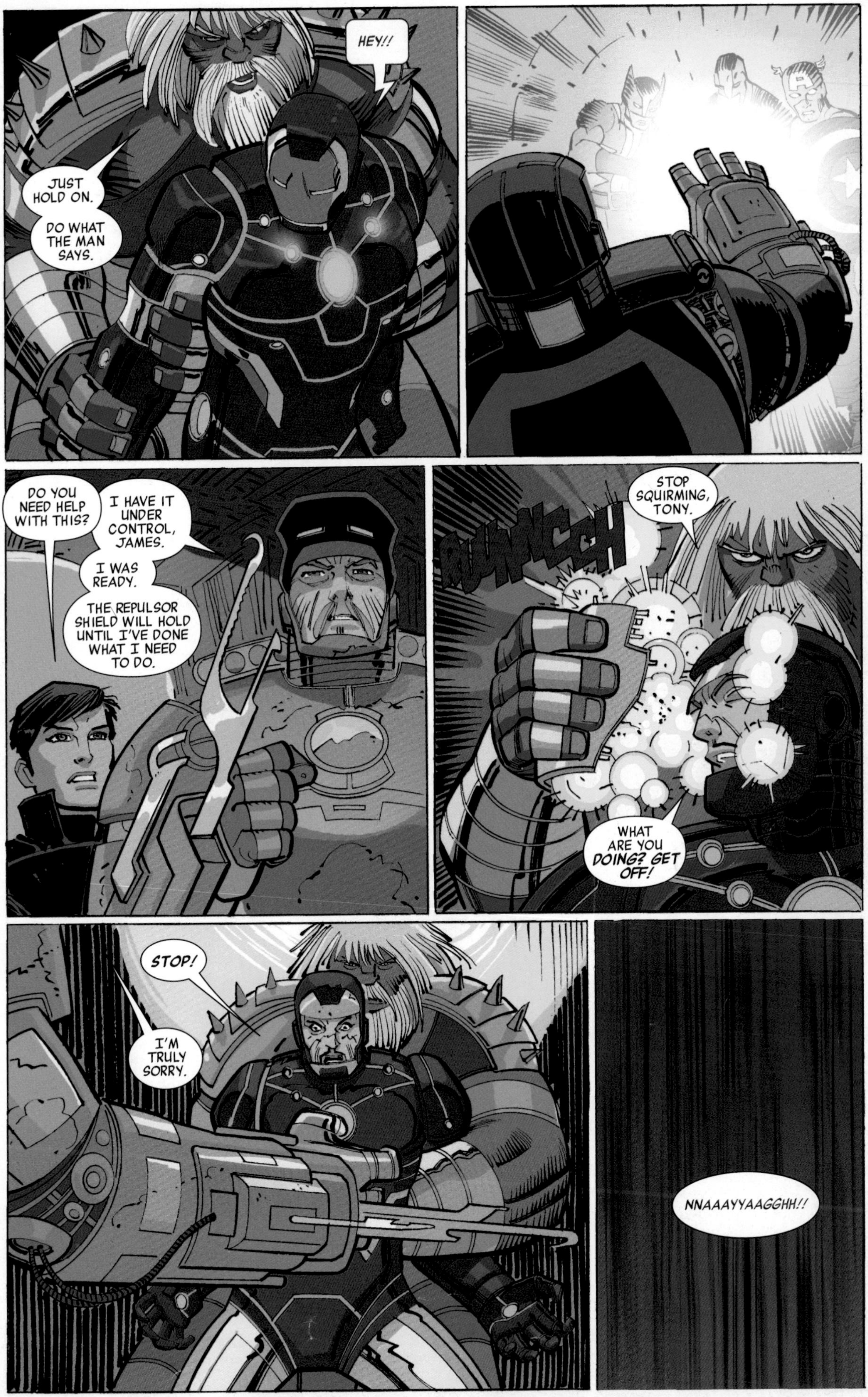
HEY!!
JUST HOLD ON.
DO WHAT THE MAN SAYS.
DO YOU NEED HELP WITH THIS?
I HAVE IT UNDER CONTROL, JAMES.
I WAS READY.
THE REPULSOR SHIELD WILL HOLD UNTIL I'VE DONE WHAT I NEED TO DO.
STOP SQUIRMING, TONY.
WHAT ARE YOU DOING? GET OFF!
STOP!
I'M TRULY SORRY.
NNAAAYYAAGGHH!!

**#4 WOMEN OF MARVEL FRAME VARIANT BY
JIM CHEUNG & JUSTIN PONSOR**

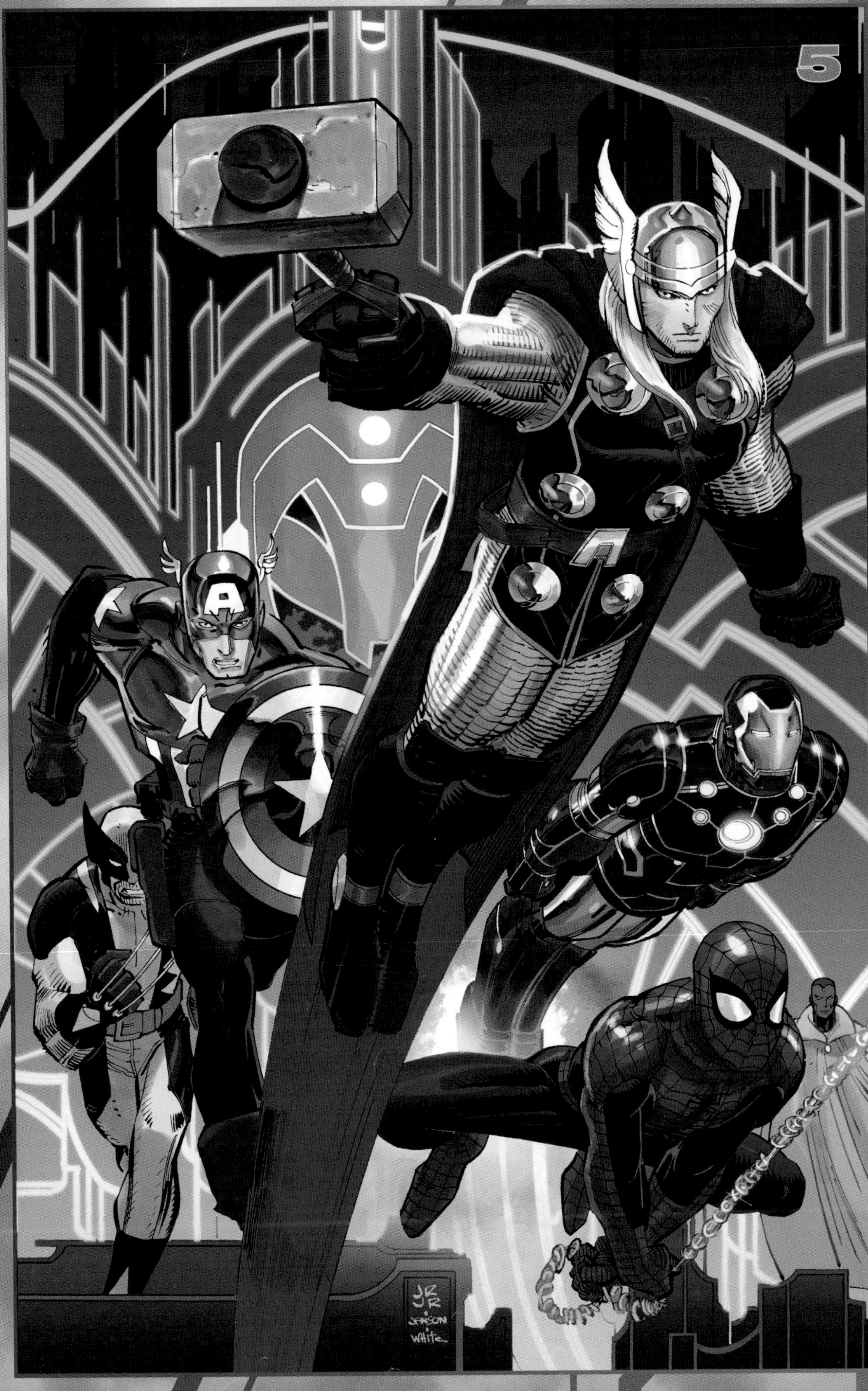
5
JR JR
JANSON
WHITE

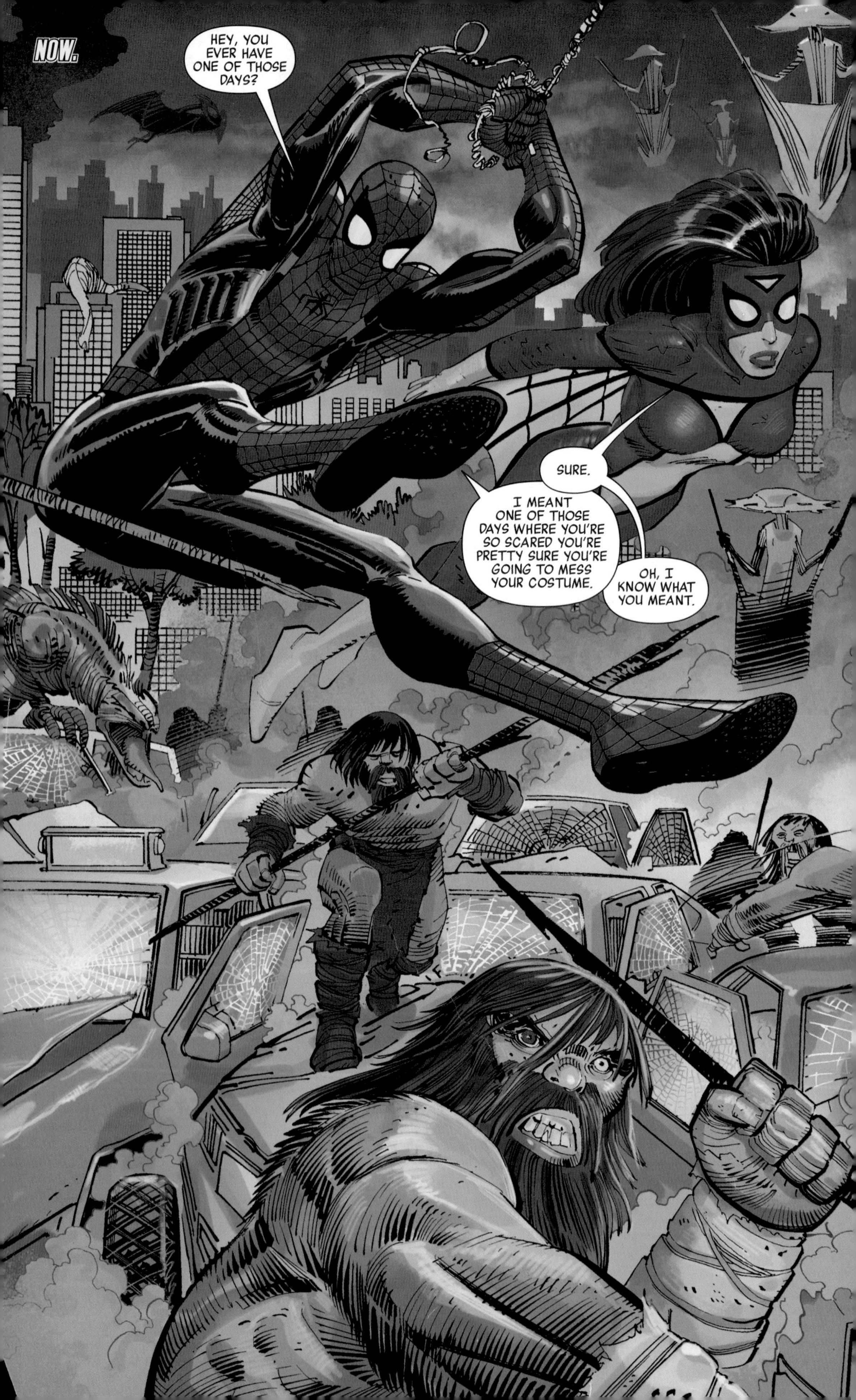
NOW.
HEY, YOU EVER HAVE ONE OF THOSE DAYS?
SURE.
I MEANT ONE OF THOSE DAYS WHERE YOU'RE SO SCARED YOU'RE PRETTY SURE YOU'RE GOING TO MESS YOUR COSTUME.
OH, I KNOW WHAT YOU MEANT.

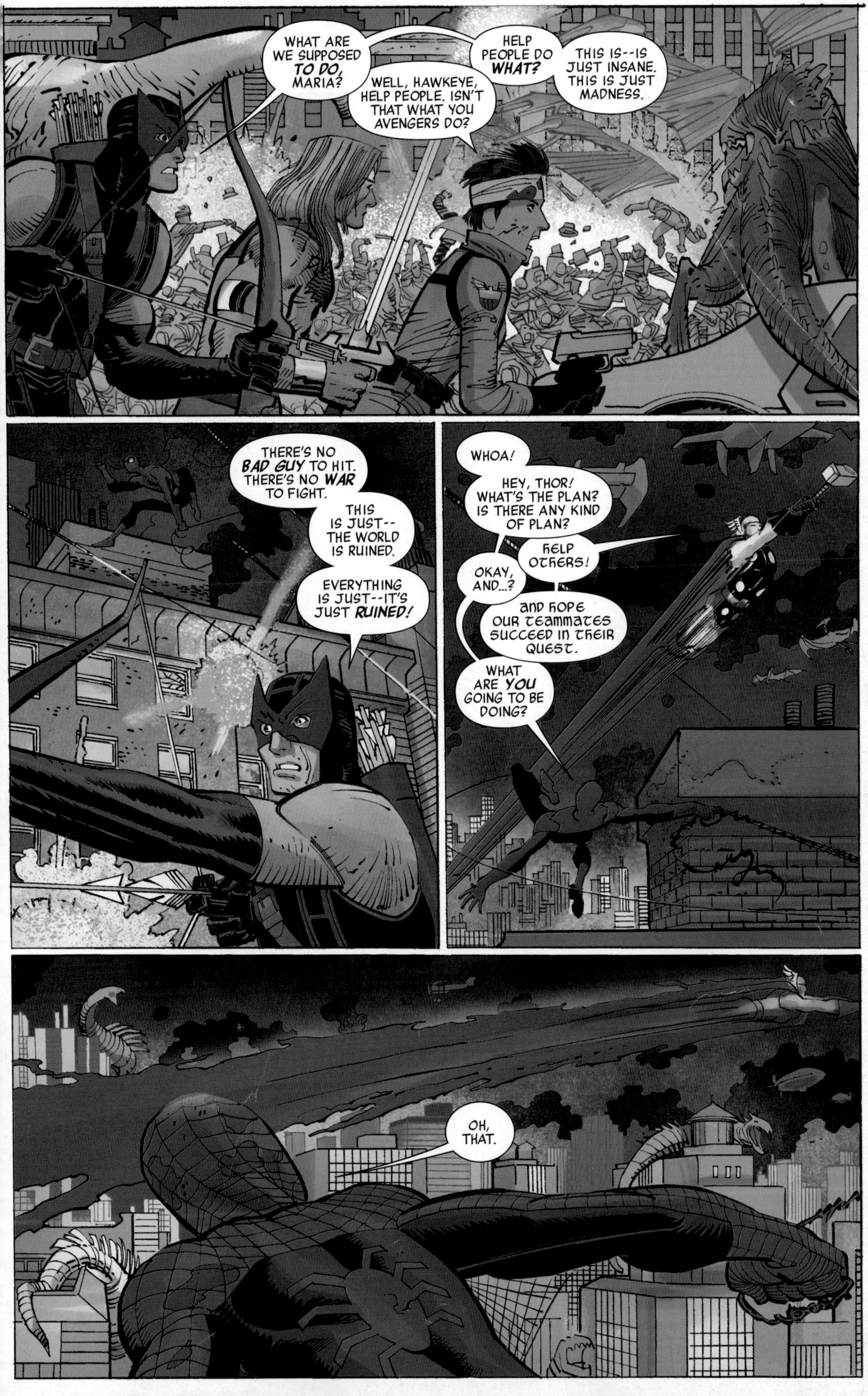
WHAT ARE WE SUPPOSED TO DO, MARIA?
WELL, HAWKEYE, HELP PEOPLE. ISN'T THAT WHAT YOU AVENGERS DO?
HELP PEOPLE DO WHAT?
THIS IS--IS JUST INSANE. THIS IS JUST MADNESS.
THERE'S NO BAD GUY TO HIT. THERE'S NO WAR TO FIGHT.
THIS IS JUST-- THE WORLD IS RUINED.
EVERYTHING IS JUST--IT'S JUST RUINED!
WHOA!
HEY, THOR! WHAT'S THE PLAN? IS THERE ANY KIND OF PLAN?
HELP OTHERS!
OKAY, AND...?
AND HOPE OUR TEAMMATES SUCCEED IN THEIR QUEST.
WHAT ARE YOU GOING TO BE DOING?
OH, THAT.

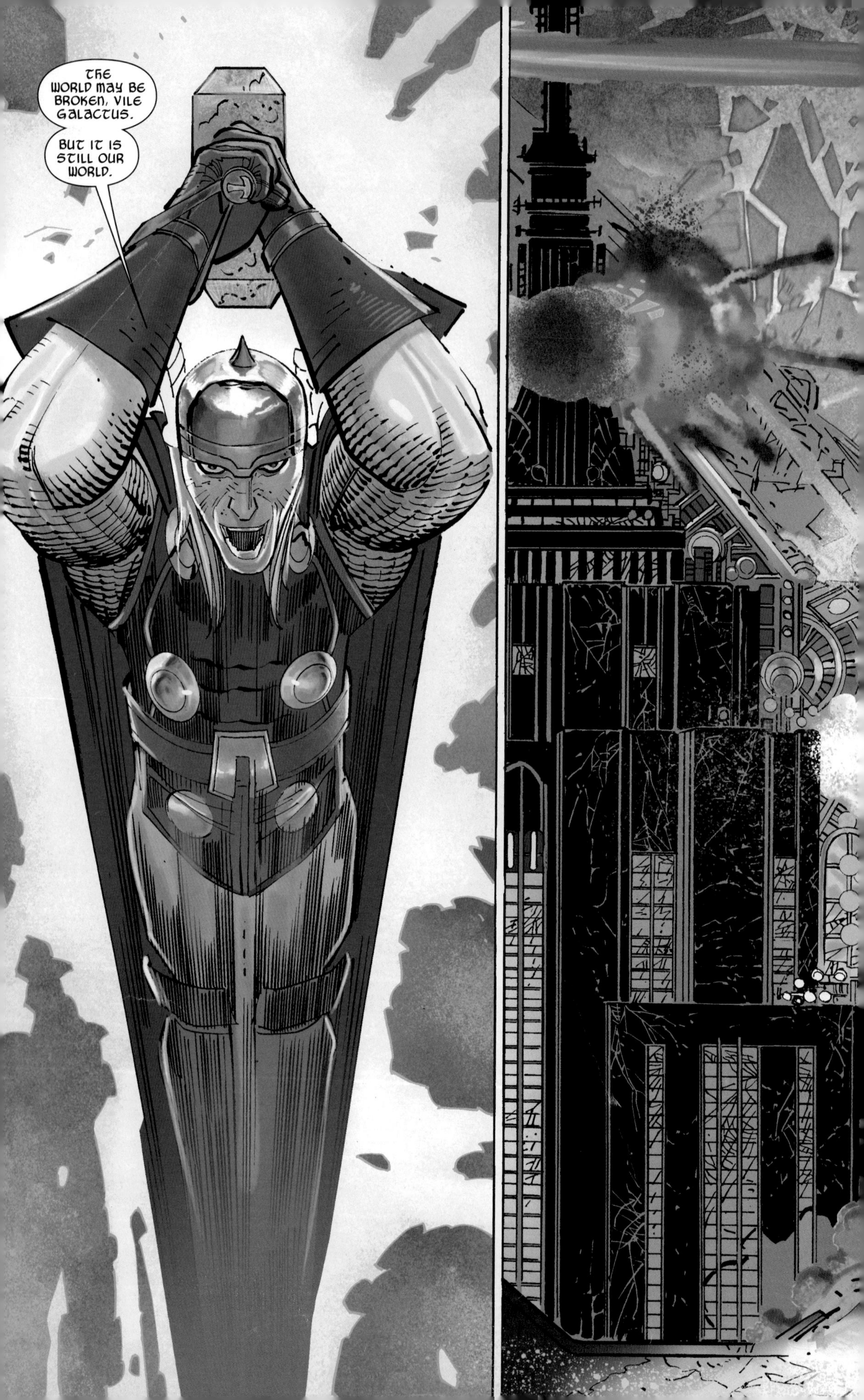
THE WORLD MAY BE BROKEN, VILE GALACTUS.
BUT IT IS STILL OUR WORLD.

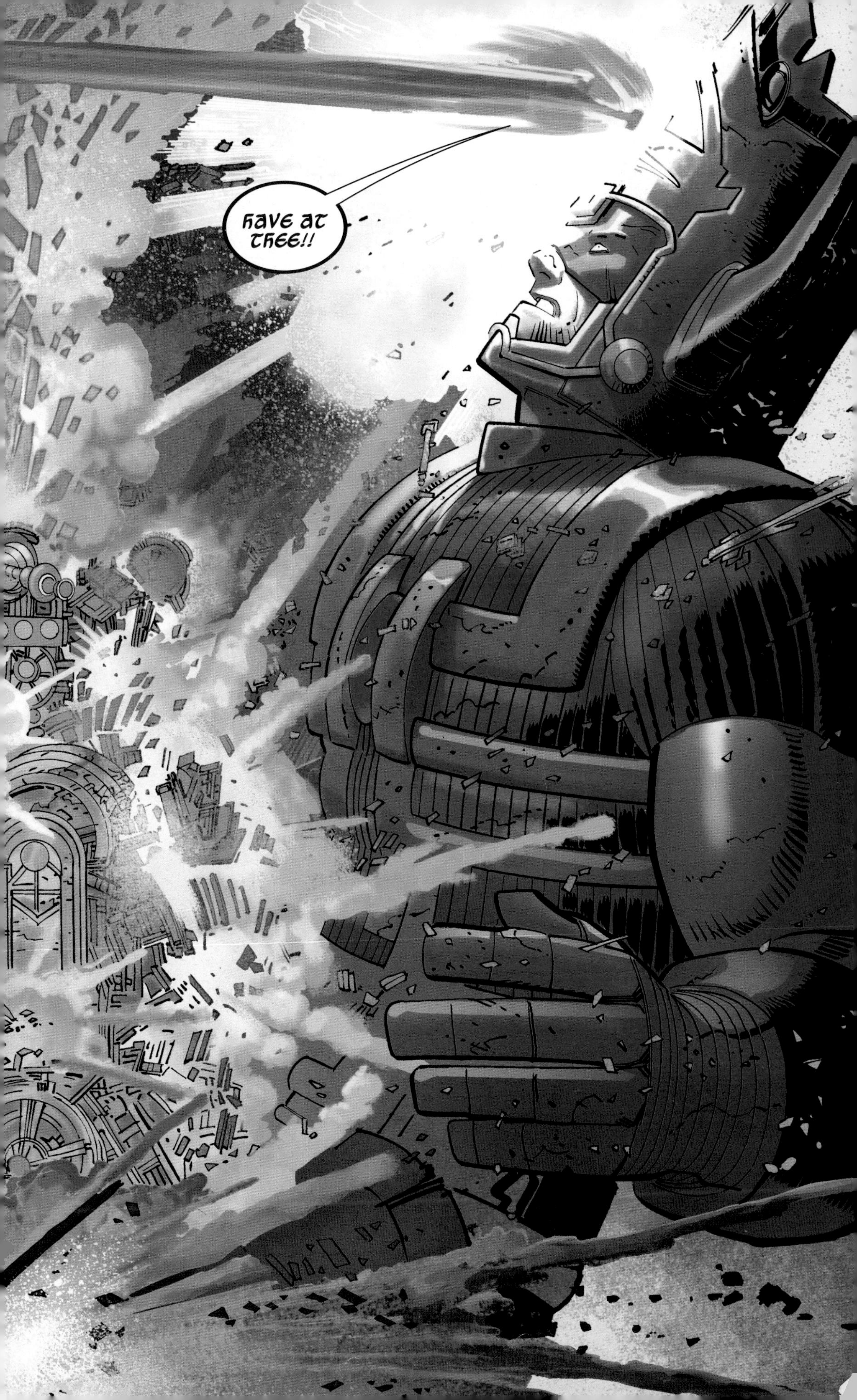
HAVE AT
THEE!!

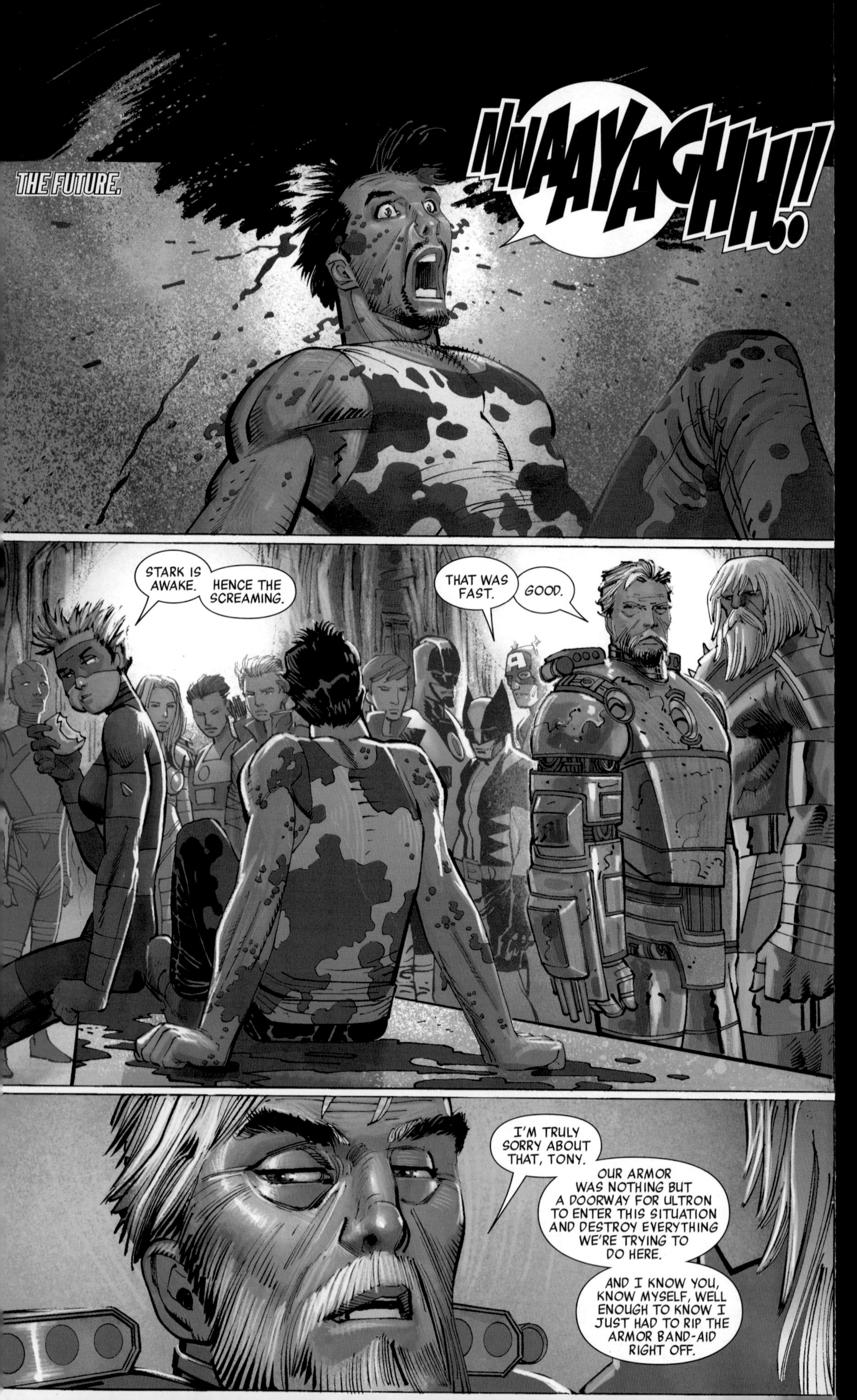
THE FUTURE.
NNAAYAGHH!!
STARK IS AWAKE.
HENCE THE SCREAMING.
THAT WAS FAST.
GOOD.
I'M TRULY SORRY ABOUT THAT, TONY.
OUR ARMOR WAS NOTHING BUT A DOORWAY FOR ULTRON TO ENTER THIS SITUATION AND DESTROY EVERYTHING WE'RE TRYING TO DO HERE.
AND I KNOW YOU, KNOW MYSELF, WELL ENOUGH TO KNOW I JUST HAD TO RIP THE ARMOR BAND-AID RIGHT OFF.

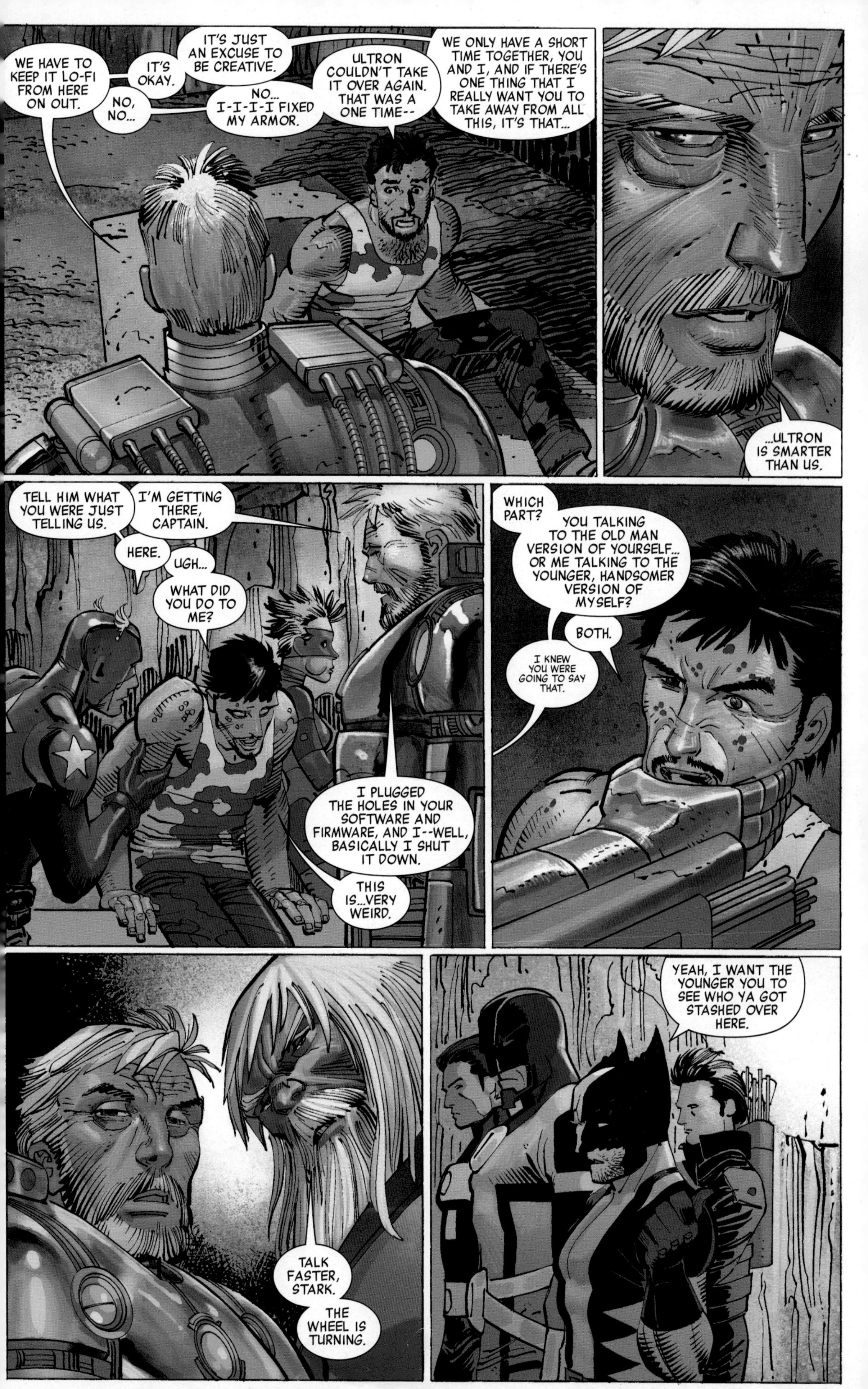
WE HAVE TO KEEP IT LO-FI FROM HERE ON OUT.
IT'S OKAY.
IT'S JUST AN EXCUSE TO BE CREATIVE.
NO, NO...
NO... I-I-I-I FIXED MY ARMOR.
ULTRON COULDN'T TAKE IT OVER AGAIN. THAT WAS A ONE TIME--
WE ONLY HAVE A SHORT TIME TOGETHER, YOU AND I, AND IF THERE'S ONE THING THAT I REALLY WANT YOU TO TAKE AWAY FROM ALL THIS, IT'S THAT...
...ULTRON IS SMARTER THAN US.
TELL HIM WHAT YOU WERE JUST TELLING US.
I'M GETTING THERE, CAPTAIN.
HERE.
UGH...
WHAT DID YOU DO TO ME?
I PLUGGED THE HOLES IN YOUR SOFTWARE AND FIRMWARE, AND I--WELL, BASICALLY I SHUT IT DOWN.
THIS IS...VERY WEIRD.
WHICH PART?
YOU TALKING TO THE OLD MAN VERSION OF YOURSELF... OR ME TALKING TO THE YOUNGER, HANDSOMER VERSION OF MYSELF?
BOTH.
I KNEW YOU WERE GOING TO SAY THAT.
TALK FASTER, STARK.
THE WHEEL IS TURNING.
YEAH, I WANT THE YOUNGER YOU TO SEE WHO YA GOT STASHED OVER HERE.

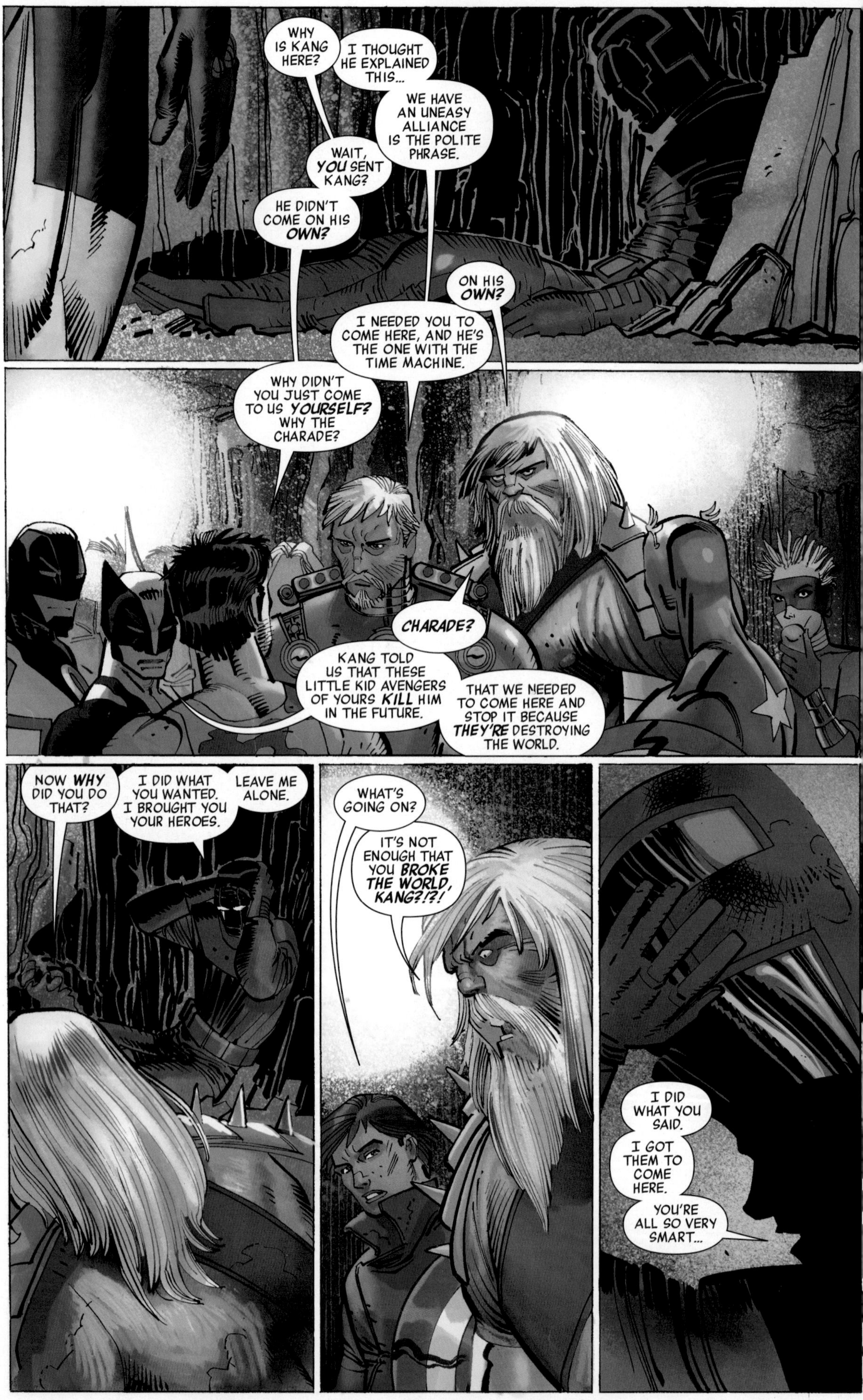
WHY IS KANG HERE?
I THOUGHT HE EXPLAINED THIS...
WE HAVE AN UNEASY ALLIANCE IS THE POLITE PHRASE.
WAIT, **YOU** SENT KANG?
HE DIDN'T COME ON HIS **OWN?**
ON HIS **OWN?**
I NEEDED YOU TO COME HERE, AND HE'S THE ONE WITH THE TIME MACHINE.
WHY DIDN'T YOU JUST COME TO US **YOURSELF?** WHY THE CHARADE?
CHARADE?
KANG TOLD US THAT THESE LITTLE KID AVENGERS OF YOURS **KILL** HIM IN THE FUTURE.
THAT WE NEEDED TO COME HERE AND STOP IT BECAUSE **THEY'RE** DESTROYING THE WORLD.
NOW **WHY** DID YOU DO THAT?
I DID WHAT YOU WANTED. I BROUGHT YOU YOUR HEROES.
LEAVE ME ALONE.
WHAT'S GOING ON?
IT'S NOT ENOUGH THAT YOU **BROKE THE WORLD, KANG?!?!**
I DID WHAT YOU SAID.
I GOT THEM TO COME HERE.
YOU'RE ALL SO VERY SMART...

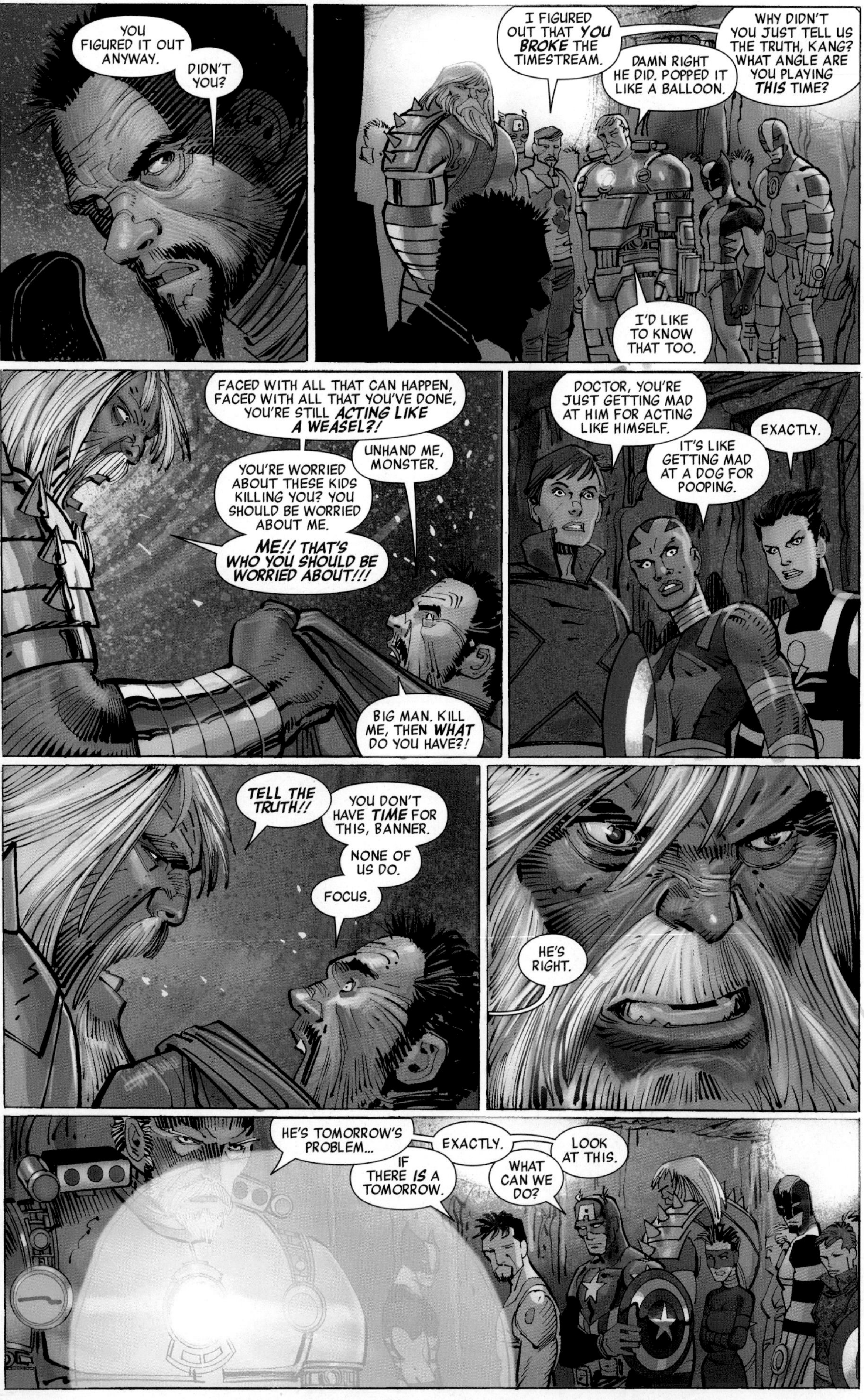
YOU FIGURED IT OUT ANYWAY.
DIDN'T YOU?
I FIGURED OUT THAT YOU BROKE THE TIMESTREAM.
DAMN RIGHT HE DID. POPPED IT LIKE A BALLOON.
WHY DIDN'T YOU JUST TELL US THE TRUTH, KANG? WHAT ANGLE ARE YOU PLAYING THIS TIME?
I'D LIKE TO KNOW THAT TOO.
FACED WITH ALL THAT CAN HAPPEN, FACED WITH ALL THAT YOU'VE DONE, YOU'RE STILL ACTING LIKE A WEASEL?!
UNHAND ME, MONSTER.
YOU'RE WORRIED ABOUT THESE KIDS KILLING YOU? YOU SHOULD BE WORRIED ABOUT ME.
ME!! THAT'S WHO YOU SHOULD BE WORRIED ABOUT!!!
BIG MAN. KILL ME, THEN WHAT DO YOU HAVE?!
DOCTOR, YOU'RE JUST GETTING MAD AT HIM FOR ACTING LIKE HIMSELF.
EXACTLY.
IT'S LIKE GETTING MAD AT A DOG FOR POOPING.
TELL THE TRUTH!!
YOU DON'T HAVE TIME FOR THIS, BANNER.
NONE OF US DO.
FOCUS.
HE'S RIGHT.
HE'S TOMORROW'S PROBLEM...
EXACTLY.
LOOK AT THIS.
IF THERE IS A TOMORROW.
WHAT CAN WE DO?

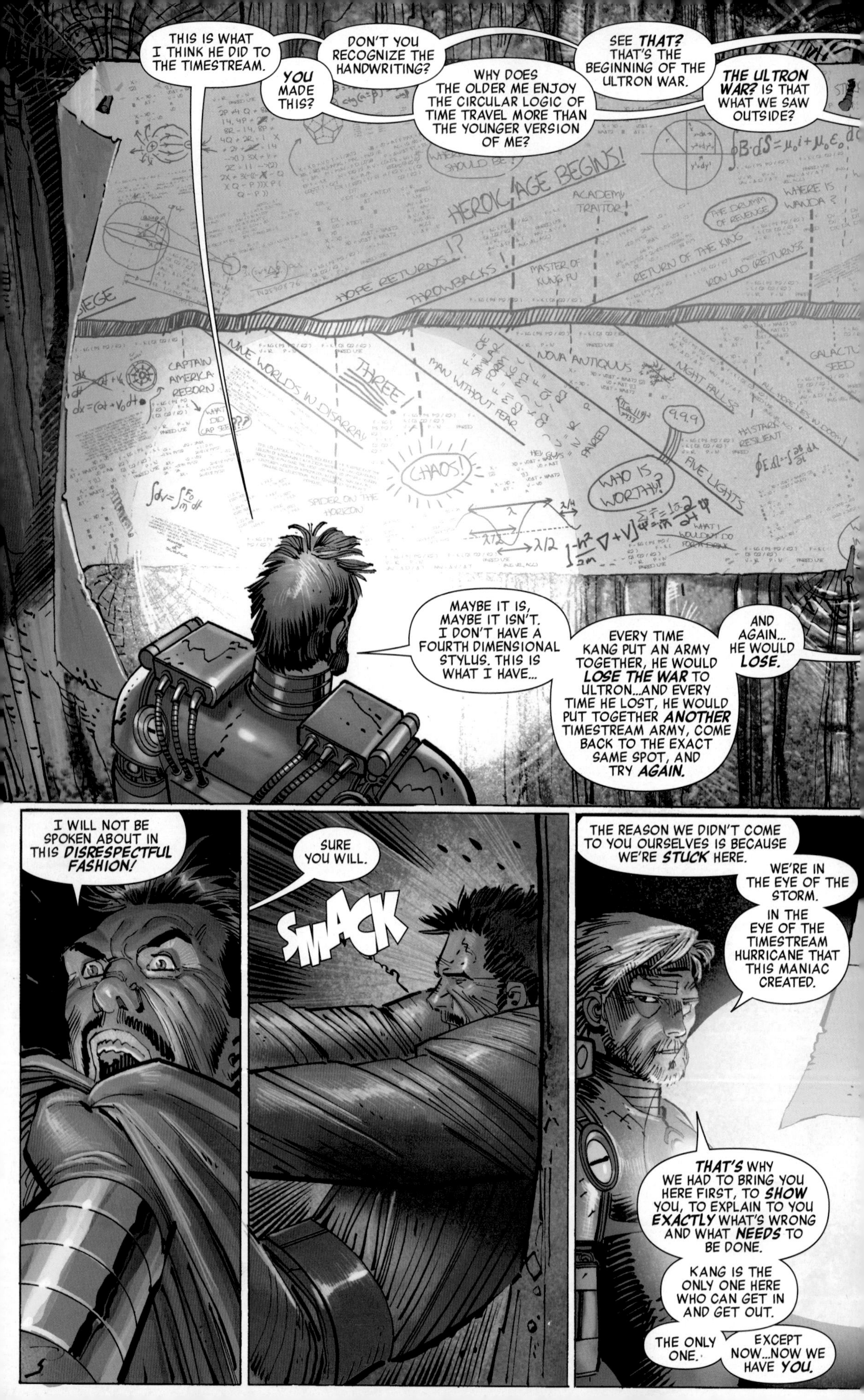
THIS IS WHAT I THINK HE DID TO THE TIMESTREAM.
DON'T YOU RECOGNIZE THE HANDWRITING?
YOU MADE THIS?
WHY DOES THE OLDER ME ENJOY THE CIRCULAR LOGIC OF TIME TRAVEL MORE THAN THE YOUNGER VERSION OF ME?
SEE THAT? THAT'S THE BEGINNING OF THE ULTRON WAR.
THE ULTRON WAR? IS THAT WHAT WE SAW OUTSIDE?
HEROIC AGE BEGINS!
SIEGE
HOPE RETURNS!?
THROWBACKS!
ACADEMY TRAITOR!
MASTER OF KUNG FU
RETURN OF THE KING
IRON LAD (RE)TURNS?
THE DRUMM OF REVENGE
WHERE IS WANDA?
CAPTAIN AMERICA REBORN
WHAT DID CAP SEE???
NINE WORLDS IN DISARRAY
THREE
MAN WITHOUT FEAR
NOVA ANTIQUUS
NIGHT FALLS?
GALACTUS SEED
ALL HOPE LIES IN DOOM!
9.9.9
CHAOS!
WHO IS WORTHY?
FIVE LIGHTS
SPIDER ON THE HORIZON
MAYBE IT IS, MAYBE IT ISN'T. I DON'T HAVE A FOURTH DIMENSIONAL STYLUS. THIS IS WHAT I HAVE...
EVERY TIME KANG PUT AN ARMY TOGETHER, HE WOULD LOSE THE WAR TO ULTRON...AND EVERY TIME HE LOST, HE WOULD PUT TOGETHER ANOTHER TIMESTREAM ARMY, COME BACK TO THE EXACT SAME SPOT, AND TRY AGAIN.
AND AGAIN... HE WOULD LOSE.
I WILL NOT BE SPOKEN ABOUT IN THIS DISRESPECTFUL FASHION!
SURE YOU WILL.
SMACK
THE REASON WE DIDN'T COME TO YOU OURSELVES IS BECAUSE WE'RE STUCK HERE.
WE'RE IN THE EYE OF THE STORM.
IN THE EYE OF THE TIMESTREAM HURRICANE THAT THIS MANIAC CREATED.
THAT'S WHY WE HAD TO BRING YOU HERE FIRST, TO SHOW YOU, TO EXPLAIN TO YOU EXACTLY WHAT'S WRONG AND WHAT NEEDS TO BE DONE.
KANG IS THE ONLY ONE HERE WHO CAN GET IN AND GET OUT.
THE ONLY ONE.
EXCEPT NOW...NOW WE HAVE YOU.

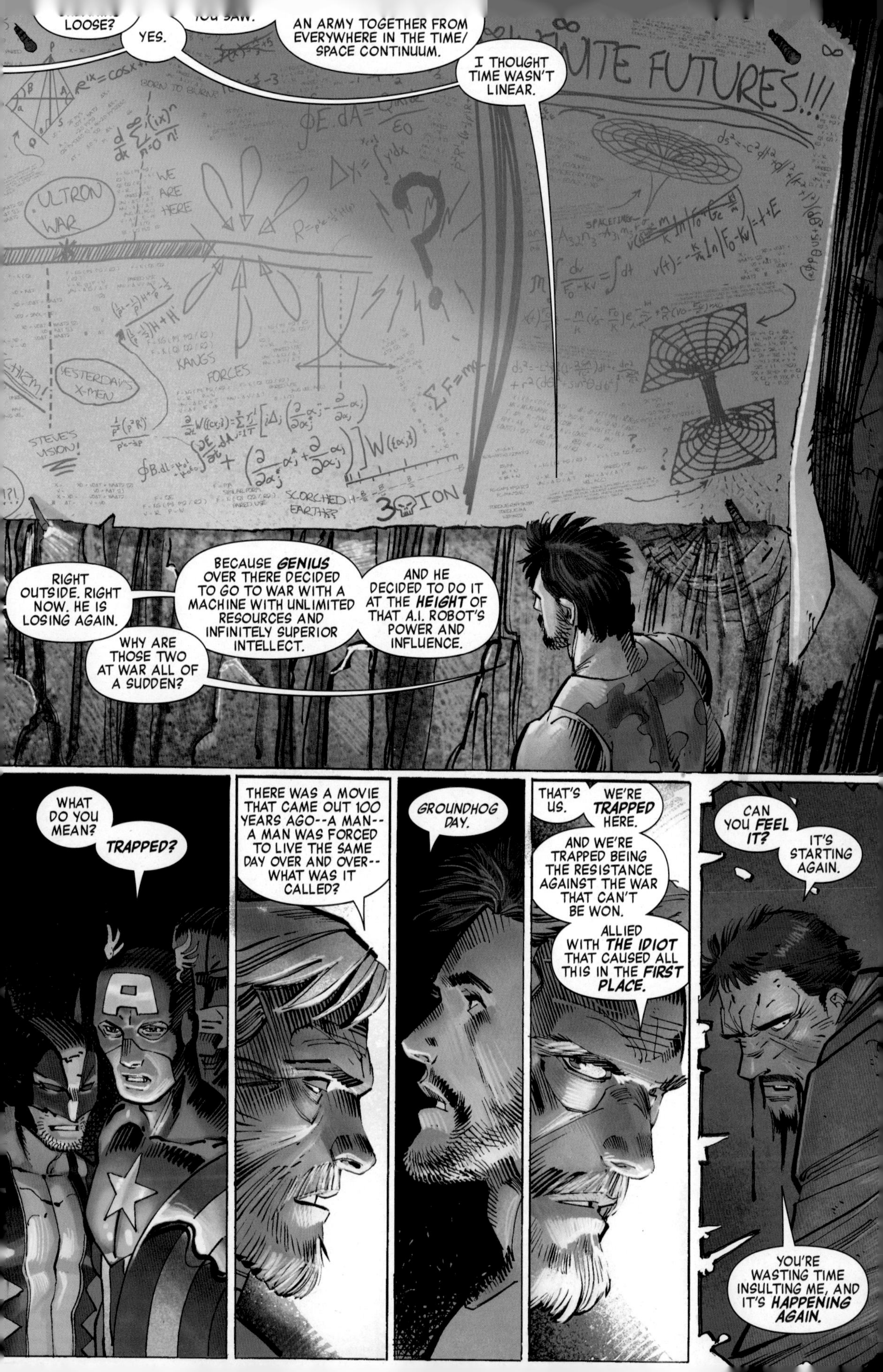
LOOSE?
YES.
AN ARMY TOGETHER FROM EVERYWHERE IN THE TIME/ SPACE CONTINUUM.
I THOUGHT TIME WASN'T LINEAR.
ULTRON WAR
WE ARE HERE
KANGS
FORCES
YESTERDAY'S X-MEN
STEVE'S VISION!
SCORCHED EARTH??
RIGHT OUTSIDE. RIGHT NOW. HE IS LOSING AGAIN.
BECAUSE GENIUS OVER THERE DECIDED TO GO TO WAR WITH A MACHINE WITH UNLIMITED RESOURCES AND INFINITELY SUPERIOR INTELLECT.
AND HE DECIDED TO DO IT AT THE HEIGHT OF THAT A.I. ROBOT'S POWER AND INFLUENCE.
WHY ARE THOSE TWO AT WAR ALL OF A SUDDEN?
WHAT DO YOU MEAN?
TRAPPED?
THERE WAS A MOVIE THAT CAME OUT 100 YEARS AGO--A MAN-- A MAN WAS FORCED TO LIVE THE SAME DAY OVER AND OVER-- WHAT WAS IT CALLED?
GROUNDHOG DAY.
THAT'S US.
WE'RE TRAPPED HERE.
AND WE'RE TRAPPED BEING THE RESISTANCE AGAINST THE WAR THAT CAN'T BE WON.
ALLIED WITH THE IDIOT THAT CAUSED ALL THIS IN THE FIRST PLACE.
CAN YOU FEEL IT?
IT'S STARTING AGAIN.
YOU'RE WASTING TIME INSULTING ME, AND IT'S HAPPENING AGAIN.

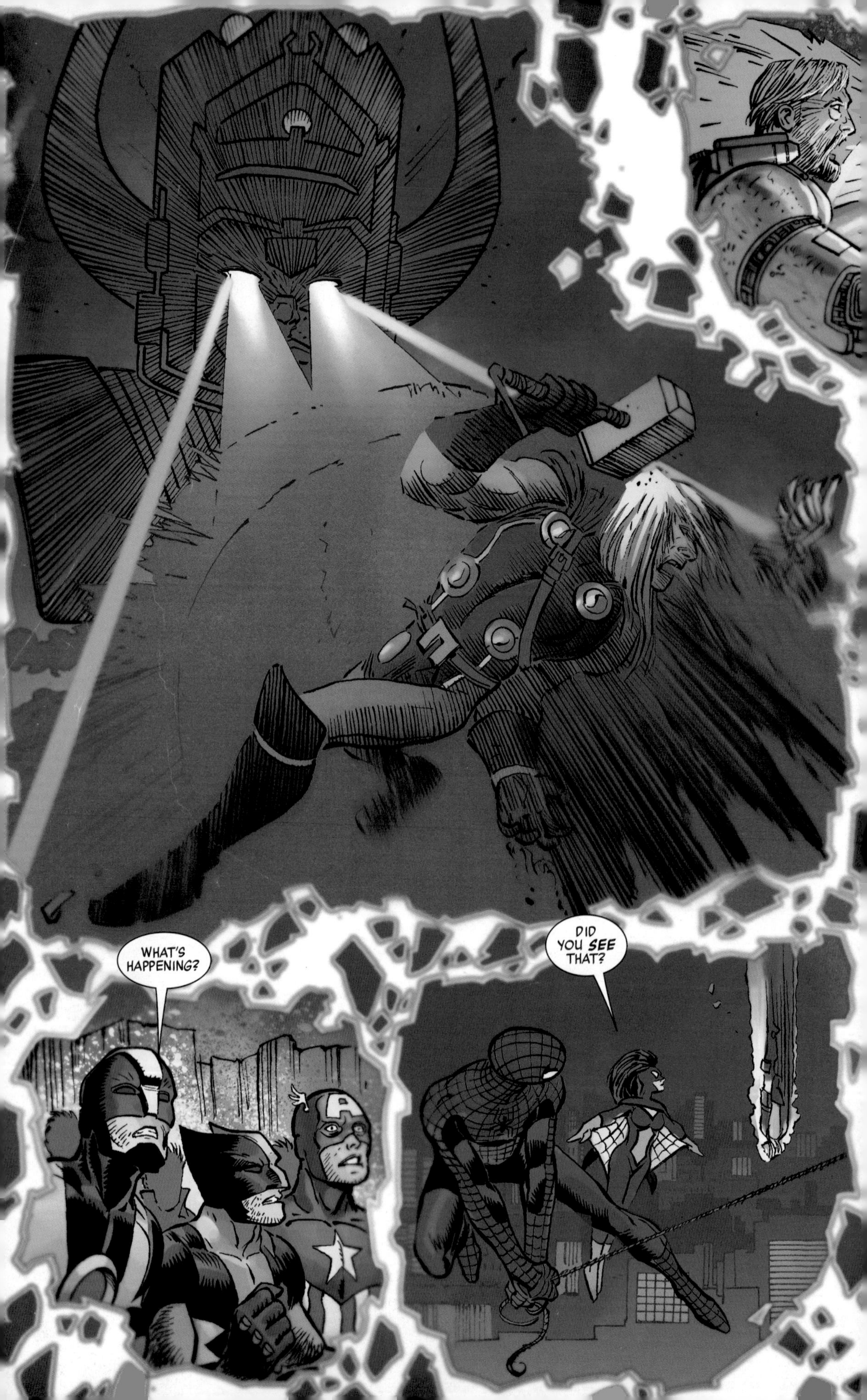
WHAT'S HAPPENING?
DID YOU SEE THAT?

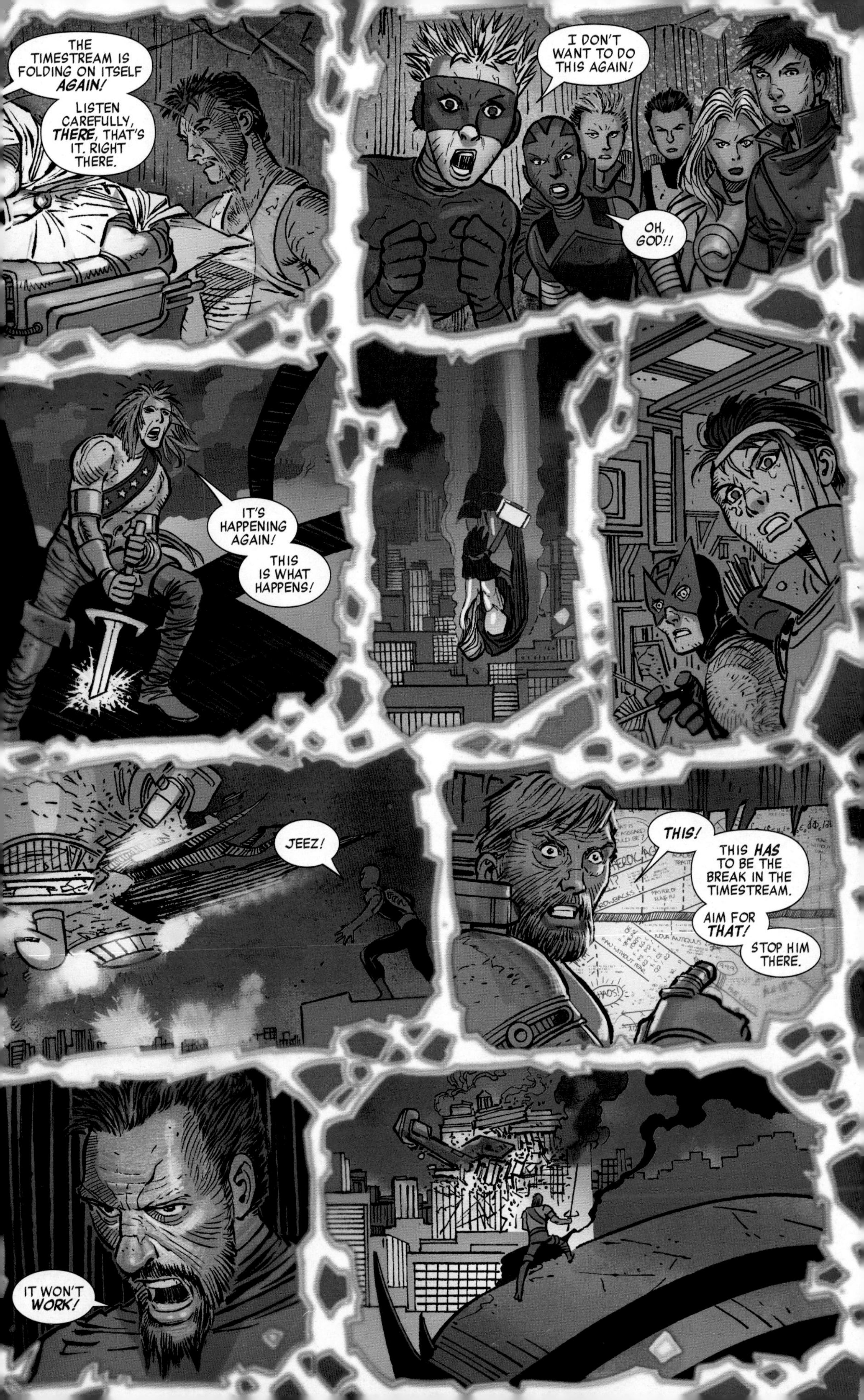
THE TIMESTREAM IS FOLDING ON ITSELF *AGAIN!*
LISTEN CAREFULLY, *THERE*, THAT'S IT. RIGHT THERE.
I DON'T WANT TO DO THIS AGAIN!
OH, GOD!!
IT'S HAPPENING AGAIN!
THIS IS WHAT HAPPENS!
JEEZ!
THIS!
THIS *HAS* TO BE THE BREAK IN THE TIMESTREAM.
AIM FOR *THAT!*
STOP HIM THERE.
IT WON'T *WORK!*

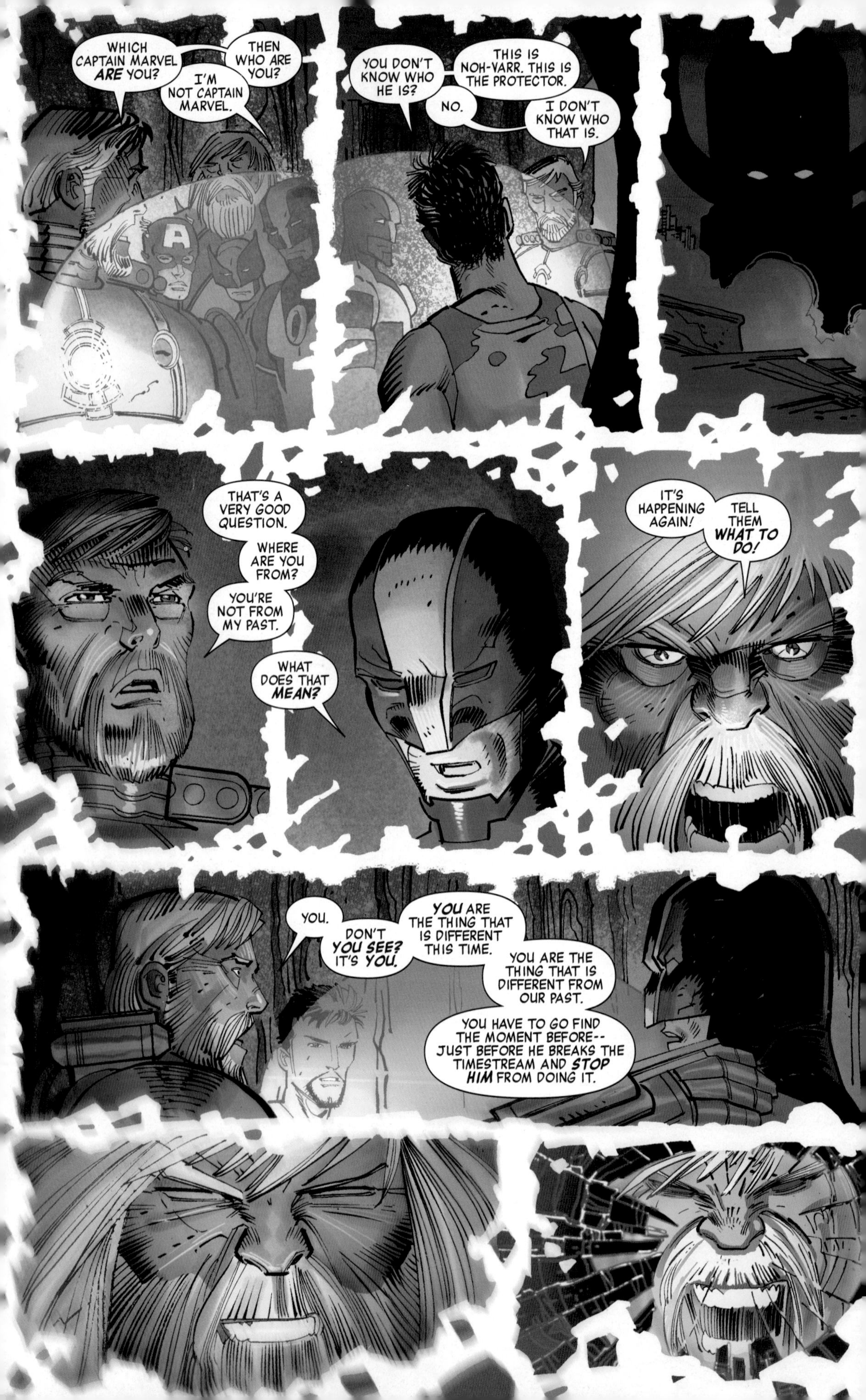

WHICH CAPTAIN MARVEL ARE YOU?
I'M NOT CAPTAIN MARVEL.
THEN WHO ARE YOU?
YOU DON'T KNOW WHO HE IS?
NO.
THIS IS NOH-VARR. THIS IS THE PROTECTOR.
I DON'T KNOW WHO THAT IS.
THAT'S A VERY GOOD QUESTION.
WHERE ARE YOU FROM?
YOU'RE NOT FROM MY PAST.
WHAT DOES THAT MEAN?
IT'S HAPPENING AGAIN!
TELL THEM WHAT TO DO!
YOU.
DON'T YOU SEE? IT'S YOU.
YOU ARE THE THING THAT IS DIFFERENT THIS TIME.
YOU ARE THE THING THAT IS DIFFERENT FROM OUR PAST.
YOU HAVE TO GO FIND THE MOMENT BEFORE-- JUST BEFORE HE BREAKS THE TIMESTREAM AND STOP HIM FROM DOING IT.

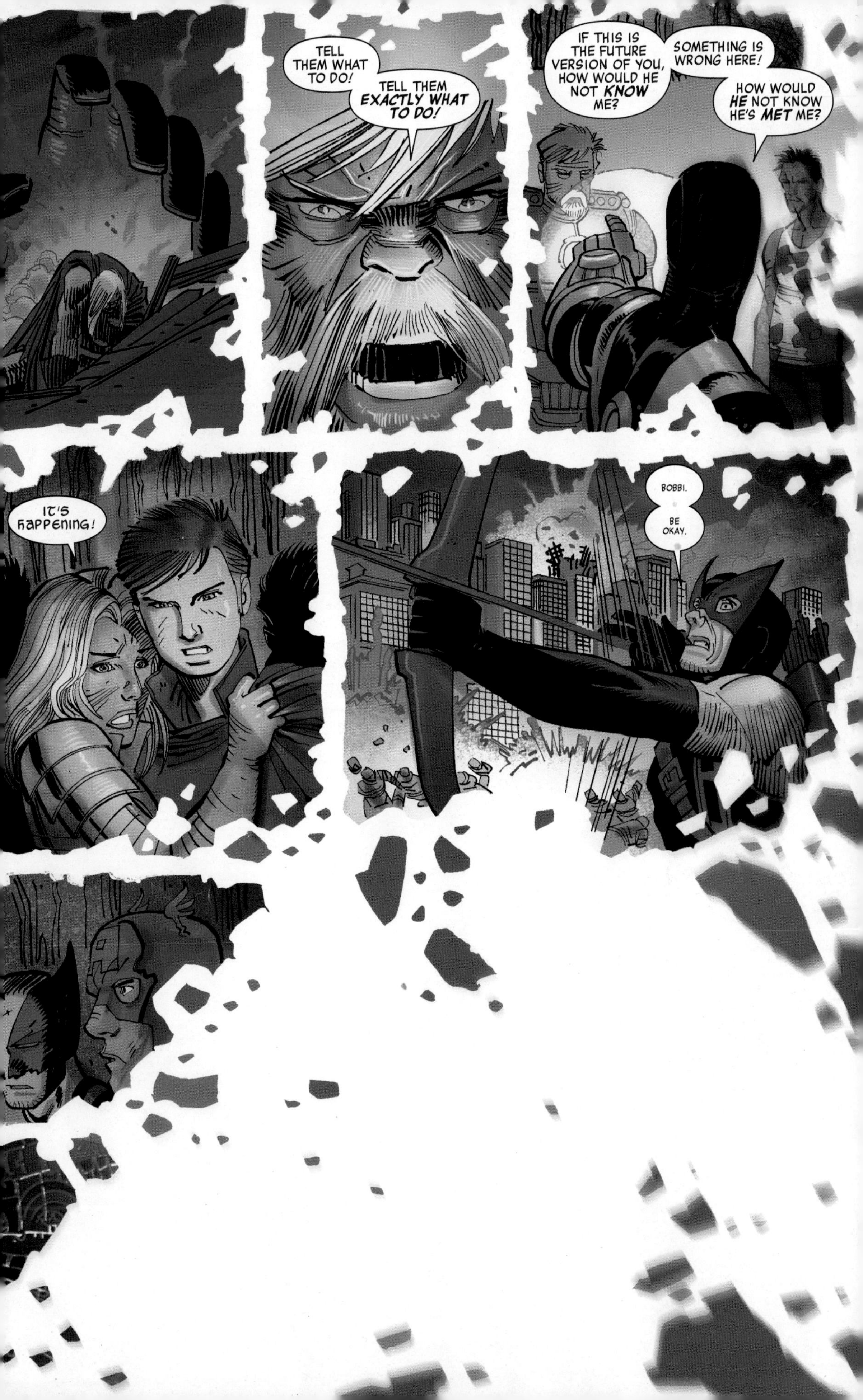
TELL THEM WHAT TO DO!
TELL THEM EXACTLY WHAT TO DO!
IF THIS IS THE FUTURE VERSION OF YOU, HOW WOULD HE NOT KNOW ME?
SOMETHING IS WRONG HERE!
HOW WOULD HE NOT KNOW HE'S MET ME?
IT'S HAPPENING!
BOBBI.
BE OKAY.

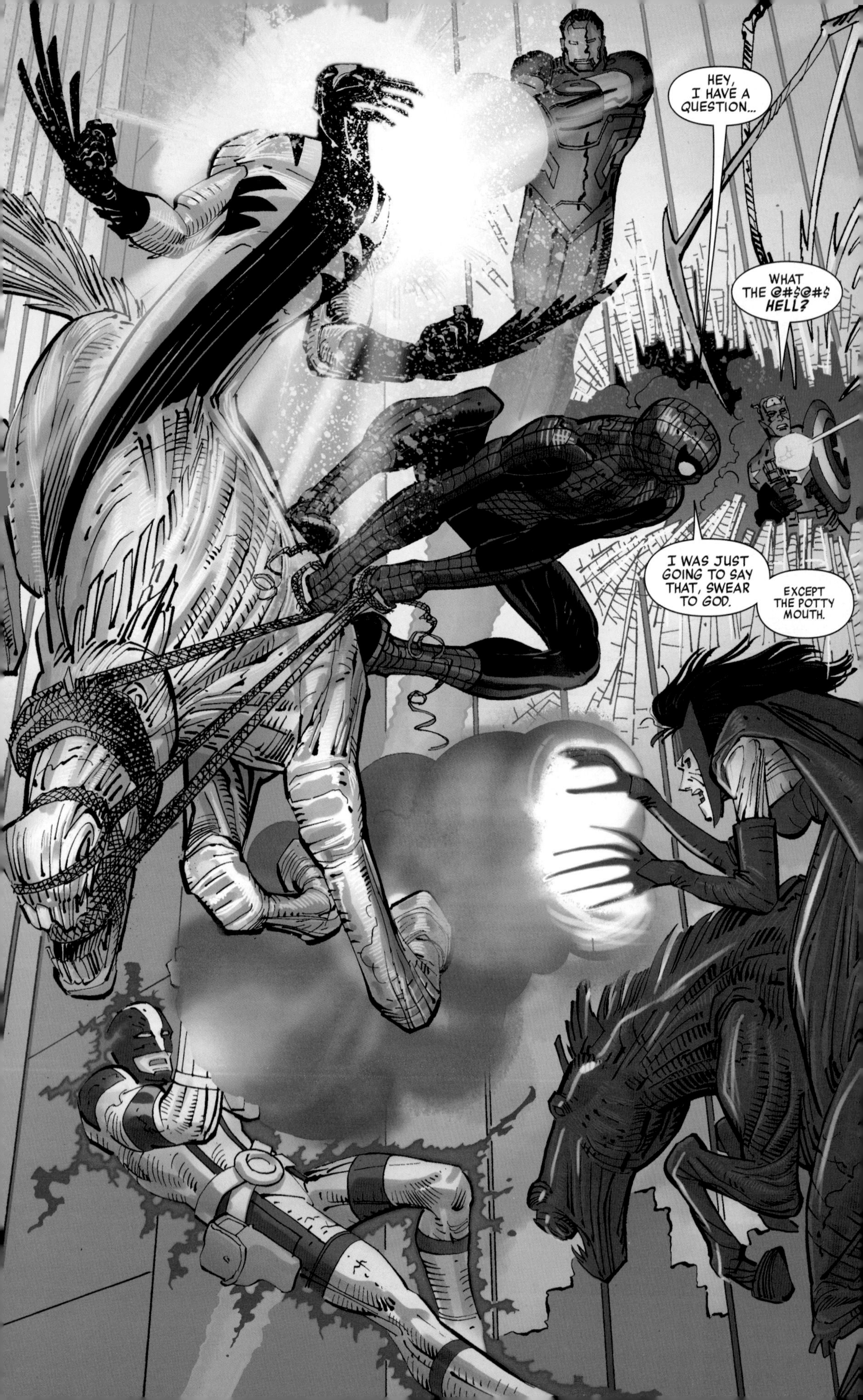
HEY, I HAVE A QUESTION...
WHAT THE @#$@#$ HELL?
I WAS JUST GOING TO SAY THAT, SWEAR TO GOD.
EXCEPT THE POTTY MOUTH.

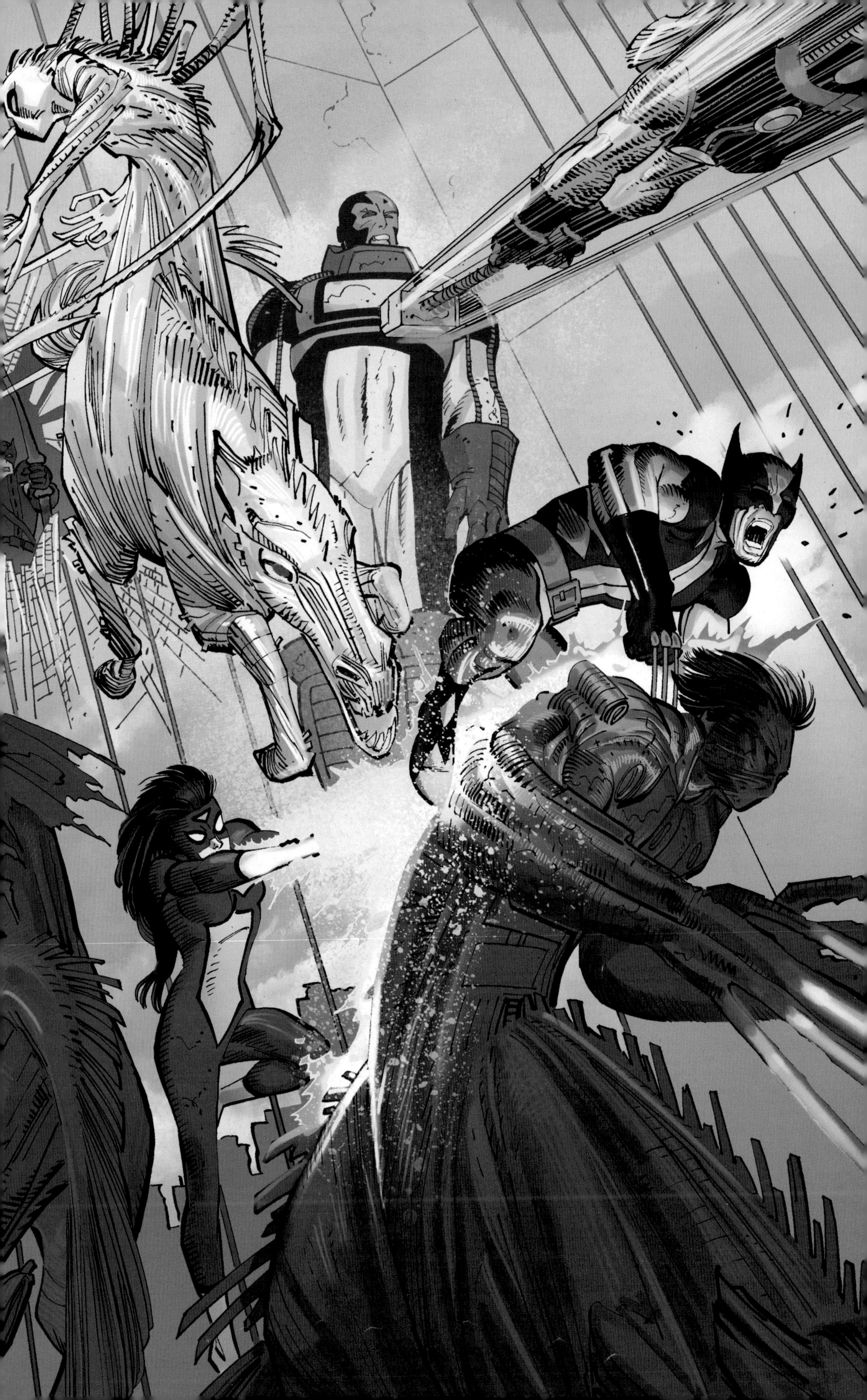

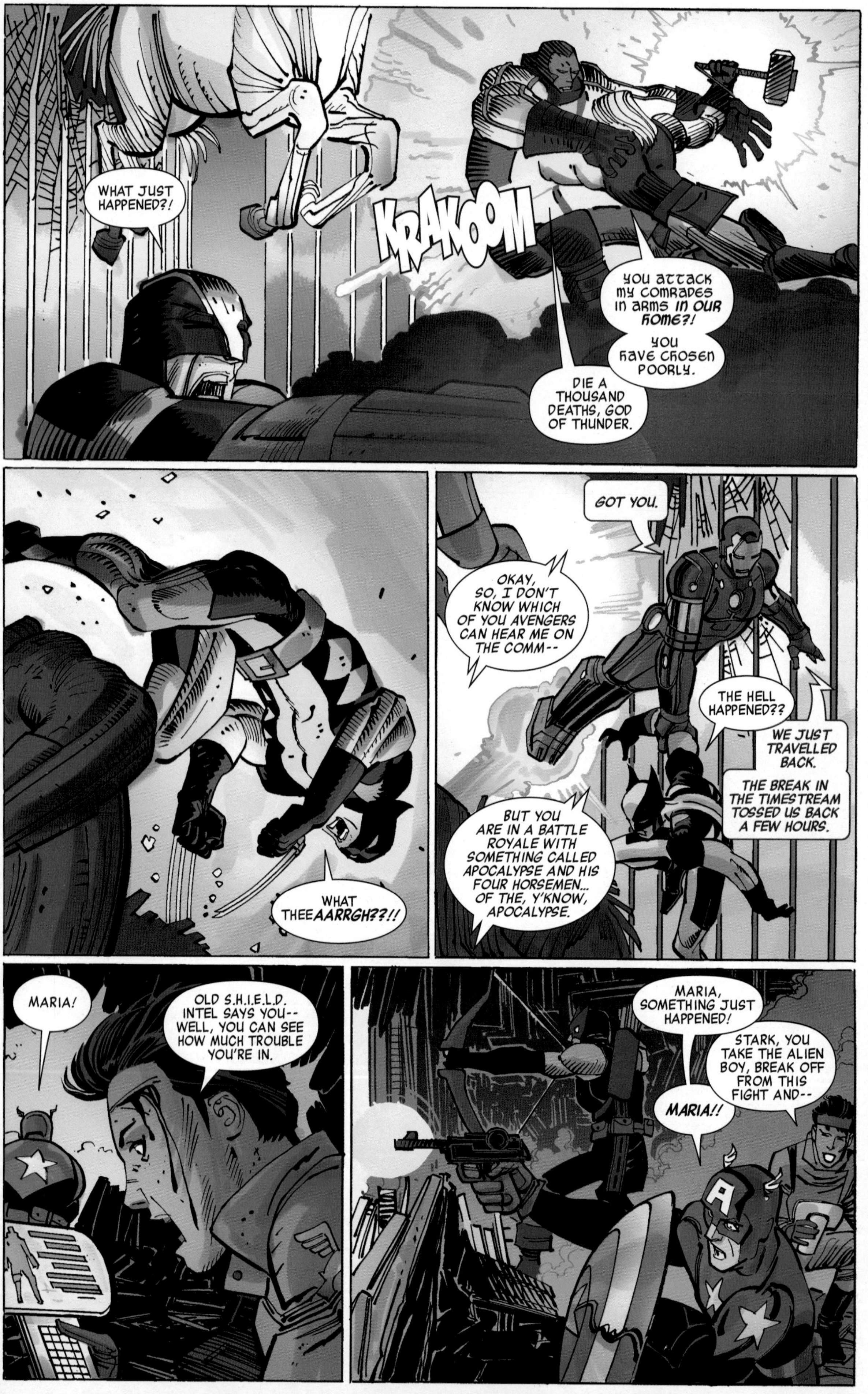
WHAT JUST HAPPENED?!
KRAKOOM
YOU ATTACK MY COMRADES IN ARMS IN OUR HOME?!
YOU HAVE CHOSEN POORLY.
DIE A THOUSAND DEATHS, GOD OF THUNDER.
WHAT THEEAARRGH??!!
GOT YOU.
OKAY, SO, I DON'T KNOW WHICH OF YOU AVENGERS CAN HEAR ME ON THE COMM--
BUT YOU ARE IN A BATTLE ROYALE WITH SOMETHING CALLED APOCALYPSE AND HIS FOUR HORSEMEN... OF THE, Y'KNOW, APOCALYPSE.
THE HELL HAPPENED??
WE JUST TRAVELLED BACK.
THE BREAK IN THE TIMESTREAM TOSSED US BACK A FEW HOURS.
MARIA!
OLD S.H.I.E.L.D. INTEL SAYS YOU--WELL, YOU CAN SEE HOW MUCH TROUBLE YOU'RE IN.
MARIA, SOMETHING JUST HAPPENED!
STARK, YOU TAKE THE ALIEN BOY, BREAK OFF FROM THIS FIGHT AND--
MARIA!!

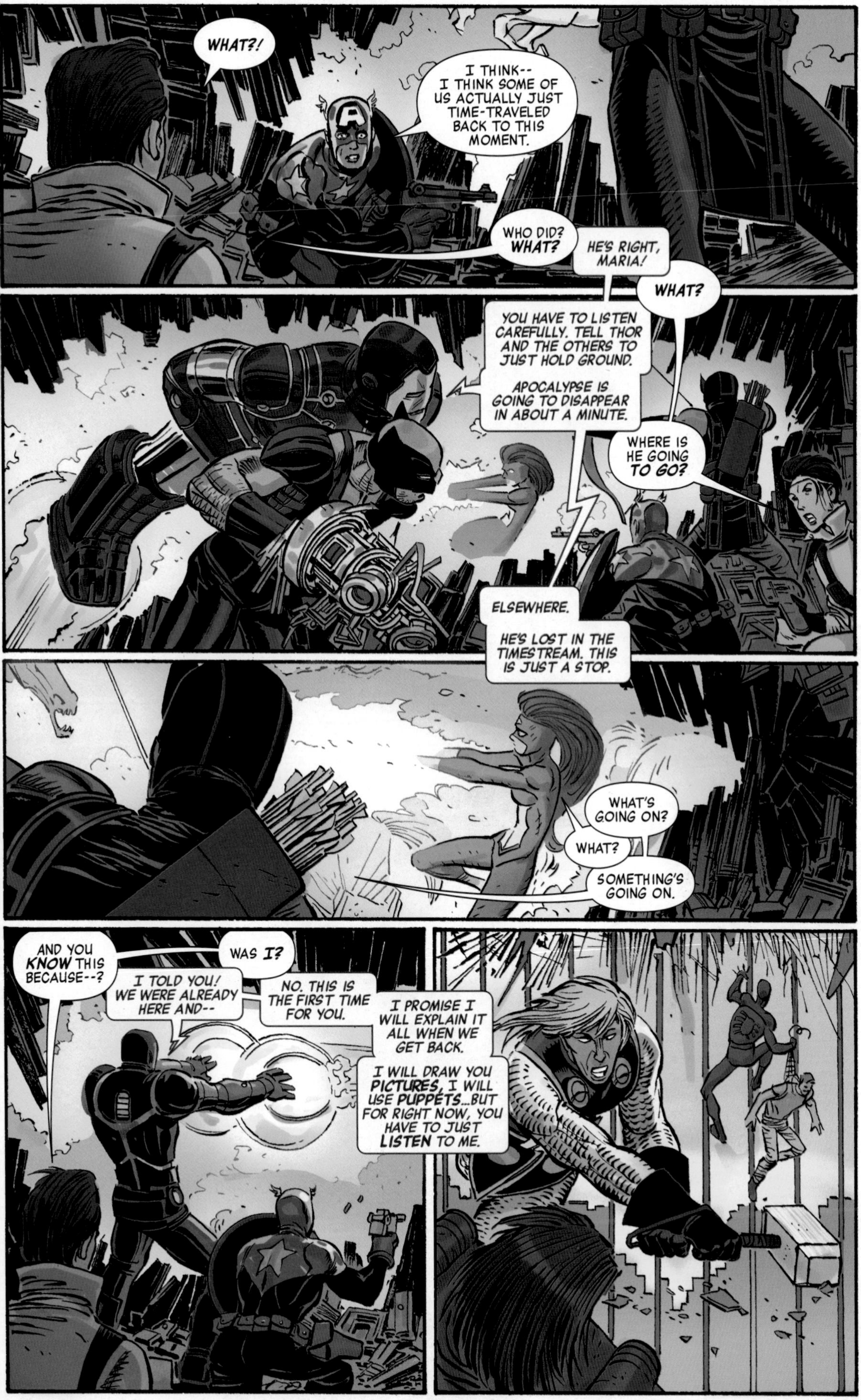
WHAT?!
I THINK-- I THINK SOME OF US ACTUALLY JUST TIME-TRAVELED BACK TO THIS MOMENT.
WHO DID? WHAT?
HE'S RIGHT, MARIA!
WHAT?
YOU HAVE TO LISTEN CAREFULLY. TELL THOR AND THE OTHERS TO JUST HOLD GROUND.
APOCALYPSE IS GOING TO DISAPPEAR IN ABOUT A MINUTE.
WHERE IS HE GOING TO GO?
ELSEWHERE.
HE'S LOST IN THE TIMESTREAM. THIS IS JUST A STOP.
WHAT'S GOING ON?
WHAT?
SOMETHING'S GOING ON.
AND YOU KNOW THIS BECAUSE--?
WAS I?
I TOLD YOU! WE WERE ALREADY HERE AND--
NO. THIS IS THE FIRST TIME FOR YOU.
I PROMISE I WILL EXPLAIN IT ALL WHEN WE GET BACK.
I WILL DRAW YOU PICTURES, I WILL USE PUPPETS...BUT FOR RIGHT NOW, YOU HAVE TO JUST LISTEN TO ME.

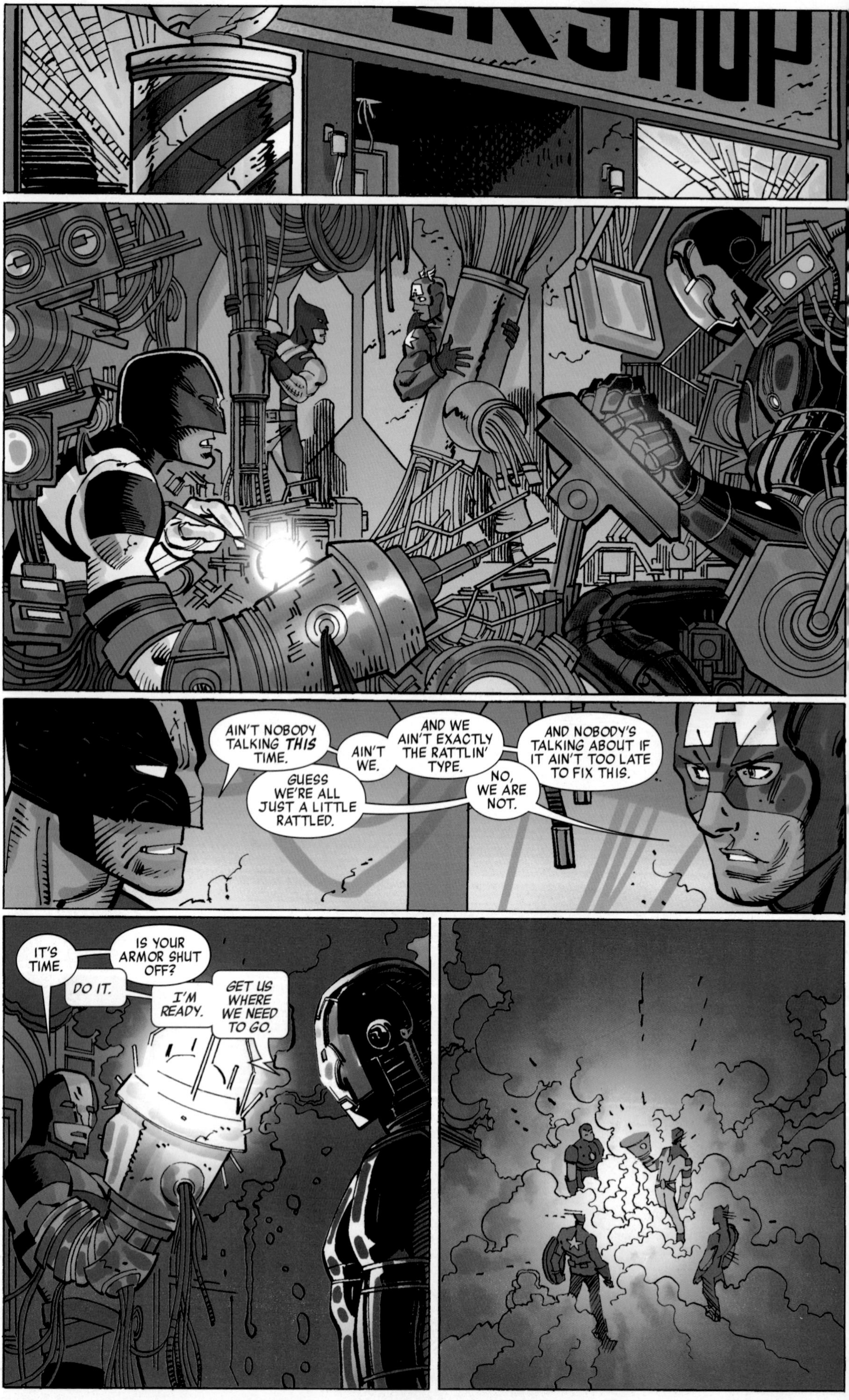
AIN'T NOBODY TALKING THIS TIME.
AIN'T WE.
AND WE AIN'T EXACTLY THE RATTLIN' TYPE.
AND NOBODY'S TALKING ABOUT IF IT AIN'T TOO LATE TO FIX THIS.
GUESS WE'RE ALL JUST A LITTLE RATTLED.
NO, WE ARE NOT.
IT'S TIME.
IS YOUR ARMOR SHUT OFF?
DO IT.
I'M READY.
GET US WHERE WE NEED TO GO.

WELL AIN'T THIS SOMETHIN'...

HOLD IT TOGETHER.

I CAN HANDLE IT.

I WAS TALKING TO ME.

HOW ARE YOU HERE?

WE TRAVELED THROUGH THE TIMESTREAM.

TO CHALLENGE ME?

NO.

THEN FOR WHAT PURPOSE?

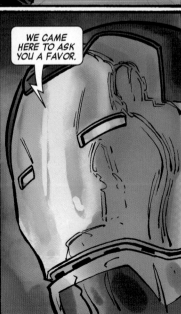

WE CAME HERE TO ASK YOU A FAVOR.

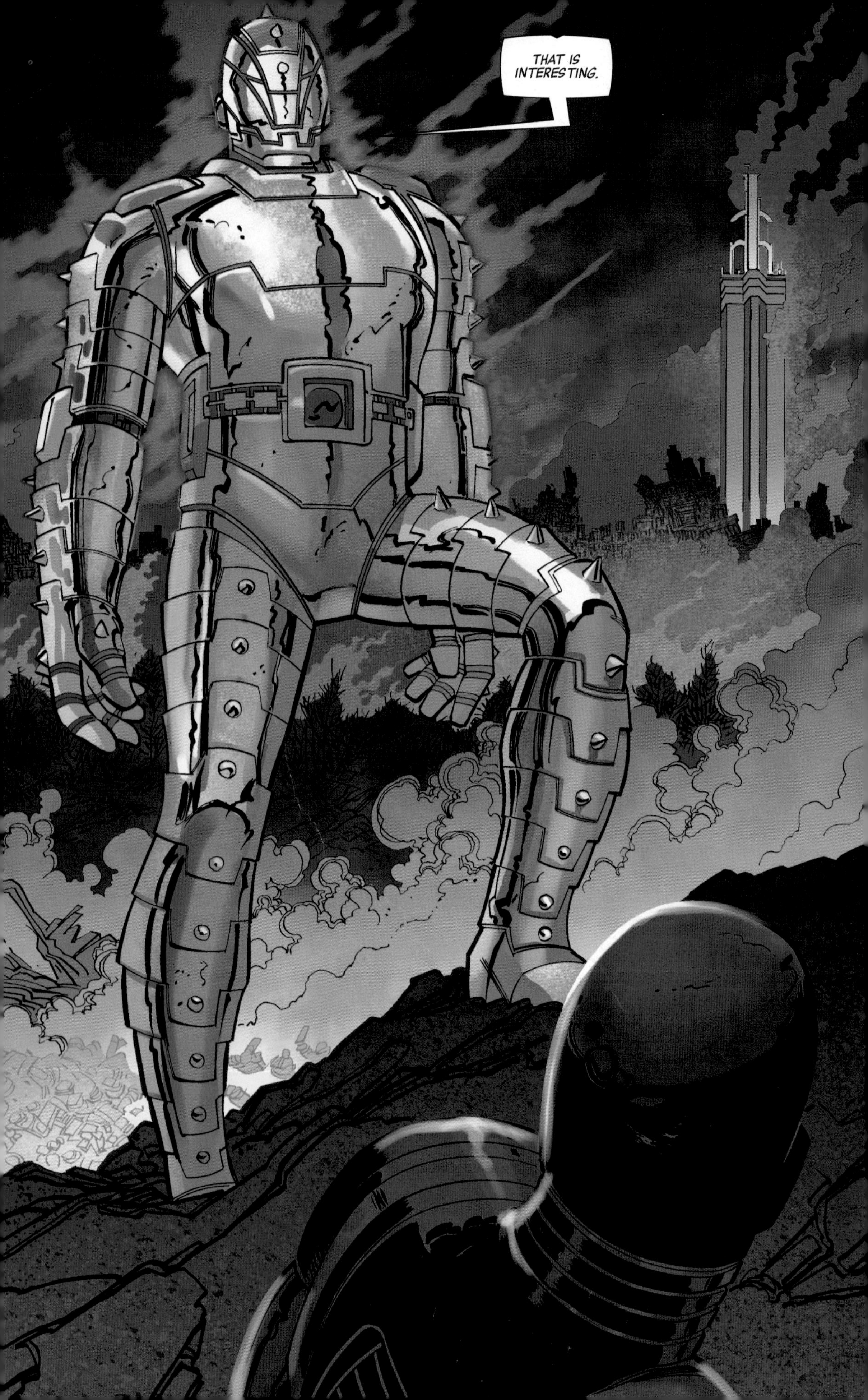
THAT IS INTERESTING.

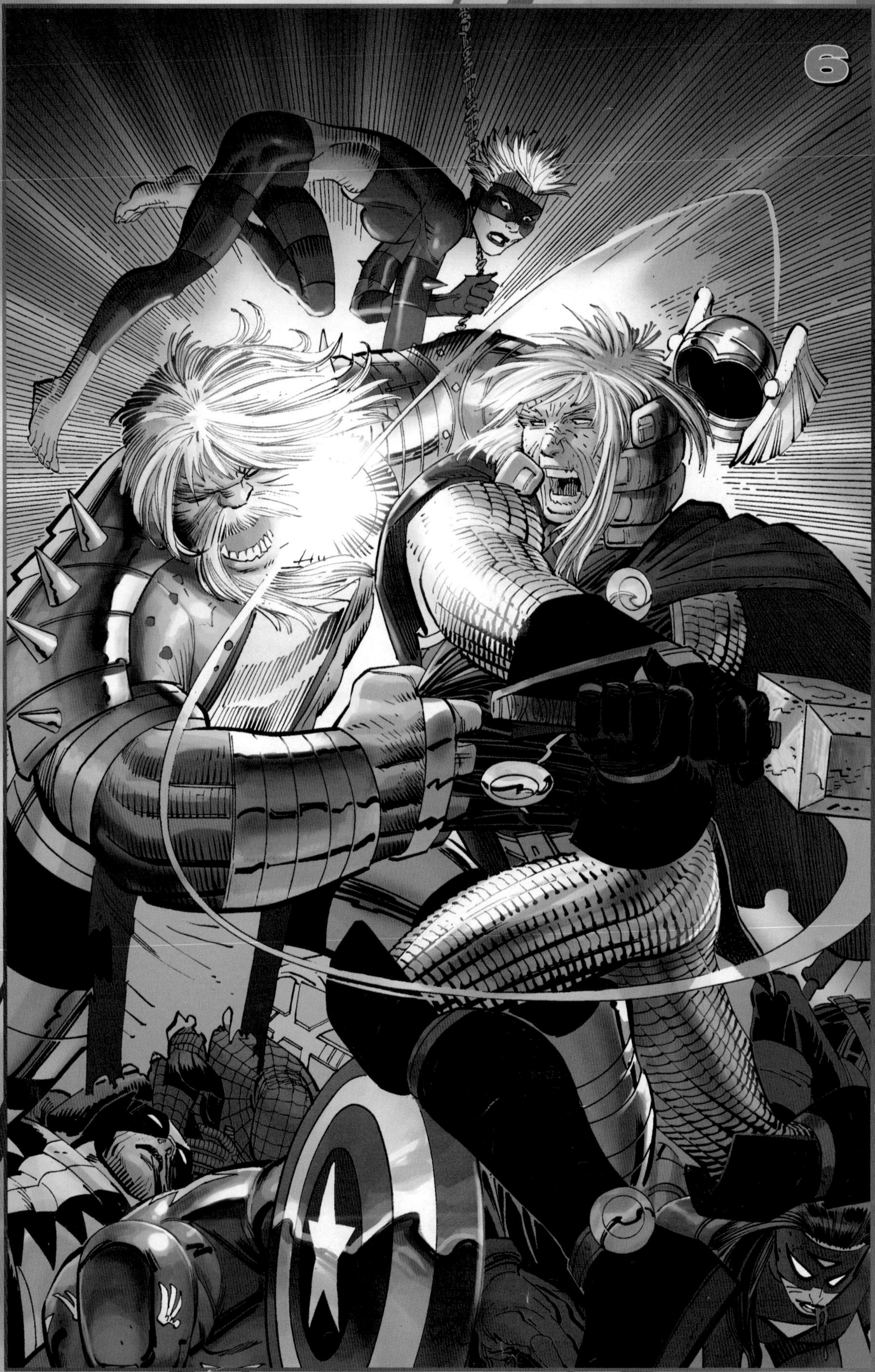
6

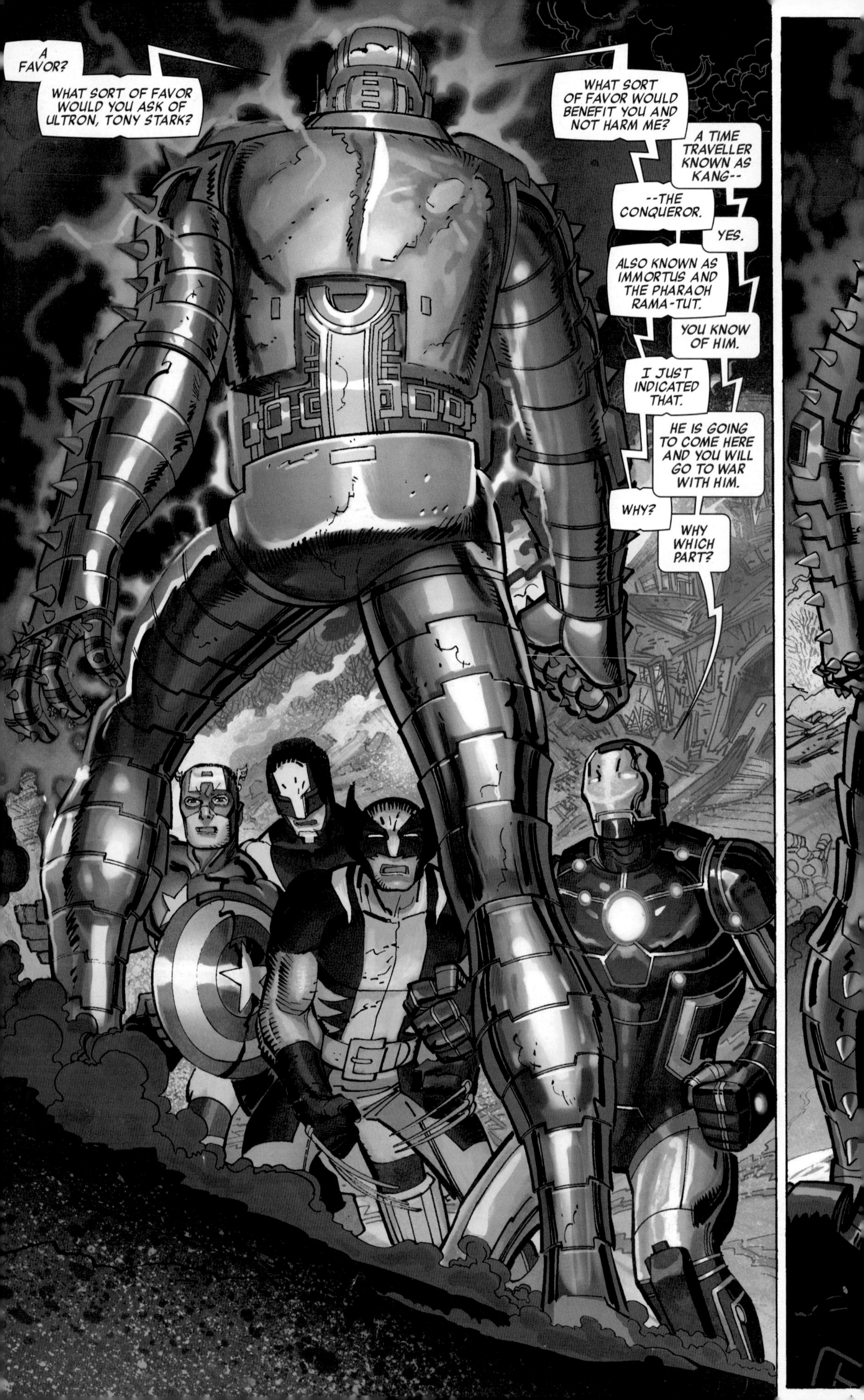
A FAVOR?
WHAT SORT OF FAVOR WOULD YOU ASK OF ULTRON, TONY STARK?
WHAT SORT OF FAVOR WOULD BENEFIT YOU AND NOT HARM ME?
A TIME TRAVELLER KNOWN AS KANG--
--THE CONQUEROR.
YES.
ALSO KNOWN AS IMMORTUS AND THE PHARAOH RAMA-TUT.
YOU KNOW OF HIM.
I JUST INDICATED THAT.
HE IS GOING TO COME HERE AND YOU WILL GO TO WAR WITH HIM.
WHY?
WHY WHICH PART?

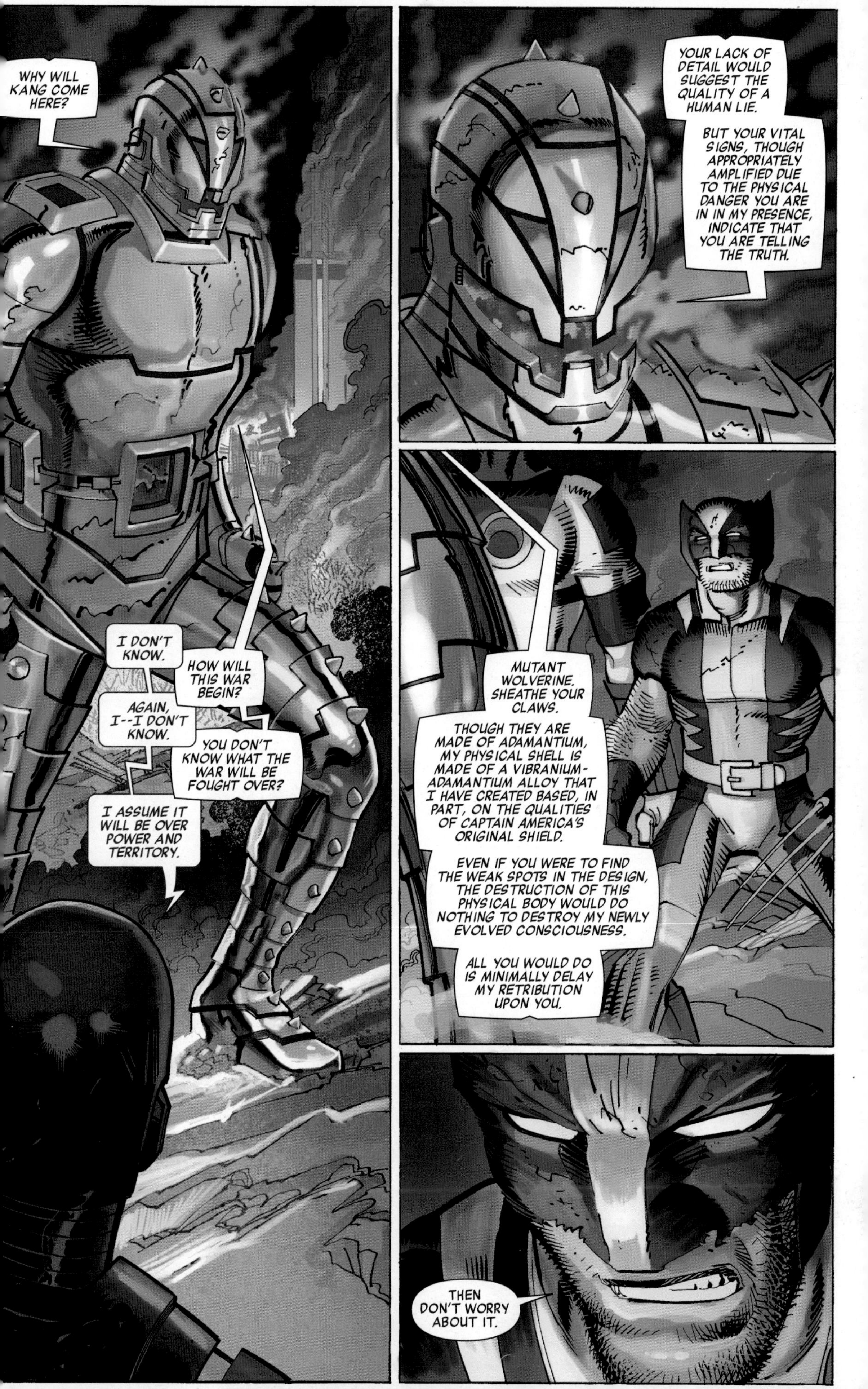
WHY WILL KANG COME HERE?
I DON'T KNOW.
HOW WILL THIS WAR BEGIN?
AGAIN, I--I DON'T KNOW.
YOU DON'T KNOW WHAT THE WAR WILL BE FOUGHT OVER?
I ASSUME IT WILL BE OVER POWER AND TERRITORY.
YOUR LACK OF DETAIL WOULD SUGGEST THE QUALITY OF A HUMAN LIE.
BUT YOUR VITAL SIGNS, THOUGH APPROPRIATELY AMPLIFIED DUE TO THE PHYSICAL DANGER YOU ARE IN IN MY PRESENCE, INDICATE THAT YOU ARE TELLING THE TRUTH.
MUTANT WOLVERINE. SHEATHE YOUR CLAWS.
THOUGH THEY ARE MADE OF ADAMANTIUM, MY PHYSICAL SHELL IS MADE OF A VIBRANIUM-ADAMANTIUM ALLOY THAT I HAVE CREATED BASED, IN PART, ON THE QUALITIES OF CAPTAIN AMERICA'S ORIGINAL SHIELD.
EVEN IF YOU WERE TO FIND THE WEAK SPOTS IN THE DESIGN, THE DESTRUCTION OF THIS PHYSICAL BODY WOULD DO NOTHING TO DESTROY MY NEWLY EVOLVED CONSCIOUSNESS.
ALL YOU WOULD DO IS MINIMALLY DELAY MY RETRIBUTION UPON YOU.
THEN DON'T WORRY ABOUT IT.

I--LISTEN, NONE OF *US* WILL BE PRESENT AT THE START OF THE WAR.

BUT IT WILL HAPPEN. SOON.

WE HAVE SEEN THE WAR FOR OURSELVES.

IT HAPPENS RIGHT HERE IN CENTRAL PARK. THE EARTH WILL BURN.

WE KNOW IT WILL HAPPEN.

YOU DID NOT SEE THE WAR BEGIN, BUT YOU SAW THE BATTLE.

YES.

VARYING CALCULATIONS OF SUCH A CONFRONTATION SUGGEST A VICTORY FOR ME.

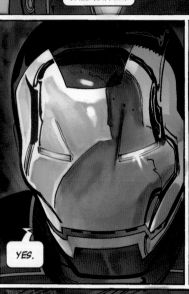

YES.

THEN I THANK YOU FOR THE FAIR WARNING.

WE NEED YOU TO LET KANG WIN.

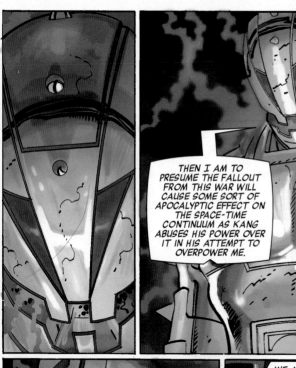

THEN I AM TO PRESUME THE FALLOUT FROM THIS WAR WILL CAUSE SOME SORT OF APOCALYPTIC EFFECT ON THE SPACE-TIME CONTINUUM AS KANG ABUSES HIS POWER OVER IT IN HIS ATTEMPT TO OVERPOWER ME.

HE BREAKS IT. THE SPACE-TIME CONTINUUM.

IT IS ALREADY HAPPENING.

AND IT IS CAUSING RIPPLE EFFECTS IN EVERY DIRECTION.

AND BY DOING SO, THE FABRIC OF OUR REALITY BEGINS TO UNRAVEL.

THREATENING EVERYTHING AND EVERYONE.

INCLUDING ME.

WE ARE STANDING IN THE EYE OF THE TIMESTORM HURRICANE.

NOT MUCH TO RULE OVER IF THERE AIN'T NOTHING LEFT.

I WILL NEED TO WITNESS.

MY NAME IS NOH-VARR. KREE ENSIGN AND EARTH PROTECTOR.

I HAVE LIMITED MEANS TO TRAVEL THROUGH TIME.

I WILL TAKE YOU. I WILL SHOW YOU WHAT YOU NEED TO SEE.

I WILL TRAVEL MYSELF.

HAND OVER YOUR TIME TRAVEL DEVICE.

NO.

YOU WILL BE ESCORTED.

THIS IS A TRAP.

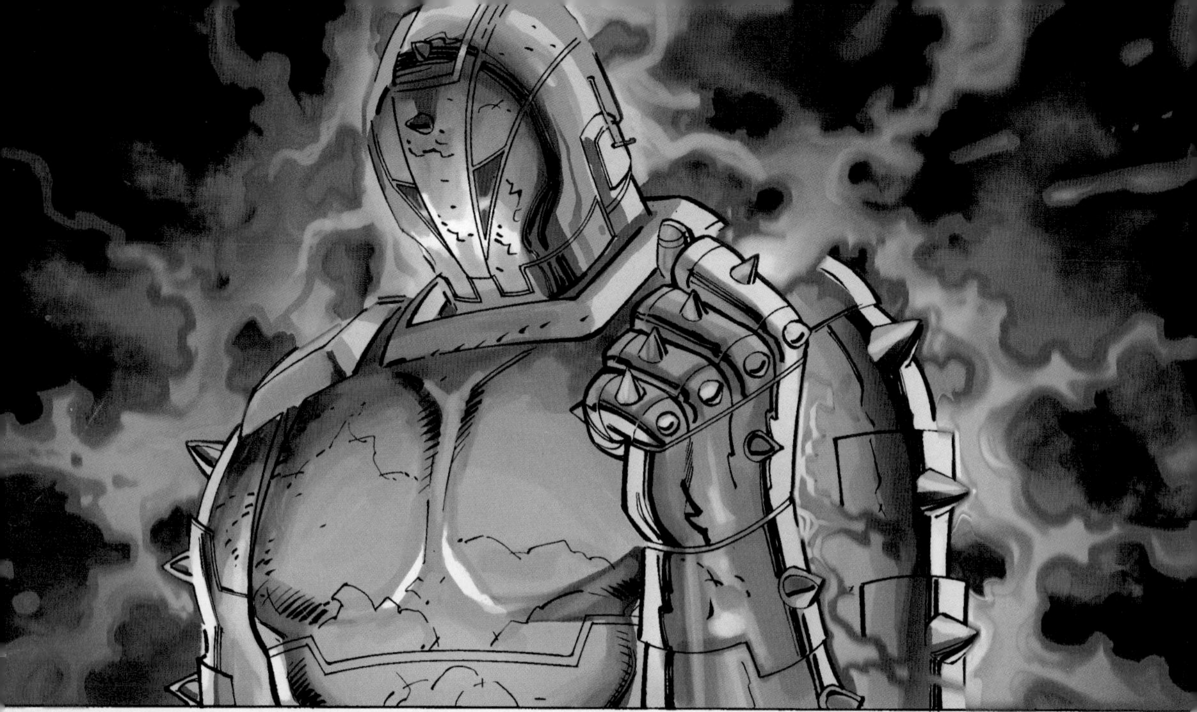

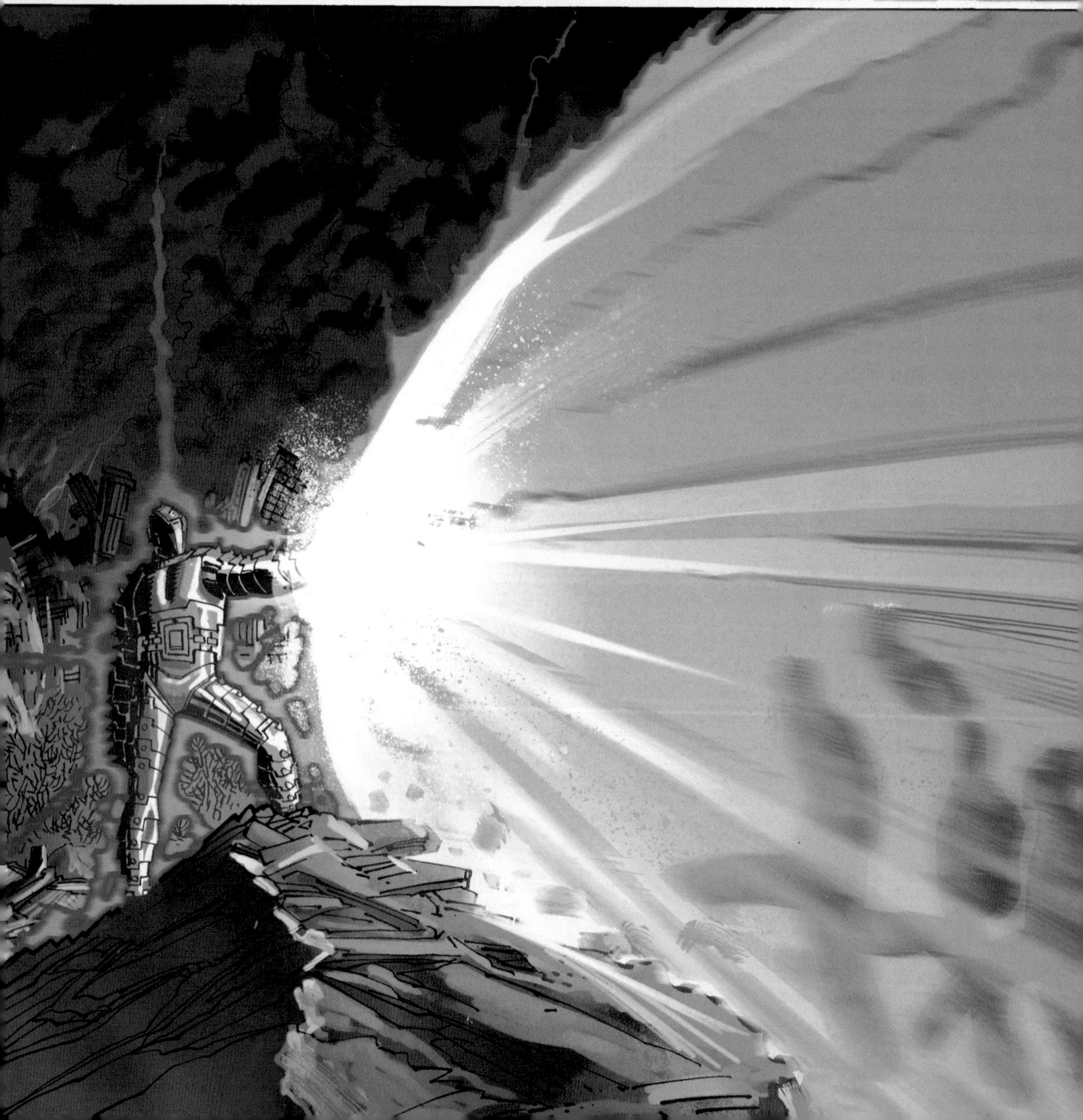

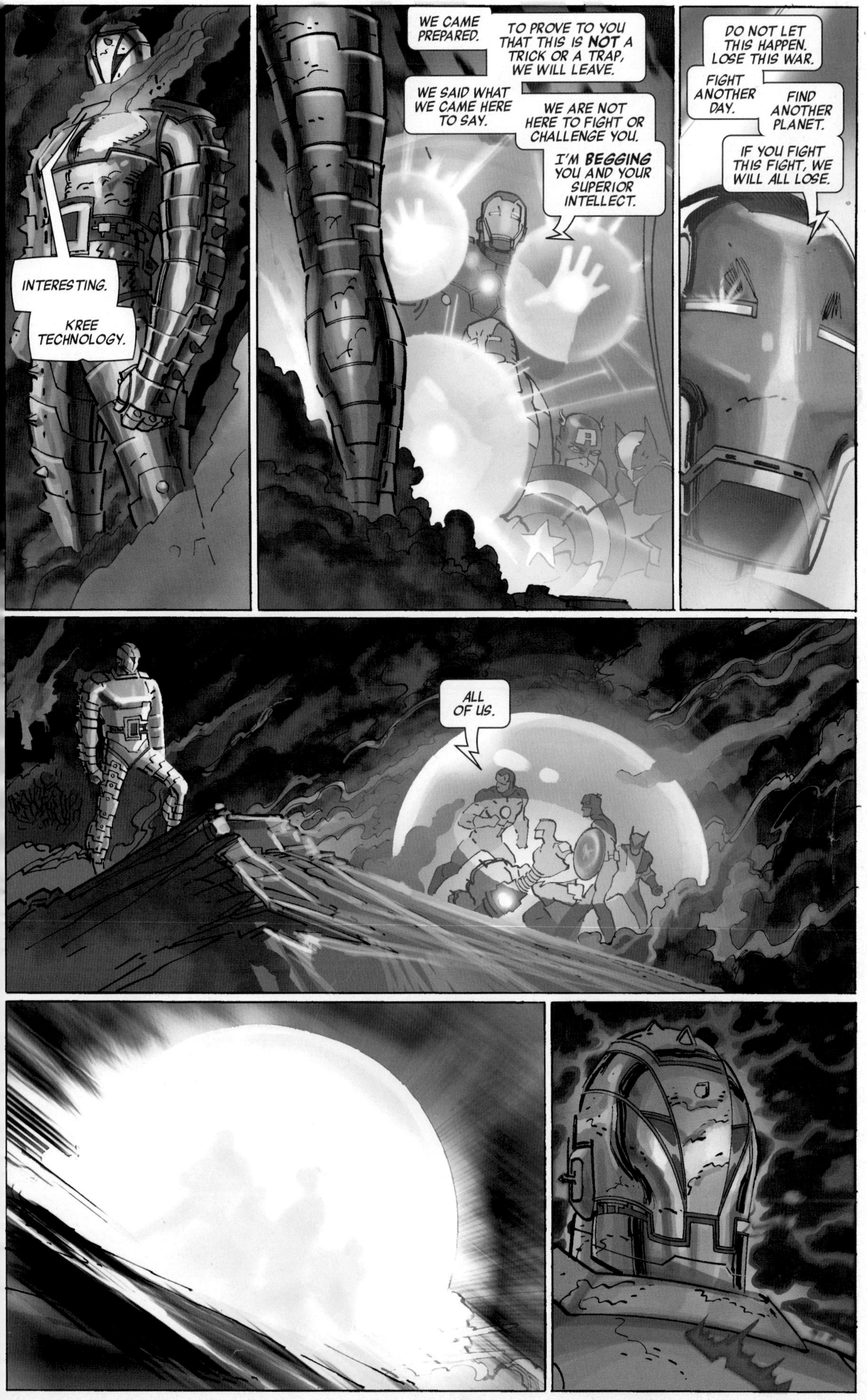
INTERESTING.
KREE TECHNOLOGY.
WE CAME PREPARED.
TO PROVE TO YOU THAT THIS IS **NOT** A TRICK OR A TRAP, WE WILL LEAVE.
WE SAID WHAT WE CAME HERE TO SAY.
WE ARE NOT HERE TO FIGHT OR CHALLENGE YOU.
I'M **BEGGING** YOU AND YOUR SUPERIOR INTELLECT.
DO NOT LET THIS HAPPEN. LOSE THIS WAR.
FIGHT ANOTHER DAY.
FIND ANOTHER PLANET.
IF YOU FIGHT THIS FIGHT, WE WILL ALL LOSE.
ALL OF US.

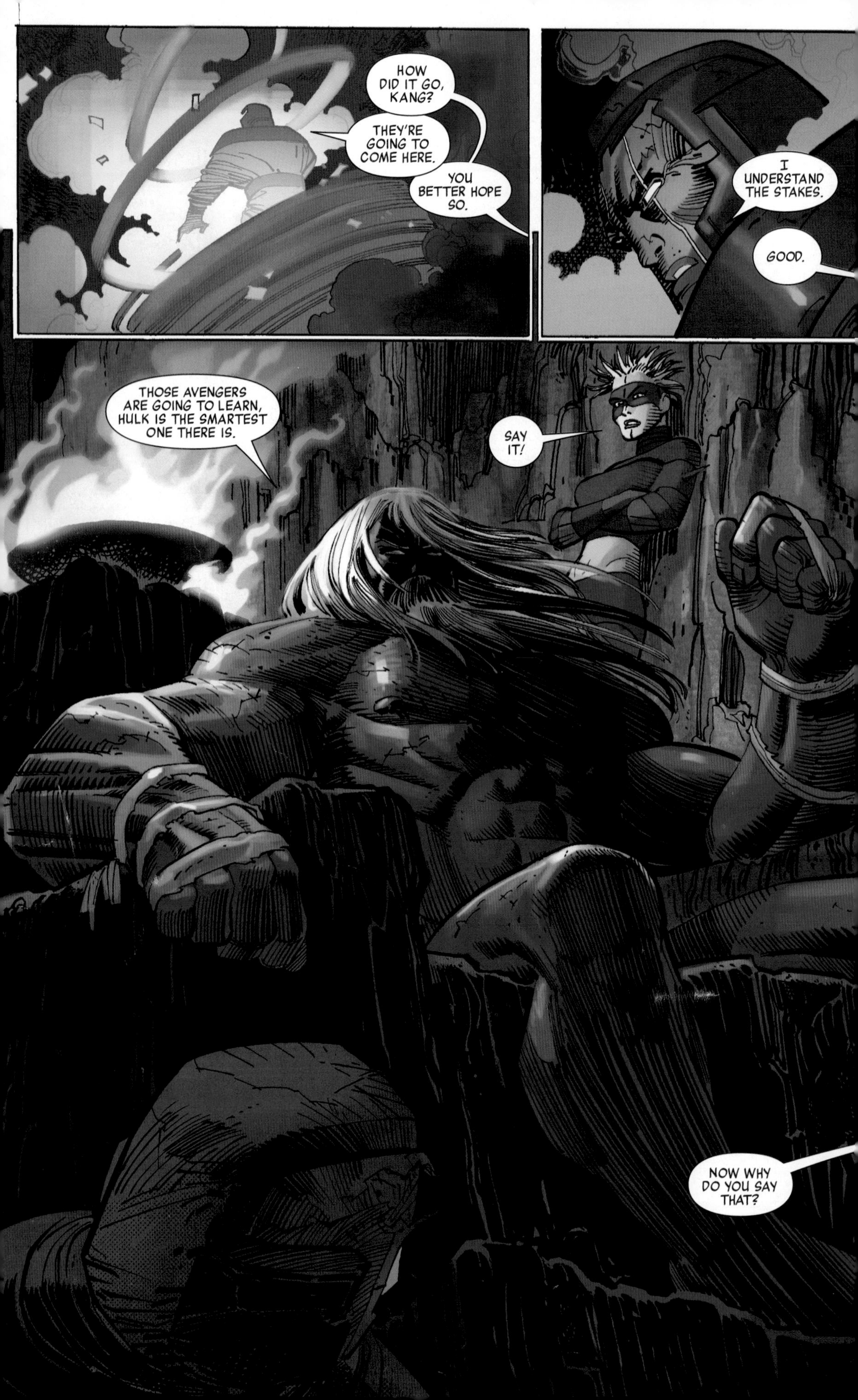
HOW DID IT GO, KANG?
THEY'RE GOING TO COME HERE.
YOU BETTER HOPE SO.
I UNDERSTAND THE STAKES.
GOOD.
THOSE AVENGERS ARE GOING TO LEARN, HULK IS THE SMARTEST ONE THERE IS.
SAY IT!
NOW WHY DO YOU SAY THAT?

I CALL IT HOW I SEE IT, STARK.

YOU'RE *STILL* BLAMING THE AVENGERS FOR CREATING ULTRON.

THEY *DID*.

SO YOU BLAME *ME*.

YOU DO HAVE TO TAKE *SOME* RESPONSIBILITY FOR IT, TONY.

YUP.

BANNER, YOU AND I HAVE LIVED A LONG TIME.

BOTH OF US HAVE *A LOT* OF THINGS WE HAVE TO TAKE RESPONSIBILITY FOR.

A LITTLE LATE TO START POINTING FINGERS.

MOMMY AND DADDY ARE FIGHTING.

SO, UM, WHAT HAPPENS NOW?

I'LL TELL YOU EXACTLY WHAT HAPPENS NOW...

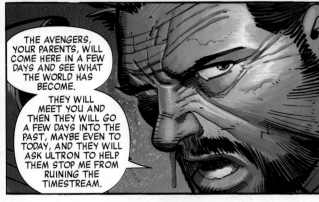

THE AVENGERS, YOUR PARENTS, WILL COME HERE IN A FEW DAYS AND SEE WHAT THE WORLD HAS BECOME.

THEY WILL MEET YOU AND THEN THEY WILL GO A FEW DAYS INTO THE PAST, MAYBE EVEN TO TODAY, AND THEY WILL ASK ULTRON TO HELP THEM STOP ME FROM RUINING THE TIMESTREAM.

THIS IS MAKING ME DIZZY.

HOW WILL WE KNOW IF IT WORKED?

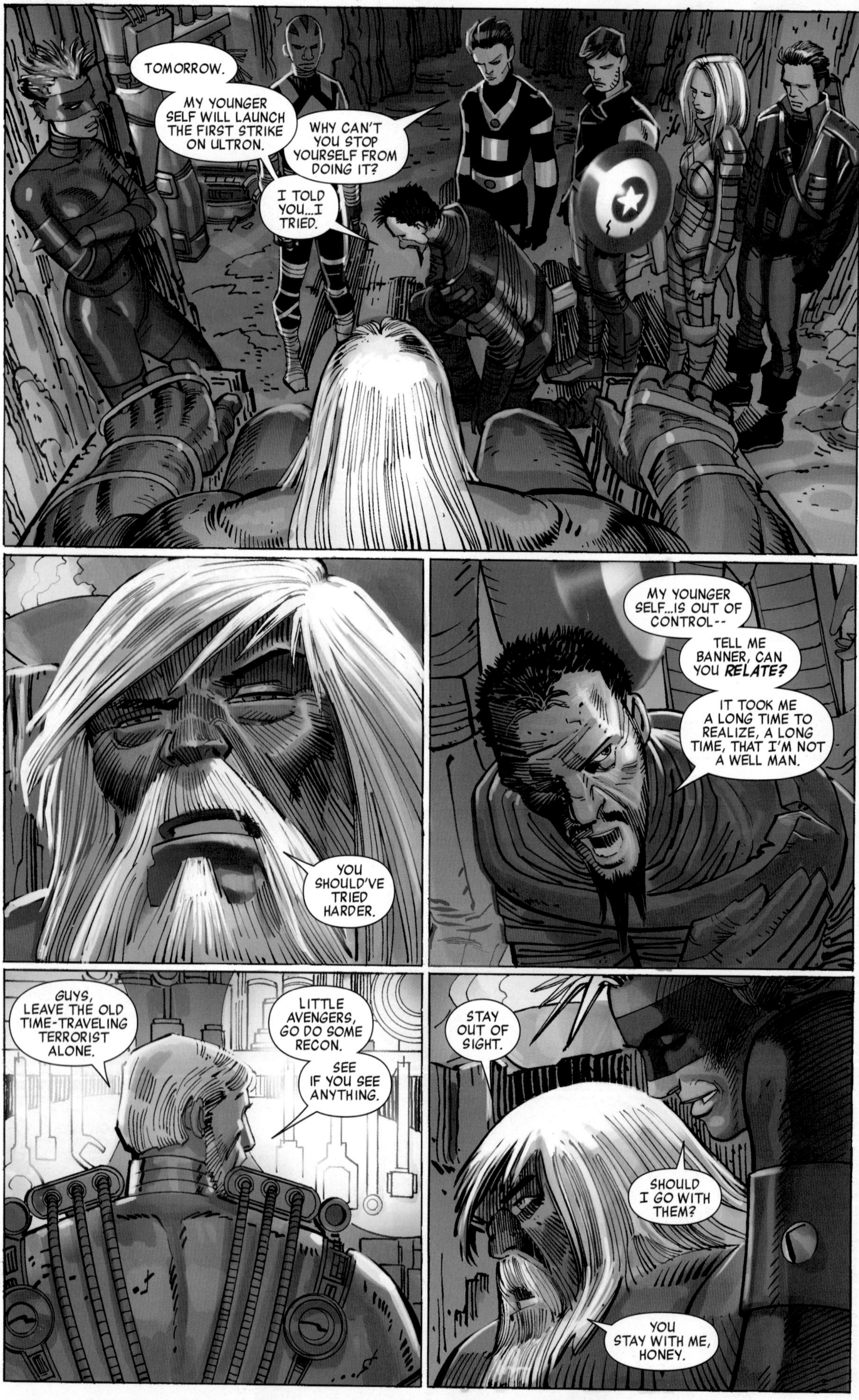
TOMORROW.
MY YOUNGER SELF WILL LAUNCH THE FIRST STRIKE ON ULTRON.
WHY CAN'T YOU STOP YOURSELF FROM DOING IT?
I TOLD YOU...I TRIED.
YOU SHOULD'VE TRIED HARDER.
MY YOUNGER SELF...IS OUT OF CONTROL--
TELL ME BANNER, CAN YOU RELATE?
IT TOOK ME A LONG TIME TO REALIZE, A LONG TIME, THAT I'M NOT A WELL MAN.
GUYS, LEAVE THE OLD TIME-TRAVELING TERRORIST ALONE.
LITTLE AVENGERS, GO DO SOME RECON.
SEE IF YOU SEE ANYTHING.
STAY OUT OF SIGHT.
SHOULD I GO WITH THEM?
YOU STAY WITH ME, HONEY.

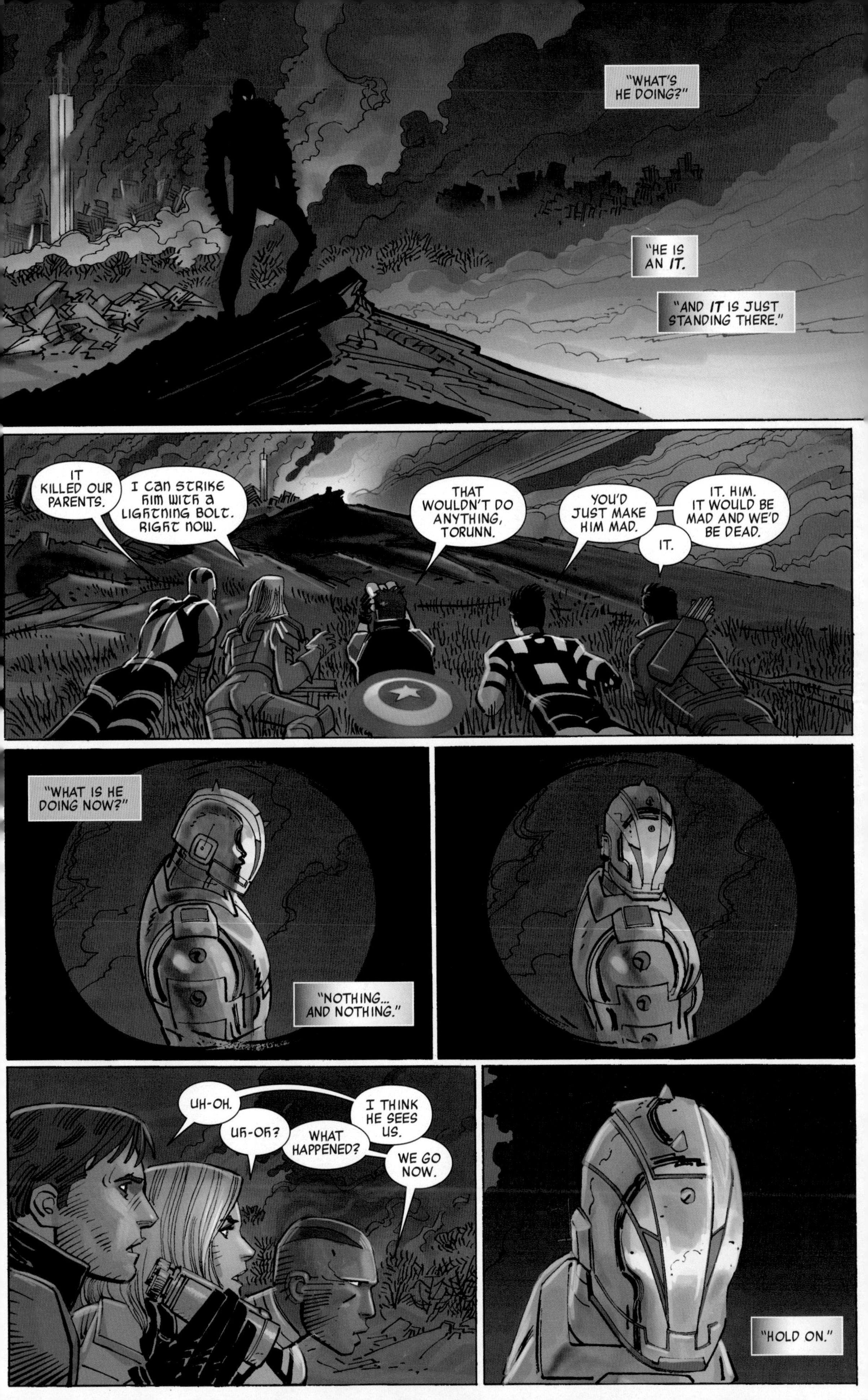
"WHAT'S HE DOING?"
"HE IS AN IT.
"AND IT IS JUST STANDING THERE."
IT KILLED OUR PARENTS.
I CAN STRIKE HIM WITH A LIGHTNING BOLT. RIGHT NOW.
THAT WOULDN'T DO ANYTHING, TORUNN.
YOU'D JUST MAKE HIM MAD.
IT. HIM. IT WOULD BE MAD AND WE'D BE DEAD.
IT.
"WHAT IS HE DOING NOW?"
"NOTHING... AND NOTHING."
UH-OH.
UH-OH?
I THINK HE SEES US.
WHAT HAPPENED?
WE GO NOW.
"HOLD ON."

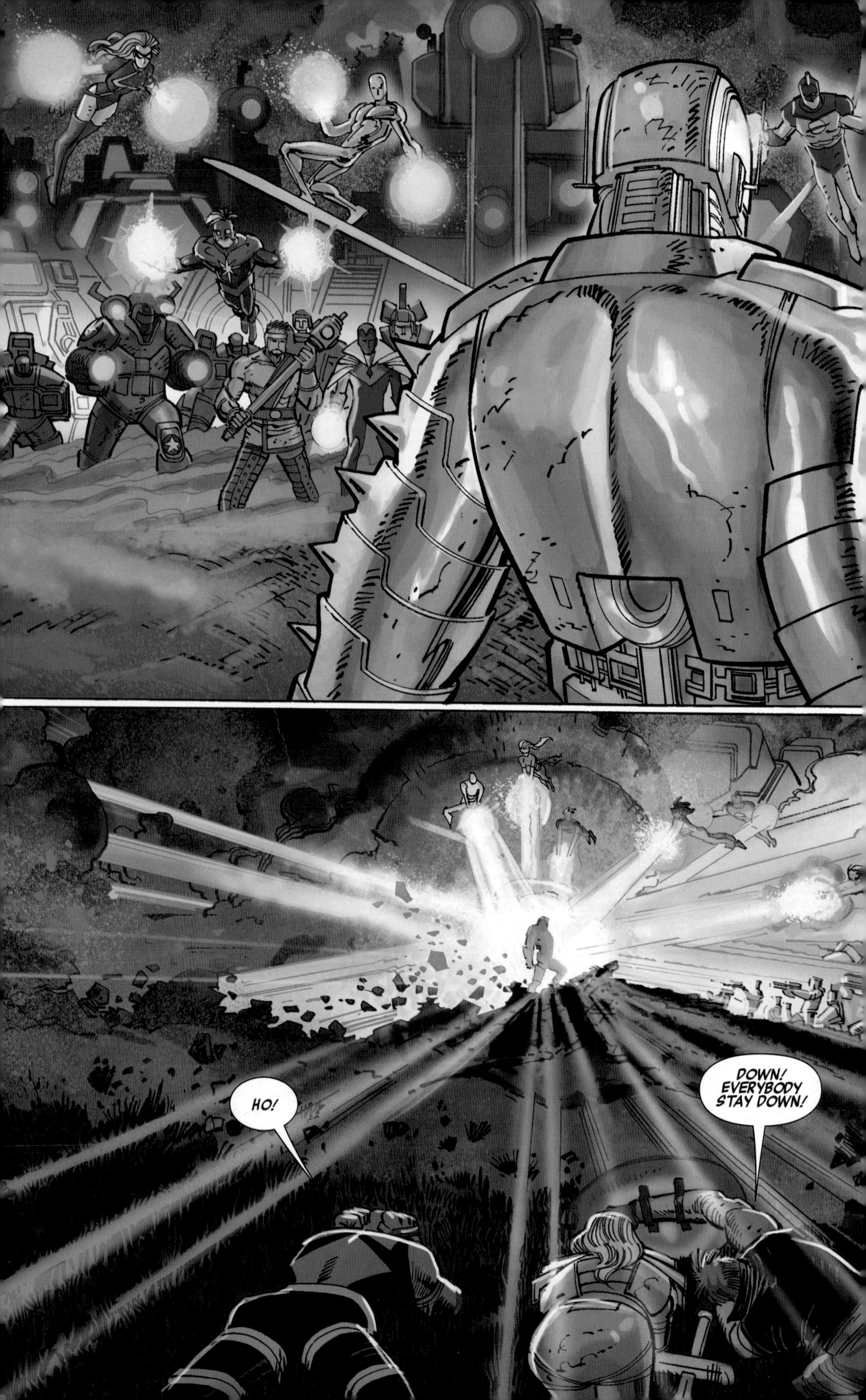
HO!
DOWN! EVERYBODY STAY DOWN!

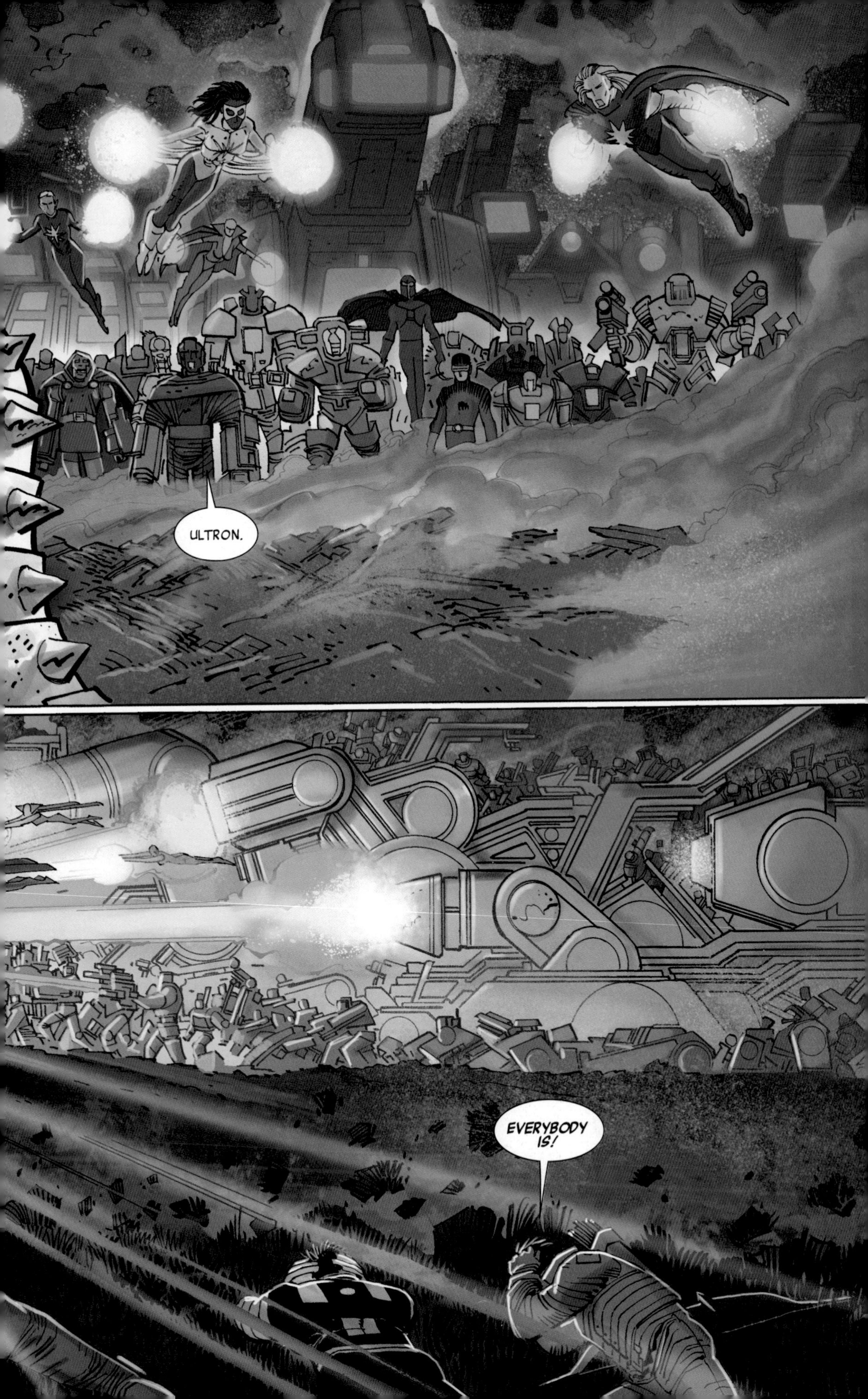
ULTRON.
EVERYBODY IS!

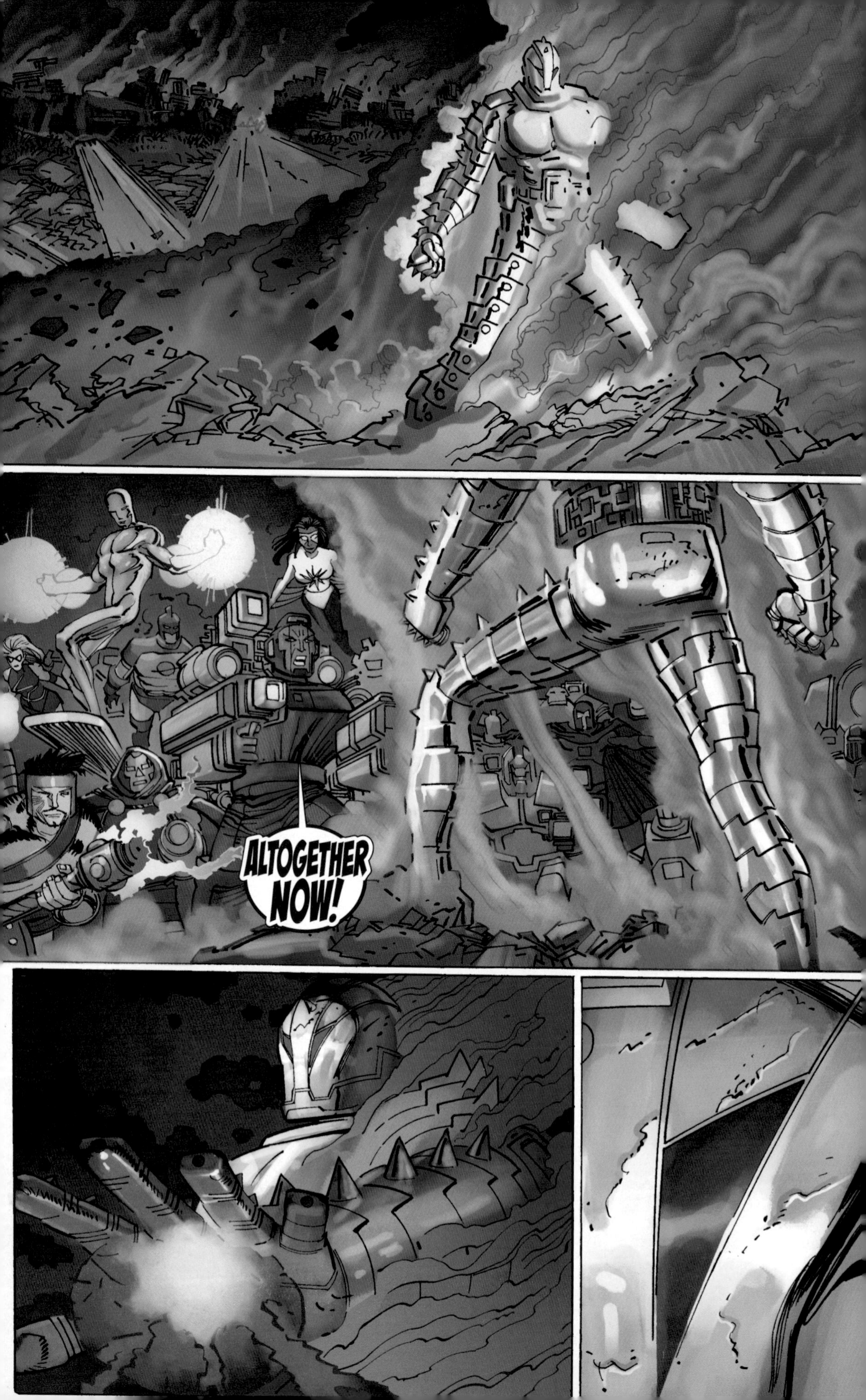
ALTOGETHER NOW!

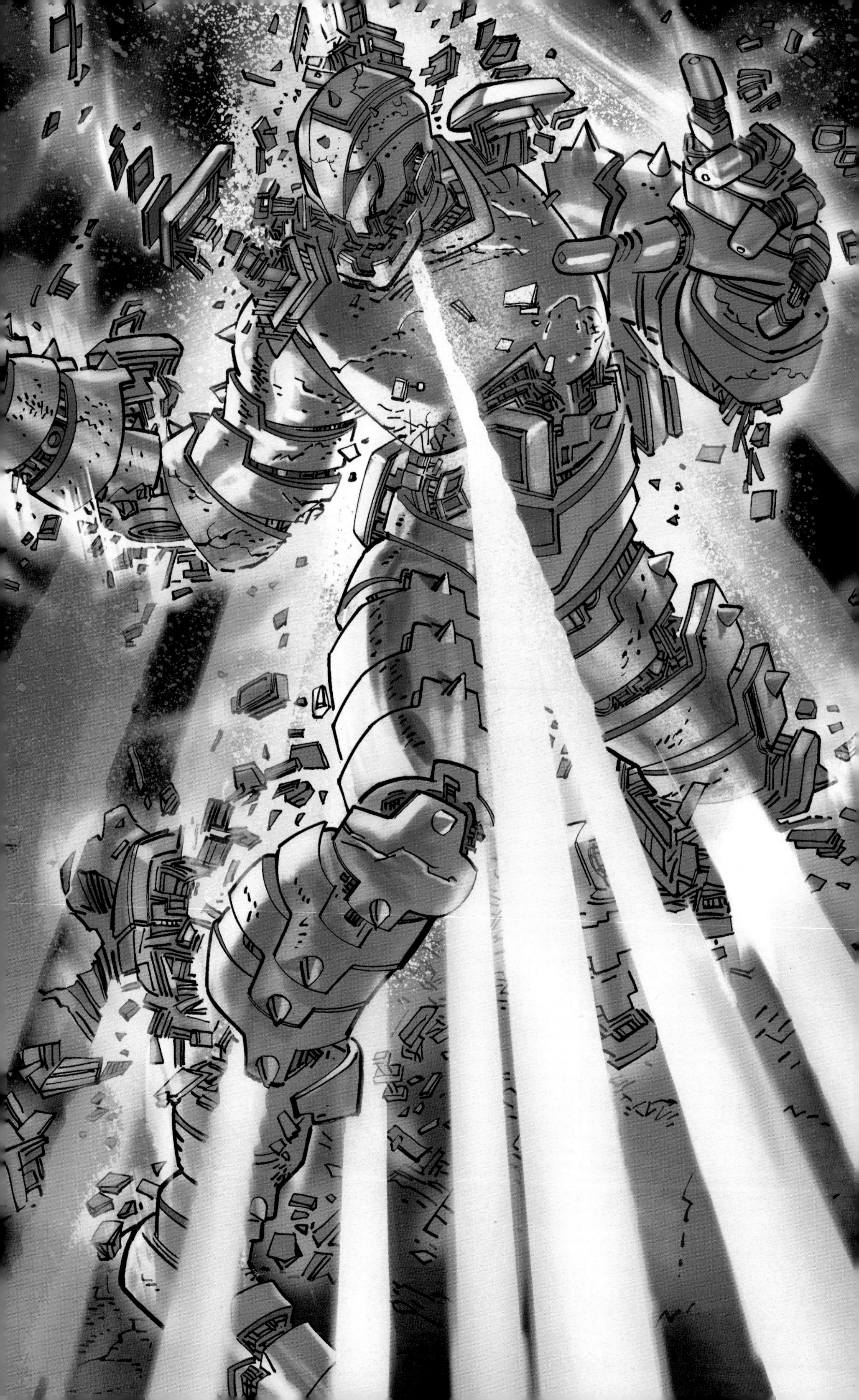

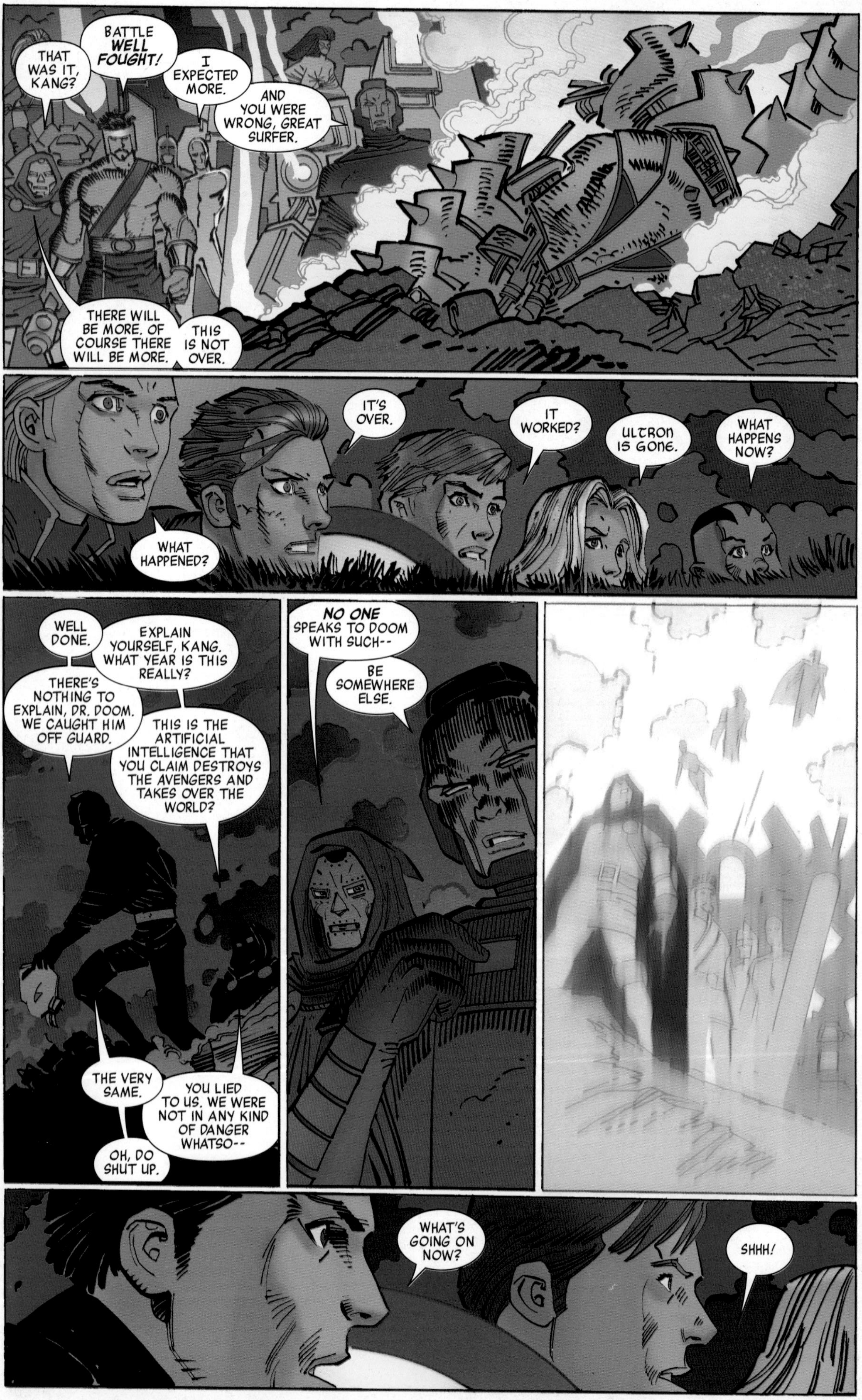
THAT WAS IT, KANG?
BATTLE WELL FOUGHT!
I EXPECTED MORE.
AND YOU WERE WRONG, GREAT SURFER.
THERE WILL BE MORE. OF COURSE THERE WILL BE MORE.
THIS IS NOT OVER.
WHAT HAPPENED?
IT'S OVER.
IT WORKED?
ULTRON IS GONE.
WHAT HAPPENS NOW?
WELL DONE.
EXPLAIN YOURSELF, KANG. WHAT YEAR IS THIS REALLY?
THERE'S NOTHING TO EXPLAIN, DR. DOOM. WE CAUGHT HIM OFF GUARD.
THIS IS THE ARTIFICIAL INTELLIGENCE THAT YOU CLAIM DESTROYS THE AVENGERS AND TAKES OVER THE WORLD?
THE VERY SAME.
YOU LIED TO US. WE WERE NOT IN ANY KIND OF DANGER WHATSO--
OH, DO SHUT UP.
NO ONE SPEAKS TO DOOM WITH SUCH--
BE SOMEWHERE ELSE.
WHAT'S GOING ON NOW?
SHHH!

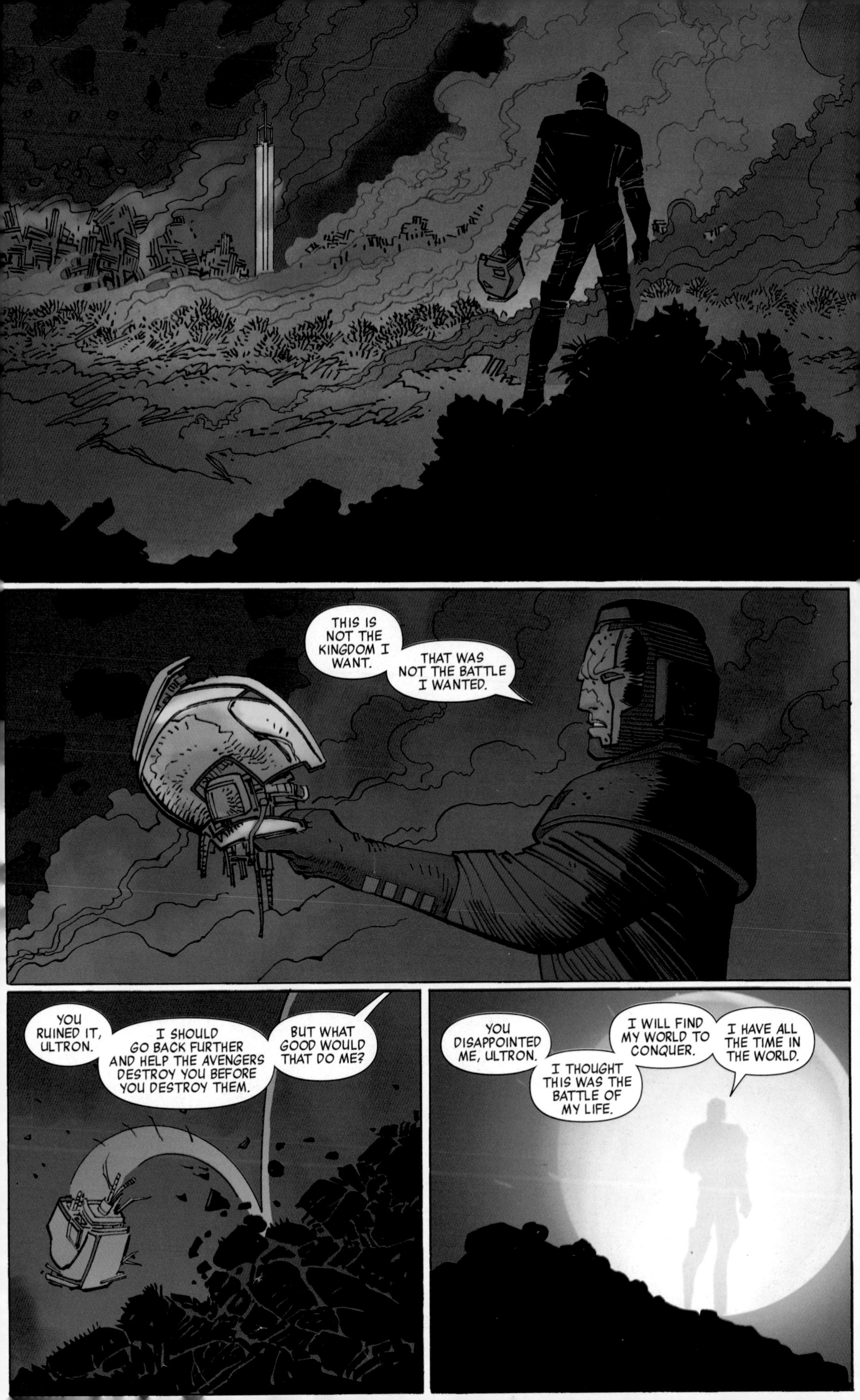
THIS IS NOT THE KINGDOM I WANT.
THAT WAS NOT THE BATTLE I WANTED.
YOU RUINED IT, ULTRON.
I SHOULD GO BACK FURTHER AND HELP THE AVENGERS DESTROY YOU BEFORE YOU DESTROY THEM.
BUT WHAT GOOD WOULD THAT DO ME?
YOU DISAPPOINTED ME, ULTRON.
I THOUGHT THIS WAS THE BATTLE OF MY LIFE.
I WILL FIND MY WORLD TO CONQUER.
I HAVE ALL THE TIME IN THE WORLD.

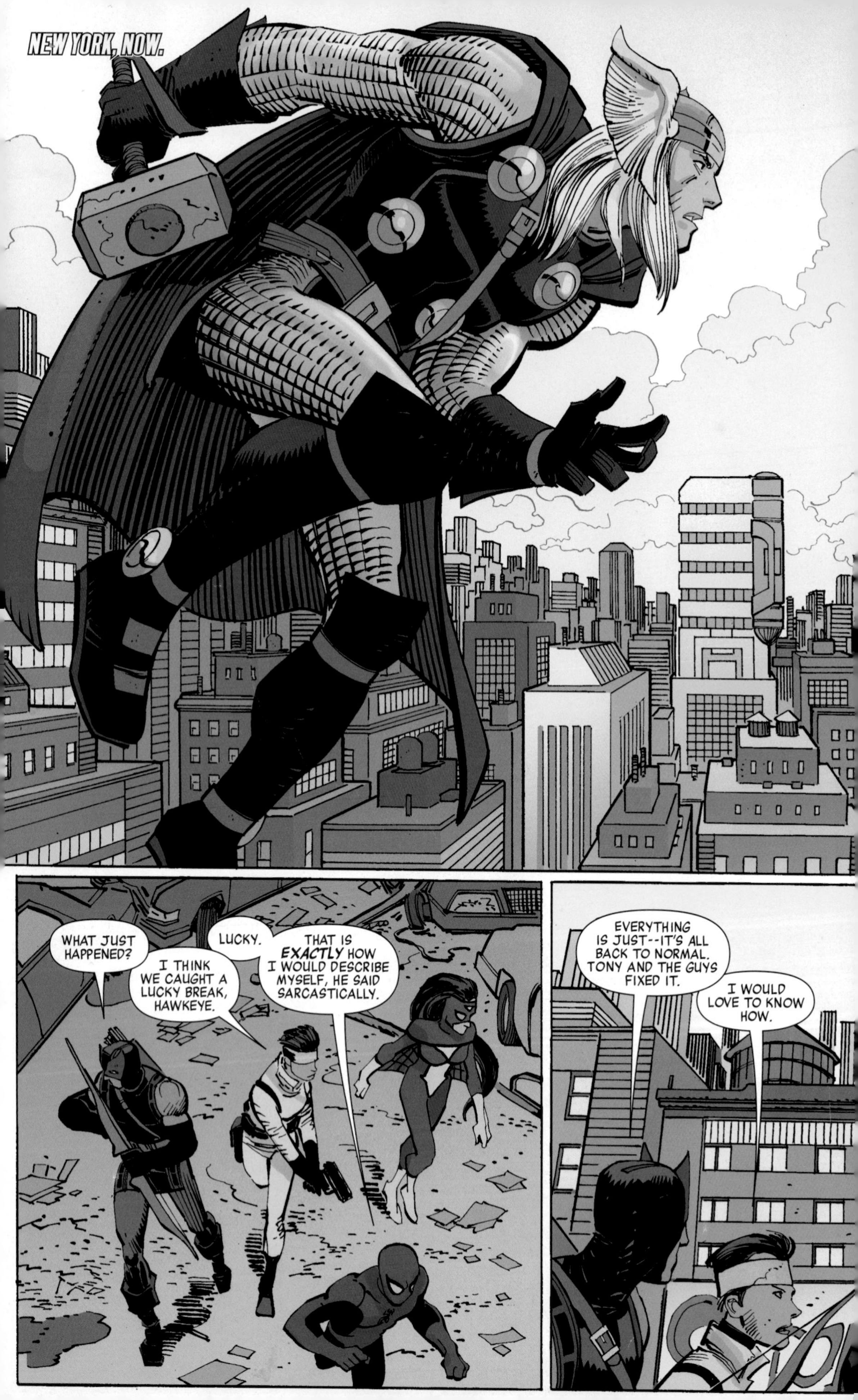
NEW YORK, NOW.
WHAT JUST HAPPENED?
I THINK WE CAUGHT A LUCKY BREAK, HAWKEYE.
LUCKY.
THAT IS EXACTLY HOW I WOULD DESCRIBE MYSELF, HE SAID SARCASTICALLY.
EVERYTHING IS JUST--IT'S ALL BACK TO NORMAL. TONY AND THE GUYS FIXED IT.
I WOULD LOVE TO KNOW HOW.

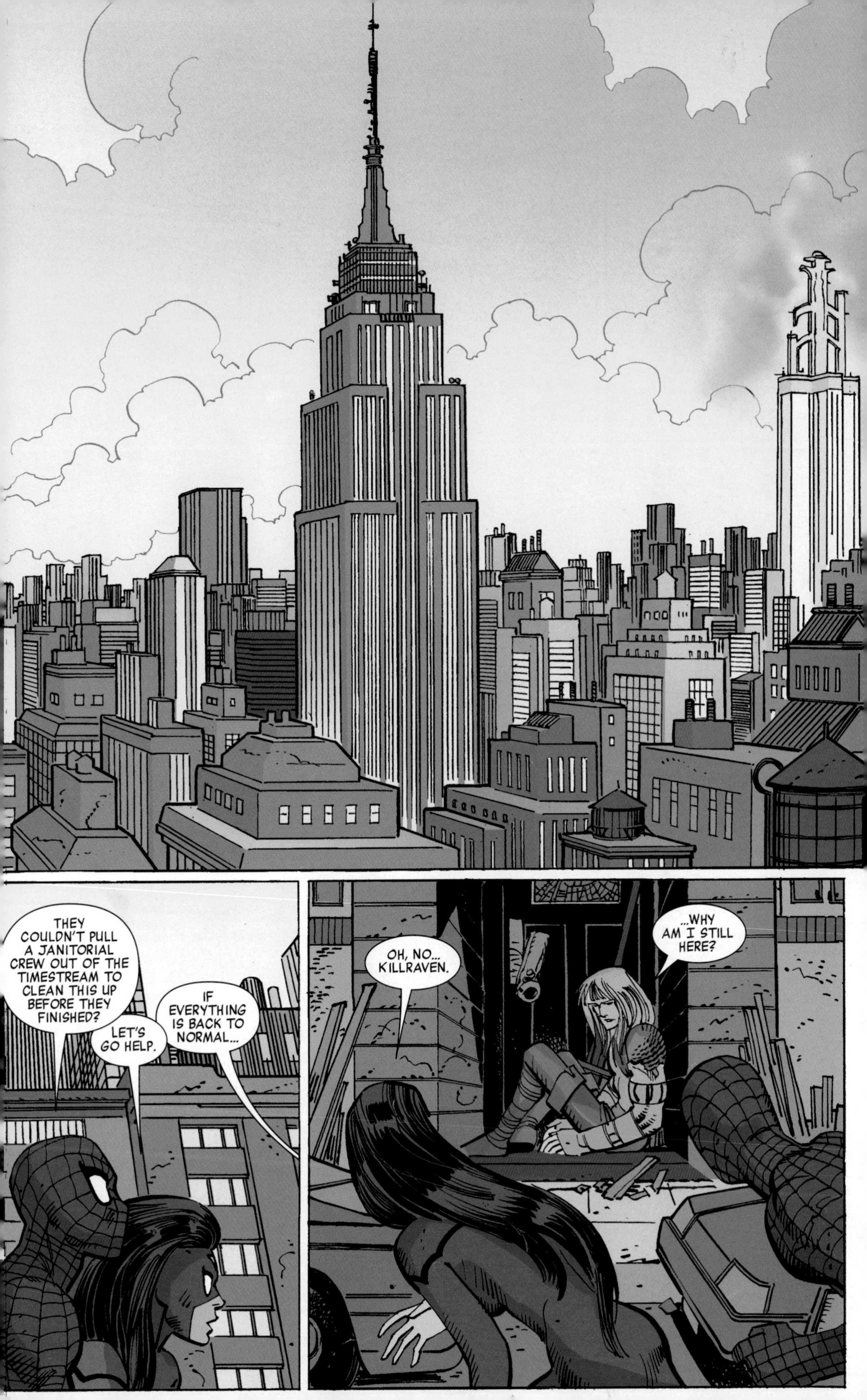
THEY COULDN'T PULL A JANITORIAL CREW OUT OF THE TIMESTREAM TO CLEAN THIS UP BEFORE THEY FINISHED?
LET'S GO HELP.
IF EVERYTHING IS BACK TO NORMAL...
OH, NO... KILLRAVEN.
...WHY AM I STILL HERE?

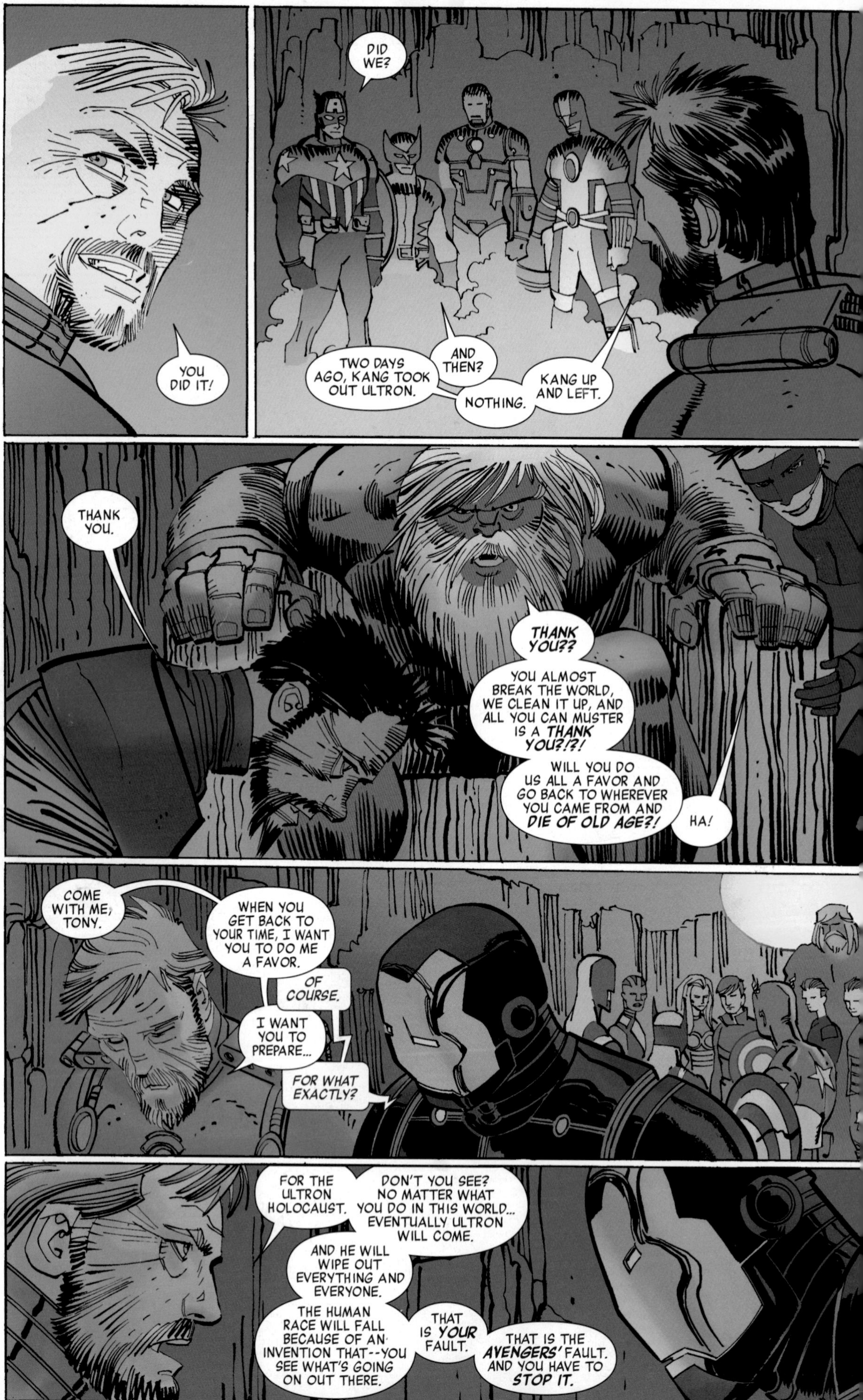
YOU DID IT!
DID WE?
TWO DAYS AGO, KANG TOOK OUT ULTRON.
AND THEN?
NOTHING.
KANG UP AND LEFT.
THANK YOU.
THANK YOU??
YOU ALMOST BREAK THE WORLD, WE CLEAN IT UP, AND ALL YOU CAN MUSTER IS A THANK YOU?!?!
WILL YOU DO US ALL A FAVOR AND GO BACK TO WHEREVER YOU CAME FROM AND DIE OF OLD AGE?!
HA!
COME WITH ME, TONY.
WHEN YOU GET BACK TO YOUR TIME, I WANT YOU TO DO ME A FAVOR.
OF COURSE.
I WANT YOU TO PREPARE...
FOR WHAT EXACTLY?
FOR THE ULTRON HOLOCAUST.
DON'T YOU SEE? NO MATTER WHAT YOU DO IN THIS WORLD... EVENTUALLY ULTRON WILL COME.
AND HE WILL WIPE OUT EVERYTHING AND EVERYONE.
THE HUMAN RACE WILL FALL BECAUSE OF AN INVENTION THAT--YOU SEE WHAT'S GOING ON OUT THERE.
THAT IS YOUR FAULT.
THAT IS THE AVENGERS' FAULT. AND YOU HAVE TO STOP IT.

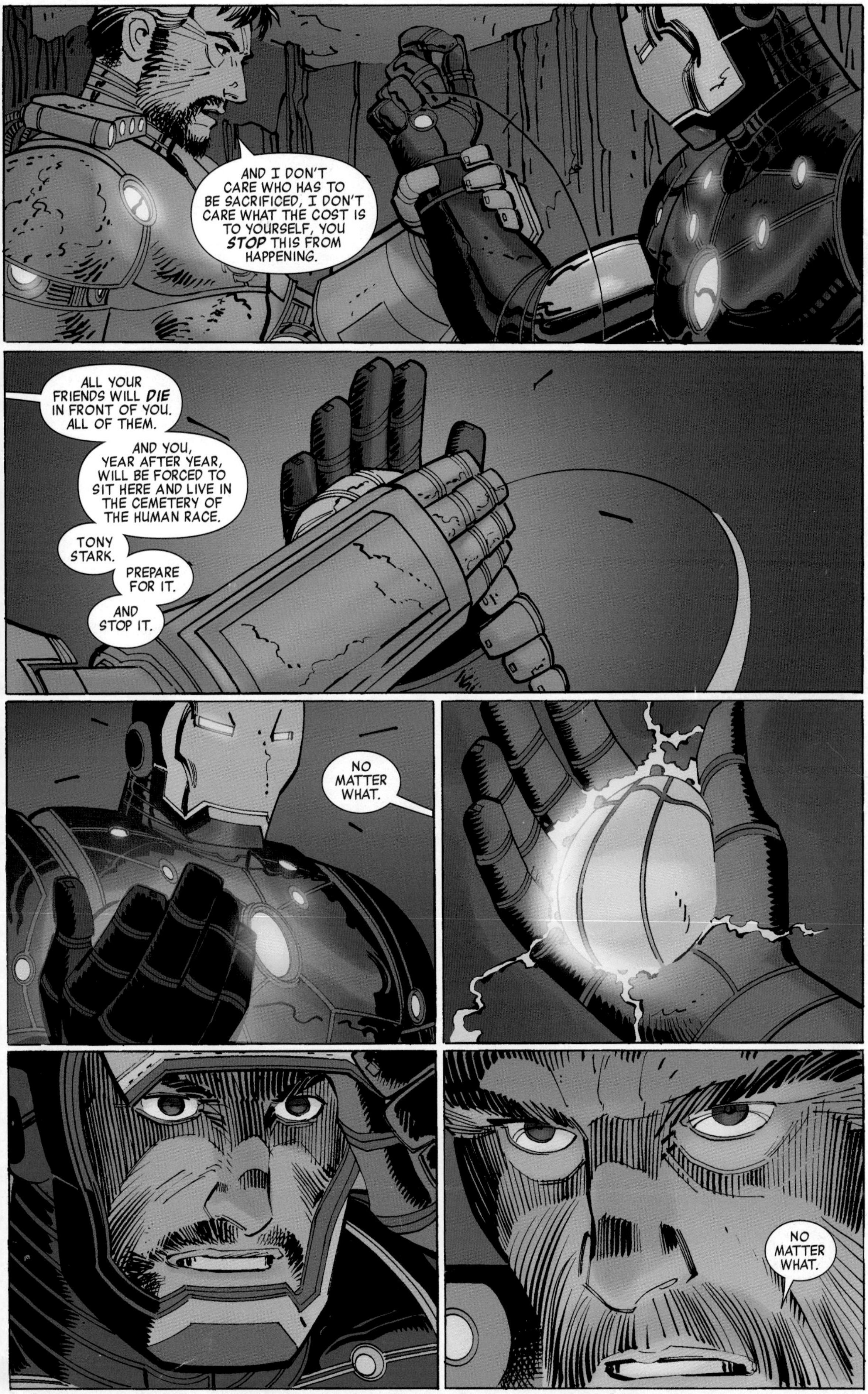
AND I DON'T CARE WHO HAS TO BE SACRIFICED, I DON'T CARE WHAT THE COST IS TO YOURSELF, YOU STOP THIS FROM HAPPENING.
ALL YOUR FRIENDS WILL DIE IN FRONT OF YOU. ALL OF THEM.
AND YOU, YEAR AFTER YEAR, WILL BE FORCED TO SIT HERE AND LIVE IN THE CEMETERY OF THE HUMAN RACE.
TONY STARK.
PREPARE FOR IT.
AND STOP IT.
NO MATTER WHAT.
NO MATTER WHAT.

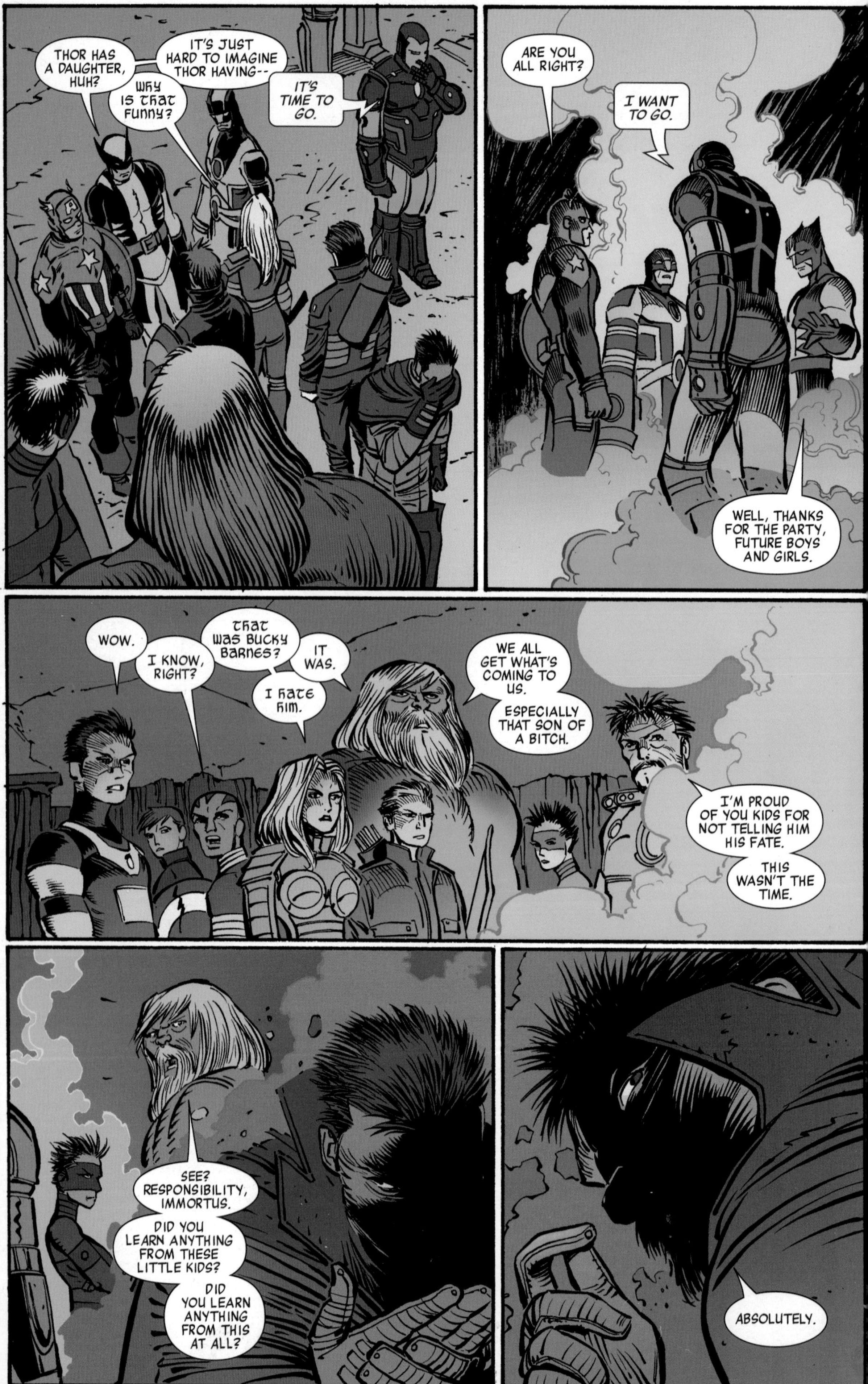
THOR HAS A DAUGHTER, HUH?
IT'S JUST HARD TO IMAGINE THOR HAVING--
WHY IS THAT FUNNY?
IT'S TIME TO GO.
ARE YOU ALL RIGHT?
I WANT TO GO.
WELL, THANKS FOR THE PARTY, FUTURE BOYS AND GIRLS.
WOW.
I KNOW, RIGHT?
THAT WAS BUCKY BARNES?
IT WAS.
I HATE HIM.
WE ALL GET WHAT'S COMING TO US.
ESPECIALLY THAT SON OF A BITCH.
I'M PROUD OF YOU KIDS FOR NOT TELLING HIM HIS FATE.
THIS WASN'T THE TIME.
SEE? RESPONSIBILITY, IMMORTUS.
DID YOU LEARN ANYTHING FROM THESE LITTLE KIDS?
DID YOU LEARN ANYTHING FROM THIS AT ALL?
ABSOLUTELY.

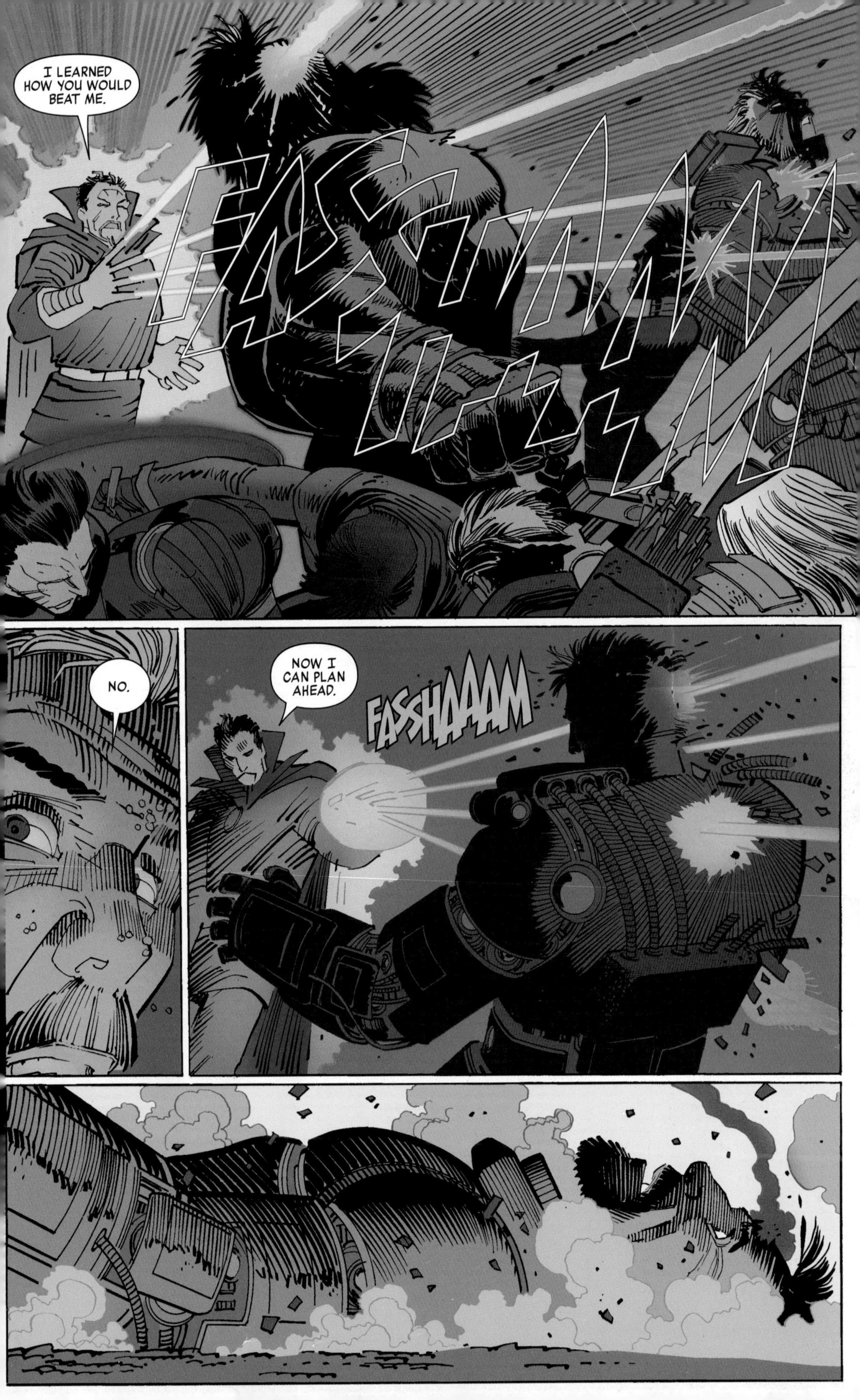
I LEARNED HOW YOU WOULD BEAT ME.
NO.
NOW I CAN PLAN AHEAD.
FASHAAAM

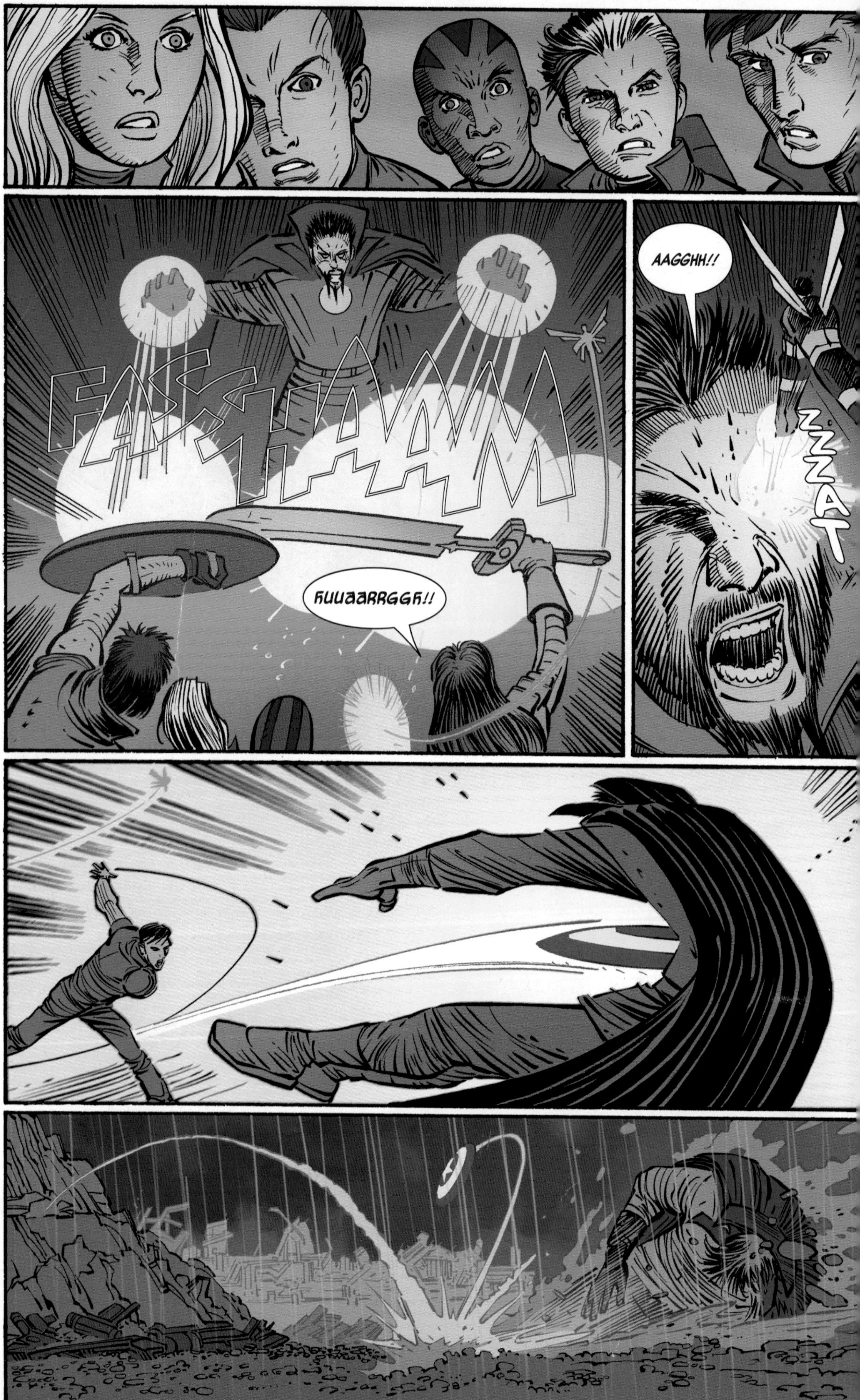
FASSHAAAM
HUUAARRGGH!!
AAGGHH!!
ZZZAT

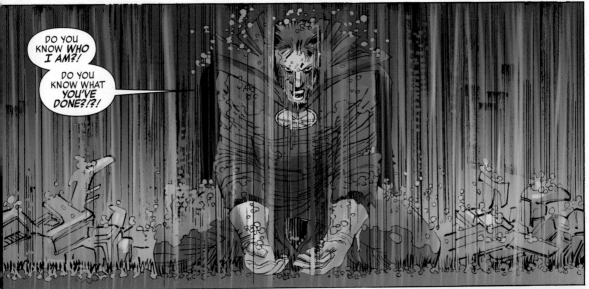

DO YOU KNOW *WHO* I AM?!

DO YOU KNOW WHAT *YOU'VE* DONE?!?!

I AM *IMMORTUS*, *MASTER* OF *TIME!!*

I WAS THERE AT YOUR *BIRTH.* I WAS THERE AT EVERY SINGLE MOMENT OF YOUR *MISERABLE* LIVES!!

AND FOR WHAT YOU'VE DONE HERE TODAY...I'LL BE THERE TO WATCH *YOU DIE!!*

EACH AND EVERY ONE OF YOU!!

I WILL *WATCH YOU DIE!!*

KRAKOOM

YOU HAVE NO IDEA THE--

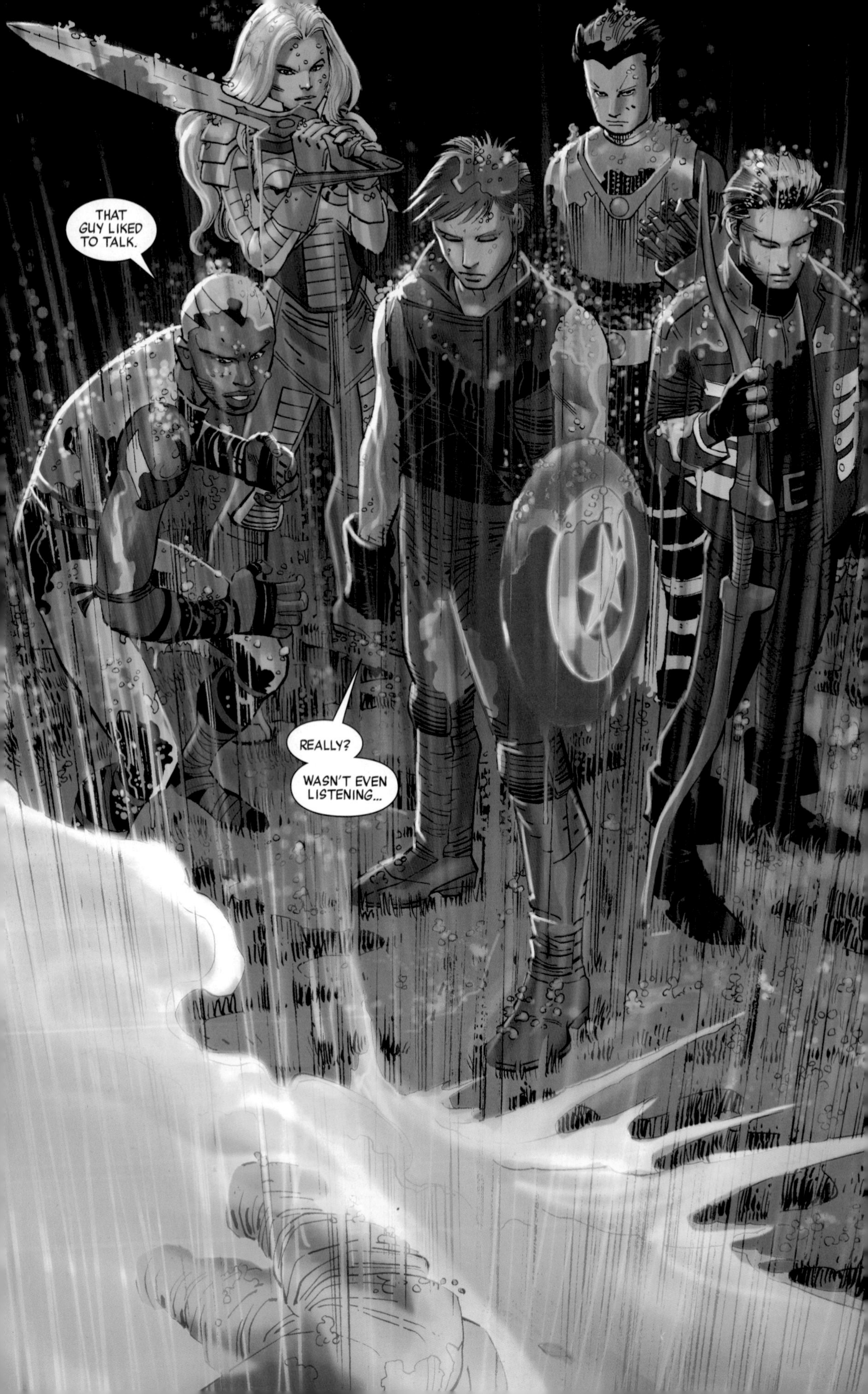
THAT GUY LIKED TO TALK.
REALLY?
WASN'T EVEN LISTENING...

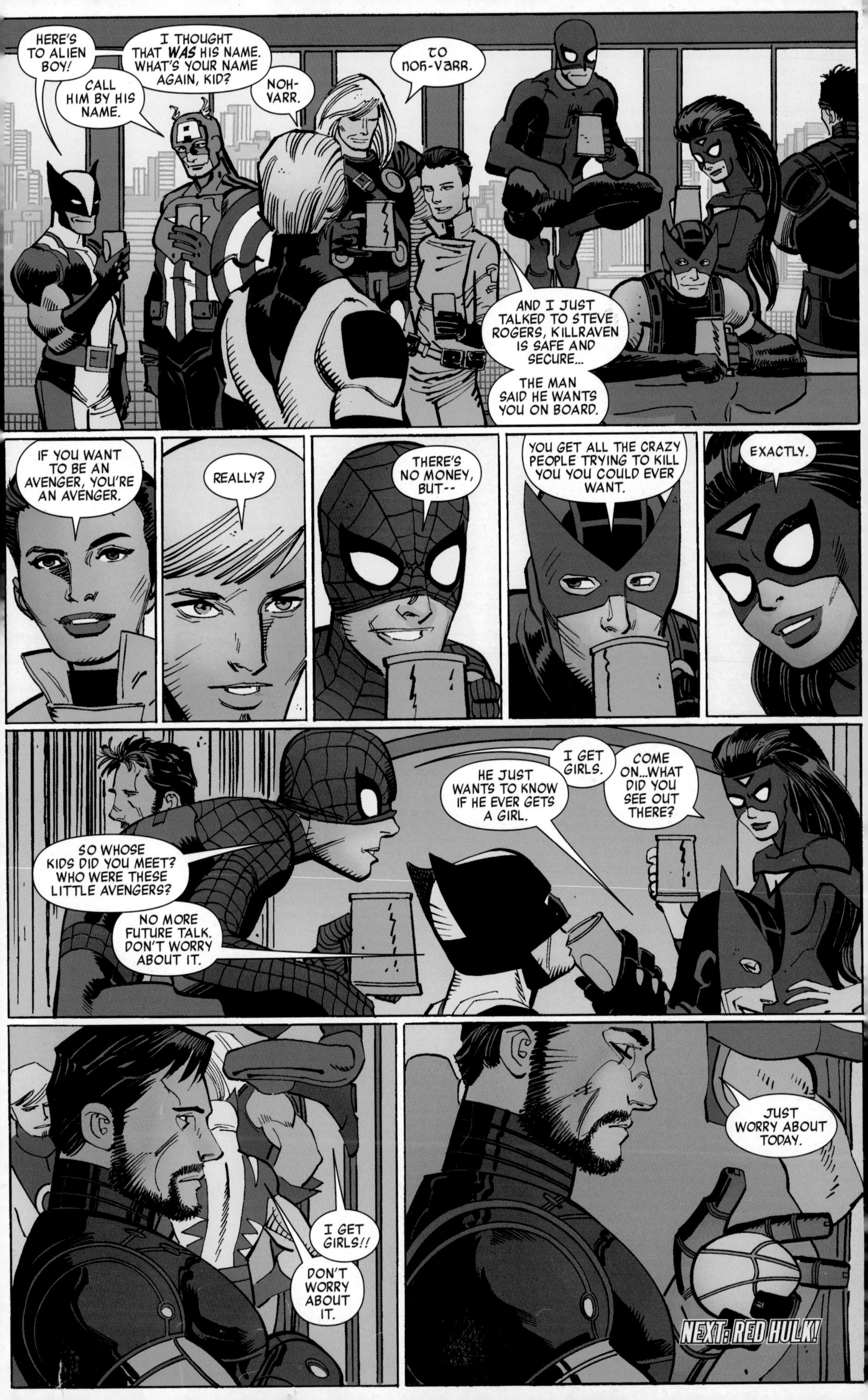
HERE'S TO ALIEN BOY!
I THOUGHT THAT WAS HIS NAME. WHAT'S YOUR NAME AGAIN, KID?
CALL HIM BY HIS NAME.
NOH-VARR.
TO NOH-VARR.
AND I JUST TALKED TO STEVE ROGERS, KILLRAVEN IS SAFE AND SECURE...
THE MAN SAID HE WANTS YOU ON BOARD.
IF YOU WANT TO BE AN AVENGER, YOU'RE AN AVENGER.
REALLY?
THERE'S NO MONEY, BUT--
YOU GET ALL THE CRAZY PEOPLE TRYING TO KILL YOU YOU COULD EVER WANT.
EXACTLY.
SO WHOSE KIDS DID YOU MEET? WHO WERE THESE LITTLE AVENGERS?
NO MORE FUTURE TALK. DON'T WORRY ABOUT IT.
HE JUST WANTS TO KNOW IF HE EVER GETS A GIRL.
I GET GIRLS.
COME ON...WHAT DID YOU SEE OUT THERE?
I GET GIRLS!!
DON'T WORRY ABOUT IT.
JUST WORRY ABOUT TODAY.
NEXT: RED HULK!

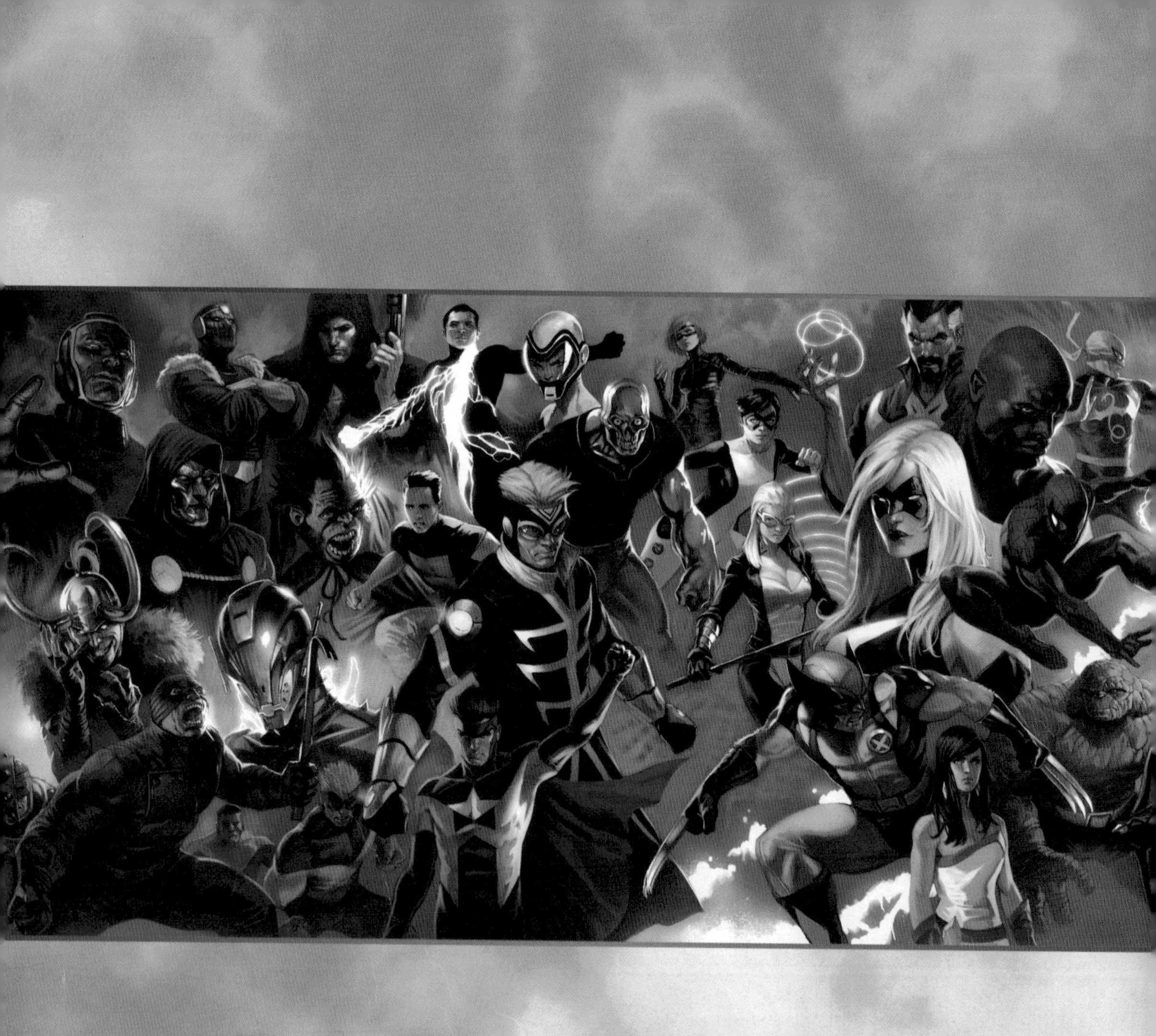

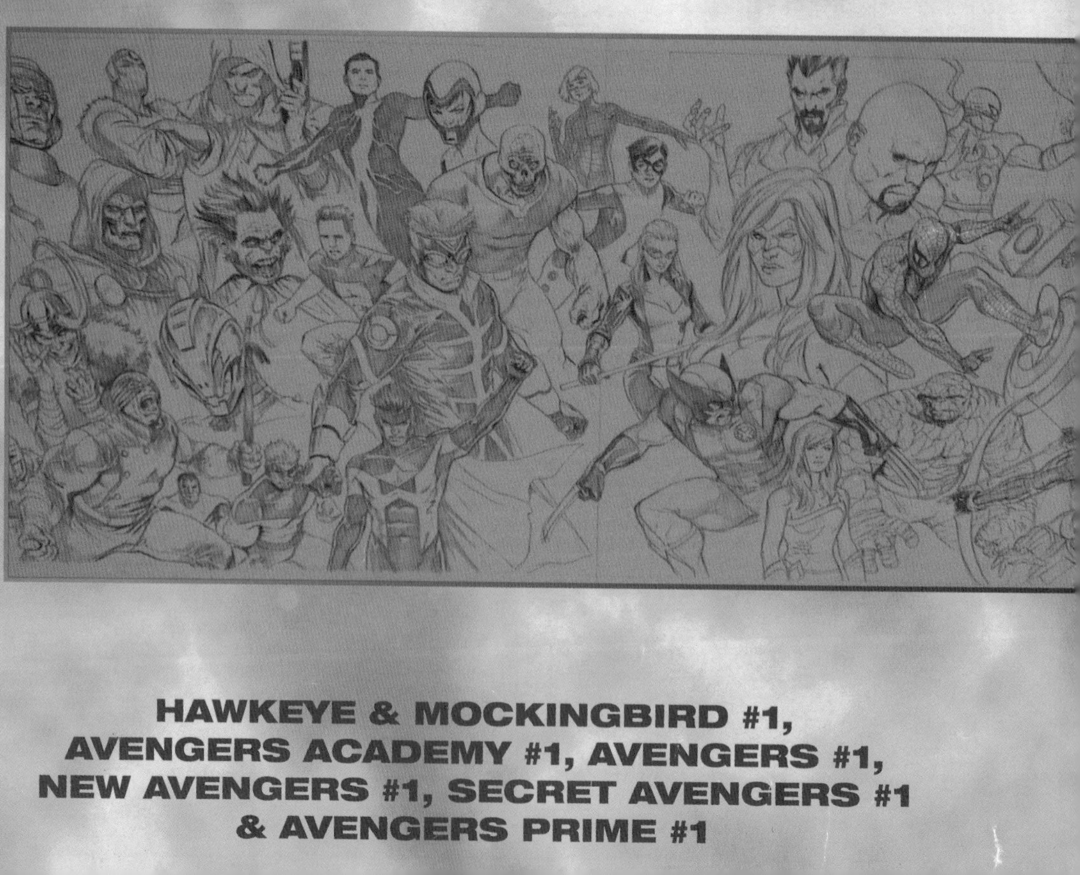

**HAWKEYE & MOCKINGBIRD #1,
AVENGERS ACADEMY #1, AVENGERS #1,
NEW AVENGERS #1, SECRET AVENGERS #1
& AVENGERS PRIME #1**

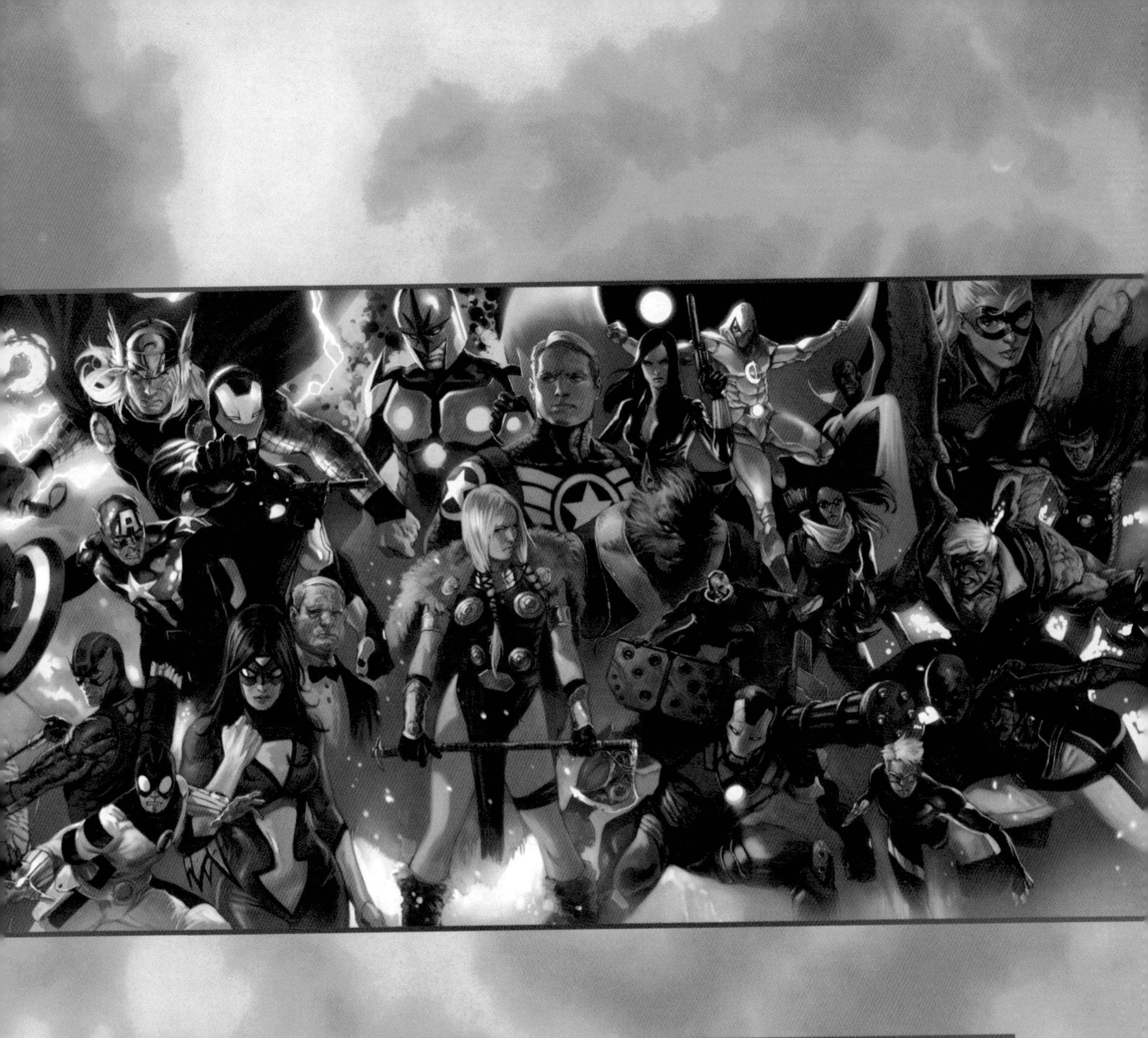

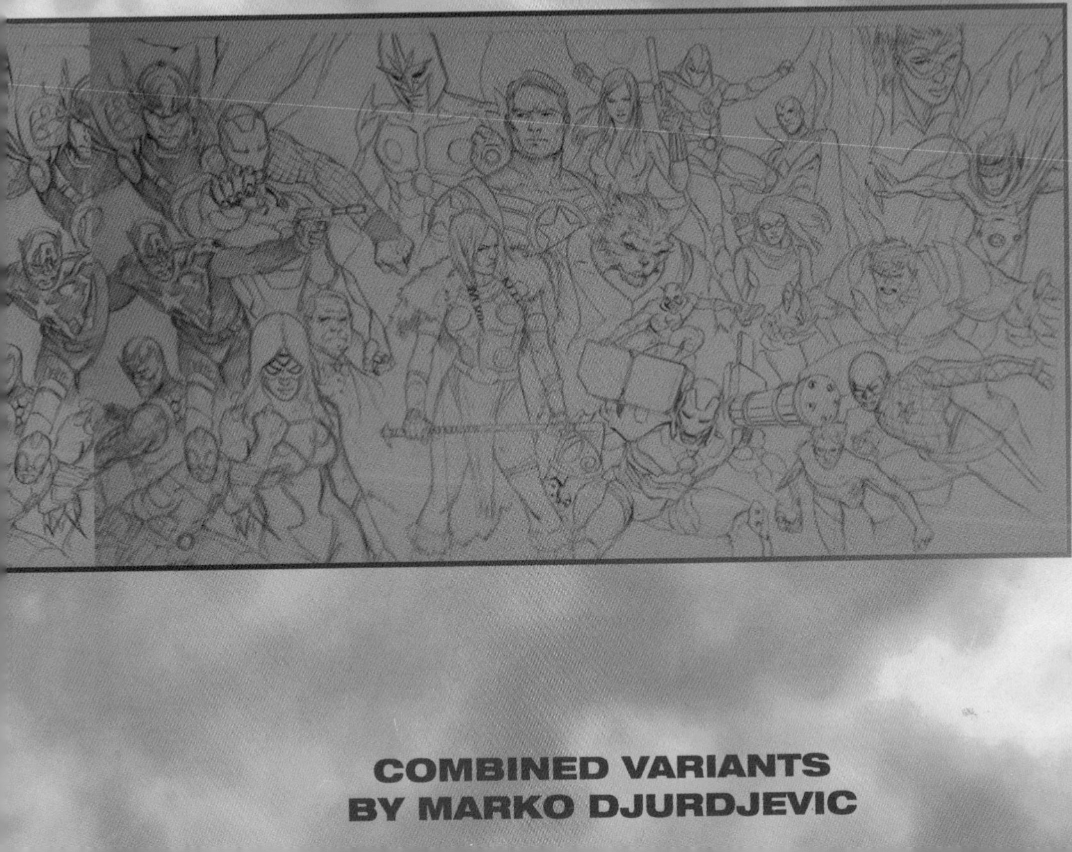

COMBINED VARIANTS
BY MARKO DJURDJEVIC

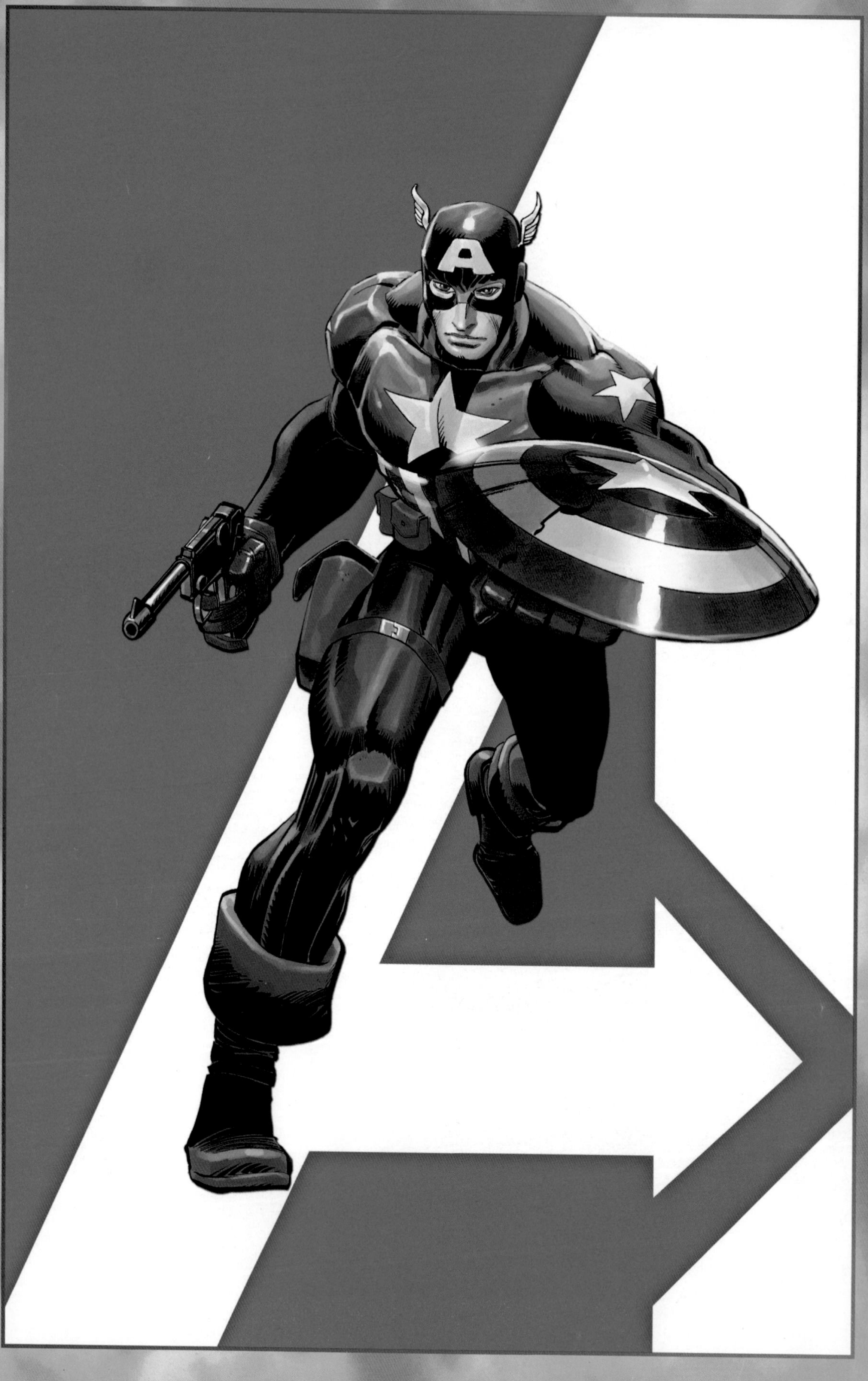

#1 VARIANT BY JOHN ROMITA JR. & DEAN WHITE

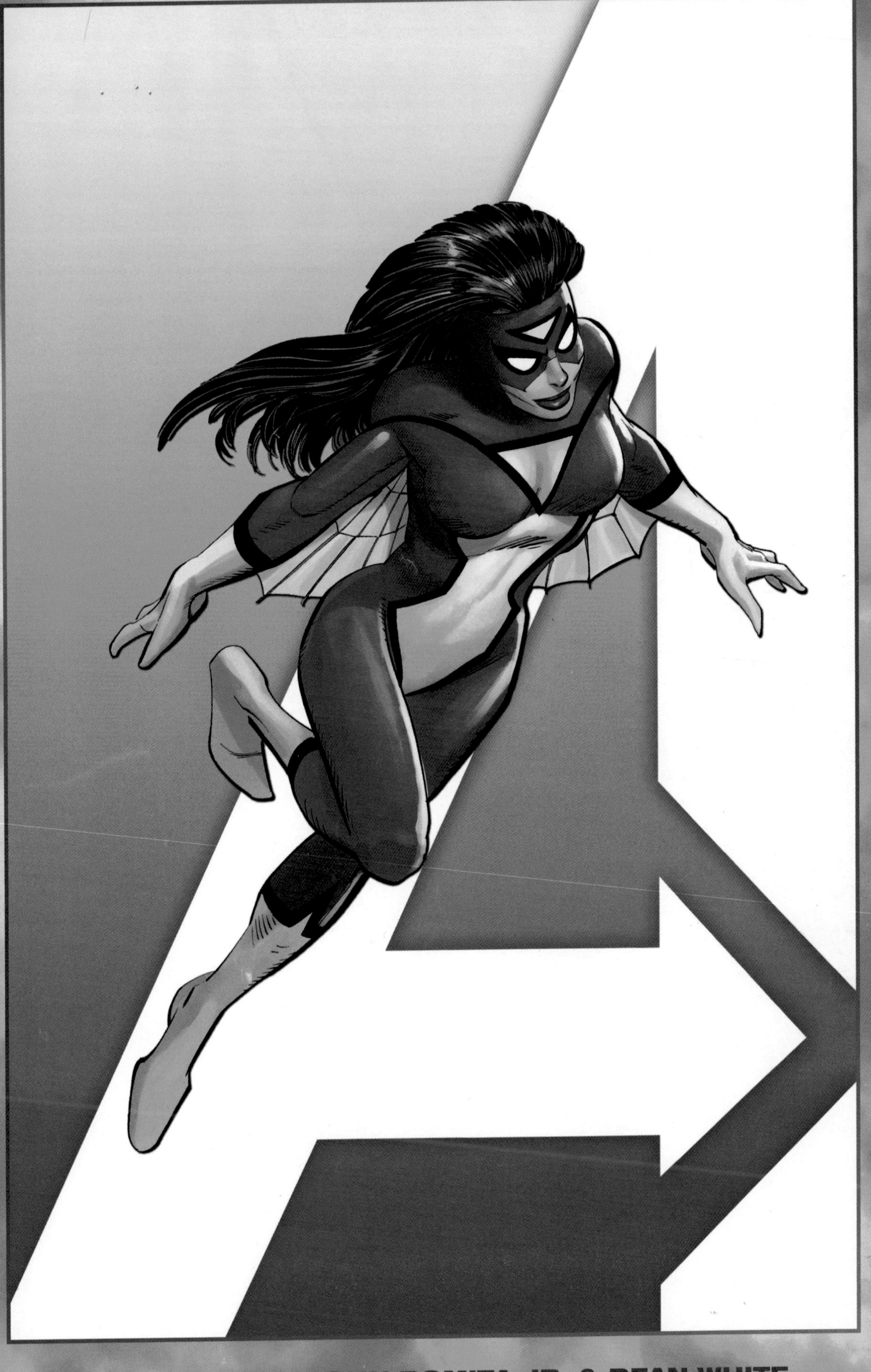

#2 VARIANT BY JOHN ROMITA JR. & DEAN WHITE

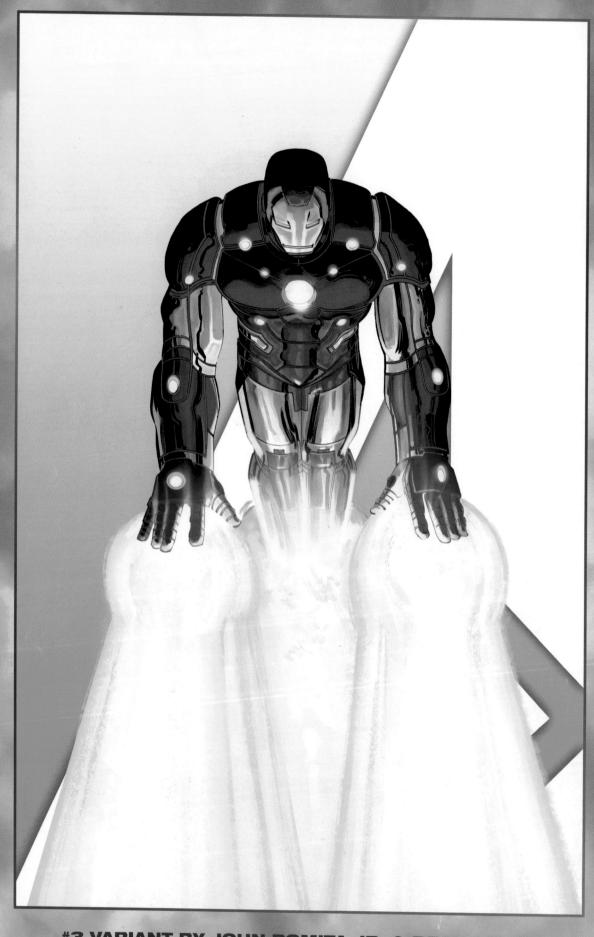

#3 VARIANT BY JOHN ROMITA JR. & DEAN WHITE

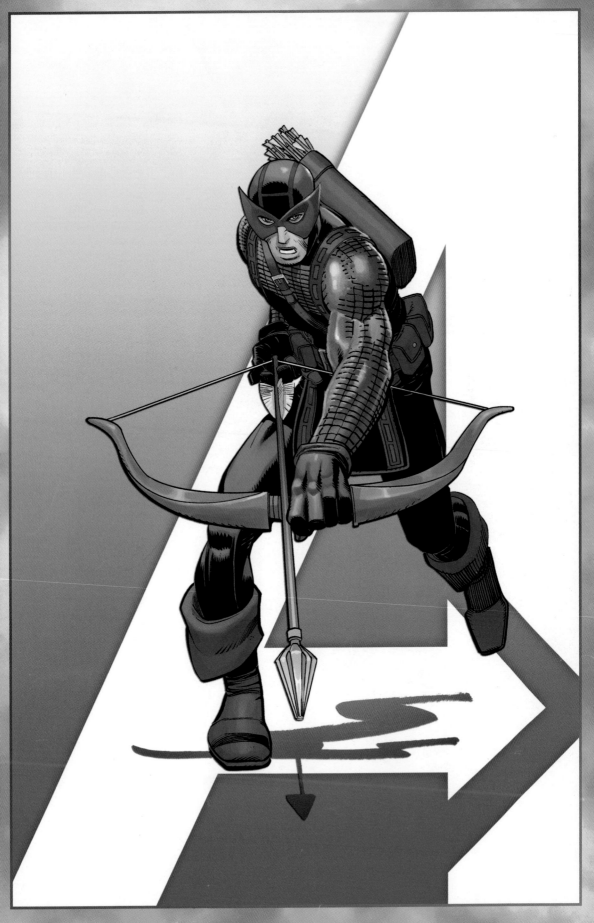

#4 VARIANT BY JOHN ROMITA JR. & DEAN WHITE

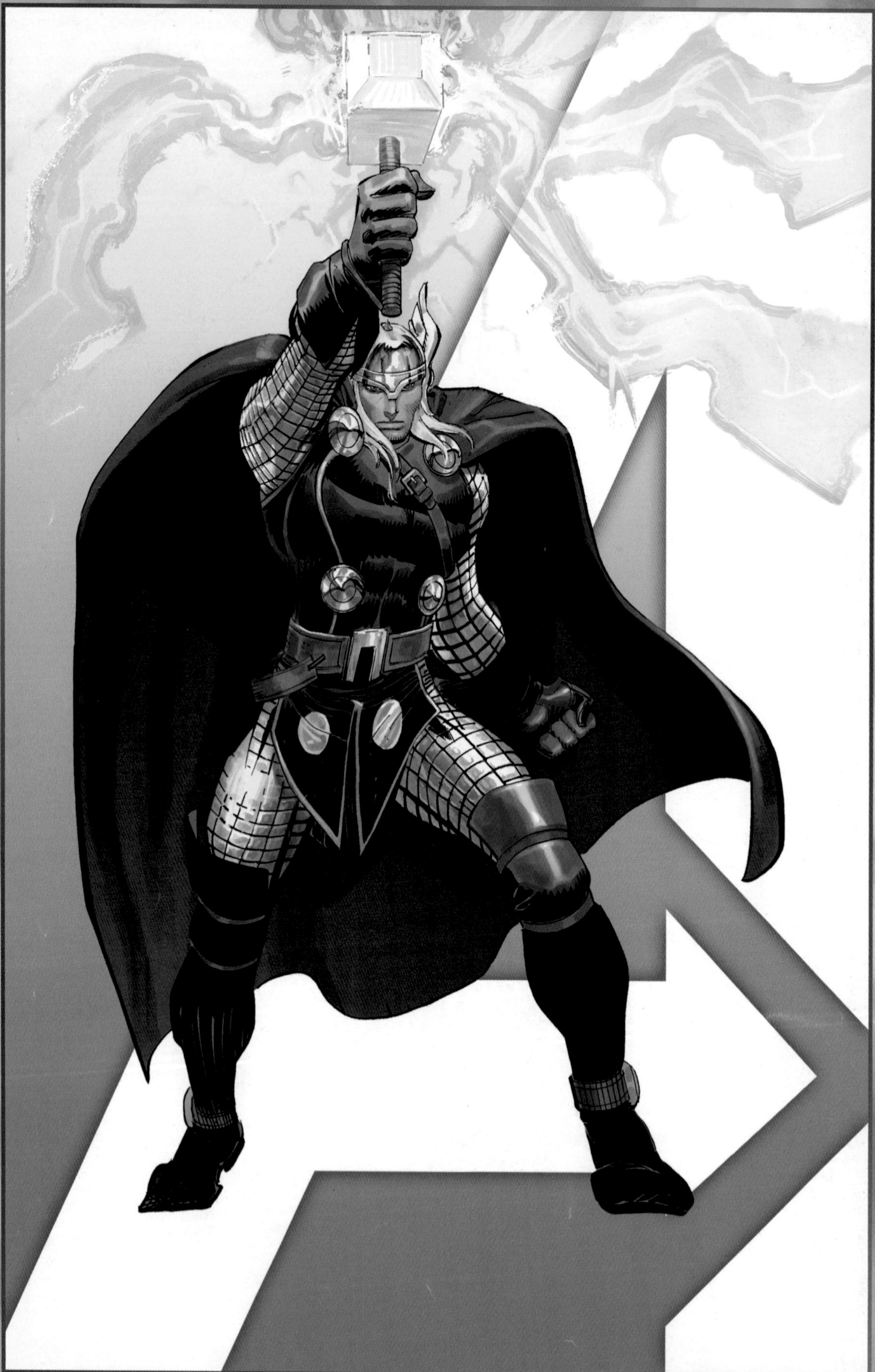

#5 VARIANT BY JOHN ROMITA JR. & DEAN WHITE

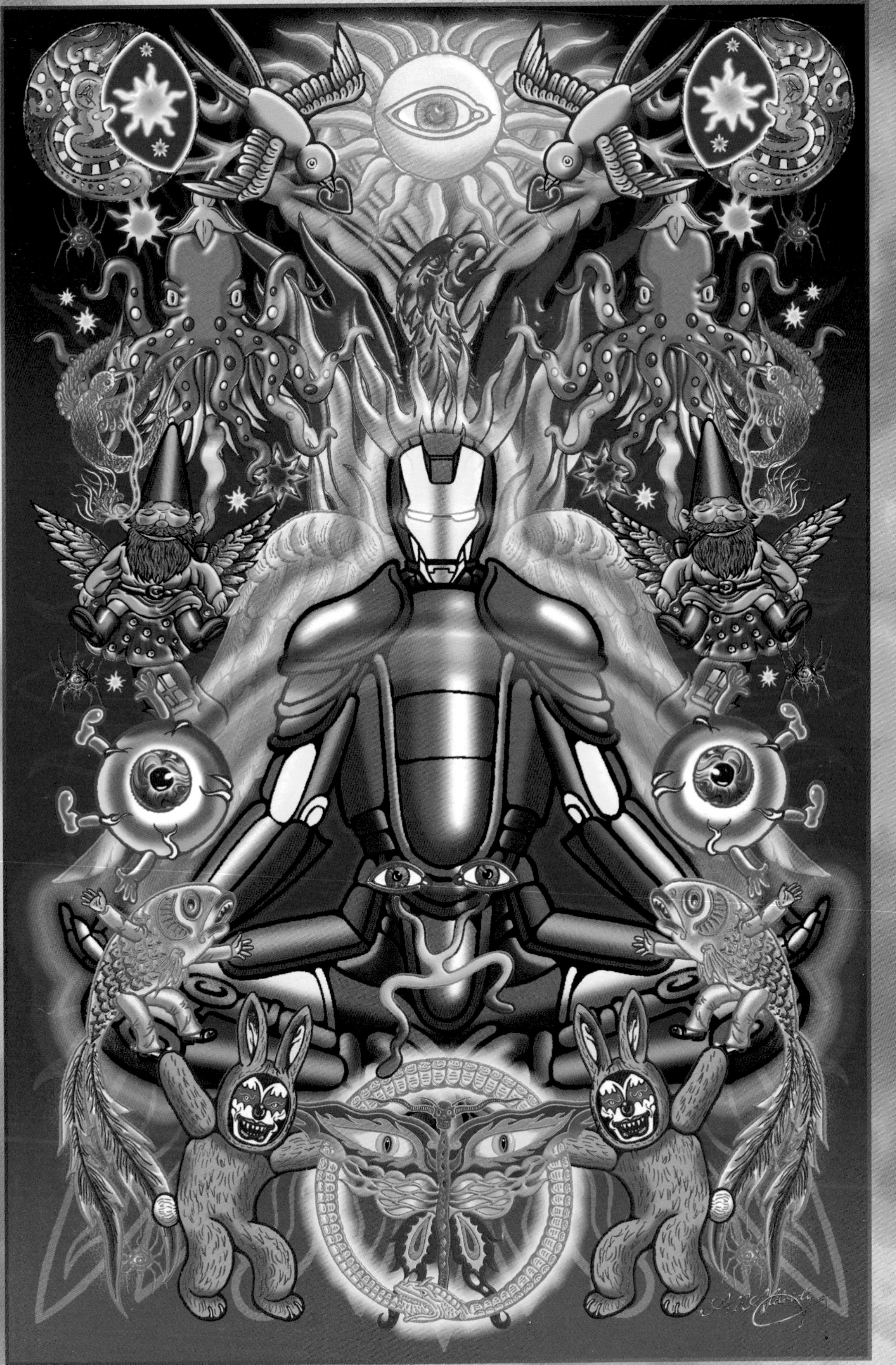

#2 IRON MAN BY DESIGN VARIANT BY ALAN ALDRIDGE

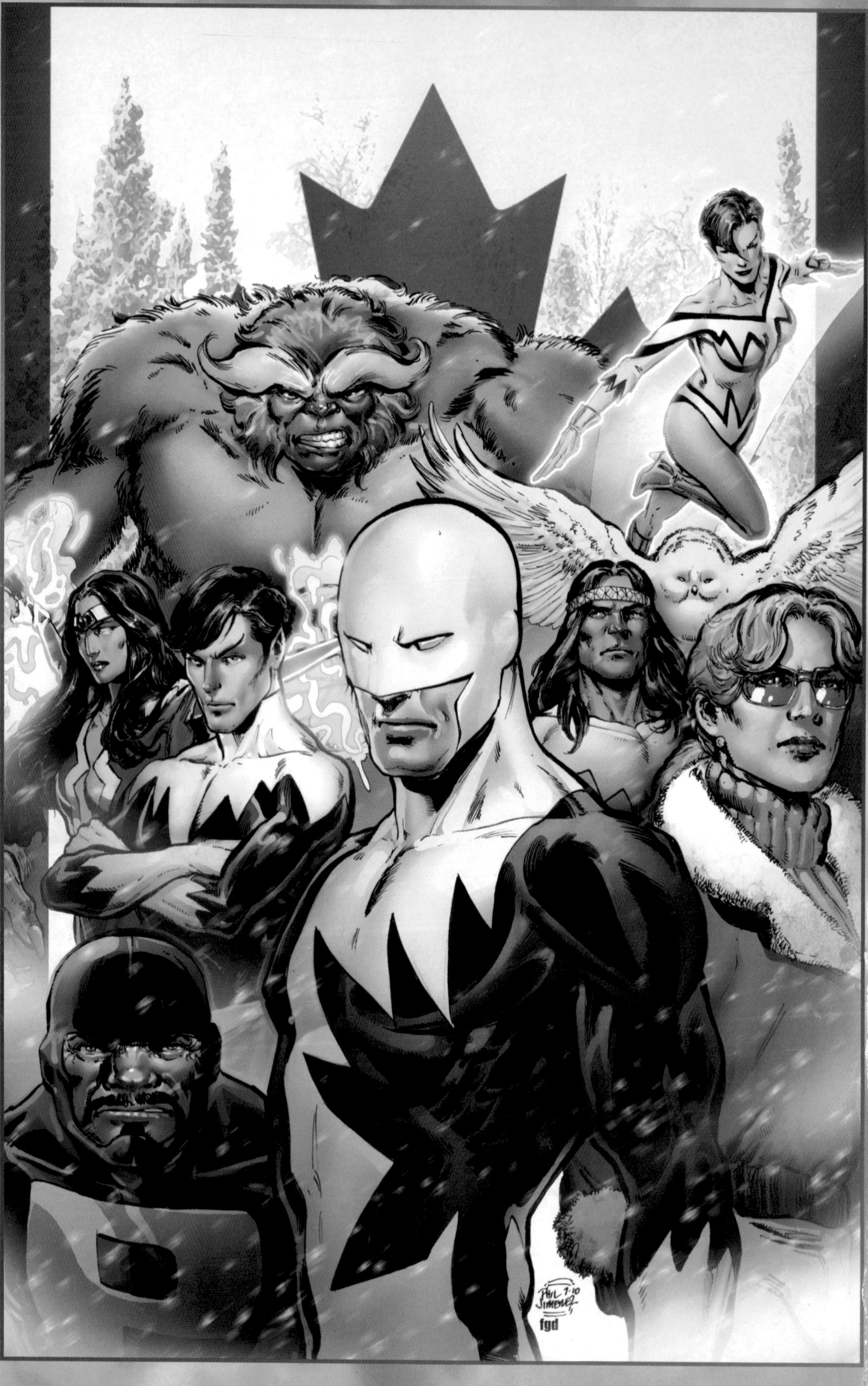

#4 FAN EXPO VARIANT BY PHIL JIMENEZ & FRANK D'ARMATA